Econometric Analyses on Global Finance and Economic Development

Yekeen Oku Abdul-Maliq
University of Abuja, Nigeria

IGI Global
PUBLISHER of TIMELY KNOWLEDGE

A volume in the Advances in Finance, Accounting, and Economics (AFAE) Book Series

Published in the United States of America by
IGI Global
Business Science Reference (an imprint of IGI Global)
701 E. Chocolate Avenue
Hershey PA, USA 17033
Tel: 717-533-8845
Fax: 717-533-8661
E-mail: cust@igi-global.com
Web site: http://www.igi-global.com

Library of Congress Cataloging-in-Publication Data

Names: Abdul-Maliq, Yekeen, 1961- editor.
Title: Econometric analyses on global finance and economic development / edited by Yekeen Abdul-Maliq.
Description: Hershey, PA : Business Science Reference, [2024] | Includes bibliographical references and index. | Summary: "This book contributes to the literature on economic history and political economy in the context of international politics, economic diplomacy, and international relations in general"-- Provided by publisher.
Identifiers: LCCN 2023049105 (print) | LCCN 2023049106 (ebook) | ISBN 9798369316108 (hardcover) | ISBN 9798369316115 (ebook)
Subjects: LCSH: Economic development--Developing countries--Econometric models. | Finance--Developing countries--Econometric models.
Classification: LCC HC59.7 .E253 2024 (print) | LCC HC59.7 (ebook) | DDC 338.9009172/4--dc23/eng/20231020
LC record available at https://lccn.loc.gov/2023049105
LC ebook record available at https://lccn.loc.gov/2023049106

This book is published in the IGI Global book series Advances in Finance, Accounting, and Economics (AFAE) (ISSN: 2327-5677; eISSN: 2327-5685)

British Cataloguing in Publication Data
A Cataloguing in Publication record for this book is available from the British Library.

Advances in Finance, Accounting, and Economics (AFAE) Book Series

ISSN:2327-5677
EISSN:2327-5685

Editor-in-Chief: Ahmed Driouchi, Al Akhawayn University, Morocco

MISSION

In our changing economic and business environment, it is important to consider the financial changes occurring internationally as well as within individual organizations and business environments. Understanding these changes as well as the factors that influence them is crucial in preparing for our financial future and ensuring economic sustainability and growth.

The **Advances in Finance, Accounting, and Economics (AFAE)** book series aims to publish comprehensive and informative titles in all areas of economics and economic theory, finance, and accounting to assist in advancing the available knowledge and providing for further research development in these dynamic fields.

COVERAGE

- Statistical Analysis
- Investments and Derivatives
- Economics of Agriculture and Biotechnology
- Internet Banking
- Labor Economics
- Economics of Natural and Environmental Resources
- Applied Finance
- Borrowing and Lending
- Fiscal Policy
- Economics of Migration and Spatial Mobility

IGI Global is currently accepting manuscripts for publication within this series. To submit a proposal for a volume in this series, please contact our Acquisition Editors at Acquisitions@igi-global.com or visit: http://www.igi-global.com/publish/.

The Advances in Finance, Accounting, and Economics (AFAE) Book Series (ISSN 2327-5677) is published by IGI Global, 701 E. Chocolate Avenue, Hershey, PA 17033-1240, USA, www.igi-global.com. This series is composed of titles available for purchase individually; each title is edited to be contextually exclusive from any other title within the series. For pricing and ordering information please visit http://www.igi-global.com/book-series/advances-finance-accounting-economics/73685. Postmaster: Send all address changes to above address.

Titles in this Series

For a list of additional titles in this series, please visit:
www.igi-global.com/book-series/advances-finance-accounting-economics/73685

Democratization of Africa and Its Impact on the Global Economy
Ndwakhulu Tshishonga (University of KwaZulu-Natal, South Africa) and Icarbord Tshabangu (Leeds Trinity University, UK)
Information Science Reference • copyright 2024 • 487pp • H/C (ISBN: 9798369304778) • US $240.00 (our price)

Digital Currency Assets and Challenges to Financial System Stability
Adekunle Alexander Balogun (University of Ibadan, Nigeria) and Yusuf Olatunji Oyedeko (Federal University Oye-Ekiti, Nigeria)
Business Science Reference • copyright 2024 • 227pp • H/C (ISBN: 9798369307700) • US $275.00 (our price)

Algorithmic Approaches to Financial Technology Forecasting, Trading, and Optimization
Amandeep Singh (Chitkara Business School, Chitkara University, India) Sanjay Taneja (Graphic Era University (Deemed), India) and Pawan Kumar (Chandigarh University, India)
Business Science Reference • copyright 2024 • 266pp • H/C (ISBN: 9798369317464) • US $275.00 (our price)

Fintech Applications in Islamic Finance AI, Machine Learning, and Blockchain Techniques
Mohammad Irfan (Business School, NSB Academy, Bangalore, India) Seifedine Kadry (Noroff University College, Norway) Muhammad Sharif (Department of CS, COMSATS University Islamabad, Wah Cantt, Pakistan) and Habib Ullah Khan (Qatar University, Qatar)
Business Science Reference • copyright 2024 • 334pp • H/C (ISBN: 9798369310380) • US $265.00 (our price)

For an entire list of titles in this series, please visit:
www.igi-global.com/book-series/advances-finance-accounting-economics/73685

IGI Global
PUBLISHER of TIMELY KNOWLEDGE

701 East Chocolate Avenue, Hershey, PA 17033, USA
Tel: 717-533-8845 x100 • Fax: 717-533-8661
E-Mail: cust@igi-global.com • www.igi-global.com

Editorial Advisory Board

Table of Contents

Detailed Table of Contents

This study evaluates macroeconomic variables' effect on economic development in Mauritius from 1981 to 2019. The study employs the vector error correction (VECM) model for estimation. The long-run estimated results indicates a positive feedback between the variables, export, LOG(EXPT), external debt, LOG(DEBT), foreign direct investment (FDI), interest rate (INTR), the per capita GDP growth and a negative feedback between the per capita growth of the economy and the gross fixed capital formation LOG(GFCF(-1)), import (LOG(IMP)), and exchange rate (EXCH). The impulse response function (IRF) result indicates that the response of PERCAP to itself increases instantly and significantly and decreases in the short-run but continues with a positive sign along the horizons in the long-run. The response of GFCF to per capita shock increases immediately and continues to a positive shock in both short-run and the long-run horizon. The monetary policy variable,s INTR and EXCH, respond to per capita increase continues with the positive signs in both the short and long-run.

This study set out to investigate how financial reforms embarked upon after the change in economic policy affected economic development in Tanzania by analysing the finance and development nexus. The study utilized autoregressive distributive lag technique to evaluate data on how gross domestic product was used to measure economic development and seven variables proxied finance. The study established that there is a long-run relationship between finance and development in Tanzania for the period studied and that this relationship is able to return to equilibrium at an above average speed in the event of volatility. The study concluded that all the dependent variables except financial openness are leading indicators of economic development in Tanzania. Consequently, it is recommended that the switch in economic policy is in the right direction and the trajectory is sustained because it is creating the desired turnaround in the economy.

This chapter employed Johansen-Juselius Cointegration test, short-run and long-run causality tests, and error correction modelling to examine the finance and economic development of Uruguay between 1981 and 2019. The result shows that gross fixed capital formation and government expenditure have positive and statistically significant relationships with gross domestic product per capita, while the degree of openness exhibits a negative but statistically significant sign in relationship with gross domestic product per capita. The study therefore recommends that since gross capital formation and government expenditure influenced the economy of Uruguay the most, the Uruguay's government should focus on building more capacity in capital stock, which is believed to attract more investment. They should also spend on real sectors of the economy to boost the economic growth and increase the gross domestic product per capita and by extension the welfare of the economy.

The study provides a deeper understanding of the current role of finance in improving economic development in Vietnam between 1981 and 2019. The study employed the autoregressive distributed lag (ARDL) modelling technique. Based on the long run model estimates, trade openness (TOP) and foreign direct investment (FDI) exert positive but insignificant impact of economic development in Vietnam, while gross capital formation (GFKF) is significant at 10%. Also, exchange rate was found to have negatively influenced economic development, while human development was also important to economic development. This study found that human development and external borrowing is seen to positively impact on economic development in Vietnam. It is recommended that external debt ratio at the threshold of 105% of annual GDP is manageable and beneficial; it is important to attract multinational corporations from developed countries; the government should strengthen and encourage the competitiveness of exports to maintain a sustainable balance with imports and improving the high-quality labor in Vietnam.

Ultimately, the study aimed to determine the significance of finance to the Brazilian economy from 1981 to 2019. On account of the nature of data stationarity, the study then adopted the autoregressive distributed lag (ARDL) modelling technique which possesses the ability to produce both long-run and short-run parameter estimates. The empirical outcome of the Brazilian growth model which has been achieved is the product of conscious and purposeful reforms to address financial and other macroeconomic deficiencies and crisis in the country. Given the theoretical assumptions and the empirical evidence, it could be concluded that credit, FDI, and human development were economically significant to the economic development of Brazil in the long-run. Although trade openness, gross capital formation, and external borrowing did not significantly account for the economic development of the

This chapter examined the effect of finance in the development of the Ethiopian economy post-Cold War. The result of the autoregressive distributed lag (ARDL) estimates shows that human development is positive and statistically significant both in the short-run and in the long-run while GDPPC, real interest rate, GDPPC, and exchange rates had significant but negative impacts on the Ethiopian economy. Finally, the result also shows that the gross fixed capital formation (GFCF) is statistically significant but negative in the short-run and positive in the long-run. The study therefore recommended that real interest rate in Ethiopia should be stabilized by the monetary authority in order to enhance private investment and by extension improve the GDPPC. Ethiopian authorities should improve on the capital accumulation to enhance total factor productivity.

This chapter x-rayed Nigeria's political and economic history from independence to date. Nigeria has been managed under four different paradigms: free market 1960-1972; socialist inclined; mixed economy, posture, structural adjustment, 1986-1994; and quasi-capitalist approach. Based on 39 multivariate time series data, econometric analyses reveal that foreign direct investment, domestic savings (GFCF) capital expenditure, private consumption, and economic openness made a positive and significant impact on the Nigerian economy. On the other hand, import, exchange rate, foreign debt, monetary management indicators, and reinterest rates had negative and significant impacts on the Nigerian economy during the period. The study therefore recommends that Nigeria adopt export focused policy, institute FDI-friendly policies, and improve on her good governance image. In summary, the study concluded that the Nigerian economy could have done better.

War in any form and at any point in time in human existence is horrific. Among all the expectations of human race and nation, war is not one, including cold war. No doubt, cold war has always been with humanity. The author in this study set out to explore the effect of the post-cold war on the Indian economic growth and development. Due to the nature of the variables of the study, a quantitative econometric model formed the research methodology. The data scope covered the period of 39 years. The overall empirical results show that some macroeconomic variables have significant effect and positive relationship with the Indian economic development.

Foreword

World War II ended Eurocentricity thereby creating a bi-polar global political and economic world. The balance of power and balance of terror that emerged between the Western capitalist nations and the Communist/Socialist East, what political historians call the Cold War; resulted into pockets of wars, some of which was as devastating as World Wars I and II.

The collapse of the Soviet Union in 1991 resulted in a de facto Washington Hegemony. The Russian invasion of Ukraine in February 2022 rekindled the East-West rivalry and hostility. As this book opines, this can be regarded as the beginning of the second Cold War.

Although, this book is essentially a book of readings in Economic, the chapters deep-dive into the historical backgrounds of World Wars I and II, as well as the paradigm adoptions and shifts the Cold War occasioned gives the book a rare combination of global and political historical and economic content and context.

The book covers very important and strategic key economic player nations like India, Bangladesh, Nigeria, and Mexico amongst others.

It is in the light that the book will be of immense value to historians, economists as well as policy makers and other global players in world economy and politics.

The book is therefore highly recommended for scholars in history, economics, political science, and international relations among others.

Munirat Yusuf-Habib
University of Abuja, Nigeria

Preface

As World War II drew to a close, from 1944 to 1945, the alliances and pacts between friends, half friends, former friends and foes, fostered or forged by the exigencies of war to present a common front against Hitler's Nazi began to falter. Well before Normandy Landings (D-Day: June 6th 1944), the defeat of Hitler was assured. However, the war raged on in the pacific with Japan making waves. Intimidated by Hiroshima, 6th August 1945 and Nagasaki 9th August 1945 nuclear bombing and Japanese defeat by Russia in Manchuria, August 15th 1945, World War II came to an end quickly but eventfully.

It is often said that when one door closes another one opens. It will appear that in the heads of men, especially leaders of the so called super powers, when one war ends, another must start. Thus, World War II gave birth to the Cold War; a war of hardline diametrically opposed ideological positions, manifesting in deep seated hostilities, economic maneuvers, political and economic propaganda yet without copious resort to the use of military arsenals or hardware. A war fought without military fire-arms but with equally lethal ammunitions of economic and political actions, propaganda, espionage, sabotage and proxy or agent soldiers and ammunitions.

The Cold War is sometimes said to have started in earnest on March, 12th 1947 with the US President, Harry Truman's open declaration; (the Truman's Doctrine) on the floor of Congress to the effect that the US will support any people or country fighting or resisting Communism not only economically but also militarily. This is argued to have pitched the USSR and her own allies against the US and her allies. Thus, the war-but-no-war between the West and the East, between Capitalism and Communism, between Democracy, political liberalism and multipartism against authoritarianism, central control and one-party system was born. The Four hottest episodes of Cold War were: (i) the Korean war, 1950-1953, (ii) the Vietnamese war, (1955-1975), (iii), the development of the H-bomb in 1954 creating the era of the mutual assured destruction (MAD), and (iv), the 1962 Cuban missile crises.

The cold war is also often accepted to have ended in 1991 with the dissolution of the Soviet Union. In the thirty-year period, 1991-2020, the world can be said to have enjoyed some sort of global peace: fragile and tense, but peace nonetheless.

In that period, world population increased by almost fifty percent, from 5.3 billion in 1990 to 7.84 billion in 2020. World nominal GDP grew from less than US$23 trillion to US$85 trillion and real GDP *per capita* grew from world average of US$4,319 to US$10,896.

Unfortunately, just as the world was beginning to think that perhaps it has found global peace, (*pax mundial*), and just as the search for chapter contributions to this book began, the world woke up to the not-so-unexpected invasion of Ukraine by Russia. It is in this light that we can now talk more appropriately, of Cold War I, (1947-1990) and Post-Cold War I, (1991 to 2021) and Cold War II from February 2022 to God knows when.

This book takes a critical look at some twelve countries' macroeconomic management paradigms and outcomes in the Post-Cold War I era; five countries from Africa, four from Asia and one and two from North and South America respectively.

All the countries in this compendium but one (Ethiopia), are former colonies; some have at one time or another being pure communist/socialist, while others have once been communist/socialist inclined. However, from literature reviews and empirical evidence, all these countries have seen to have moved towards a market economy philosophy to different degrees.

THE TWELVE COUNTRIES IN FOCUS

Bangladesh

A south east Asia country, Bangladesh, as part of the British Raj, obtained independence from Great Britain on August 14th 194 as part of Pakistan, Bangladesh seceded from Pakistan to become an autonomous People's Republic of Bangladesh in 1971. Bangladesh is recognized as hosting the largest Muslim population proportion in the world, with ninety-one percent of its population of about 170 million as at 2021, being Muslims. With a nominal GDP of US$460 billion, Bangladesh is the second largest economy in south Asia and 35th in the world as well as 138th on the bases of real GDP per Capital. Bangladesh is regarded as one of the fairly peaceful and fast-growing economy in the world.

Brazil

Brazil is the largest economy in south America with a population of (215m) as well as by normal GDP of US$1.9 trillion in 2022. Brazil is ranked 11th in the world by nominal GDP but 78th by real GDP per Capita. Brazil was under Portuguese colonozation for about three hundred years, until 1822 when it gained independence. Brazil has had some rough economic and political upheavals including military rules, economic crisis in the 1980s, 1990s and even between 2014 and 2019. Brazil has however remained a fairly well-to-do economy especially since some major economic reforms in the late 1990s after the 1981-1993 period of stagnation, hyper-inflation and crisis. Being among the first twenty economies by normal GDP is not a mean achievement.

Empirical reviews as well as econometric analysis in this chapter reveal that the Brazilian economy is fairly strong and resilient, with large export market and fair share of global FDI. Brazil is projected as one of the worlds ten largest economy in the near future.

Ethiopia

Ethiopia is regarded as Africa oldest nation, and the only non-former colony in History not haven been colonized by any country in history. A landlock country in the horn of Africa, Ethiopia has a population of about 124 million (2022 estimate). After the overthoron of emperor Hailey Selassie, the Father of modern Ethiopia on September 12th 1974, Ethiopia has undertaken several political and socio-economic reforms with a homegrown reform Agenda since the 1990s, of which liberalization, privatization and globalization are pivotal.

Ethiopia has had its own fair share of internal crises, prominent among which are the secession of Eretria in 1993 after almost thirty years of armed struggle and the famine of 1983-1985, among others. In order to modernize her economy and integrate it into the world economy, Ethiopia adopted the English language in 1994 as a medium of learning, especially in secondary schools.

Five things Ethiopia may be remembered for today are: (i), Ethiopia is the only African country that escaped colonialization, (ii), Ethiopia is regarded as the birthplace of the coffee beans (iii), Ethiopia is one of the few countries not on the Gregorian calendar, (iv), Ethiopia has its one peculiar form of Christianity; Ethiopian Orthodox Christianity, and (v), in modern terms, Ethiopia has Africa's best Airline, the Ethiopian Airline; all clear evidence of better tomorrow for Ethiopians.

Ghana

The Republic of Ghana, (Gold Coast in colonial era) is one of the four former British colonies in West Africa. Romanticized as the Black Star, Ghana is one of West Africa's economy power houses and an example of the fairly developed socially dynamic countries in Africa. Ghana obtained independence from Great Britain on the 6th of March 1958 after about sixty-six-year period of colonization. Ghana inherited the British system of Government, education as well as the free economy management philosophy. However, under Dr. Khame Nkurumah, Ghana's first leader, as well as the originator of the concept of neo-colonialism, Khame Nkurumah immediately steered Ghana into Socialism, (African Socialism), and the non- aligned moment.

The solidity and quality of education in Ghana today can all be traced to Kwame Nkrumah. He insisted that all Ghanaian children go to school and encouraged women too to attend school.

Unfortunately, like most newly decolonized countries that wanted to distance themselves from their former colonial masters, Ghana embarked on several anti-free-market policies. This, like in most other countries, also failed to spur economic development as much and as fast as Ghanaians would have cherished. Therefore, on February 24th 1966, in what should effectively be classified as a *coup-d'état*, Nkrumah was forced out of government and out of Ghana.

Subsequently, the one-time world's largest producer of Cocoa, gradually lost her agricultural and industrial lead in West Africa. The coming to power of Flt. Lieutenant John Jerry Rawlings in 1979 and 1981 is generally regarded as what brought Ghana back from the brink of economic catastrophe and political strangulation.

After Ghana's economic adjustment in the 1980s, under IMF tutelage, considered to be one example of the success, especially in Africa, the Ghanaian economy seem to have done better in the late 1990s and early 2000s. The severe global financial crises and especially the COVID-19 pandemic, as well as some apparently not firm grasp of the nation's economic fundamentals by recent administrations seem to be having a slowing down effect on the Ghanaian economy. Corruption accusation, poor and declining quality of governance have also contributed to the not-so-impressive outcomes in the Ghanaian economy in recent times. Nevertheless, with a nominal GDP of US$72.84 billion in 2020 and *per capita* real GDP of US$2176 Ghana ranks 77th and 145th in the world and in Africa respectively.

India

India, with the largest population of 1.41 billion in the world (from 2023), is the third largest economy in Asia and 5th in the world by nominal GDP of US$3.4trillion.

On the bases of real GDP per Capita, India ranks 139th in the world. India obtained independence from Britain on 15th August 1947. Like many former colonies, India attempted to distance itself from her colonial masters in her immediate post colonial days. India once attempted a socialist or quasi-socialist economic management philosophy; the mixed economy paradigm since 1990s. However, India has embarked on a steady series of economic reforms prominent among which are: liberalization and opening up in general. India's economic strides can be gleaned from her strong economic powers, with nuclear capability as well as the prominent roles Indian professionals, diplomats and politicians are currently playing in the world. With a real GDP per Capita of US $... however, India can be said to still be in the developing countries bracket. However, with the way India has progressed in recent times, politically and economically, India can realistically be classified among a World emerging super powers.

Indonesia

A neighbor of and contender to China, India, Japan and Bangladesh. Indonesia is another trillion-dollar economy in south east Asia. Indonesia is a former British colony which gained independence on August 17th 1945. With a population of about 274 million, a nominal GDP of about US$3.30 trillion, (16th in rank globally), but 112th on real GDP bases. Indonesia is another east Asian power house. Indonesia too has gone through some period of turmoil, especially economic crisis of late 1970s and early 1980s. Empirical review and econometric analysis in this study reveal not only that Indonesia has some impressive growth record but also that the country has been on a positive growth trajectory in the twenty-first century, though still with much room and need for improvement.

Mauritius

A former colony of Netherlands, France and then Britain until it became independent in 1968. Mauritius is a small island east of Madagascar in the southern east of Africa, Mauritius is a small economy with only a population of about 1.3million people and a nominal GDP of only US$29 billiom. Mauritius is a small country and a small economy by all Standards. However, at 141st position by nominal GDP but 73rd by real GDP per Capita, and as one of the three fastest growing African economies in the 21st century. Mauritius has been recognized as an economy to recon with. The strength and growth of the Mauritius economy has been attributed to political stability, sound firm and consistent macroeconomic management, openness and steady FDI flows as well as other factors. The chapter on Mauritius suggest that she is a small but dynamic and progressive economy with great tourism assets and destination of significance and exciting macroeconomic management disposition, hence the impressive growth outcomes.

Mexico

Mexico (the united Mexican states) is one of the three largest economies by population as well as by GDP, with the GDP of US US$1.4 trillion, 14th largest in the world and 63rd rank in real GDP bases (2022) in North America. With a history dating back to the pre-Aztec times, Mexico is an old country. Colonized by Spain for about three hundred years 1521-1821/1824, New Spain, as the Spaniards chose to call Mexico during the colonial era, has had a rough political history in her early post-colonial periods relatively fair political and economic outcomes. In later life especially after World War II, Mexico has had a

Bogged down by internal crises after a decade of war of independence as well as wars with Spain, the United State of America and other foreign interferences, Mexico went into a period of socio-political upheavals, the Mexican Revolution 1910 to 1920. After World War II and more so, since the last quarter of the 20th century, Mexico has experienced a more tranquille socio-political existence, has undertaken much opening up of her economy and more market-oriented reforms of which entry into the North America Free and Trade Agreement in 1994 Improvement in the Mexican-US relationship and among other reforms were prominent. The combined effect of the above have been a more dynamic pace of socio economic growth. Mexico's admission into the OECD is a testimony to her rising status as an economic power in her own rights.

Empirical reviews in this study as well as the econometric analyses suggest that Mexico has made tremendous progress in the areas of socio-political stability as well as the area of economic development. There is however a consensus in empirical literature that the Mexican economy has not benefited enough from her geographical advantage and resources endowments. Large informal sector, growing inequality, less than transparent governance stance (Corruption), declining total factor productivity, poor financial resource management, fiscal and monetary are factors identified in theory and empirical studies as holding down the Mexican economy post-Cold War and more so in the 21st century. Addressing these are considered as must-do if Mexico wishes to reap full benefits of her relation with the USA, Canada as well as the world as a whole.

Nigeria

The Federal Republic of Nigeria, is a country in the West African region. With a population of 219 million (2022 estimate), Nigeria obtained Independence from Britain on October 1st 1960. With a rather catastrophic coup delte in 1966 followed by a 30-month civil war (July 1967- January 15th 1970), Nigeria came under military rule with a unitary form of government, although it was tagged as a federation of 12, 19, 24 and later 30 states plus a semi-autonomous Federal Capital Territory from 1966 to 1993 except 1997-1983. Currently as a federation, Nigeria tasted socialism or quasi-socialism, (mixed economy) from 1972/1974 to 1886 via the Nigerian Enterprise promotion Decree (NEPD). This resulted into Nigeria's economy declined steadily until in 1986 when the nation adopted the structural adjustment programme(SAP).

Apparent lack of full-hearted adherence to the true tenet of SAP seem to have affected Nigeria's effort in achieving a faster rate of development. Since 1999, after release to Civil Rule, Nigeria has pursued a more market based economic management policy becoming Africa's largest economy by nominal GDP in 2014; However, high level of informal sector, low savings and poor capital formation capabilities have contributed to the relatively low pace of development and increasing incidence of poverty in the country. Poor governance, corruption and weak institutions are often cited as the most important hinderances to Nigeria economic development. Greater level of transparency and less uncertainties in her economic policy stance are often canvassed as Nigeria's hope for improved economic performance.

Nigeria is currently ranked as the 6th largest country in the world by population. With a nominal GDP of US$477 billion in 2022, Nigeria is ranked as the first in African and 31st in the world, hence is often romanticized as the Giant of Africa. However, with a real GDP *per capita* of US$2,184 (less than one sixth of world average), Nigeria, at 154th among the first fifty from the rear globally.

Tanzania

Outcome of the union of Tanganyika and Zanzibar on the 26th of April 1964. Tanzania was born as a nation in the east African region. Noted for housing the tallest mountain in Africa; Mount Kilimanjaro, as well as the second largest Lake in the world, Lake Tanganyika the world most treasured Parks, Tanzania is one of the tourism destinations in Africa. With a nominal GDP of US$75.7 billion described as all-time high and real GDP *per capita* of US$1253 in 2022 respectively, Tanzania is ranked globally as 75th and 166th respectively on the bases of nominal and real GDP. Relatively free of corruption; building on the legacy of its founding Father,

Mualim Julius Nyerere, Tanzania's economy has progressed fairly better, especially after the failure of Ujamaa, (Africa Socialism) and subsequent economic reforms.

Empirical review and the data analysis in this chapter show that pro-market reforms in East African countries, of which Tanzania is one, has resulted in some appreciable economic growth and development in the region as much as in Tanzania itself.

Uruguay

A Spanish colony from 1516-181, the Republic of Uruguay is the second smallest country in South America. With a population of only 3.5 million (2022), 79th in the world; with real GDP per Capita of US$1821in 2022 47th in the world as well as a robust social security system, high quality health and educational services, Uruguay rates as highly developed. These outcomes have been driven by political stability disciplined stable as well as sustainable macroeconomic management.

As per countries in this compendium of countries experiences post-Cold War, Uruguay will stand out; small in size 132nd ranked in population but stable, dynamic and progressive positioned as the 47th most developed economy by real GDP *per capita* in 2022, (at 44% higher than world's average), Uruguay is the most developed among the twelve countries in this study.

Vietnam

As far as this book goes, Vietnam, has a special position on the world politics and economic history in relation to the cold war and post-cold war.

Vietnam, (the Socialist Republic of Vietnam), was one country in which the cold war actually got hot. The Cuban crises, dangerous as it got, did not result into a civil-cum-proxy war. The Korean crises that resulted into war lasted only about five years and resulted into the partitioning of Korea into North and south Korea till date.

Unlike the above, the Vietnamese war lasted for about twenty years (1955-1975) but ended up with a one Vietnam.

Three other key facts are relevance to this book regarding Vietnam, vis-à-vis the cold war episode are: (i) as said above, the cold war got really hot in Vietnam. (ii) Although, Vietnam emerged in 1975 as a strong and united socialist country, today Vietnam is described as a mixed socialist oriented market economy. and (iii) Vietnam has grown steadily after some major left-to-right economic reforms, including opening up; and thereby becoming the 13th largest economy in Asia, 36th in the world with a nominal GDP of US$409, (described as an all-time high in the Vietnamese economic history) and real GDP *per Capita* of US$13457 in 2022, 11th in rank, higher than world's average.

SUMMARY AND OVERVIEW

In relation to world politics and macroeconomic management paradigms, the countries reviewed in this book and especially the cases of Vietnam, it can be averred that war, cold or hot, is inimical to economic progress and that a competitive free market economic orientation and globally focused economic management paradigm produce faster and better developmental dividends than other-wise.

The three big take-aways from this book are: (i) as it is often said, there is neither a good war nor a bad peace, (ii) as in almost everything in life, unity cooperation and competitive collaboration are better than war and confrontations, and (iii) all said and done, the free market economic management philosophy has proven that liberalism or neoliberalism as it is now variously couched has continued to outperform closed, regimental and centrally planned economic management approach.

Yekeen Oku Abdul-Maliq
University of Abuja, Nigeria

Chapter 1
Finance and Development in Bangladesh:
A Post-Cold War Evaluation

Edward Ogbonnia Eleje
Department of Banking and Finance, Federal University, Wukari, Nigeria

Habila Abel Haruna
https://orcid.org/0000-0002-7281-2230
Department of Banking and Finance, Federal University, Wukari, Nigeria

Hyeladi Stanley Dibal
https://orcid.org/0000-0002-8860-5009
Department of Banking and Finance, Federal University, Wukari, Nigeria

ABSTRACT

This study evaluates the role of finance in the economic development of Bangladesh post-Cold War from 1981-2019. Using the ARDL model and Granger causality test, the findings show that gross fixed capital formation and balance of payment are positive and significant to real gross domestic product (RGDP) in the short run and long run, and a bidirectional relationship exists between them. Foreign direct investment (FDI) has a long-run and short-run negative and significant effect, while external borrowing (EXB) has a long-term positive and significant effect on RGDP. While a bidirectional causality exists between FDI and RGDP, there is no causality between EXB and RGDP. Exchange rates (EXR) have a positive and significant effect, while interest rates (INTR) were insignificant. A unidirectional causality exists between EXR and RGDP whereas no causality exists between INTR and RGDP. The findings of this study, therefore, underscore the relevance of finance in Bangladesh's economy post-Cold War and thus contribute to existing debate on the role of finance in economic development of nations.

DOI: 10.4018/979-8-3693-1610-8.ch001

1. INTRODUCTION

Bangladesh is a country located in the south-east Asian region with a population of over 160million people in 55.598 sq. miles and is surrounded by India on all sides, except Burma (Myanmar) bordering the far southeast region and Bay of Bengal to the south (Ahmed, 2011). The economy is agrarian and nearly half of the population is engaged in agriculture and farming. Bangladesh got its independence from Pakistan on 16th December 1971 which gave birth to the first parliamentary era that lasted until 1975. Between 1975 and 1990, the country experienced military rule before the current parliamentary era which started in 1991. It is currently a unitary parliamentary constitutional republic based on the Westminster system (World Factbook, 2022). The country has seen remarkable development progress under several unfavourable conditions, including weak governance and political instability, inequalities within the country, the downsides of rapid urbanization, and exposure to several natural disasters (Sawada et al, 2018). The end of the British control in 1947 saw the partitioning of Bengal based on religion rather than language or ethnic origin. The eastern and western parts of Bengal became part of Pakistan (East Pakistan) and India, respectively with no significant difference in per capita income between the west and East Pakistan.

The post-independence differences in economic growth between the two parts of Pakistan became obvious and widened in favour of West Pakistan. As noted by Bose (1953) during the period 1959-1960 and 1969-1970, East Pakistan's per capita income increased by 1.5 per cent per annum, compared to the 3.6 per cent increase experienced in West Pakistan, and this resulted in a 61 per cent higher per capita income in West Pakistan by 1969-1970. In the early 1970s, Bangladesh was heavily dependent on foreign aid due to a lack of domestic resources needed for capital formation; the saving and investment rates were stuck below 5 and 15 per cent of GDP, respectively. In the late 1970s, remittances from migrant workers contributed significantly to foreign exchange reserves, which gradually reduced dependence on foreign aid and strengthened national savings (Taslim, 2008).

The post-war economic management in Bangladesh targeted a review of the war-ravaged economy in an overall framework of extensive state control and socialist ideology (Mahmud, 2008). There was a policy shift towards privatization and promotion of the private sector in the wake of the military rule in the country (Mahmud et al., 2008). The economic reform process was targeted at opening the domestic economy for foreign investments and making the domestic economy market-based (Ahluwalia & Mahmud, 2004). Some of the notable economic reforms introduced to drive the post-cold war Bangladesh economy include the introduction of the Foreign Private Investment Act of 1980 which provided confidence to the investors especially foreign investors about safety of their investment. Also, the Readymade

Garment (RMG) sector was introduced in 1980 representing Bangladesh's largest export-earning sector. Other major sectors like Textiles, Pharmaceuticals, Leather, and Jute etc. also got energized during the same period. Government provided policy boosts like Back-to-Back LC and Bonded Warehouse Facilities to export oriented RMG sector and achieved a revolutionary boom in export earnings. Currently, 84% of Bangladesh's export earnings come from this sector. The agricultural sector is also a success story making Bangladesh self-sufficient in food grain production shortly after independence.

The introduction of microfinance framework in Bangladesh successfully served as another booster for the economy. According to Mohajan (2013), the microfinance system helped the poor and the ultra-poor to develop their financial conditions. The Grameen Bank is the first microfinance institution in Bangladesh, which was established in 1976. It gives loans to those people whom the government or any commercial bank will not give loan facility. At present, Grameen Bank is the largest micro-finance bank in Bangladesh and probably the biggest microcredit organization in the world (Mohajan, 2013). At present, it provides small loans of about $600 million to more than 10 million rural poor (95% are women) in Bangladesh (Islam et al., 2012).

This study therefore, espouses the finance and development nexus in Bangladesh with a specific focus on the role of Gross Fixed Capital Formation, Net Import and Export, Foreign Direct Investment, and External Borrowing in the development process in Bangladesh through the finance-growth theoretical lens proposed by Levine (2005) while accounting for the moderating role of exchange rate and interest rate for a period of 39 years ranging from 1981-2019. The Auto-Regressive Distributed Lag (ARDL) model approach proposed by Pesaran and Shin (1999) and Pesaran et al. (2001) was adopted to investigate the long-run and short-run relationship between finance and development in Bangladesh post-cold war. This provides a nuanced perspective of the finance-development nexus in Bangladesh, especially during the post-cold war period.

The rest of the chapter is organised as follows; the introduction is followed by section two which discusses the Economic management philosophy in Bangladesh during the Cold War: 1947 to 1980; section three discussed the political, social and economic reforms in Bangladesh post-cold war; section four provided empirical insights into the finance-development nexus; the methodology adopted is presented in section five while the results and discussions are presented in section six; the conclusion is reported in section seven.

Figure 1. Map of Bangladesh

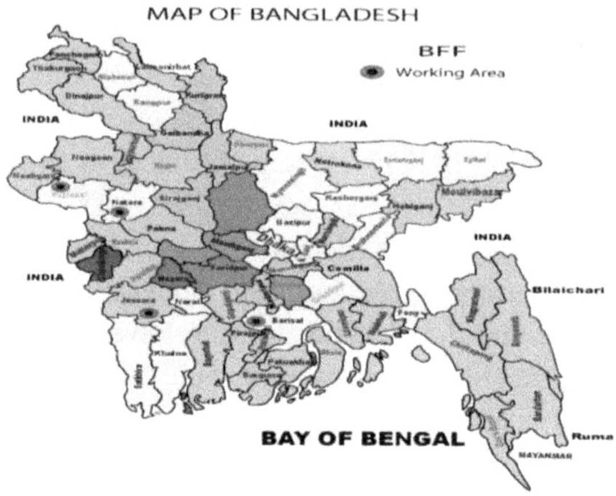

2. POLITICAL, SOCIAL, AND ECONOMIC REFORMS IN BANGLADESH POST-COLD WAR

Bangladesh is a country in Southern Asia, bordering the Bay of Bengal between Burma and India with geographical coordinates 24 00 N, 90 00 E and a total area of 48,460 sq km. As of 2022, it has a population of 165,650,475, a population growth rate of 0.93% and an urban population of 39.7% of the total population. The country is blessed with natural gas, arable land, timber and coal. Figure 1 shows the map of Bangladesh.

After the war of independence, Bangladesh was poor, overpopulated and emerged from its war of independence desperately poor, overpopulated, and revolving from devastating damage the war caused to economic, institutional and physical capital (Faaland & Parkinson, 1976). Certain economic reforms have become pertinent for the country to recover from the devastating aftermath effect of the war of independence. As part of the economic reforms, in the mid-1980s, Bangladesh embarked on market-oriented liberalization policy reforms known as the Structural Adjustment due to the macroeconomic imbalances attributed to the decline in foreign aid and preceding episodes of the deterioration in the country's terms of trade (Ahluwalia & Mahmud, 2004; Kalirajan & Salim, 1997). The post-war economic management in Bangladesh was predominantly targeted at reviving a war-ravaged economy in an overall framework of extensive state control and with an avowed ideology of socialism (Ahmed, 2005; Mahmud, 2008). With the change of government and the birth of the military regime, the country had a policy shift towards privatization and promotion of the private sector (Mahmud et al., 2008). This gradual approach to the economic reform process was guided by trade liberalization and economic deregulation to make the domestic economy market-based and various procedures to open up the domestic economy and attract foreign direct investment (Ahluwalia & Mahmud, 2004; Kalirajan & Salim, 1997). The gradual recovery of the Bangladesh economy (GDP per capita income) started in the late 1970s.

The transformation and improvement in both economic performance and human capital development indicators started in the early 1990s due to the economic reforms and transition to democracy. Despite a reduced and declining dependence on foreign aid, the economy was showing a glimpse of transiting from stabilization to growth (Mahmud et al., 2008; Ahluwalia & Mahmud, 2004). More so, this economic transformation is also partly attributed to the slow population growth rate coupled with a sustained increase in GDP growth. The growth of GDP per capita had been slow as compared to the standard of contemporary South Asia in the 1980s, at about 3.7 per cent a year; but it accelerated to 4.4 per cent in the first half of the 1990s, and to 5.2 per cent in the second half. Agriculture, industry, and services sectors contributed to the growth acceleration of the economy since the early 1990s. Despite prolonged political instability, insufficient power supplies, and slow implementation of some economic reforms, Bangladesh's economy has grown roughly 6% per year since 2005. It has been recorded that more than half of the GDP is generated through the service sector (World Factbook, 2022; Mahmud et al., 2008). The improvement in human capital development was beyond expectation in the 1990s, this placed Bangladesh among the top performers according to the United Nations Development Programme (UNDP) Human Capital Development Index.

As mentioned by Chowdhury (2002), the reformation of the financial sector was also part of the liberalization and privatization process that started in 1975 with the change of administration. This led to the privatization of state-owned enterprises in 1976 due to deteriorating economic conditions. The liberalization of the financial sector took place in 1982 with the privatization of two Nationalized Commercial Banks (NCBs) and permitting of Private Commercial Banks (PCBs) to operate in the country. With the introduction of the structural adjustment programme in the mid-1980s, the privatization and liberalization process gained momentum which gave birth to the financial sector reform agenda launched in 1984 with the appointment of the National Commission of Money, bank and Credit (NCMBC). The commission submitted a report in 1986 and in response to that, the government launched the Financial Sector Reforms Programme in 1990 under a Financial Sector Adjustment Credit of the International Development Agency. To further the course of the financial sector transformation agenda, the government launched the Banking Reform Committee in 1996 and by 1997, they reported powerful recommendations concerning setting up and operation of Commercial Banks addressing major issues like interest rate liberalization; loan classification and provision; capital adequacy; introduction of instruments for indirect monetary management; legal reforms; strengthening of central bank; strengthening of bank supervision; improving the operational efficiency of commercial banks; and reforms in foreign exchange regimes.

3. FINANCE AND DEVELOPMENT

Gross Fixed Capital Formation and Economic Growth

The concept of gross fixed capital formation dates back to the National Bureau of Economic Research (NBER) studies of Simon Kuznets on capital formation in the 1937s, where standard measures for it were adopted in the 1950s. It can be classified as gross private domestic investment and gross public domestic investment and GFCF General Government Sector (Ajose & Oyedokun 2018; Ali, 2015). It consists of resident producers' investments, deducting disposals, in fixed assets during a given period. It also includes certain additions to the value of non-produced assets realized by producers or institutional units (IMF 2022). Gross Fixed Capital Formation (GFCF) forms a significant fragment of economic growth. Empirical evidence has shown that gross fixed capital formation has a significant effect (Tabassum & Ahmed, 2014; Bahname, 2012; Abdullahi et al., 2012), a not significant effect (Ajose & Oyedokun 2018; Nweke et al., 2017) and long-run significant relationship (Biplob & Halder 2018; Ali, 2015) on economic growth. Some recent empirical evidence by Meyer and Sunusi (2019) revealed a long-run relationship exists between gross fixed capital formation and economic growth, with causality running from economic growth to gross fixed capital formation. This is also reported by Ajose and Oyedokun (2018). On the contrary, other studies revealed a bidirectional causality (Biplob & Halder, 2018; Nweke et al., 2017). Boamah et al. (2018) investigated the relationship between gross fixed capital formation and economic growth of 18 Asian countries. Using panel data from 1990 to 2017, they documented a significant positive impact of gross fixed capital formation on economic growth. Nazir et al. (2020) investigate the causal relationship between financial innovation and economic growth in China, India, and Pakistan over the period of 1970-2016. Using an Autoregressive Distributed Lag (ARDL) bound testing and Granger causality-based Error Correction Model (ECM), this study finds that gross fixed capital formation contributes considerably positively to the economic growth in China, India, and Pakistan.

Trade and Economic Growth

Early studies have investigated both the export-led growth and import-led growth in trying to link trade and economic growth. Empirical evidence has established the existence of export-led growth (Selvanathan et al., 2020; Khanom, 2019; Emmanuel, 2017; Ahmed & Uddin, 2009) and import-led growth (Selvanathan et al., 2020: Awokuse, 2007). Other studies have established a positive association between exports and GDP but the opposite is seen between imports and GDP (Khanom, 2019; Akhter, 2015). Ahamad (2018) investigated the impact of international trade on the economic growth of Bangladesh and found a strong positive relationship between international trade and economic growth. Ahmed and Uddin (2009) investigated the causal nexus between export, import, remittance and GDP growth in Bangladesh from 1976 to 2005. Using the vector error correction model (VECM), the study indicates exports, imports and remittance impact GDP growth in the short run but has no long-run impact. Also, the result revealed a unidirectional causal effect. Meraj (2013) investigated the effect of globalization and trade openness on economic growth in Bangladesh and the results showed a long-run association between exports, imports and GDP of Bangladesh. A bidirectional causality export to GDP was established but there is no evidence of causality from imports to GDP and vice-versa. A study by Shirazi & Manap (2005) also reported empirical evidence of a long-run bidirectional relationship between imports and output growth in Bangladesh. Selvanathan et al. (2020) examined the causal relationship between economic growth, imports and exports in Bangladesh during the period 1970-2017. Empirical evidence supports the export-led growth and growth-led exports hypotheses. A revealed significant short-run and long-run unidirectional causality from imports to economic growth was also confirmed.

Foreign Direct Investment and Economic Growth

FDI inflows and outflows are globally recognized in the growth of an economy (Temiz & Gokmen, 2014; Thilakaweera, 2011). It is an investment made to acquire lasting interest in an enterprise operating in an economy other than that of the investor with the intention of having a stake in the management of the enterprise (Organisation for Economic Co-operation and Development [OECD], 2021). In the absence of adequate domestic investment, FDI inflow coming from industrially advanced countries is widely utilized to accelerate industrialization that can foster sustained economic growth and reduce the unemployment rate in developing countries (Hussain & Haque 2016). According to Sarker and Khan (2020), FDI is an important factor that can influence economic growth in a developing country like Bangladesh due to capital inadequacy as a result of insufficient domestic savings both in the private and public sectors. Empirical literature has revealed mixed results on the relationship between foreign direct investment and economic growth in Bangladesh. This relationship revealed foreign direct investment has a significant relationship (Oyegoke & Aras, 2021; Sarker & Khan, 2020; Rajib & Rahman, 2020; Asaduzzaman, 2019; Qamruzzaman & Jianguo, 2017; Adhikary, 2015) and no significant relationship (Jamil & Hasan, 2015; Rahman, 2015; Tabassum & Ahmed, 2014; Shimul et al., 2009) economic growth. Asaduzzaman (2019) investigates the empirical relationship between some economic variables and economic growth in Bangladesh between 1973-2017 using the Johansen cointegration test and VECM analysis. The results revealed a long-run and short-run significant relationship between foreign direct investment, real effective exchange rate and trade openness, and economic growth where the study further suggests utilizing foreign direct investment and trade openness can augur well for the development of Bangladesh's economy. Sarker and Khan (2020) also found a long-run significant relationship between foreign direct investment and economic growth and further inferred a unidirectional relationship running from GDP Granger caused FDI while Dritsakis et al. (2006) revealed a unidirectional causal relationship running from the ratio of foreign direct investments to GDP to per capita GDP. Tabassum and Ahmed (2014) on the other hand examine the relationship between foreign direct investments and the economic growth of Bangladesh covering 1972–2011 and found a not significant relationship.

External Debt and Economic Growth

When government fails to meet their developmental objective through infrastructural development, poverty reduction and sustained economic growth, external borrowing becomes a way out for most developing economies. Bangladesh particularly relies on external borrowing since independence to manage the saving-investment gap and fiscal deficit (Dey &Tareque, 2019; Yeasmin, et al., 2015). Empirical evidence has shown external debt has an adverse effect (Yeasmin, et al., 2015; Yeasmin & Chowdhury, 2014), negative effect (Dey &Tareque, 2019; Kharusi & Ada, 2018; Ramzan & Ahmad, 2014; Ali & Mustafa, 2012), positive effect (Rahman et al., 2012) and an indirect positive effect (Saifuddin, 2016) on economic growth. A study by Hossain and Shirin (2016) investigates the effects of different types of debts on economic growth in Bangladesh using time series data spanning from 2000 to 2015. Using the ARDL model shows that there exists a long-run relationship between external debt and economic growth. Findings revealed the existence of a bidirectional causality between public sector external debt and economic growth while causality between private external debt and economic growth is insignificant. This however is contrary to the work of Korkmaz (2015) which shows a unidirectional causality running from economic growth to external debt. Dey and Tareque (2019) examine the impact of external debt on economic growth in Bangladesh using time series data from 1980 to 2017. Employing the ARDl model, the study results reveal a negative impact of external debt on GDP growth. It further revealed that macroeconomic policies index has a positive impact on economic growth which indicates that this adverse effect of debt can be mitigated or even nullified by sound macroeconomic policies and appropriate human resource policy.

Macroeconomic Variables and Economic Growth

Monetary policy through its macroeconomic variables is a fundamental factor of macroeconomic management that stimulates economic stability and promotes economic development (Van Dan & Binh, 2018). Scholars have tried to establish a link between these variables and economic growth. Empirical evidence has been established that exchange rate has a negative effect (Saxena & Bansal, 2019; Van Dan & Binh, 2018), long-run impact (Ali et al., 2015) and bidirectional causality between interest rate and economic growth (Hossin, 2020; Uddin, et al., 2014). Empirical evidence on exchange rate have established a not significant (Rajib & Rahman, 2020; Halder, 2019), negative causal relationship (Karahan, 2020), long-run significant effect (Asaduzzaman, 2019; Razzaque, et al., 2017), and positive effect (Khan, 2021; Islam & Hossain, 2019; Uddin, et al., 2014) on economic growth. Other studies by Chowdhury et al. (2019) investigate the impact of macroeconomic variables on the economic growth in Bangladesh from 1987-2015. The results revealed that interest rate and exchange rate are statistically significant determinants of economic growth while on the contrary, Etale and Imbazi, (2020) examined the influence of some selected microeconomic variables on economic growth in Nigeria between 1999 and 2018 and discovered that interest rate and exchange rate not significant determinant of economic growth.

4. METHODOLOGY

Data and Measurement of Variables

The study utilized data covering the period of 39 years from 1981-2019. Using the finance-growth nexus proposed by Levine (2005), the objective of the study was to investigate the role of finance on the development of the Bangladesh economy after the cold war. As a dependent variable, real gross domestic product per capita (Ajose & Oyedokun 2018; Nweke et al., 2017) was used as a proxy for development while gross fixed capital formation (Nazir et al., 2020; Ajose & Oyedokun 2018; Boamah et al., 2018; Ali, 2015), net import and export (Selvanathan et al., 2020;

Table 1. Variables measurement and source

Variables	Measurement	Symbol	Source
Development	Real Gross Domestic Product Per Capita	RGDP	World Governance Indicators
Finance	Gross Fixed Capital Formation Net Import and Export Foreign Direct Investment External Borrowing	GFCF BOP FDI EXB	World Governance Indicators World Governance Indicators World Governance Indicators World Governance Indicators
Moderator Variables	Exchange Rate Interest Rate	EXR INTR	World Governance Indicators World Governance Indicators

Source: Authors' Compilation 2022

Khanom, 2019), foreign direct investment (Haruna et al., 2023; Sarker & Khan, 2020; Rajib & Rahman, 2020; Asaduzzaman, 2019), and external borrowing (Dey &Tareque, 2019: Hossain & Shirin, 2016) were used as proxies for finance in the independent variables. Macroeconomic variables proxied by exchange rate and interest rate (Chowdhury et al., 2019; Etale & Imbazi, 2020) were introduced as control variables to see the role they play in determining economic development. Table 1 gives the variables measurement and source as used in this study.

The Autoregressive Distributed Lag (ARDL) Model

The Auto-Regressive Distributed Lag (ARDL) model approach proposed by Pesaran and Shin (1999) and Pesaran et al. (2001) was adopted to investigate the long-run and short-run relationship between finance and development in Bangladesh post-cold war. The ARDL is a model whose assumptions are based on the ordinary least square (OLS) model that can suit both non-stationary time series as well as times series with mixed order of integration (Pesaran & Shin, 1999; Pesaran, Shin & Smith, 2001; Nkoro & Uko, 2016; Shrestha & Bhatta, 2018) which include lags of both the dependent and independent variables as regressors (Adediran, 2020). This method determines the co-integrating relationships between series with different orders of integration while the reparameterized result gives the long-run relationship and the short-run dynamics of the considered variables (Nkoro & Uko, 2016; Pesaran et al. 2001; Pesaran and Shin, 1999). More so, the ARDL technique takes a sufficient number of lags to take into consideration the data-generating process in a general-to-specific modelling framework (Shrestha & Bhatta 2018; Ghouse et al., 2019) which is why it can potentially deal with many misspecification and autocorrelation problems and come up an appropriate model that can be interpreted (Ghouse et al., 2019). Additionally, this model has the potential to simultaneously estimate both long-run and short-run co-integrating relationships thereby providing an unbiased estimation for the study (Pesaran et al. 2001; Qamruzzaman & Wei, 2018). The ARDL model is therefore presented below:

$$y_t = \sum_{j=1}^{p} \gamma_j y_{t-j} + \sum_{j=0}^{q} \left('_j x_{t-j} \right) + \mu_t \tag{1}$$

where x_t is a k x 1 vector of multiple regressors; γ_j is the autoregressive parameter; δ_t is the symmetric distributed lag parameters; ε is an *iid* process with zero mean and constant variance. To investigate the relationship between investigate the long-run and short-run relationship between finance and development in Bangladesh post-cold war, the study is modelled using the Levine (2005) finance-growth nexus and proposed below

$$Y = f(G,T) \tag{2}$$

$$\text{Development} = f(GFCF, BOP, FDI, EXB, EXR, INTR) \tag{3}$$

$$RGDP_{it} = \delta'_1 GFCF_{i,t-j} + \delta'_2 BOP_{i,t-j} + \delta'_3 FDI_{i,t-j} + \delta'_3 EXB_{i,t-j} + \delta'_2 EXR_{i,t-j} + \delta'_3 INTR_{i,t-j} + \varepsilon_t \tag{4}$$

Where RGDP is real gross domestic product per capita, GFCF is gross fixed capital formation, BOP is net import and export, FDI is foreign direct investment, EXB is external borrowing, EXR is exchange rate, INTR is real interest rate, x_{it}, and δ_{ij} are k x 1 coefficient vectors.

This study, therefore, specifies the panel ARDL model ARDL (2 1 2 1 2 3 3) below

$$RGDP_{it} = \sum_{j=1}^{p} \gamma_{ij} RGDP_{i,t-j} + \sum_{j=0}^{q} \delta'_{ij} GFCF_{i,t-j} + \sum_{j=0}^{q} \delta'_{ij} BOP_{i,t-j} + \sum_{j=0}^{q} \delta'_{ij} FDI_{i,t-j} + \sum_{j=0}^{q} \delta'_{ij} EXB_{i,t-j} + \sum_{j=0}^{q} \delta'_{ij} EXR_{i,t-j} + \sum_{j=0}^{q} \delta'_{ij} INTR_{i,t-j} + \varepsilon_t \tag{5}$$

The estimated error correction form (cointEq(-1)) corresponding to the long-run estimates measures the speed of adjustment whereby short-run dynamics converge to the long-run equilibrium path in the models without losing the long-run information and avoids problems such as spurious relationships resulting from non-stationary time series data (Shrestha & Bhatta 2018). The coefficient of CointEq(-1) describes how deviations from that long-run relationship affect the changes in them in the next period and is expected to be negative and significant. When that happens, it implies that each year the disequilibrium in the series is being corrected and it takes two years to return to equilibrium. Following Pesaran et al. (2001), the error correction form for the model is presented as:

$$RGDP_{it} = \sum_{j=1}^{p}\gamma_{ij} RGDP_{i,t-j} + \sum_{j=0}^{q}\delta'_{ij}\, GFCF_{i,t-j} + \sum_{j=0}^{q}\delta'_{ij}\, BOP_{i,t-j}$$
$$+\sum_{j=0}^{q}\delta'_{ij}\, FDI_{i,t-j} + \sum_{j=0}^{q}\delta'_{ij}\, EXB_{i,t-j} + \sum_{j=0}^{q}\delta'_{ij}\, EXR_{i,t-j} + \sum_{j=0}^{q}\delta'_{ij}\, INTR_{i,t-j} + ect_t + \varepsilon_t \quad (6)$$

Unit Root Test

This study applied the Augmented Dickey-Fuller (ADF) test proposed by Dickey and Fuller (1979), Philip Perron (PP) test proposed by Phillips and Perron (1988) and Kwiatkowski–Phillips–Schmidt–Shin (KPSS) tests proposed by Kwiatkowski et al. (1992) to determine the order of integration of the variables used in this study to ensure that none of the variables is integrated into order two I(2) because when this happens, the estimations are not consistent (Asteriou & Monastiriotis, 2004).

ARDL Bound Test for Co-Integration

To determine the presence of a long-run relationship between the variables, the computed F statistics obtained from the estimation in equation 1 are weighed against the asymptotic critical value bounds of Pesaran et al. (2001) and Banerjee et al. (1998) which state that if the computed F-statistic falls outside the critical value bounds, a conclusive inference can be drawn and there would be no need to know the integration/ co-integration status of the underlying regressors. However, if the F-statistic falls inside these bounds, the inference is inconclusive and knowledge of the order of the integration of the underlying variables is required before conclusive inferences can be made. The null hypothesis of no co-integration is therefore represented by $\beta1 = \beta2 = 0$ and the alternative hypothesis of a co-integrating relationship by $B1 \neq \beta2 \neq 0$.

5. RESULTS AND DISCUSSIONS

Descriptive and Correlation Matrix

The long-run relationship between finance and development in Bangladesh post-cold war was investigated using time series data from 1981-2019. Table 2 presents the descriptive statistics and correlation matrix which gives the detailed features of each of the variables. The descriptive statistic shows that the mean of the variables in each distribution in the data set is very close to their corresponding median while the standard deviation shows how far the observations are from the sample mean.

Table 2. Descriptive statistics and correlation matrix

	RGDP	GFCF	BOP	FDI	EXB	EXR	INTR
Mean	590.2741	21.97487	5.433846	0.776923	28.42333	52.97282	5.940256
Median	413.0800	12.71000	2.550000	0.240000	28.49000	52.14000	5.760000
Maximum	1797.320	88.83000	24.94000	3.210000	44.48000	85.66000	14.82000
Minimum	204.4200	2.920000	1.450000	0.050000	16.58000	17.99000	-5.480000
Std. Dev.	436.5132	23.89794	5.761202	0.967327	7.926247	20.44018	3.840007
Skewness	1.457083	1.535740	2.010779	1.309336	0.336021	0.027277	-0.585524
Kurtosis	4.055426	4.339292	6.679019	3.296675	2.067296	1.646864	4.935208
Observations	39	39	39	39	39	39	39
Correlation							
RGDP	1.000000						
GFCF	0.998870	1.000000					
	0.0000						
BOP	0.957865	0.960639	1.000000				
	0.0000	0.0000					
FDI	0.944472	0.939348	0.937192	1.000000			
	0.0000	0.0000	0.0000				
EXB	-0.719636	-0.719184	-0.669030	-0.720227	1.000000		
	0.0000	0.0000	0.0000	0.0000			
EXR	0.846719	0.839551	0.775072	0.822489	-0.700992	1.000000	
	0.0000	0.0000	0.0000	0.0000	0.0000		
INTR	-0.171692	-0.178541	-0.192273	-0.158872	0.443964	-0.008568	1.000000
	0.2960	0.2768	0.2409	0.3340	0.0046	0.9587	

Table 3. Unit root test

		RGDP	GFCF	BOP	FDI	EXB	EXR	INTR
Level								
		T-Stat (P-Value)	T-Stat (P-Value)	T-Stat (P-Value)	T-Stat (P-Value)	T-Stat (P-Value)	T-Stat (P-Value)	T-Stat (P-Value)
PP	With Constant	8.7063 (1.0000)	9.4950 (1.0000)	4.7292 (1.0000)	1.6239 (0.9993)	-1.2760 (0.6307)	-0.8983 (0.7780)	-3.8515 (0.0054)***
	Constant & Trend	3.7507 (1.0000)	3.5425 (1.0000)	1.1792 (0.9999)	-1.0796 (0.9194)	-3.6532 (0.0384)**	-2.5173 (0.3185)	-3.7145 (0.0334)**
ADF	With Constant	2.3154 (0.9999)	1.4140 (0.9987)	3.0617 (1.0000)	0.0612 (0.9573)	-0.7041 (0.8331)	-0.3137 (0.9130)	-3.8515 (0.0054)***
	Constant & Trend	1.1864 (0.9999)	-0.7540 (0.9609)	2.5313 (1.0000)	-0.3841 (0.9837)	-3.5373 (0.0512)*	-3.2568 (0.0894)*	-3.4882 (0.0583)*
KPSS	With Constant	0.6495 **	0.6455 **	0.6258 **	0.6138 **	0.485 **	0.7609)***	0.1435
	Constant & Trend	0.1879 **	0.1881 **	0.2225 ***	0.1905 **	0.1526 **	0.1037	0.1433 *
First Difference								
PP	With Constant	-1.6245 0.4604	-1.6490 0.4482	-5.5503 0.0000	-6.9966 0.0000	-4.3374 0.0015 ***	-9.1037 0.0000	-12.6158 0.0000
	Constant & Trend	-2.8862 0.1783	-2.5933 0.2853	-6.5247 0.0000	-12.7355 0.0000	-4.0713 0.0146 **	-8.7927 0.0000	-16.6595 0.0000
ADF	With Constant	-1.7792 0.3846	-1.6490 0.4482	1.4950 0.9988	-0.7822 0.8102	-5.1464 0.0002 ***	-5.5399 0.0000	-9.1636 0.0000
	Constant & Trend	-2.9354 0.1637	-2.4831 0.3341	-0.3921 0.9828	-1.9500 0.6046	-5.1944 0.0008 ***	-5.4467 0.0004 ***	-9.1088 0.0000
KPSS	With Constant	0.6008 **	0.5811 **	0.5062 **	0.5242 **	0.4367 *	0.3921 *	0.5000 **
	Constant & Trend	0.1748 **	0.1725 **	0.1276 *	0.1463 **	0.1803 **	0.3947 ***	0.5000 ***

Table 4. Bounds test for cointegration

Dependent Variables	F-Statistics	Outcome	Decision
RGDP	10.84761	Cointegration	Estimate ECM (Error Correction Model)

The correlation matrix on the other hand checks for multi-collinearity among our independent variables.

Preliminary assessments of the model conducted using the PP, ADF and KPSS unit root tests are presented in Table 3. The results show that the variables are a mixture of I(0) and I(1). To check the presence of co-integration, the bound test was performed and revealed the presence of a long-run relationship between the variables at 5% statistical significance with F-statistics of 10.84761 as presented in Table 4.

The bound test of cointegration established the existence of a long-run relationship in the model. The short run and long run estimates in Table 5, gross fixed capital formation and net import revealed a positive and significant short-run relationship with real gross domestic product per capita. Alternatively, a negative significant

Table 5. Short run and long run estimates

Variable	Coefficient	Std. Error	t-Statistic	Prob.
Short Run Coefficients				
D(RGDP(-1))	-0.216445	0.142670	-1.517106	0.1500
D(GFCF)	17.008033	2.332093	7.293032	0.0000
D(BOP)	3.014484	1.144407	2.634102	0.0188
D(BOP(-1))	-5.957219	1.693612	-3.517463	0.0031
D(FDI)	-10.016953	5.635825	-1.777371	0.0958
D(EXB)	-0.010695	0.540126	-0.019802	0.9845
D(EXB(-1))	-1.282725	0.573309	-2.237405	0.0409
D(EXR)	-2.242561	0.814935	-2.751830	0.0148
D(EXR(-1))	-2.723477	0.854632	-3.186725	0.0061
D(EXR(-2))	-1.776237	0.759897	-2.337470	0.0337
D(INTR)	-1.085855	0.452447	-2.399959	0.0298
D(INTR(-1))	0.559628	0.286462	1.953581	0.0697
D(INTR(-2))	0.827764	0.302613	2.735388	0.0153
CointEq(-1)	-0.356263	0.128765	-2.766775	0.0144
Long Run Coefficients				
GFCF	11.904091	1.423540	8.362313	0.0000
BOP	40.853637	10.170575	4.016846	0.0011
FDI	-48.001429	19.253361	-2.493145	0.0248
EXB	3.224855	1.511433	2.133641	0.0498
EXR	2.500966	0.842159	2.969708	0.0095
INTR	-6.941521	4.034640	-1.720481	0.1059
C	49.932308	50.970392	0.979634	0.3428

long-run relationship was revealed between foreign direct investment and real gross domestic product per capita at a 10% level of significance while exchange rate and real interest rate are significant with real gross domestic product per capita at a 5% level of significance. Furthermore, external borrowing although negative is not significant in the long run. The long-run dynamics revealed that all variables have a significant relationship with real gross domestic product per capita except for real interest rate which is not significant. Gross fixed capital formation, net import, external borrowing and exchange rate revealed a positive effect while foreign direct investment has a negative effect on real gross domestic product per capita. External borrowing and real interest rates do not have any causal relationship with real gross domestic product per capita.

The coefficient of error correction terms CointEq(-1)) revealed to be negative and significant at the 5% level which shows the variables are co-integrated. The coefficient shows about 35.6 per cent of the disequilibrium in real gross domestic product per capita is offset by the short-run adjustment in the same year. This implies that each year the disequilibrium in the series is being corrected and it takes two years to return to equilibrium.

To infer causality, the Granger causality test developed by Granger (1969) was employed and the results revealed that gross fixed capital formation, net import and foreign direct investment have a bidirectional relationship with real gross domestic product per capita while exchange rate has a unidirectional relationship with real gross domestic product per capita. External borrowing and real interest rates do not

Table 6. Granger causality test

Null Hypothesis:	Obs	F-Statistic	Prob.
GFCF does not Granger Cause RGDP	37	2.75253	0.0789
RGDP does not Granger Cause GFCF		4.42164	0.0202
BOP does not Granger Cause RGDP	37	8.08539	0.0014
RGDP does not Granger Cause BOP		17.2258	8.E-06
FDI does not Granger Cause RGDP	37	7.87434	0.0017
RGDP does not Granger Cause FDI		5.37137	0.0097
EXB does not Granger Cause RGDP	37	0.61263	0.5482
RGDP does not Granger Cause EXB		0.34329	0.7120
EXR does not Granger Cause RGDP	37	6.95433	0.0031
RGDP does not Granger Cause EXR		2.09592	0.1395
INTR does not Granger Cause RGDP	37	0.31064	0.7352
RGDP does not Granger Cause INTR		0.31136	0.7346

Table 7. Summary of findings

Variable	Short-Run	Long-Run	Causality
GFCF	+ sig.	+ sig.	Bidirectional Causality @ 10%
BOP	+ sig.	+ sig.	Bidirectional Causality
FDI	- sig. @ 10%	- sig.	Bidirectional Causality
EXB	- n.s	+ sig.	No Causality
EXR	- sig.	+ sig.	Unidirectional
INTR	- sig.	- n.s	No Causality

Source: Authors' computations, 2022 (Eviews 9)

have any causal relationship with real gross domestic product per capita. Generally, it can, therefore, be concluded finance affects development in Bangladesh post-cold war and there is a causality in most of the variables used in the study. The summary of findings is presented in Table 7 while the Granger causality test is presented in Table 6.

The diagnostic tests performed showed that the model is strong and stable as presented in Table 8. No problem with autocorrelation, serial correlation and heteroscedasticity was discovered. The Ramsey Regression Specification Error Test (RESET) test by Ramsey (1969) shows the model is correctly specified. The Cumulative Sum (CUSUM) and Cumulative Sum of Squares (CUSUMSQ) of recursive residuals plots proposed by Brown et al. (1975) show the stability of the model. These are presented in Figure 2 for the CUSUM plot and Figure 3 for the CUSUMSQ plot. The figures show that both CUSUM and CUSUM square lie within 5% critical bounds of parameter stability, which shows the stability of coefficients and thus implies the long-run relationships among the variables

Table 8. Diagnostic tests

Specification	Stat (*p*-Values)	Conclusion
Durbin–Watson (autocorrelation)	2.344303	No Autocorrelation
Bruesch–Godfrey (Serial Correlation)	5.476931 (0.1400)	No Serial Correlation
Bruesch–Pagan (heteroscedasticity)	14.96092 (0.7786)	No Heteroscedasticity
Jarque–Bera (normality)	0.818621(0.664108)	Normality
Ramsey RESET Test	1.275350 (0.2777)	No Model specification error
R^2	0.999951	
F-statistics	15222.90 (0.0000)	

Source: Authors' computations, 2022 (Eviews 9)

Figure 2. CUSUM plot map

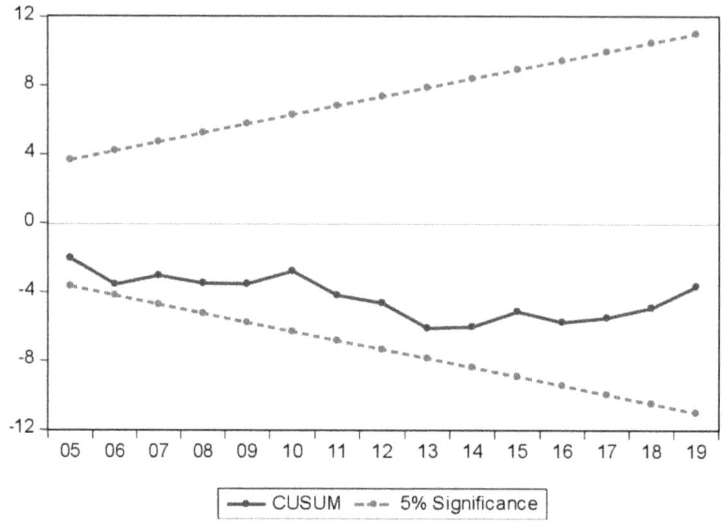

Figure 3. CUSUMSQ plot map

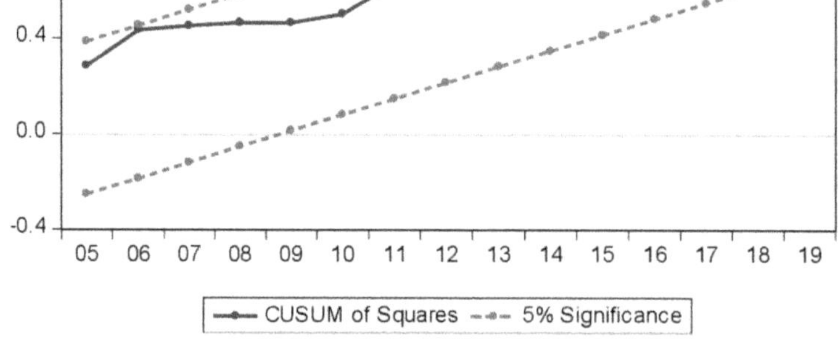

Discussion of Findings

This study is an attempt to explain the finance-development nexus in the Bangladesh context. The role of gross fixed capital formation, net import-export, foreign direct investment, and external borrowing in the development process in Bangladesh while controlling for exchange rate and interest rate was evaluated. Gross fixed capital formation (GFCF) exhibits a positive and significant impact on the economic development process in Bangladesh both in the short run and long run. There is also a bidirectional causality between the GFCF and the real gross domestic product (RGDP). This means that while the GFCF potentially influences the RGDP, the RGDP in turn influences the GFCF as reported in the Granger causality test in Table 6 at a 10% level of significance. These findings agree with Tabassum and Ahmed (2014); Bahname (2012); Abdullahi et al. (2012), Meyer and Sunusi (2019); Boamah et al. (2018); Nazir et al. (2020). Meyer and Sunusi (2019) revealed a long-run relationship exists between gross fixed capital formation and economic net import and export growth, with causality running from economic growth to gross fixed capital formation. Similar findings were reported by Ajose and Oyedokun (2018). Boamah et al. (2018) and Nazir et al. (2020) documented a significant positive impact of GFCF on economic growth. Also, consistent with the findings of this study Biplob and Halder (2018) and Nweke et al. (2017) revealed a bidirectional causality running between GFCF and economic growth. Nevertheless, while consensus seems to exist among scholars to some extent that there is a positive relationship between GFCF and economic growth, some scholars (Ajose & Oyedokun 2018; Nweke et al., 2017) found such relationship not to be significant.

The net import and export proxied by balance of payment (BOP) contribution to economic growth process in Bangladesh is positive and significant both in the short-run and long-run while there is a bidirectional causality between BOP and RGDP. This agrees with evidence documented by Selvanathan et al. (2020); Khanom (2019); Emmanuel (2017) and Ahmed and Uddin (2009). These scholars established the existence of export and import-led growth while Khanom (2019) and Akhter (2015) revealed otherwise. Also, consistent with this study Meraj (2013) found a long-run association among exports, imports and GDP in Bangladesh with a bidirectional causality running between export and GDP established. Selvanathan et al. (2020) nevertheless, confirmed unidirectional causality from imports to economic growth.

Foreign direct investment (FDI)was found to contribute negatively to the economic growth process in Bangladesh in the short run and long run and there is a bidirectional causality running between FDI and RGDP. Scholars appeared unanimous as to the magnitude of the relationship between FDI and economic growth (Oyegoke & Aras, 2021; Sarker & Khan, 2020; Rajib & Rahman, 2020; Asaduzzaman, 2019; Qamruzzaman & Jianguo, 2017; Adhikary, 2015) but fail to agree on the direction of such relationship. Asaduzzaman (2019) found a long-run and short-run significant relationship between foreign direct investment, real effective exchange rate and trade openness and economic growth and suggested that the utilization of foreign direct investment and trade openness foster the development of Bangladesh's economy. Sarker and Khan (2020) also found a long-run significant relationship between foreign direct investment and economic growth but inferred a unidirectional relationship running from GDP to FDI. Tabassum and Ahmed (2014) on the other hand examine the relationship between foreign direct investments and the economic growth of Bangladesh covering 1972–2011 and found a not significant relationship.

External borrowing (EXB) was found to be negative and not significant in the short-run while in the long-run there is a significant positive relationship with economic growth in Bangladesh. Also, this study found no causality between external borrowing and RGDP in Bangladesh. Although Bangladesh relies on external borrowing to manage the saving-investment gap and fiscal deficit, Empirical evidence has shown external debt have an adverse effect on her economic growth process (Yeasmin, et al., 2015; Yeasmin & Chowdhury, 2014), negative effect (Dey &Tareque, 2019; Kharusi & Ada, 2018; Ramzan & Ahmad, 2014; Ali & Mustafa, 2012). This agrees with the findings of this study only in the short-run though the result is not significant. The findings of this study reported a positive and significant impact of external borrowings on economic growth in Bangladesh in the long run and argued that external borrowings contributed significantly and positively to the Bangladesh economic growth process in the long run. However, the Granger causality test failed to support this argument as there seems to be no causality between external borrowing and RGDP in Bangladesh over the study period.

The macroeconomic indicators (exchange rate and interest rate) introduced as disturbances in the model indicated a significant negative effect in the short-run while in the long run, exchange rate exhibited a positive and significant and interest rate exhibited a negative but not significant effect. Also, there is a unidirectional causality running from exchange rate to RGDP and no causality between interest rate and RGDP. Contrary to the findings of this study, Rajib and Rahman (2020) and Halder (2019) reported a not significant effect of exchange rate on economic growth. Similarly, Etale and Imbazi (2020) espousing the influence of some selected microeconomic variables on economic growth in Nigeria between 1999 and 2018 concluded that interest rate and exchange rates are not significant determinants of economic growth. The findings of this study find support from the works of Asaduzzaman (2019); Razzaque, et al. (2017) who found a significant effect in the long run. Also, the works Khan (2021); Islam and Hossain, (2019); and Uddin et al. (2014) found exchange rate to have a positive effect on economic growth.

6. CONCLUSION

This study explored the role of finance in the economic development process in Bangladesh. The study specifically focused on the effect of gross fixed capital formation, foreign direct investment, and external borrowing on the real gross domestic product with exchange rates and interest rates as disturbances in the model. Findings show that gross fixed capital formation (GFCF) exhibits a positive and significant impact on the economic development process in Bangladesh both in the short-run and long-run. There is also a bidirectional causality between the GFCF and the real gross domestic product (RGDP). The implication is that gross fixed capital formation is an important factor in Bangladesh's economic growth process. Similarly, the net of import and export proxied by balance of payment (BOP) contributes positively and significantly to the economic growth process in Bangladesh both in the short run and long run while a bidirectional causality between BOP and RGDP exists. This means that an improved net import-export would enhance economic development in Bangladesh. Foreign direct investment (FDI) was found to contribute negatively to the economic growth process in Bangladesh in the short run and long run and there is a bidirectional causality running between FDI and RGDP. By implication, foreign direct investment deteriorates economic growth in Bangladesh. External borrowing (EXB) was found to be negative and not significant in the short-run while in the long-run there is a significant positive relationship with economic growth in Bangladesh. Also, this study found no causality between external borrowing and RGDP in Bangladesh. The disturbances in the model (exchange rate and interest rate) exhibit a significant negative effect in the short run while in the long run, exchange rate exhibits a positive and significant and interest rate exhibits a negative but not significant effect. Also, there is a unidirectional causality running from exchange rate to RGDP and no causality between interest rate and RGDP. The findings of this study underscore the importance of finance in the economic development process in Bangladesh as highlighted by the Levine (2005) finance-growth theoretical framework.

The results of this study have contributed to existing debates on the role of finance in economic development. Particularly, gross fixed capital formation, net import-export, and to some extent external borrowings are important factors in the economic development of Bangladesh.

REFERENCES

Abdullahi, Y. Z., Aliero, H. M., & Yusuf, M. A. (2012). Does FDI cause economic growth? Evidence from selected countries in Africa and Asia. *African Journal of Social Sciences*, *2*(4), 114–124.

Adediran, O. S. (2020). Autoregressive distributed lag approach to external credit and economic growth in Nigeria. In P. O. Alege (Ed.), *Applied Econometric Analysis: Emerging Research and Opportunities*. Covenant University. doi:10.4018/978-1-7998-1093-3.ch003

Adhikary, B. K. (2015). Dynamic Effects of FDI, Trade Openness, Capital Formation and Human Capital on the Economic Growth Rate in the Least Developed Economies: Evidence from Nepal, *International Journal of Trade. Economics and Finance*, *6*(1), 1–7.

Ahamad, M. H. (2018). Impact of international trade on economic growth in Bangladesh. *International Journal of Scientific Research*, *7*(11), 1624–1627.

Ahluwalia, I. J., & Mahmud, W. (2004). Economic transformation and social development in Bangladesh. *Economic and Political Weekly*, *39*(36), 4009–4011. https://www.jstor.org/stable/4415501

Ahmed, H. A., & Uddin, Md. G. S. (2009). Export, imports, remittance and growth in Bangladesh: An empirical analysis. *Trade and Development Review, 2*(2), 79-92. http://www.tdrju.net

Ahmed, K. S. (2011). *Economical development of Bangladesh- Problems & solutions*. Arcada University of Applied Sciences. https://www.theseus.fi/bitstream/handle/10024/38338/Ahmed_Kazi%20Siam.pdf

Ahmed, S. (2005). Development performance and policy reforms since independence. In S. Ahmed (Ed.), *Transforming Bangladesh into a middle-income economy*. Macmillan India Ltd. for the World Bank.

Ajose, K. (2018). Capital formation and economic growth in Nigeria. *International Accounting and Taxation Research*, *2*(2), 131–142.

Akhter, M. (2015). The impact of export and import on economic growth in Bangladesh. *World Vision*, *9*(1), 66–81.

Ali, G. (2015). Gross fixed capital formation and economic growth of Pakistan. *IMPACT Journal of Research in Humanities. Arts and Literature*, *1*(2), 21–30.

Ali, M. A., Saifullah, M. K., & Kari, F. B. (2015). The impact of key macroeconomic factors on economic growth of Bangladesh: A VAR Co-integration analysis. *International Journal of Management Excellence*, *6*(1), 667–673. doi:10.17722/ijme.v6i1.820

Ali, R., & Mustafa, U. (2012). External debt accumulation and its impact on economic growth in Pakistan. *Pakistan Development Review*, *51*(4), 79–96. doi:10.30541/v51i4IIpp.79-96

Asaduzzaman Md. (2019). *FDI an opportunity for economic growth of Bangladesh: A VECM analysis*. MPRA Paper No. 110328, 1-28.

Asteriou, D., & Monastiriotis, V. (2004). What do unions do at the large scale? Macro-economic evidence from a panel of OECD countries. *Journal of Applied Econometrics*, *7*(1), 2746.

Awokuse, T. O. (2007). Causality between exports, imports, and economic growth: Evidence from Transition economies. *Economics Letters*, *94*(3), 389–395. doi:10.1016/j.econlet.2006.08.025

Bahname, M. (2012). Foreign direct investment and economic growth: Evidence from Southern Asia. *Atlantic Review of Economics*, *2*(2), 34–48.

Banerjee, A., Dolado, J., & Mestre, R. (1998). Error-correction mechanism tests for cointegration in a single-equation framework. *Journal of Time Series Analysis*, *19*(3), 267–283. doi:10.1111/1467-9892.00091

Biplob, M. (2018). Financial sector development and economic growth: Empirical evidence from Bangladesh. *Asian Economic and Financial Review*, *8*(6), 799–814. doi:10.18488/journal.aefr.2018.86.799.814

Boamah, J., Adongo, F. A., Essieku, R., & Lewis, J. A. Jr. (2018). Financial depth, gross fixed capital formation and economic growth: Empirical analysis of 18 Asian economies. *SSRN*, *2*(4), 120–130. doi:10.2139/ssrn.3424688

Brown, R. L., Durbin, J., & Evans, J. M. (1975). Techniques for testing the constancy of regression relationships over time. *Journal of the Royal Statistical Society. Series B. Methodological*, *37*(2), 149–192. doi:10.1111/j.2517-6161.1975.tb01532.x

Chowdhury, A. (2002). Politics, society and financial sector reform in Bangladesh. *International Journal of Social Economics*, *29*(12), 963–988. doi:10.1108/03068290210447003

Chowdhury, A. H. M. Y., Hamid, M. K., & Akhi, R. A. (2019). Impact of macroeconomic variables on economic growth: Bangladesh perspective. *Information Management and Computer Science*, *2*(2), 19–22. doi:10.26480/imcs.02.2019.19.22

Dey, S. R., & Tareque, M. (2020). External debt and growth: Role of stable macroeconomic policies. *Journal of Economics, Finance and Administrative Science*, *25*(50), 185–204. doi:10.1108/JEFAS-05-2019-0069

Dibal, H. S., Iyortsuun, A. S., & Haruna, H. A. (2021), Asymmetric impact of financial market development on entrepreneurship in Nigeria. In Entrepreneurial finance, innovation and development. Routledge. doi:10.4324/9781003134282-10

Dickey, D. A., & Fuller, W. A. (1979). Distribution of the estimators for autoregressive time series with a unit root. *Journal of the American Statistical Association*, *74*(366a), 427–431. doi:10.1080/01621459.1979.10482531

Dritsakis, N., Varelas, E., & Adamopoulos, A. (2006). The main determinants of economic growth. An empirical investigation with Granger causality analysis for Greece. *European Research Studies*, *9*(3-4), 47–58.

Emmanuel, I. (2017). Balance of Payments Constrained Economic Growth in Nigeria. *African Journal of Economic Review*, *5*(2), 1–13.

Etale, L. M., & Imbazi, L. I. (2020). Influence of selected macroeconomic variables on economic growth in Nigeria (1999 – 2018). *Advances in Social Sciences Research Journal*, *7*(8), 315–325. doi:10.14738/assrj.78.8811

Faaland, J., & Parkinson, J. R. (1976). *Bangladesh: the test case of development*. C. Hurst.

Ghouse, G., Khan, S. A., & Rehman, A. U. (2018). *ARDL model as a remedy for spurious regression: Problems, performance and prospectus*. MPRA Paper No. 83973, Pakistan Institute of Development Economics. https://mpra.ub.uni-muenchen.de/83973/

Granger, C. W. J. (1969). Investigating causal relations by econometric models and cross-spectral methods. *Econometrica*, *37*(3), 424–438. doi:10.2307/1912791

Halder, P. (2019). Analysis of the impact of exchange rate, inflation, export and import on gross domestic product in Bangladesh. *Business, Management and Economics Research*, *5*(12), 170-175.

Haruna, H. A., Dibal, H. S., & Isichei, E. E. (2023). Foreign direct investments and stock market development in Sub-Saharan Africa: Does regulatory quality moderate? *Global Business Review*, *0*(0), 1–20. doi:10.1177/09721509231163712

Hossain, M. A., & Shirin, S. (2016). Impact of debts on economic growth of Bangladesh: An application of ARDL model. *Asia-Pacific Journal of Business*, *7*(1), 1-10. https://imr.kangwon.ac.kr/apjb.7.7.201606.1

Hossin, Md. S. (. (2020). Interest rate deregulation, financial development and economic growth: Evidence from Bangladesh. *Global Business Review*, 1–14. doi:10.1177/0972150920916564

Hussain, M. E., & Haque, M. (2016). Foreign direct investment, trade, and economic growth: An empirical analysis of Bangladesh. *Economies*, *4*(2), 1–14. doi:10.3390/economies4020007

Islam, J. N., Mohajan, H. K., & Datta, R. (2012). Aspects of microfinance of Grameen Bank of Bangladesh. *International Journal of Economic Research*, *3*(4), 76–96.

Islam, T., & Hossain, M. T. (2019). Exchange rates and economic growth in Bangladesh: An econometric analysis. *Trade and Development Review*, *2*(2), 79–92.

Istiak, K. M. (2012). Foreign aid to Bangladesh: Some iconoclastic issues. *Journal of Developing Areas*, *46*(1), 331–343. doi:10.1353/jda.2012.0005

Jamil, T., & Hasan Md, S. B. (2015). Foreign direct investment and economic growth: Evidence from Bangladesh. *Journal of Business Studies*, *36*(2), 171–180.

KalirajanK. P.SalimR. (1997). Economic reforms and capacity realization in Bangladesh: An empirical analysis. doi:10.2139/ssrn.1222343

Karahan, O. (2020). Influence of exchange rate on the economic growth in the Turkish economy. *Financial Asset and Investing*, *11*(1), 21–34. doi:10.5817/FAI2020-1-2

Khan, M. F. H. (2021). Impact of exchange rate on economic growth of Bangladesh. *European Journal of Business and Management Research*, *6*(3), 173–175. doi:10.24018/ejbmr.2021.6.3.891

Khanom, S. (2019). Does trade openness cause economic growth in Bangladesh? *IIUC Studies*, *16*, 99–110. doi:10.3329/iiucs.v16i0.50139

Kharusi, S. A., & Ada, M. S. (2018). External debt and economic growth: The case of emerging economy. *Journal of Economic Integration*, *33*(1), 1141–1157. doi:10.11130/jei.2018.33.1.1141

Korkmaz, S. (2015), The relationship between external debt and economic growth in Turkey, *Proceedings of the Second European Academic Research Conference on Global Business, Economics, Finance and Banking (EAR15Swiss Conference)*, 971-978.

Kwiatkowski, D., Phillips, P. C. B., Schmidt, P., & Shin, Y. (1992). Testing the null hypothesis of stationarity against the alternative of a unit root. *Journal of Econometrics*, *54*(1–3), 159–178. doi:10.1016/0304-4076(92)90104-Y

Levine, R. (2005), Finance and growth: Theory and evidence. In P. Aghion & S. N. Durlauf (Eds.), Handbook of Economic Growth. Elsevier.

Mahmud, W. (2008). Bangladesh. In A. Chowdhury & W. Mahmud (Eds.), *Handbook on the South Asian Economies*. Edward Elgar Publishing. doi:10.4337/9781848441293.00009

Mahmud, W., Ahmed, S., & Mahajan, S. (2008). *Economic reforms, growth, and governance: The political economy aspects of Bangladesh's development surprise. Commission on Growth and Development Working Paper; No. 22*. World Bank. http://hdl.handle.net/10986/28037

Meraj, M. (2013). Impact of globalization and trade openness on economic growth in Bangladesh. *Ritsumeikan Journal of Asia Pacific Studies*, *32*, 40–50.

Meyer, D. F., & Sanusi, K. A. (2019). A causality analysis of the relationships between gross fixed capital formation, economic growth and employment in South Africa. *Studia Universitatis Babeş-Bolyai Oeconomica*, *64*(1), 33–44. doi:10.2478/subboec-2019-0003

Mohajan, H. K. (2013). Economic development of Bangladesh. *Journal of Business Management and Administration*, *1*(4), 41–48. https://mpra.ub.uni-muenchen.de/id/eprint/50663

Nazir, M. R., Tan, Y., & Nazir, M. I. (2021). Financial innovation and economic growth: Empirical evidence from China, India and Pakistan. *International Journal of Finance & Economics*, *26*(4), 6036–6059. doi:10.1002/ijfe.2107

Nkoro, E., & Aham, K. U. (2016). Autoregressive distributed lag (ARDL) cointegration technique: Application and interpretation. *Journal of Statistical and Econometric Methods*, *5*(4), 63–91.

Nweke, G. O., Odo, S. I., & Anoke, C. I. (2017). Effect of capital formation on economic growth in Nigeria, *Asian Journal of Economics. Business and Accounting*, *5*(1), 1–16. doi:10.9734/AJEBA/2017/36075

Oyegoke, O. E., & Aras, O. N. (2021). Impact of foreign direct investment on economic growth in Nigeria. *Journal of Management, Economics, and Industrial Organization*, *5*(1), 31–38. doi:10.31039/jomeino.2021.5.1.2

Pesaran, M. H., & Shin, Y. (1999). An autoregressive distributed lag modelling approach to cointegration analysis. Econometrics and economic theory in the 20th century. In S. Strom (Ed.), *The Ragnar Frisch centennial symposium*. Cambridge University Press. doi:10.1017/CCOL521633230.011

Pesaran, M. H., Shin, Y., & Smith, R. P. (2001). Bounds testing approaches to the analysis of level relationship. *Journal of Applied Econometrics, 16*(3), 289–326. doi:10.1002/jae.616

Phillips, P. C. B., & Perron, P. (1988). Testing for a unit root in time series regression. *Biometrika, 75*(2), 335–346. doi:10.1093/biomet/75.2.335

Qamruzzaman, M., & Jianguo, W. (2017). Financial innovation and economic growth in Bangladesh. *Financial Innovation, 3*(19), 1–24. doi:10.1186/s40854-017-0070-0

Qamruzzaman, M., & Jianguo, W. (2018). Nexus between financial innovation and economic growth in South Asia: Evidence from ARDL and nonlinear ARDL approaches. *Financial Innovation, 4*(20), 1–19. doi:10.1186/s40854-018-0103-3

Rahman, A. (2015). Impact of foreign direct investment on economic growth: Empirical evidence from Bangladesh. *International Journal of Economics and Finance, 7*(2), 178–185. doi:10.5539/ijef.v7n2p178

Rahman, M. M., Bashar, M. A., & Dey, S. (2012). External debt and gross domestic product in Bangladesh: A co-integration analysis. *Management Research and Practice, 4*(4), 28–36.

Rajib, M. I., & Rahman, R. (2020). Foreign direct investment and economic growth: Evidence from Bangladesh economy. *European Scientific Journal, 16*(10), 38–55. doi:10.19044/esj.2020.v16n10p38

Ramsey, J. B. (1969). Tests for specification errors in classical linear least-squares regression analysis. *Journal of the Royal Statistical Society. Series B. Methodological, 31*(2), 350–371. doi:10.1111/j.2517-6161.1969.tb00796.x

Ramzan, M., & Ahmad, E. (2014). External debt growth nexus: Role of macroeconomic policies. *Economic Modelling, 38*, 204–210. doi:10.1016/j.econmod.2013.12.014

Razzaque, M. A., Bidisha, S. H., & Khondker, B. H. (2017). Exchange rate and economic growth. *Journal of South Asian Development, 12*(1), 42–64. doi:10.1177/0973174117702712

Saifuddin, M. D. (2016). Public debt and economic growth: Evidence from Bangladesh. *Global Journal of Management and Business Research, 16*(5), 64–73.

Sarker, F., & Khan, F. (2020). Nexus between foreign direct investment and economic growth in Bangladesh: An augmented autoregressive distributed lag bounds testing approach. *Financial Innovation, 6*(10), 1–28. doi:10.1186/s40854-019-0164-y

Sawada, Y., Mahmud, M., & Kitano, N. (2018). *Economic and social development of Bangladesh: Miracle and challenges* (1st ed.). Palgrave Macmillan Cham. doi:10.1007/978-3-319-63838-6

SaxenaH.BansalP. K. (2019), Relationship between economic factors and economic growth. Proceedings of 10th International Conference on Digital Strategies for Organizational Success. https://ssrn.com/abstract=3319961 or doi:10.2139/ssrn.3319961

Selvanathan, S., Jayasinghe, M., & Selvanathan, E. A. (2020). Exports, imports and sustainable economic growth in Bangladesh. In M. Hossain, Q. K. Ahmad, & M. M. Islam (Eds.), *Climate Adaptation for a Sustainable Economy: Lessons from Bangladesh, an Emerging Tiger of Asia* (pp. 195–218). Nova Science Publishers.

Shimul, S. N., Abdullah, S. M., & Siddiqua, S. (2009). An examination of FDI and growth nexus in Bangladesh: Engle Granger and bound testing Cointgration approach. *BRAC University Journal, 6*(1), 69–76. https://dspace.bracu.ac.bd/xmlui/handle/10361/455

Shirazi, N. S., & Abdul Manap, T. A. (2005). Export-led growth hypothesis: Further econometric evidence from South Asia. *The Developing Economies, 43*(4), 472–488. doi:10.1111/j.1746-1049.2005.tb00955.x

Shrestha, M. B., & Bhatta, G. R. (2018). Selecting appropriate methodological framework for time series data analysis. *The Journal of Finance and Data Science, 4*(2), 71–89. doi:10.1016/j.jfds.2017.11.001

Tabassum, N., & Ahmed, S. P. (2014). Foreign direct investment and economic growth: Evidence from Bangladesh. *International Journal of Economics and Finance, 6*(9), 117–135. doi:10.5539/ijef.v6n9p117

Taslim, M. A. (2008). Governance, policies and economic growth in Bangladesh. In N. Islam & M. Asaduzzaman (Eds.), *A Ship Adrift: Governance and Development in Bangladesh.* Bangladesh Institute of Development Studies.

Temiz, D., & Gokmen, A. (2014). FDI inflow as an international business operation by MNCs and economic growth: An empirical study on Turkey, *International Business Review. International Business Review, 23*(1), 45–154. doi:10.1016/j.ibusrev.2013.03.003

Thilakaweera, B. H. P. K. (2011). Economic impact of foreign direct investment in Sri Lanka. *Staff Studies-Central Bank of Sri Lanka, 41*(1&2), 89–115. https://ss.sljol.info/articles/10.4038/ss.v41i1.4684

Uddin, K. M. K., Rahman, M. M., & Quaosar, G. M. A. A. (2014). Causality between exchange rate and economic growth in Bangladesh. *European Scientific Journal, 10*(31), 11–26.

UNCTAD. (1992). Transnational corporations as engines of growth. World Investment Report. doi:10.1007/978-3-030-04200-4_67

Yeasmin, F., & Chowdhury, M. N. M. (2014). Impact of foreign debt on growth in Bangladesh: An econometrics analysis. *International Journal of Developing and Emerging Economics*, 2(4), 1–24.

Yeasmin, F., Chowdhury, M. N. M., & Hossain, M. A. (2015). External public debt and economic growth in Bangladesh: A co-integration analysis. *Journal of Economics and Sustainable Development*, 6(23), 64–74.

Chapter 2
Finance and Development in Mauritius Post Cold War

Ifeanyi Okoh
National Open University of Nigeria, Abuja, Nigeria

Ephraim Ikechukwu Ugwu
https://orcid.org/0000-0003-0522-3492
Federal University, Oye-Ekiti, Nigeria

ABSTRACT

This study evaluates macroeconomic variables' effect on economic development in Mauritius from 1981 to 2019. The study employs the vector error correction (VECM) model for estimation. The long-run estimated results indicates a positive feedback between the variables, export, LOG(EXPT), external debt, LOG(DEBT), foreign direct investment (FDI), interest rate (INTR), the per capita GDP growth and a negative feedback between the per capita growth of the economy and the gross fixed capital formation LOG(GFCF(-1)), import (LOG(IMP)), and exchange rate (EXCH). The impulse response function (IRF) result indicates that the response of PERCAP to itself increases instantly and significantly and decreases in the short-run but continues with a positive sign along the horizons in the long-run. The response of GFCF to per capita shock increases immediately and continues to a positive shock in both short-run and the long-run horizon. The monetary policy variable,s INTR and EXCH, respond to per capita increase continues with the positive signs in both the short and long-run.

DOI: 10.4018/979-8-3693-1610-8.ch002

1.0 INTRODUCTION

The paradise island called Mauritius is a small island economy vulnerable to exogenous shocks. The country has been able to craft a strong growth-oriented developmental path for itself. Natural hazards and terms-of-trade uncertainties have never prevented the economy from having strong and stable growth. Although a variety of explanations have been advanced to explain Mauritius's growth path, the country's focus on global trade activities has no doubt been a major driver of the economic performance. Aside from its success in macroeconomic management, one of the keys to Mauritius's economic success has been its rich web of trade links, effective institutions, and history of public collaboration. The combination of political stability, democratic legacy, rule of law, and quality of judicial institutions sets Mauritius apart from many Sub-Saharan African countries. The economy witnessed a heavy human capital investment as a result of great effort in promoting export trade. In 1983, Mauritius signed double taxation avoidance treaty with India which paved way for inflow of foreign direct investment and strong financial sector (Romer, 1992, Frankel, 2010, Stiglitz, 2011).

The exchange rate system of the Mauritius economy had always been considered strong compared to other developing economies. This contributed immensely in preventing anti-trade bias due from import tariffs and encouraged export trade (Iman and Minoiu, 2008). Simultaneously, Mauritius pursued a very liberal investment regime and used incentives to attract foreign direct investment (FDI). Mauritius also offset the burdens on its exporters with tariff-free access for productive inputs, with tax incentive subsidies and relaxed labor market regulations in the export sector. Furthermore, it has used export processing zones (EPZs) to export key manufacturing goods, mostly apparel and textiles. Mauritius's overall trade and investment policy has been based on a managed embrace of globalization and cultivation of market access. Additionally, the public and private sectors maintain a vibrant partnership that manifests itself in a range of areas.

The country's economy thrived equally through the creation and efficient management of the Export Processing Zone (EPZ). This led the country to transit from low income to a middle income economy (Subramanian and Roy, 2001). The most thriving factor for the Mauritius story was the promotion of environmental friendliness and incentives for FDI inflows. Alongside successful trade policy and adaptability, another major reason for the economic success has been its business climate and incentives for foreign companies to locate there. Mauritius has no capital controls, a relatively stable currency, a low flat corporate tax rate of 15 percent, labor for larger firms, the thrust of the reforms has been to alleviate these constraints.

The Mauritius economy for the past thirty years have witnessed sustained economic development, having maintained a track record of sustained growth. The economy

Figure 1. The growth of Mauritius economy from 1981 to 2017
Source: *Statistics Mauritius, under the aegis of the Ministry of Finance and Economic Development*

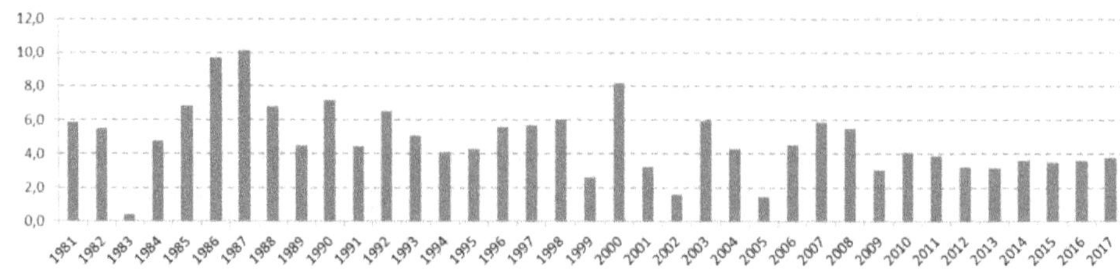

is among the economies in Africa maintaining a technology oriented approach. The Mauritius economy between 1980s and the year 2000 witnessed sustained growth, thus propelling the economy from low income to an upper middle income status. The economy equally achieved a full employment with increase wage prices compared to other developing economies. This resulted to a shift from labour intensive to a capital intensive growth approach. The Figure 1 shows the Mauritius growth from 1981 to 2017.

However, during the 2009 global financial crises, the Mauritius recorded a slightest fall in economic growth but continued to maintain a positive growth. However, as a result Corona measures and COVID 19 global pandemic, the economy recorded a fall in its Gross Domestic Product (GDP) by 14% as result of a decline in the both tourism and hospitality industries. The rate of unemployment rose to 9.2%, with an increase in the public debt from 65% to 95% of the growth rate between 2019 and 2020. Also, there was an increase in external debt during the periods from 15% to 20%.

Achievement of economic development has always been the goals for human being, societies and countries. The drivers of economic growth and development are the macroeconomic variables such as, exchange rate, investment, export and import and the rate of interest (Shukla, 2017). This study therefore evaluates the macroeconomic development of Mauritius for the past 40 years. The fundamental goals of macroeconomic policy is always to achieve a sustainable development, maintenance of price stability and full employment. Thus, the main objective of this study is to evaluate the interaction effect between macroeconomic variables which include, gross fixed capital formation, foreign divestment investment, exports and imports, exchange rate and rate of interest on economic development of Mauritius.

2.0 LITERATURE REVIEW

The effect of core macroeconomic variables such as exchange rate, the GDP, investment, exports and imports and the rate of interest on economic development has been the focus of many macroeconomic researchers. Madhou, Sewak,Moosa, Ramiah and Gerth (2021) evaluate monetary policy effect on inflation targeting in Mauritius by highlighting challenges faced by the monetary authority towards implementing fledged inflation targeting approach. The study developed a forecasting model and a policy system in support of transition towards full-fledged inflation targeting in Mauritius. Svirydzenka and Petri (2014) examined the Mauritius economy and noted that the economy was pronounced a miracle as a result of efforts towards full development. The study utilized growth accounting method to evaluate past and future growth of the economy. The empirical results project a future growth of 4 to 5% as the economy adopts a proactive policies. The study equally predict that with 5% growth, the economy could reach high income level by 2021.

Other studies which include a study by Shukla (2020) on the interaction effect between macroeconomic variables and economic growth of India from 1978 to 2018, utilized the multiple linear regression model approach for estimation. The empirical result show that real interest, foreign direct investment and consumption expenditure impacts positively on economic growth. Dan and Binch (2019) evaluate the effect off macroeconomic variables on economic growth for a selected 68 developing economies from 1996 to 2016. Using the Generalized Method of Moment (GMM) estimation procedures, the result shows that domestic investment, trade openness and labour indicate a positive and significant effect on economic growth. The results also show that money supply, inflation and interest rate indicate a negative effect on growth. Chingoiro and Mbulawa (2017) evaluate effect of electricity consumption on economic growth of Botswwana from 1980 to 2014 using VECM econometrics approach .The result shows that electiricity consumption, human capital and inflation impacts positively on economic growth. Mbulawa (2015) examines the effects of macroeconomic variables on economic growth in Botswana from 1975 to 2012. Employing the Vector Error Correction (VECM) techniques for evaluation, the results indicate that foreign direct investment and inflation impacts positively on economic growth. Sharma, Singh and Singh (2011) evaluate the effect of macroeconomic variables on economic performance of Sri Lanka and India from 2002 to 2009 using Vector Auto regression approach. The study find that exchange rate and rate of interest positively impact on economic growth of both economies. Garrison and Lee (1995) investigate the impact of macroeconomic variables on economic growth of selected countries. The empirical results indicate foreign direct investment impacted positively the growth while large budget deficit shows a negative effect on the growth of the economy.

3.0 METHODOLOGY OF THE RESEARCH

3.1 Methodological Framework

This study in line with Olayungbo and Quadri (2019), adopts the two-gap model propounded by Harrod–Domar, which states that emerging economies face shortages of domestic saving to meet up the domestic investment opportunities or shortfall of foreign exchange to finance imported intermediate and capital (Todaro and Smith, 2012). The model was further expanded by Chenery and Strout (1966). The model assumes that emerging economies utilizes external inflow of funds to attain equilibrium in the saving investment gap. According to Olayungbo and Quadri (2019), the two-gap approach of external assistance indicate that foreign finance (loans, or grants) plays a critical role in enhancing local resources in order to reduce domestic saving and foreign exchange bottlenecks.

3.2 Model Specification

The data on Percapita Gross Domestic Product is utilized as the dependent variable. While the data on gross fixed capital formation, import, export, external debt, foreign direct investment, interest rate and exchange rate are utilized as the independent variables. The model that capture the impact of macroeconomic variables on economic growth in Mauritius are therefore specified as follows:

$$\text{PERCAP}= \text{F(GFCF, IMP, EXPT, DEBT, FDI,INTR,EXCH)} \quad (1)$$

The variables are defined as follows:

PERCAP = Percapita Gross Domestic Product
GFCF = Gross fixed capital formation
IMP = Import
EXPT = Export
DEBT = External debt
FDI = Foreign Direct Investment
INTR = Real interest rate
EXCH = Exchange rate
The relationship between the independent variables and dependent variable in the equation, are specified in the linear form as follows:

$$\text{PERCAP} = \alpha_0 + \alpha_1\text{GFCF} + \alpha_2\ \text{IMP} + \alpha_3\text{EXPT} + \alpha_4\text{DEBT} + \alpha_5\text{FDI} + \alpha_6 INTR + \alpha_7 EXCH + \mu_t \tag{2}$$

where

α_o = the intercept
α_s = the estimated parameters
μ_t = the stochastic terms

For statistical reasons, we further transform the equations into logarithms as follows:

$$\text{LOG(PERCAP)} = \lambda_0 + \lambda_1\text{LOG(GFCF)} + \lambda_2\ \text{LOG(IMP)} + \lambda_3\text{LOG(EXPT)} + \lambda_4\text{LOG(DEBT)} + \lambda_5\text{FDI} + \lambda_6 INTR + \lambda_7 EXCH + \nu_t \tag{3}$$

where

λ_0 = the intercept terms
λ_s = the estimated parameters
ν_t = the stochastic terms

3.3 Estimation Procedures

Since a cointegration can be established, the study in line with study conducted by Loto and Alao (2016) utilized the augmented form of causality which comprises of the Vector Error Correction (VECM). Therefore, this study utilized a multivariate K[th] order VECM stated as follows:

$$\begin{bmatrix} \Delta Y_t \\ \Delta X_t \end{bmatrix} = \begin{bmatrix} \phi_{10} \\ \phi_{20} \end{bmatrix} + \sum_{t=1}^{p} \begin{bmatrix} \alpha_{11} & \alpha_{12} \\ \alpha_{21} & \alpha_{22} \end{bmatrix} \begin{bmatrix} \Delta Y_{t-1} \\ \Delta X_{t-1} \end{bmatrix} + \begin{bmatrix} \lambda_1 \\ \lambda_2 \end{bmatrix} \begin{bmatrix} ECT_{h,t-1} \end{bmatrix} + \begin{bmatrix} \mu_{1t} \\ \mu_{2t} \end{bmatrix} \tag{4}$$

where

Y_t = Log(NGDP)
X_t = Log(REM), EXCH POPGR Log(PUBEXP) Log(GFCF)
ECT = Error Correction term

3.4 Diagnostic and Stability tests

In order to ascertain the robustness of the estimated output, diagnostics and stability tests procedures are conducted. Among the tests conducted include, serial correlation test, and the CUSUM and CUSUMSQ tests to ascertain if the VECM estimated results are stable.

4.0 RESULTS AND DISCUSSION

From the trend analysis of the percapita GDP growth of Mauritius from (1981-2019), it can be observed that from 1981 to 2000, the percapita growth of indicates a dramatic upward trend; and also from 2000 to 2019, the is a fluctuations which clearly indicate that there are ups and down in the percapita GDP of the economy of Mauritius during the period under study.

Figure 2. The trend of the per capita GDP growth in Mauritius from 1980- 2019
Source: Authors' own compilation from the Stata 11 result

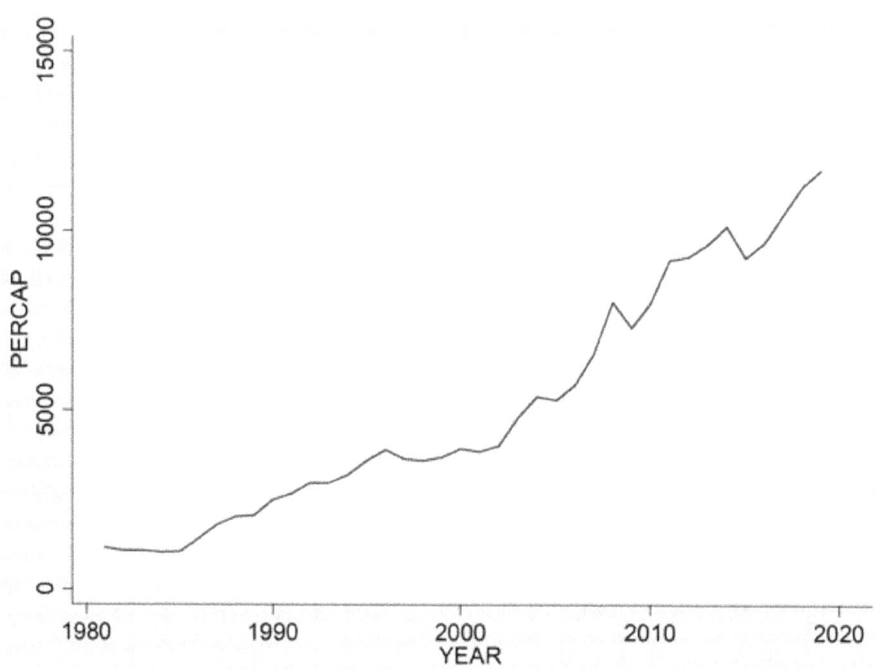

4.1 The Descriptive Statistics

To evaluate the effect of macroeconomic variables on economic growth of Mauritius the variables are evaluated using the descriptive statistics shown in table 1 below.

Table 1. The descriptive statistics

	PERCAP	GFCF	IMP	EXPT	DEBT	FDI	INTR	EXCH
Mean	5104.427	1.344590	3.738462	3.221795	52.95359	13.07179	8.764103	23.63667
Median	3899.440	1.080000	2.850000	2.850000	49.49000	0.040000	7.440000	26.25000
Maximum	11702.49	2.809000	8.010000	6.280000	95.07000	59.00000	16.79000	35.54000
Minimum	1027.990	0.190000	0.510000	0.510000	18.74000	-0.030000	1.070000	8.940000
Std. Dev.	3310.906	0.829991	2.506287	1.909970	21.65522	18.93416	4.164464	8.336419
Skewness	0.532139	0.267530	0.413533	0.168201	0.395962	0.936839	0.250206	-0.182152
Kurtosis	1.946373	1.783325	1.755441	1.722273	1.982848	2.250669	2.049830	1.530811
Jarque-Bera	3.644580	2.870704	3.628567	2.836848	2.700329	6.617269	1.874006	3.723256
Probability	0.161655	0.238032	0.162955	0.242095	0.259198	0.036566	0.391800	0.155419
Sum	199072.7	52.43900	145.8000	125.6500	2065.190	509.8000	341.8000	921.8300
Sum Sq. Dev.	4.17E+08	26.17764	238.6961	138.6234	17820.05	13623.09	659.0249	2640.843
Observations	39	39	39	39	39	39	39	39

Source: Authors' compilation from the Eviews result

The results of the descriptive statistics indicate that all of the variables have positive mean values with 39 observations. The result show a minimum FDI value of -0.030000 and maximum value of 11702.49 by PERCAP. The highest variation of 3310.906 is recorded by the PERCAP while the least standard deviation of 1.909970 is recorded by EXPT. The normality test result for the variables showed that four of the variables have values greater than 0.05 level of significance.

4.2 Correlation

The correlation test result are presented in Table 2.

The correlation test results shows that there is positive relationship between the percapita GDP growth and six variables under study, and the interest rate indicate a negative value of -0.000462 to the percapita GDP growth.

Table 2. The correlation matrix

	PERCAP	GFCF	IMP	EXPT	DEBT	FDI	INTR	EXCH
PERCAP	1.000000	0.966839	0.990806	0.977203	0.780505	0.890602	-0.000462	0.884998
GFCF	0.966839	1.000000	0.982548	0.979253	0.757516	0.890659	0.059459	0.875047
IMP	0.990806	0.982548	1.000000	0.990820	0.783971	0.905550	0.005538	0.883294
EXPT	0.977203	0.979253	0.990820	1.000000	0.744225	0.869441	0.106308	0.917146
DEBT	0.780505	0.757516	0.783971	0.744225	1.000000	0.856375	-0.369830	0.596441
FDI	0.890602	0.890659	0.905550	0.869441	0.856375	1.000000	-0.265381	0.698756
INTR	-0.000462	0.059459	0.005538	0.106308	-0.369830	-0.265381	1.000000	0.318543
EXCH	0.884998	0.875047	0.883294	0.917146	0.596441	0.698756	0.318543	1.000000

Source: Authors' compilation from the Eviews result

4.3 The Stationarity Test

In order to test for the unit root among the variables under consideration, we conducted a stationarity test procedures using the Augmented Dickey-Fuller (ADF) test procedures presented in table 3 as follows:

The result shows that the variables are not integrated of order zero I(0); however, at first difference, all the estimated variables are integrated of order one I(1) at 5% significance level . Therefore a Johansen cointegration test procedure is conducted to ascertain if there exist a long run relationship between the variables under consideration.

Table 3. The ADF unit root test procedures

Augmented Dickey Fuller ADF Test						
Variable	Level Difference	Probability	Order of Integration	First Difference	Probability	Order of Integration
PERCAP	1.242617	0.9979	I(0)	-6.095652	0.0000	I(1)**
GFCF	-0.082439	0.9442	I(0)	-5.130718	0.0002	I(1)**
IMP	0.068125	0.9589	I(0)	-6.265269	0.0000	I(1)**
EXPT	-0.523903	0.8753	I(0)	-6.622579	0.0000	I(1)**
FDI	-0.541920	0.8713	I(0)	-10.15619	0.0000	I(1)**
DEBT	-0.881216	0.7834	I(0)	-6.114686	0.0000	I(1)**
INTR	-1.684764	0.4304	I(0)	-10.32890	0.0000	I(1)**
EXCH	-1.121738	0.6972	I(0)	-5.945191	0.0000	I(1)**
Note: * ** *** indicate stationarity at either 1%, 5% and 10% respectively						

Source: Authors' compilation from the Eviews result

4.4 Cointegration

The cointegration test results is presented in the Table 4.

From the cointegration test results in table 4 above, the trace likelihood ratio and the Maximum Eigenvalue test results showed three and two cointegrating equations respectively at 5% significant level

4.5 Lag Length Selection

In order determine the lag order of the VECM model estimation, the study conducted lag length selection criterion. From the following criterions, Akaike Information Criterion (AIC), Schwarz Criterion (SC) and Hannan-Quinn information criterion (HQ), the tests indicated 1 lag for both AIC and SC and HQ test procedures respectively.

From the test result above, we utilized the AIC test results since it is supported with the final prediction error. Therefore the VAR model with a constant and VAR (1) lags is estimated.

Table 4. Summary of cointegration estimate

Trace Test					
Null Hypothesis	**Alternative Hypothesis**	**Eigenvalue**	**Statistics**	**95% Critical Value**	**Prob.****
None *	r≤1	0.882292	229.2964	159.5297	0.0000
At most 1 *	r≤2	0.777364	152.2726	125.6154	0.0004
At most 2*	r≤3	0.648748	98.19277	95.75366	0.0336
At most 3	r≤4	0.476130	60.52777	69.81889	0.2195
At most 4	r≤5	0.428863	37.25338	47.85613	0.3357
At most 5	r≤6	0.193235	17.08886	29.79707	0.6335
At most 6	r≤7	0.165304	9.358837	15.49471	0.3332
Maximum Eigenvalue test					
None *	r≤1	0.882292	77.02383	52.36261	0.0000
At most 1 *	r≤2	0.777364	54.07984	46.23142	0.0060
At most 2	r≤3	0.648748	37.66500	40.07757	0.0912
At most 3	r≤4	0.476130	23.27439	33.87687	0.5096
At most 4	r≤5	0.428863	20.16452	27.58434	0.3299
At most 5	r≤6	0.193235	7.730021	21.13162	0.9195
At most 6	r≤7	0.165304	6.504737	14.26460	0.5493
* denotes hypothesis rejection at 0.05 significance level					

Source: Authors' compilation from the Eviews result

Table 5. The VAR lag length selection for the model

Lag	LogL	LR	FPE	AIC	SC	HQ
1	-1.412363	NA	5.01e-09*	3.535803*	6.322256*	4.518158*
* indicates lag order selected by the criterion						

Source: Authors' compilation from the Eviews result

4.6 The VECM Estimation Procedures

The long-run coefficient results from the VECM output shows that deviations from the long-run affect changes in variables under consideration. From the results, the coefficient of LOG(GFCF(-1)) is negative and is statistically significant. Also, the variables LOG(IMP) and EXCH coefficients are negative significant at 5% levels. This indicates a negative feedback between the percapita income of the Mauritius economy and the gross fixed capital formation, import and the rate of exchange during the period understudy. Other variables which include, LOG(EXPT), LOG(DEBT),FDI and INTR show positive signs and are statistically significant at 5% level. This implies a positive feedback between export, foreign inflow and the percapita GDP growth in the economy. The FDI positive feedback conforms to findings of Shukla (2020) on the interaction effect between macroeconomic variables and output growth of India which show that real interest and foreign direct investment impacts positively on the Indian economy. Also, Mbulawa (2015) in a study of the economy of Botswana noted that foreign direct investment and inflation impacts positively on economic growth. On the other hand, Sharma et al (2011) on the effect of macroeconomic

Table 6. The long-run VECM estimation

Variable	CointEq1	Std Error	T-Statistic
LOG(PERCAP(-1))	1.000000		
LOG(GFCF(-1))	-0.325610	0.19901	-1.63616
LOG(IMP(-1))	-3.102932	0.38500	-8.05954
LOG(EXPT(-1))	3.198261	0.34361	9.30781
LOG(DEBT(-1))	0.453787	0.06116	7.41993
D(FDI(-1))	0.016969	0.00304	5.57904
INTR(-1)	0.013966	0.013966	1.99905
EXCH(-1)	-0.054684	0.00601	-9.09151
C	-8.692592		

Source: Authors' compilation from the Eviews result

Table 7. The VECM estimation results

Error Correction:	D(LOG (PERCAP))	D(LOG (GFCF))	D(LOG (IMP))	D(LOG (EXPT))	D(LOG (DEBT))	D(FDI,2)	D(INTR)	D(EXCH)
CointEq1	-0.225630	-0.269717	-0.117152	-0.309841	-0.089451	-11.56347	-4.586493	3.640856
Std error	0.07092	0.11484	0.10931	0.09879	0.18423	11.6189	2.51716	1.52495
t-statistic	-3.18148	-2.34857	-1.07175	-3.13650	-0.48555	-0.99523	-1.82209	2.38752
R-squared	**0.557991**	0.576184	0.361454	0.454362	0.342471	0.682311	0.463349	0.441118
Adj. R-squared	0.404988	0.429478	0.140419	0.265487	0.114864	0.572341	0.277585	0.247658

Source: Authors' compilation from the Eviews result

variables on economic performance of Sri Lanka and India find that exchange rate and rate of interest positively impact on economic growth of both economies.

4.7 The Short-Run VECM Test Procedures

From the short-run estimated result above, the error correction term is -0.225630 with correct negative sign for the variable LOG(PERCAP) with a t-statistic value of -3.18148 that is significant statistically. It shows that as the percapita GDP growth deviates from equilibrium, its adjustment through macroeconomic variables amount to 22% annually. Thus, 22% of the disequilibrium in the percapita GDP growth is corrected annually.

4.8 Impulse Responses Function (IRF)

The IRF show effects of a shock to one endogenous variable on others in the model. The figure 3 below shows the response of other macroeconomic aggregates to percapita GDP growth shocks.

The IRF result from the Figure 2 show that the response of PERCAP to itself increases instantly and significantly and decreases in the short-run, but continues with the positive sign along the horizons in the long-run. The response of GFCF to percapita GDP growth shock increases immediately and continues to fluctuate to a positive shock in both short-run and the long-run horizon. The response of the IMP and EXPT increases instantly and significantly and continues with the positive signs along the horizons in the long-run. The response of DEBT to PERCAP shock decreases immediately and continues to decline along the horizon in both short and long-run to a positive shock. On the other hand, the response of the variable FDI to percapita growth shock decreases immediately and continues to fluctuate along the horizon in both short and long-run to a negative shock.The monetary policy variables,

Figure 3. The IRF results
Source: *Authors' computation from the Eviews result*

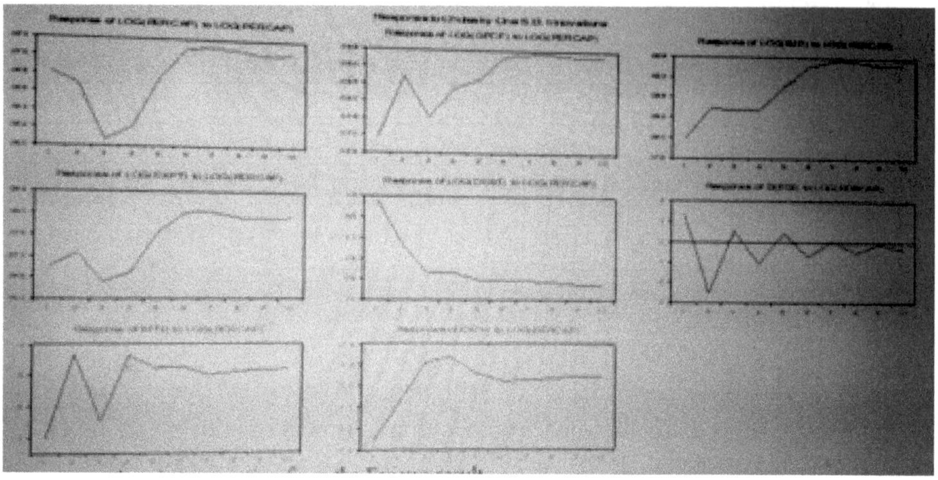

INTR and EXCH response to percapita GDP growth shock show an instant increase and continues with the positive signs in both the short and long-run.

4.9 Variance Decompositions

The variance decomposition provides complementary information on the dynamic variable in the system. The variance decomposition results are therefore presented in the tables below:

The results from the table above indicates that shocks to the PERCAP itself increased from the beginning but continues to a long-run period. Also, the result indicate that shock to Log(GFCF), LOG(IMP), LOG(EXPT) and EXCH accounts for all the variability in the overall periods.

4.10 Diagnostic Test

Ascertaining the robustness of the estimated parameters, a diagnostic test is therefore conducted. To evaluate the robustness of the estimated VECM results, a VEC residual serial correlation test is shown in Table 9.

From the table, both the VEC residual serial correlation LM test estimate showed the absence of serial correlation in the VEC estimates. This is because the null hypothesis of both tests are accepted.

Table 8. The variance decomposition of LOG(PERCAP)

	S.E.	LOG (PERCAP)	LOG (GFCF)	LOG (IMP)	LOG (EXPT)	LOG (DEBT)	D (FDI)	INTR	EXCH
1	0.068222	100.0000	0.000000	0.000000	0.000000	0.000000	0.000000	0.000000	0.000000
2	0.107009	79.73645	0.220000	1.195840	0.119441	12.24568	1.036824	0.023894	5.421867
3	0.144230	61.62064	8.154452	2.950434	0.126832	14.36643	3.106983	0.857918	8.816318
4	0.175921	53.87756	14.94566	5.380046	0.808165	10.52848	4.441530	0.589516	9.429046
5	0.204123	50.96572	19.11487	6.049629	1.070227	7.868230	4.927345	0.685691	9.318288
6	0.228529	50.27364	20.81034	6.277424	1.149606	6.349964	4.884659	0.743904	9.510470
7	0.250620	49.86451	21.42968	6.531167	1.246635	5.492077	4.811092	0.725221	9.899620
8	0.271542	49.28174	21.87959	6.865805	1.357197	4.920673	4.793599	0.689693	10.21170
9	0.291406	48.62136	22.41802	7.143578	1.454442	4.450027	4.837612	0.672045	10.40291
10	0.310165	48.09102	22.94917	7.340978	1.524616	4.042459	4.871312	0.670387	10.51006

Source: Authors' computation from the Eviews result

Table 9. Diagnostic tests

VEC Residual Serial Correlation LM Tests		
Null Hypothesis: no serial correlation at lag order h		
Included observations: 36		
Lags	LM-Stat	Prob
1	54.00142	0.8091
Probs from chi-square with 64 df.		

Source: Authors' computation from the Eviews result

4.11 Stability test

In order to evaluate stability level of the estimated VECM model, the study utilizes the Cumulative Sum (CUSUM) and the Cumulative Sum of Squares (CUSUMSQ) tests to evaluate the residuals shown in the Figures 4 and 5.

From the two figures above, the CUSUM and CUSUMSQ tests results showed that it is within the restricted lines, though it had deviated a little. Hence, the null hypothesis for CUSUM and CUSUMSQ are rejected and the ARDL model is effective and stable overtime.

Figure 4. The CUSUM test result
Source: Authors' computation from the Eviews result

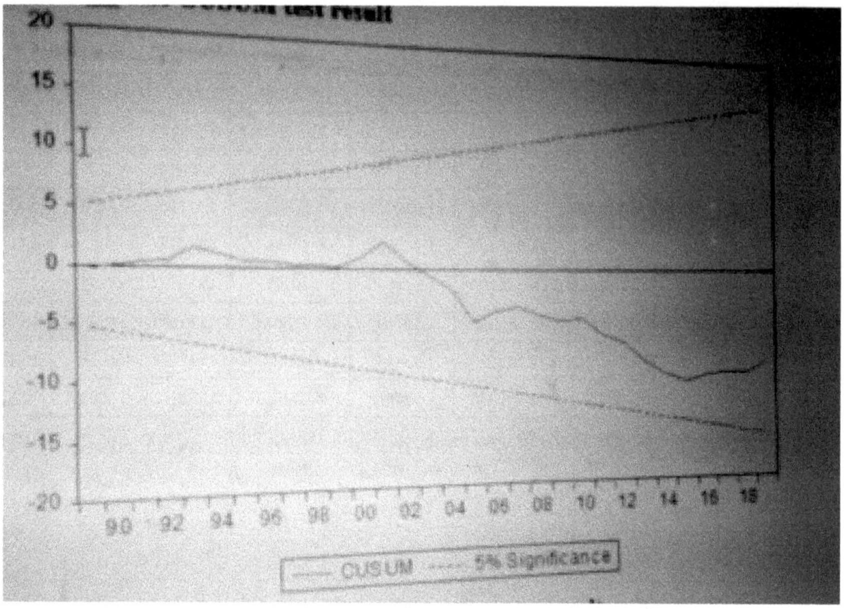

Figure 5. The CUSUMQ test result
Source: Authors' computation from the Eviews result

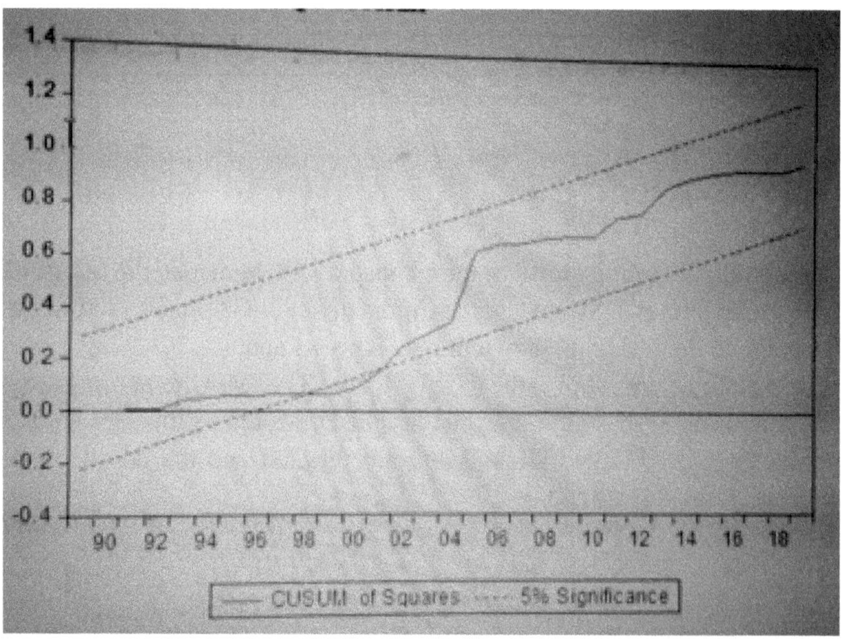

5.0 CONCLUSION AND RECOMMENDATIONS

This study evaluates the effect of macroeconomic variables on economic development in Mauritius. The macroeconomic variables are evaluated to ascertain both the short-run and long-run effect of the macro aggregates on economic development. The study becomes crucial for policy purposes, especially as the country is just recovering from the effect of the COVID 19 pandemic which affected major sectors of the Mauritius economy. The long-run coefficient results from the VECM output indicates a positive feedback between the variables, export, LOG(EXPT), external debt, LOG(DEBT),foreign direct investment (FDI) and interest rate (INTR) and the percapita GDP growth; while there exists a negative feedback between the percapita growth of the Mauritius economy and the gross fixed capital formation LOG(GFCF(-1)), import, (LOG(IMP)), and exchange rate, (EXCH) during the period under review. The short-run estimated result shows 22% of the disequilibrium in the percapita GDP growth is corrected annually. The IRF result show that the response of PERCAP to itself increases instantly and significantly and decreases in the short-run, but continues with the positive sign along the horizons in the long-run. The response of GFCF to percapita GDP growth shock increases immediately and continues to fluctuate to a positive shock in both short-run and the long-run horizon. The response of the IMP and EXPT increases instantly and significantly and continues with the positive signs along the horizons in the long-run. The monetary policy variables, INTR and EXCH response to percapita GDP growth shock show an instant increase and continues with the positive signs in both the short and long-run. On the other hand, the response of the variable FDI to percapita growth shock decreases immediately and continues to fluctuate along the horizon in both short and long-run to a negative shock. The variance decomposition results indicates that shocks to the PERCAP itself increased from the beginning but continues on the increase in the long run period. the result indicate also that shock to Log(GFCF), LOG(IMP), LOG(EXPT) and EXCH accounts for most of the variability in the overall periods.

REFERENCES

Chenery, H. B., & Strout, A. M. (1966). Foreign Assistance and Economic Development. *The American Economic Review*, *56*, 679–733.

Chingoiro, S., & Mbulawa, S. (2017). Electricity consumption and Economic growth in Botswana: A Vector Error Correction approach. Advances in Management & Applied Economics, 7(2).

Dan, D. V., & Binch, V. D. (2019). The Effect of Macroeconomic Variables on Economic Growth: A Cross-Country Study. *International Econometric Conference of Vietnam, ECONVN 2019: Beyond Traditional Probabilistic Methods in Economics*, 919–927.

Garrison, C.B., & Lee, F. (1995). The effect of macroeconomic variables on economic growth rates: A cross-country study. *Journal of Macroeconomics, 17*(2), 303-317. https://doi.org/ doi:10.1016/0164-0704(95)80103-0

Loto, M. A., & Alao, A. A. (2016). Remittances and the Growth of the Nigerian Economy. EJBE, 6(2).

Madhou, A., Sewak, T., Moosa, I., Ramiah, V., & Gerth, F. (2021). Towards Full-Fledged Inflation Targeting Monetary Policy Regime in Mauritius. *Journal of Risk and Financial Management*, *14*(3), 126. doi:10.3390/jrfm14030126

Mbulawa, S. (2015). Effect of Macroeconomic Variables on Economic Growth in Botswana. Journal of Economic and Sustainable Development, 6(4).

Olayungbo, D. O., & Quadri, A. (2019). Remittances, financial development and economic growth in sub-Saharan African countries: Evidence from a PMG-ARDL approach. *Financial Innovation*, *5*(1), 9. doi:10.1186/s40854-019-0122-8

SharmaG. D.SinghS.SinghG. (2011). Impact of Macroeconomic Variables on Economic Performance: An Empirical Study of India and Sri Lanka. http://dx.doi.org/ doi:10.2139/ssrn.1836542

Shukla, S. (2017). Innovation and economic growth: A case of India. *Humanities & Social Science Review*, *5*(2), 64–70. doi:10.18510/hssr.2017.521

Shukla, S. (2020). The Impact of Macroeconomic Variables on Economic Growth: Empirical Evidence from India'. *International Journal of Current Advanced Research*, *09*(06), 22628–22632. doi:10.24327/ijcar.2020.22632.4471

Svirydzenka, K., & Petri, M. (2014). *Mauritius: The Drivers of Growth—Can the Past be Extended?* International Monetary Fund (IMF) Working Paper WP/14/134.

Todaro, M. P., & Smith, S. (2012). *Economic Development* (11th ed.). Pearson Education Inc.

Chapter 3
Finance and Development in Tanzania Post Cold War

Nneka Maureen Nwala
https://orcid.org/0000-0002-1183-1059
Nasarawa State University, Keffi, Nigeria

ABSTRACT

This study set out to investigate how financial reforms embarked upon after the change in economic policy affected economic development in Tanzania by analysing the finance and development nexus. The study utilized autoregressive distributive lag technique to evaluate data on how gross domestic product was used to measure economic development and seven variables proxied finance. The study established that there is a long-run relationship between finance and development in Tanzania for the period studied and that this relationship is able to return to equilibrium at an above average speed in the event of volatility. The study concluded that all the dependent variables except financial openness are leading indicators of economic development in Tanzania. Consequently, it is recommended that the switch in economic policy is in the right direction and the trajectory is sustained because it is creating the desired turnaround in the economy.

1. INTRODUCTION

Tanzania ranks as the third fastest growing economy in Africa after Ethiopia (8%) and Ivory Coast (7.5%), and an average real GDP growth rate of 6.3% over the past decade (2010-2019) The real GDP of Tanzania grew by 4.8% in 2020 reaching USD 64.4 billion versus USD 60.8 billion in 2019 and it is projected to grow at +5.1% in 2022 and 6.0% in 2026 (International Monetary Fund, 2021).This can be attributed

DOI: 10.4018/979-8-3693-1610-8.ch003

to the post-1990s economic reform which was a shift towards market based economy. Prior to this reform there were other major reforms but economic development in these eras was slow. It was basically characterized by poor education, low level of technology and the dependence on foreigners and largely depended on agriculture through export of cash crops such as cotton.

The United Republic of Tanzania an east African country was the result of the amalgamation of Tanganyika and Zanzibar in 26th April 1964. Tanganyika is the mainland covering more than 99 percent of the combined territories' total area while Zanzibar is an island, it is the 31st largest country in the world but 14th in Africa and surrounded by Kenya, Uganda, Rwanda, Burundi, Zambia, Malawi and the Republic of Congo. Its capital city which is Dodoma is centrally located on the mainland is the De jure and the largest city and port is Dar Es Salaam which is the De facto capital city (Gupta, 2019). According to the Tanzanian National Bureau of Statistics, total population is estimated at 59.7 million people in 2020. The official language in Tanzania is Swahili and English.

Figure 1. Map of Tanzania depicting its major cities
Source: *Tanzania-CIA WFB Map.png*

After the infamous Berlin conference where, European colonisers deliberated on how to share African territories which held in 1884-1885 German East Africa was established. However, Tanzania was only the colony of the Germans till the World War 1 began. Though the German colonization period was brief the Tanganyika area experienced development in major cash crops, they created a novel structure of production of export crops and commenced the construction of railroads network. Although they succeeded in disrupting the traditional agricultural practices, it became the prominent cause of impoverishment and population decline in some areas.

At the end of WWI, League of Nations asked Britain to administer the territory on its behalf. The British administration utilized the principle of 'indirect rule, most of the administrative tasks, including tax collection, were done by Native Authorities who were mere tools used by the central government with no say whatsoever in its decisions. A Legislative Council was created in 1926, but its members were essentially selected within the European and Asian minority however after the World War II the United Nations urged the participation of more natives. Two educated Tanganyika chiefs were appointed to the Legislative Council in 1945. Due to several internal and external pressures the British administration exchanged the indirect rule with a local multi-tier formal structure, allowing for elections of officials into the Legislative council from region to district to village level this change made way for more Tanganyika participation in government.

Tanganyika educated elites formed a political party, Tanganyika African National Union (TANU) from Tanganyika African Association (TAA) a social club for educated indigenous civil servants. Being the first African in Tanganyika to get a university degree Julius Nyerere became the president of TAA in 1953. He was able to mobilize grassroots support and thus TANU won all the seats of the Legislative Council in 1958, this same feat was repeated again at the Legislative council elections in 1960. One year later, independence was declared with TANU as the party of government and Nyerere as Prime Minister (Bourguignon, 2018).

Tanzania since the mid- 1980 has been a capitalist economy after Ujamaa ideology, a socialist model based on freedom, self-reliance and family-hood failed as a remedy to poverty and underdevelopment. Following all these reforms, Tanzania has witnessed over three decades of economic liberalisation and neo-liberal policies fully driven by the private sector transiting it from low-income to lower-middle-income status in July 2020. Liberalization of the economy, is expected to increase efficiency, productivity as well as stimulate growth. Ngowi (2009) is of the view that since the advent of neo-liberal policies era, there have been impressive economic growth in the country because from 2007 to 2018, the national poverty rate fell from 34.4 to 26.4 percent, while the extreme poverty rate dropped from 12 to 8 percent. However, Mandalu, Thakhathi, and Costa (2018) noted that this economic growth has failed to reduce poverty considerably amongst the rural people who are the majority in the country. Therefore, this study investigated the effect of the financial reforms and liberalization on the development of Tanzania post-cold war. Especially as most of the liberalization that took place was financial in nature as a result of the switch in political ideology (see Roger Nord et al. 2009).

2. ECONOMIC, SOCIAL, AND POLITICAL REFORM FROM 1960-1980, 1981-2020

The then president Mwl. Julius Kambarage Nyerere in 1967 introduced the system called Ujamaa (socialism) meaning family hood where by all means of production were owned and shared by all community members. Making Tanzania a socialist oriented nation both economically and politically. Ujamaa was conceived to rectify the economic affairs that was inherited from the colonial economic system. After independence in 1961 the bulk of economic activities in Tanganyika's was controlled by British colonial masters and Asian businessmen. Industries, plantations, banks, mines and relatively large commercial activities were owned by the British and Asians (Ngowi, 2009). In the mid-1960s a number of imbalances were experienced, leading to market failures; being a capitalist economy, the government had no power to intervene over the market forces. The people's independence expectations were not met as they lived in more or less the same situation as before independence; they continued to labour for the same colonial masters they had worked for before independence. To a large extent, Ujamaa model succeeded in building a cohesive, post-independence nation, and furthered Swahili as the official national language.

After 18 years it was obvious that Ujamaa was no longer achieving the objectives for which it was set and it became imperative for Tanzania to change its economic policy. Although Tanzania started a National Economic Survival Program in 1982 and continued up to 1986 during which time there was a change in political leadership in 1985, as economic conditions worsened, Tanzania accepted the conditions of the International Monetary Fund and World Bank Structural adjustment programme called the economic recovery programmes in 1986. This phase which lasted from 1986 to1995 was characterized by banking sector liberalization, currency devaluation, reductions in budget deficit liberalization of the economy, increasing efficiency and productivity and stimulating growth (Twinoburyo & Odhiambo, 2018). This period also witnessed (i) Liberalisation of exchange and trade regimes. (ii) Liberalisation of agricultural marketing system and domestic prices, and (iii) initiation of parastatals and civil services reforms. The outcomes of these policies and actions saw the dominance of public monopolies, insolvency of large state-owned and state-run banks, weakness of budgetary management, fiscal deficits, elusive macroeconomic stability and low economic growth (Robinson et al., 2011).

According to Mandalu, Thakhathi, and Costa (2018) the second phase of structural reformation was implemented from 1996 to 2005. Several of the parastatals and large state owned banks were fully privatized. The financial sector became fully liberalized, regulatory framework became market oriented others include, Trade reform, regional integration, Reversal of fiscal dominance of monetary policy, Fiscal consolidation, and Sizable finance assistance from donors.

3. EMPIRICAL REVIEW

Saganga (2021) used ARDL and bound testing to investigate the effect of financial development on Tanzania's economic growth from 1980 to 2017. Economic growth was measured as real Gross domestic product growth percentage and four financial development variables namely domestic credit to private sector as percentage of GDP; deposit money bank assets as percentage of GDP; deposit money bank to deposit money bank assets and central bank assets percentage; and liquid liabilities as percentage of GDP were aggregated to two proxies Financial system depth, and financial system liquidity and efficiency. The study found a negative relationship between financial liquidity and efficiency and economic growth however financial depth was found not to have any long run relationship with economic growth but had a positive effect in the short run. The outcome of this study emphasized the fact that the Tanzianian economy was formerly state-dominated which very later was liberalized and this was captured in the data used for the study.

Similarly, Simba and Çankal (2020) analysed the causal relationship between financial development institutions and economic growth in Tanzania from 1989 to 2018. Annual percentage growth of Gross Domestic Product (GDP) was used to measure economic growth and Four proxies of financial development institutions was utilized, Broad Money as a percentage of GDP, Domestic credit for private sector as a percentage of GDP), Domestic credit provided by financial sector as a percentage of GDP, and Domestic credit to the private sector by banks as a percentage of GDP. Autoregressive Distributed Lag (ARDL), Vector Error Correction Model (VECM), and Granger Causality test were used to analyse the data of the study. The study found that there is positive short and long run relationship between the dependent and independent variables of the study and that causality runs from economic growth to financial development institution in Tanzania. This study is however different from Saganga (2021) because the independent variables was not aggregated and they used a short time frame.

Nwala and Fodio (2019) investigated the effect of macroeconomic variables on financial sector development in Nigeria from 1984 to 2017. Macroeconomic variables were proxied by inflation, money supply, financial openness, trade openness and government expenditure and financial sector development was proxied by private sector credit to GDP and Total market capitalization. The study utilized Autoregressive distributive lag model to analyse the data. The study found that financial sector development depends on money supply, interest rate, financial openness and inflation in Nigeria while, exchange rate, trade openness and total government expenditure are not significant. One can reasonably infer that Tanzania and Nigeria have likely pursued distinct economic policies following the Cold War. Divergences in regulatory structures, fiscal strategies, and monetary measures could exert notable impacts on the respective outcomes within the financial sectors of the two nations.

Likewise, Maganya (2018) empirically ascertain the relationship between financial development and economic growth in Tanzanian using Vector Error Correction Model. Economic growth the endogenous variable of the study was proxied by the growth of Real GDP per capita and financial development was proxied by Broad Money, Domestic Credit to private sector to GDP and Bank Deposit to GDP. The study found that all variables have long-run linear relationship with growth of real GDP per capita corroborating the studies of Simba and Çankal (2020). However, the study did not determine causality or indicate the period studied.

In contrast to studies that singularly examine a specific country, Bumann, Hermes, and Lensink (2012) employed a meta-regression analysis methodology to investigate the correlation between financial liberalization and economic growth, aggregating findings from 60 empirical studies. These studies were sorted into different categories including: 1) financial openness was measured (de jure versus de facto measures); 2) if the study was published as a working paper or as a peer-reviewed academic journal article; 3) the time periods covered by the original studies (i.e. before the 1970s, and in the 1980s, 1990s and 2000s); 4) the type of countries included in the analysis (developed countries, developing countries and a mixed set of developed and developing countries; 5) the number of countries taken into account in the analysis; 6) whether or not panel data are used; 7) if potential endogeneity problems have been treated; 8) whether or not fixed effects are used; 9)whether or not a set of relevant conditioning variables has been included, resulting in 441 t-statistics. The study concluded that on average, there is a positive effect of financial openness on growth, the significance of this effect is weak.

4. DATA ANALYSIS

This study adopted the ex-post facto research design as the data used for the analysis is historical in nature. Data collected was from Annual World Bank and International Monetary Fund (IMF) national accounts data from 1981 to 2019, include gross domestic product which is the proxy for development in Tanzania for the period studied.

Model Specification

Unit Root Test

Augumented Dickey Fuller (ADF) test was used to detect the stationarity properties of the data. The ADF procedure attempts to retain the validity of the tests based on white – noise errors in the regression model by ensuring that the errors are indeed white- noise thus:

$$\Delta Y_t = \alpha + \lambda Y_{t-1} + \sum \delta_i Y_{t-i} + \varepsilon_t$$

Where:

$\lambda = \rho - 1$

This specification is then tested for:

H0: $\lambda = 0$
H1: $\lambda > 1$

Following the stationarity test on the time series, it is critical to determine if they exhibit long-run associationship between them. As a result, the bound test technique was used to assess if a linear combination existed among our variables. Pesaran and Shin (1999) demonstrated that cointegrating systems may be estimated using thc bound test, with the benefit that the variables in the stated model can be I(0), I(1), or a mix of both, and without the requirement to specify which are I(0) or I(1) (1).

If the calculated F-stat exceeds the upper limit critical value of F-tab determined by Pesaran and Shin (1999), we reject the null hypothesis of no Co-integration, indicating that a long run connection exist between the variables. On the other hand, if it is less than the lower limit, the null of no Co-integration cannot be dismissed. Finally, if it falls between these two limits, the outcome seems to be inconclusive.

The bound test for the existence of long-run relationships is then simply a test of

$$H_0 : \alpha_1 = \alpha_2 = \alpha_3 = \alpha_4 0$$

$$H_1 : \alpha_1 \neq \alpha_2 \neq \alpha_3 \neq \alpha_4 \neq 0$$

Autoregressive Distributive Lag (ARDL) technique is an appropriate model used for a small sample size and it allows flexibility about the order of integration of the variables (Pesaran & Shin 1999, Persaran et all 2001, Duasa, 2007). The reparameterized result gives the short-run dynamics and long-rum relationship of the considered variables ARDL has been found to adequately capture the dynamic attribute of financial and economic variables as it automatically includes the lagged values of the dependent variable and independent variables as regressors (explanatory variables). This procedure beyond providing the effect of independent variables, enables the model to estimate the expected dependence of contemporaneous value of the dependent variable on its previous values.

The model of this study is specified as:

$$\mathbf{GDP_t = \beta_1 + \beta_2 GDP_{t-1} + \beta_3 OPEN_t + \beta_4 GOVCAP_t + \beta_5 EXDEBT_t + \beta_6 RINTR_t + \beta_7 PRICONSU_t + \beta_8 GFCF_t + \beta_9 EXP_t + \varepsilon_t} \ldots.. \quad (1)$$

The bounds test procedure is captured with the following representation:

$$\Delta GDP_t = \alpha_0 + \alpha_1 GDP_{t-1} + \alpha_2 OPEN_{t-1} + \alpha_3 GOVCAP_{t-1} + \alpha_4 EXDEBT_{t-1} + \alpha_5 RINTR_{t-1} + \alpha_6 PRICONSU_{t-1} + \alpha_7 GFCF_{t-1} + \alpha_8 EXP_{t-1}$$

$$+\sum_{i=1}^{N1} \gamma_1 \Delta GDP_{t-i} + \sum_{j=0}^{N2} \gamma_2 \Delta OPEN_{t-j} + \sum_{k=1}^{N3} \gamma_3 \Delta GOVCAP_{t-k} + \sum_{l=1}^{N4} \gamma_4 \Delta EXDEBT_{t-l} + \sum_{m=1}^{N5} \gamma_5 \Delta RINTR_{t-m} + \sum_{n=1}^{N6} \gamma_6 \Delta PRICONSU_{t-n}$$
$$+\sum_{o=1}^{N7} \gamma_7 \Delta GFCF_{t-o} + \sum_{P=1}^{N8} \gamma_8 \Delta EXP_{t-P} + u_t \text{ -----} (1)$$

Where;

GDP = Gross Domestic Product
OPEN = Financial Liberalisation/Openness
GOVCAP = Government Capital Expenditure
EXDEBT = External Debt
RINTR = Real Interest Rate
PRICONSU = Private Consumption
GFCF = Gross Fixed Capital Formation
EXP = Trade openness (Export –Import)
$\alpha_2 - \alpha_8$ = The long run coefficients of OPEN, GOVCAP, EXDEBT, RINTR, PRICONSU, GFCF and EXP

$\gamma_2 - \gamma_8$ = The short run coefficients of OPEN, GOVCAP, EXDEBT, RINTR, PRICONSU, GFCF and EXP

α_0 = Intercept parameter estimate

Δ = First difference operator

t = a deterministic trend

Table 1. Measurement of variables

Variables	Measurement	Supporting Studies
Gross Domestic Product	It is regarded as the most closely-watched aggregate economic indicator and one which is so regularly used as a measure of the standard of living. GDP is essentially the monetary value of final goods and services—that is, those that are bought by the final user—produced within the borders of a country in a given period of time (say a quarter or a year). It counts all of the output generated within the borders of a country. GDP is composed of goods and services produced for sale in the market and also includes some nonmarket production, such as defense or education services provided by the government.	Lequiller & Blades (2007), OECD (2009), Dynan, & Sheiner (2018)
Financial Openness	Measured by qualitative indicators of restrictions on financial credits and personal capital transactions of residents and financial credits to nonresidents, as well as the use of multiple exchange rates	Various IMF reports and working papers Abiad, Detragiache, and Tressel, (2008)
Government Capital Expenditure	Total amount spent by the government on assets which are long-term in nature and allow the economy to generate revenue for many years.	Annual World Bank national accounts data, and OECD National Accounts data files
External Debt	Total debt borrowed from foreign lenders, including commercial banks, governments or international financial institutions. Typically denominated in foreign currency	Arnone, Bandiera and Presbitero (2015) Atiku and Nwala (2021).
Real Interest Rate	Nominal interest rate adjusted for inflation	Annual World Bank national accounts data
Private Consumption	It is calculated using private consumption in constant 2015 prices and World Bank population estimates. It is the market value of all goods and services, including durable products (such as cars, washing machines, and home computers), purchased by households and includes payments and fees to governments to obtain permits and licenses. Data are in constant 2015 U.S. dollars	Annual World Bank national accounts data, and OECD National Accounts data files
Gross Fixed Capital Formation	The value of acquisitions of new or existing fixed assets by the business sector, governments and "pure" households (excluding their unincorporated enterprises) *less* disposals of fixed assets. It indicates how much of the new value added in the economy is invested rather than consumed	Kuznets, Epstein and Jenks (1941). Lequiller & Blades (2007)
Trade openness	Net of imports and exports	Annual World Bank and IMF national accounts data

Source: author's compilation, 2022

If the calculated F-stat surpasses the upper limit critical value of F-tab determined by Pesaran and Shin (1999), the null hypothesis of no Co-integration will be rejected, this signals that a long run relationship exist between the variables. Conversely, if it is less than the lower limit, the null of no Co-integration cannot be rejected. Finally, if it falls between these two limits, the outcome seems to be inconclusive.

The bound test for the existence of long-run relationships is a test of:

$$H_0 : \alpha_1 = \alpha_2 = \alpha_3 = \alpha_4 0$$

$$H_1 : \alpha_1 \neq \alpha_2 \neq \alpha_3 \neq \alpha_4 \neq 0$$

Finally, after demonstrating the existence of a long-run cointegration connection, the research used the ECM technique to evaluate both the long-run impacts and the short-run dynamics. ECM was used to decide the rate at which the variables adjust towards the long-run equilibrium path in response to any short-run deviation.

The GDP data seem to have a lot of outliers as indicated by the difference between the mean (472.6654) and the median (406.5400) value and supported by the standard deviation which reports a wide spread of the GDP data. It can be observed from table 2 that the financial openness data are symmetrical in nature as the mean (42.69077) and median value (42.04000) are similar. The government capital expenditure data observed in table 2 indicates the data is skewed more to the right as the mean value (6.012564) is larger than the mean median value (2.49000). However, the standard deviation (6.544540) suggests that the data are clustered

Table 2. Descriptive statistics

	GDP	OPEN	GOVCAP	EXDEBT	RINTR	PRICONSU	GFCF	EXP
Mean	472.6654	42.69077	6.012564	76.76282	5.324872	12.68641	5.972821	3.215128
Median	406.5400	42.04000	2.490000	54.26000	5.630000	10.06000	2.660000	1.450000
Maximum	1122.120	65.69000	19.22000	165.8700	14.67000	34.70000	20.78000	9.030000
Minimum	149.1100	23.98000	0.610000	21.76000	-26.50000	2.130000	0.560000	0.140000
Std. Dev.	323.2745	10.86357	6.544540	48.12001	6.852805	10.72564	6.452884	3.261181
Skewness	0.678376	0.274144	0.961926	0.443569	-2.504385	0.829594	1.013406	0.738250
Kurtosis	2.016510	2.565052	2.338531	1.714733	13.03517	2.236090	2.557157	1.908901
Jarque-Bera	4.563046	0.795924	6.725469	3.963252	204.4127	5.421757	6.994123	5.477144
Probability	0.102129	0.671687	0.034640	0.137845	0.000000	0.066478	0.030286	0.064663
Observations	39	39	39	39	39	39	39	39

Source: Author's computation eviews output

more around the mean. The External debt data reports wide spread of the data set as the mean value (76.76282) is a lot different from the median value (54.26000) same for the standard deviation(48.12001)which tells of a highly dispersed data set. The real interest rate portrays the picture of a fairly symmetrical data set as the mean (5.324872) median (5.630000) and standard deviation (6.852805) are not far apart from each other. Private consumption data on the other hand indicates an asymmetric data that is skewed to the right because and median(10.06000) and standard deviation (10.72564) are closer in value than the mean(12.68641) meaning that there is the presence of outliers and these outliers are enough to cause much dispersion from the mean value. The gross fixed capital formation data follows the pattern of financial openness data-set where there is a remarkable difference between the mean(5.972821) and the median (2.660000) indicating the presence of outliers but the standard deviation(6.452884) allude to the fact that despite these outliers the data-set is still clustered around the mean value. Finally, the trade liberalization data equally follows the financial openness and gross fixed formation data-set where the mean (3.215128) is quite higher than the median(1.45000) value but the standard deviation(3.261181) shows that the data are clustered closely around the mean (more reliable).

Most time series data do not have constant mean and variance over time therefore Unit root test was conducted on each of the variables to avoid having spurious regression estimates using the Augmented Dickey Fuller test.

Most of the variables were not stationary at level except RINTR which was stationary @I(0) but at the first difference EXDEBT, GDP, GFCG, GOVCAP, OPEN, and PRICONSU were stationary. Because the variables were stationary at different levels the Autoregressive Distributed Lag (ARDL) cointegration technique was used to evaluate the long-run relationship between the variables.

Table 3. Unit root tests results

		LEVEL		FIRST LEVEL	
S/N	VARIABLE	ADF VALUE	CRITICAL @5%	ADF TEST VALUE	CRITICAL @ 5%
1	EXDEBT	-1.492561	-3.533083	-4.062243	-3.536601
2	GDP	-1.418693	-3.533083	-5.231840	-3.536601
3	GFCF	-0.558149	-3.533083	-6.668195	-3.540328
4	GOVCAP	-3.864279	-3.557759	-6.064190	-3.540328
5	OPEN	-2.834877	-3.536601	-3.733507	-3.536601
6	PRINCONSU	-0.992002	-3.533083	-4.633895	-3.536601
7	RINTR	-5.448426	-3.533083		

Source: Authors Computations from eviews output

Table 4. Extract of ARDL, diagnostics test, and bound test

Variable	Coefficient	Std. Error	t-Statistic	Prob.*
GDP(-1)	0.137770	0.287743	0.478796	0.6378
GDP(-2)	-0.662148	0.209452	-3.161336	0.0054
OPEN	0.111891	0.835379	0.133941	0.8949
OPEN(-1)	1.563775	0.700773	2.231499	0.0386
GOVCAP	64.22472	14.24285	4.509260	0.0003
EXDEBT	-0.873783	0.257678	-3.390985	0.0033
RINTR	-1.313116	0.496559	-2.644433	0.0165
RINTR(-1)	-0.778238	0.425585	-1.828631	0.0841
PRICONSU	17.44471	6.152012	2.835611	0.0110
PRICONSU(-1)	17.85143	11.34432	1.573602	0.1330
PRICONSU(-2)	16.00637	6.605259	2.423277	0.0261
GFCF	-54.80957	15.75496	-3.478876	0.0027
GFCF(-1)	-18.74970	7.907134	-2.371239	0.0291
GFCF(-2)	20.19940	7.877536	2.564178	0.0195
EXP	1.075524	16.47600	0.065278	0.9487
EXP(-1)	-54.64744	15.08836	-3.621827	0.0020
EXP(-2)	-38.04964	11.14829	-3.413048	0.0031
C	-727.1534	303.7837	-2.393655	0.0278
R-squared	0.999291			
Adjusted R-squared	0.998581			
F-statistic	1408.669			
Prob(F-statistic)	0.000000			
Durbin-Watson stat	2.118951			
Diagnostic Test				
Heteroskedasticity Test: ARCH	0.192930 (0.6633)			No Heteroskedasticity
B-Godfrey Serial Correlation LM	5.121903(0.5191)			No serial correlation
Ramsey RESET Test	0.042604 (0.8389)			No functional misspecification
Bounds testing procedure result (5% significance)				
F statistic	I(0) Bound			I(1) Bound
4.369247	2.11			3.15

Source: Authors computation eviews output. Note:Values in parenthesis are p-values

Table 4 presents the extract of ARDL, Diagnostics Test and Bound Test. The R-square, which was used to assess the estimated model's goodness of fit, suggests that the model is fairly suited in prediction. The R-squared 0.999291 implies that the exogenous variables explain 99% of the endogeneous variable. It indicates that OPEN, GOVCAP, EXP, GFCF, EXDEBT, RINTR and PRICONSU has substantial influence over GDP for the period studied. The F-Statistic 1408.669(0.0000) reveals that the exogenous variables jointly explains the dependent variables and that the model is proper and significant. The results of the diagnostic tests in table 4 indicate that the residuals of the ARDL specification are not affected by issues of auto-correlation, heteroscedasticity or misspecification.

The Bound test technique is a cointegration method used to assess if there is a long-run relationship among the variables where the variables are both I(0) and I(1). The value of the F-statistic is 4.369247 and this is larger than the upper (I(1)) (2.11) and lower limit (I(0)) (3.15) critical values at the 5% significance level, according to the co-integration test results.

Therefore, at the 5% significance level, the no long run relationship is rejected. Consequently, it may be deduced that the variables are co-integrated. There is a long-run co-integration association between EXDEBT, GDP, GFCG, GOVCAP, OPEN, RINTR and PRICONSU in Tanzania for the period studied

Table 5. ECM results

Variable	Coefficient	Std. Error	t-Statistic	Prob.
CointEq(-1)	-0.632425	0.098317	-6.432507	0.0000

Source: Author's computation from Eviews

The ect(-1) communicates the rate with which the dynamic model adjusts to re-establish equilibrium after a disruption. For the Ect(-1) to be considered suitable the coefficient is expected to be significant, less than one and negative. The calculated coefficient of the ect(-1) for this model in table 5 is appropriate. According to the results, if the model is in disequilibrium, it takes an average speed of 63.2425% for the model to converge back to long-run equilibrium in the current year.

The estimation results of the long-run coefficients included in the cointegration model in table 6 showed that EXDEBT, and RINTR, had negative significant relationship in the long-run with GDP however PRICONSU had positive significant long-run connection with GDP. Other variables had insignificant association with GDP: OPEN and GFCF has positive insignificant long-run relationship but GOVCAP and EXP were negative and not significant at 5% significant level.

Table 6. Extract from ECM output (long run coefficients)

Variable	Coefficient	Prob.
OPEN	1.935572	0.1886
GOVCAP	-6.093577	0.7189
EXDEBT	-1.317347	0.0008
RINTR	-3.636132	0.0171
PRICONSU	31.27197	0.0002
GFCF	15.43271	0.3251
EXP	-29.30383	0.2019
C	171.7852	0.0014

Source: Author's computation from Eviews results

The long run equation is stated thus:

EC = GDP - (1.9356*OPEN -6.0936*GOVCAP -1.3173*EXDEBT -3.6361 *RINTR + 31.2720*PRICONSU + 15.4327*GFCF -29.3038 *EXP + 171.7852)

Statistical Tests of Hypotheses

The Wald test (f-statistic) and the corresponding p-values were used to examine the two hypotheses proposed in this research. The study's threshold of significance is set at 5% for a two-tailed test. The Wald test generates a test statistic based on the unconstrained regression and examines the coefficients' joint significance. The Wald statistic assesses how close the unconstrained estimates are to fulfilling the constraints imposed by the null hypothesis. If the constraints are true, then the constrained estimates should come near to meeting the constraints.

Discussion of Findings

The computed f-statistic value for OPEN using the Wald-test in Table 7 was 3.085420, and its probability value was 0.0704. Because the probability value was more than 0.05 at the 5% confidence level, it fell in the acceptance zone, and so we may accept the initial null hypothesis that financial openness does not significantly affect GDP in Tanzania for the period studied. This findings however contradicts that of Nwala and Fodio (2019) who found significant effect in Nigeria as well as Bumann, Hermes, and Lensink (2012) who found weak significant effect.

Table 7. Summary of Wald results

Variable	F-Stat	P-Value	Significant @5%
Gdp (c1 &c2)	4.999148	0.0188	Yes
Open (c3 &c4)	3.085420	0.0704	No
Govcap (c5)	61.22472	0.0003	Yes
Exdebt(c6)	-0.873783	0.0033	Yes
Rintr (c7 & c8)	5.192305	0.0166	Yes
Priconsu (c9, c10 &c11)	11.72428	0.0002	Yes
Gfcf (c12, c13 &c14)	4.888939	0.0117	Yes
Exp (c15, c16 &c17)	9.072240	0.0007	Yes

Source: Author's computation eviews output

The f-statistic value for GOVCAP as indicated in Table 7 is 61.22472 with a probability value of 0.0003. Since the probability value is less than 0.05 it is concluded that the null hypothesis is rejected thus, government capital expenditure significantly affects GDP in Tanzania for the period studied conflicting with the findings of Nwala and Fodio (2019).

From Table 7 the F-statistic of EXDEBT is -0.873783 and a p-value of 0.0033. For a 5% confidence level, the probability value is less than 0.05. It consequently falls inside the rejection range, allowing us to reject the second null hypothesis and infer that the external debt has a considerable influence on GDP in Tanzania for the period studied.

RINTR's f-statistic is 5.192305 with a p-value of 0.0166 which is within the rejection zone as it is less than 0.05. This signifies that the null hypothesis that real interest rate does not significantly affect GDP in Tanzania is not accepted because real interest rate does significantly affect GDP in Tanzania for the period studied. This is in line with the findings of Nwala and Fodio (2019) who found that interest rate significant in Nigeria.

The computed f-statistic for PRICONSU in Table 7 is 11.72428 and its p-value is 0.0002. The p-value is less than 0.05 thus the null hypothesis falls in the rejection area. The study concludes that Private consumption does significantly affect GDP in Tanzania for the period studied and the findings aligns with that of Simba and Çankal (2020) and Maganya (2018) who found significant effect.

Table 7 also reveals that the f-statistic for GFCF is 4.888939 and p-value 0.0117. The calculated p-value denotes that the null hypothesis is in the rejection zone therefore it is accepted that gross capital formation does substantially influence GDP in Tanzania.

Finally, the f-statistic and p-value for EXP is 9.072240 and 0.0007 respectively. For a 5% confidence level, the probability value is less than 0.05 this evidently result in rejection of the null hypothesis which states that Export does not significantly affect GDP in Tanzania.

5. SUMMARY AND CONCLUSION

This study set out to investigate how financial reforms embarked upon after the change in economic policy affected economic development in Tanzania. From the analysis it is evident that these reforms carried out post-Ujaama era indeed has improved the standard of living of Tanzanians. This study established that there is a long-run relationship between finance and development in Tanzania for the period studied and this relationship is able to return to equilibrium at an above average speed in the event of volatility.

The paper concludes that Gross Capital Formation, External Debt, Real Interest Rate, Private Consumption, Trade Liberalization and Government Capital Expenditure are leading indicators of Economic development in Tanzania for the period studied.

This study therefore recommends that Tanzania should continue with the market economy reforms and multi-party democracy as this seems to be the best path in achieving its objective of moving Tanzania from the low income country to a lower-middle-income country and lifting a vast majority of its population from poverty.

REFERENCES

Abiad, A., Detragiache, E., & Tressel, T. (2008). *A New Database of Financial Reforms. mimeo*. International Monetary Fund.

Arnone, M., & Luca, B. (2015). *External debt sustainability: Theory and empiricalevidence*. http://www3.unicatt.it/unicattolica/Dipartmenti/DISES/allegati/ArnoneBandiera Presbiter033.pdf

Atiku, S. D., & Nwala, M. N. (2021). Analysis of the Effect of External Public Debt on Economic growth in Nigeria. *International Journal of Innovative Research in Accounting and Sustainability*, *6*(4), 68–82.

Balassa, B. (1989). Financial liberalization in developing countries. *Policy Research Working Paper Series 55*, The World Bank.

Bourguignon, F. (2018). *Political and Economic Development of Tanzania: A Brief Survey – Tanzania Institutional Diagnostic*. Economic Development & Institutions.

Bumann, S., Hermes, N., & Lensink, R. (2012). *Financial liberalisation and economic growth: a meta-analysis. Technical report*. EPPI-Centre, Social Science Research Unit, Institute of Education, University of London.

Duasa, J. (2007). Determinants of Malaysian Trade balance: An ARDL bound testing approach. *Global Economic Review*, *36*(1), 89–102. doi:10.1080/12265080701217405

Dynan, K., & Sheiner, L. (2018). *GDP as a Measure of Economic Well-Being*. Hutchins Center on Fiscal & Monetary Policy at Brookings, Hutchins Center Working Paper #43.

Gupta, V. (2019). A Case Study on Economic Development of Tanzania. *Journal of the International Academy for Case Studies*, *26*(1), 1–16.

Kuznets, S., Epstein, L., & Jenks, E. (1941). *National Income and Its Composition, 1919–1938* (Vol. 1). National Bureau of Economic Research.

Lequiller, F., & Blades, D. (2007). *Understanding National Accounts*. OECD Publishing., doi:10.1787/9789264027657-en

Maganya, M. H. (2018). Financial Development and Economic Growth in Tanzania: An Empirical Investigation. *International Journal of Academic Research in Business & Social Sciences*, *8*(8), 291–307. doi:10.6007/IJARBSS/v8-i8/4470

Mandalu, M., Thakhathi, D. R., & Costa, H. (2018). Investigation on Tanzania's Economic History since Independence: The Search for a Development Model *World. Journal of Social Sciences and Humanities*, *4*(1), 61–68.

Ngowi, P. H. (2009). Economic Development and change in Tanzania since independence: The Political leadership factor. *African Journal of Political Science and International Relations*, *3*(4), 259–267.

Nwala, M. N., & Fodio, I. M. (2019). Effect of Macroeconomic Variables on Financial Sector Development in Nigeria. *Journal of Accounting. Business and Social Sciences*, *1*(2), 1–12.

OECD (2009). *National Accounts of OECD Countries 2009. Volume I, Main Aggregates*. OECD Publishing. doi:10.1787/na_vol_1-2009-en-fr

Pesaran, M. H., & Shin, Y. (1999). An autoregressive distributed-lag modelling approach to co-integration analysis. In *Econometrics and Economic Theory in the 20th Century. The Ragnar-Frish Centennial Symposium*. Cambridge University Press.

Pesaran, M. H., Smith, R. J., & Shin, Y. (2001). Bounds Testing Approaches to the Analysis of Level Relationships. *Journal of Applied Econometrics, 16*(3), 289–326. doi:10.1002/jae.616

Robinson, D. O., Gaertner, M., & Papageorgiou, C. (2011). Tanzania: growth acceleration and increased public spending with macroeconomic stability. Yes Africa Can, p. 21.

Roger Nord. (2009).Tanzania: the story of an African transition. African Dept. International Monetary Fund.

Saganga, M. K. (2021). Financial development and economic growth in Tanzania: An ARDL and bound testing approach. *Asian Journal of Economics and Banking, 5*(1), 46–65. doi:10.1108/AJEB-09-2020-0063

Simba, H. M. A., & Çankal, E. (2020). Empirical Analysis of Financial Development Institutions and Economic Growth in Tanzania: Based on ARDL Model. *Journal of Business Research-Turk, 12*(2), 1962–1973. doi:10.20491/isarder.2020.955

Twinoburyo, E. N., & Odhiambo, N. M. (2018). Can monetary policy drive economic growth? Empirical evidence from Tanzania. *Contemporary Economics, 12*(2), 207–222.

Chapter 4
Finance and Development in Uruguay Post Cold War:
A Cointegration and Error Correction Analysis

Osmond Agu
Federal University, Oye-Ekiti, Nigeria

Adepoju Adeoba Asaolu
Federal University, Oye-Ekiti, Nigeria

ABSTRACT

This chapter employed Johansen-Juselius Cointegration test, short-run and long-run causality tests, and error correction modelling to examine the finance and economic development of Uruguay between 1981 and 2019. The result shows that gross fixed capital formation and government expenditure have positive and statistically significant relationships with gross domestic product per capita, while the degree of openness exhibits a negative but statistically significant sign in relationship with gross domestic product per capita. The study therefore recommends that since gross capital formation and government expenditure influenced the economy of Uruguay the most, the Uruguay's government should focus on building more capacity in capital stock, which is believed to attract more investment. They should also spend on real sectors of the economy to boost the economic growth and increase the gross domestic product per capita and by extension the welfare of the economy.

DOI: 10.4018/979-8-3693-1610-8.ch004

1. INTRODUCTION

Uruguay has its independence as far back as 1828. It had strong ties with Italy, United Kingdom and France at the earlier stages of its existence. Reputed to be the second smallest country of its continent (South America) and situated at the South-eastern coast of it. Although it shares some historical and cultural similarities with some neighbouring Latin-American countries especially Brazil and Argentina (Encyclopedia Britannica, 2011)).

Politically speaking, Uruguay developed much in the 20th century as one of the most progressive in the region due to its comparative stability, comprising advanced social legislation and relatively large middle class. However, the negative effects of nearly twelve-year military rule between 1973 and 1985 was massive on its national life. Despite the restoration of democracy, the country has been plagued with downward slide in economy and factional struggles retarded its growth; the hardship culminated in large emigration of Uruguayans to North America and European countries, among others. (Galeano, 1996)

Larger part of the country's population are crowded in its capital city, Montevideo more than its other major cities of Salto and Paysandu. Much of its commercial activities, political and social institutions are also concentrated around Montevideo.

In terms of its geography and environment, Uruguay has boundary with Brazil in the Northern and Eastern parts, the south-eastern part by the Atlantic Ocean, by Rio De la Plata in the South and the Uruguay river separates its western boundary from Argentina.

Figure 1. Map of Uruguay
Source: Encyclopedia Britannica (2011)

The country has a massive landscape of rolling land with an average elevation of approximately 383 feet. Also, there are broad valleys, plains (pampas), low plateaus and hills, and ridges such as Haedo Ridge (Cuchilla de Haedo) in the north and Grande Ridge (Cuchilla Grande) in the southeast (southward extension of the Brazilian Highlands). The highest point in the country is Mount Catedral which rises to 1,685 feet near the south eastern coast. Valleys and coastal plains have large deposits of sand, clay, and fertile alluvium. It has well-watered land despite the fact that no large rivers flow entirely within the country. With no marked rainy or dry season, its heaviest precipitation occurs between March and April with greater rainfalls in the winter with frequent thunderstorms at the summer.

Comparatively, only a small portion of the land is forested as largest number of trees grow along the watercourses. Most of the wildlife Uruguay was noted for had long disappeared with few ones like Jaguars found once in a while in remote areas. Reptiles and some aquatic lives also exist around the country. Overall, there exists some national parks and a wildlife reserve dedicated to preserve animals and bird species (Preston et al, 2011).

1.1 Ethno-Religious Perspectives

The indigenous people of Uruguay are mainly of European origin, historically regarded as descendants of 19th and 20th century immigrants from Spain and Italy and partly Britain and France. Original settlers in the country were migrants from Paraguay and Argentina. However, only small portion of direct descendants of Uruguay's indigenous peoples remain, and mestizos (of mixed European and Indian ancestry) account for less than 10% of the population. Blacks and persons of mixed Black and white ancestry make up an even smaller proportion of the total. Spanish is spoken throughout Uruguay, while Rivera and other borderland towns near Brazil speak Portuguese and Spanish. (Gonzalez-Risotto and Rodriguez, 1989).

The dominant religion is Christianity of Roman Catholic denomination having about 50% of the population. While about one-third, are adherents of other Christian faiths or are non-denominational Christians. About one-sixth of Uruguayans are agnostics or atheists. Jews, mostly in Montevideo, make up a small minority, which is nevertheless one of the larger Jewish communities in South America. (Encyclopedia Britannica, 2011)

1.2 The Economy of Uruguay

Despite the size of Uruguay, its gross national product (GDP) per capital is among the leading forces in the Latin America. The country's relatively high standard of living is attributable to proceeds from its export of agricultural produce among which is wool and beef. As a way of improving its balance of trade, the successive government have put machineries in place to grow its economy organically with the manufacturing (electricity, alcohol manufacturing, refinement of petroleum and other products (no domestic commercial source for petroleum, natural gas and other raw materials are imported)), meat and fish processing and production of cement, chemicals, textiles and tobacco among others and service (the railways and telephone company) sectors that remain dynamic and highly contributory to the economy. It is important to state now that the government of Uruguay largely controls these sectors, although attempts have been made since the 90s towards the privatisation of state-owned companies (Bayne, 1991).

Broadly speaking, cattle and sheep production remain most important economic activities, for instance beef, wool, livestock and allied products, skin and hides contribute about 40% of its income from export (10% of its GDP). Although with emphasis on livestock farming, less attention has been paid to the few arable land available for cultivation; major crops in Uruguay remain rice, wheat, sugarcane, sunflower seeds, oranges and grapes which is the source of raw material to the wine industry. Although low volume in terms of international standards, the country also produces fish with almost 50% of its catch exported. Lastly, its forestry (dominated by eucalyptus and pine trees) fills up most of the domestic needs. The county was powered (electricity) in the 80s by Negro and Uruguay plants, but as at now, mainly gas and oil-fuelled thermal plants are powering it (Encyclopedia Britannica, 2011).

The official local currency is Uruguayan Peso. Banking and financial services employ a little portion of the working public. The relaxed banking laws that provide a form of tax shield for investors has placed Uruguay on the world map as an offshore financial centre; the volume of international banking is huge and most of the banking transactions are denominated in the United States dollars (US$) and few other strong foreign currencies. The central bank regulates foreign exchange and the country's private banks, among others.

1.3 The Politics of Uruguay

Due to limited space allotted to this work, table 1 summarises Uruguay's political trajectory from 1512 to 2020.

According to the United States' Department of States, Post World War 2 Uruguay was referred to as the 'Switzerland of the Americas'. It is on record that until the dictatorship of 1973, the country had only two coups d'etat (1933 and 1942) interrupted their democracy in the 20th century. Uruguay was also reputed to be the home of lowest infant mortality and illiteracy rates (due to free and compulsory education) in South America.

Table 1. Political trajectory of Uruguay

S/N	Event	Date
1	Colonisation: This era is known as Banda Oriental. - Portuguese 1st Exploration of Uruguay. Thereafter, the 1st European explorer Juan Diaz De Solis got there in 1516, he was however killed by the natives. Nonexistence of treasures such as gold and silver made settlements to be largely limited in the 16th and 17th centuries.	1512 – 1516
2	Establishment of Colonia de Sacramento by Portuguese Colonist	1680 -1726
3	Establishment of San Felipe de Montevideo by Spanish Colonist	1726 -1750
4	Treaty of Madrid securing Spanish control over Banda Oriental	1750 -1796
5	Anglo-Spanish War	1796 – 1808
6	British Attack/ Occupation	1807 -1811
7	Struggle for Independence: Provincial Freedom under Artigas and Brazilian Province	1811 -1828
8	The Thirty-Three: 1825 - Formation of provincial government, with secession of Cisplantia province from Brazil & allegiance to the United province of Rio de la Plata. Brazil launched Cisplantie war that ended in 1828 with the signing of Treaty of Montevideo.	1825 -1828
9	Constitution of 1830 (approved in 1829)	1830
10	The Guerra Grande	1839 – 1852
11	The Uruguayan War	1864 – 1865
12	Colorado Rule	1865 – 1958
	Power Sharing Agreement	1872
	Military In Power	1875 – 1890
	Immigration (unprecedented rise in the number of immigrants)	1860 -1900
	Economy: Improvement of livestock farming production by Europeans, start of canal system & Telegraph and banks, among others	1857 – 1896
	Battle Era	1903 – 1933
	The Coup	1933
	World War II: battle of the River Plate	1939
13	Military Dictatorship	1973 – 1985
14	Luis Alberto Lacalle's Rule	1990 – 1995
15	Sanguinetti's Rule	1995 -2000
16	Battle's Reign: Coalition between Colorado & National Party under 1996 constitutional amendment (none of the parties won the 1996 election by the required majority)	2000 – 2002
17	Tabaré Vázquez's Rule	2004 – 2010
18	José Mujica's Rule	2010 – 2015
19	Tabaré Vázquez's Rule	2015 – 2019
20	Luis Lacalle Pou's Rule	2020

Source: Wikipedia

2. LITERATURE REVIEW

2.1 Economic Strategy and Management Philosophy

Uruguay is one of the most business-friendly countries, its income is also among the most evenly distributed in the Latin America and in terms of per capita income, it has one of the largest middle classes in the region (World Bank's Index Gini Report, 2021).

The main economic base of Uruguay is the agricultural sector, it accounts for over 60% of its total export with China as the most prominent of Uruguay's exports. This sector is dominated by meat, cellulose, dairy products and pharmaceuticals, among others.

The largest quantum leap in the country's economic trajectory happened between 2003 and 2019. However, the progress started slowing down in 2014 culminating in a decrease of 0.5% in 2019 alone; the downturn is attributable to recession in two of the country's trade partners (Argentina and Brazil). The covid-19 pandemic worsened the situation in the year 2020 making Uruguay witness economic recession for the first time since pre-millennium period this same period witnessed 5.9% slide in its gross domestic product (GDP) with attendant negative impact on unemployment and poverty. However, the government has stepped up with a number of economic strategies to realign the country back to the path of prosperity (International Trade Administration, 2021 and Agu & Asaolu, 2023).

It is important at this juncture to state that Uruguay is one of the most economically, socially and politically stable countries in the region, this has culminated in the growth in its foreign direct investment (FDI) from various countries in the past over 15 years largely due to the greater confidence in the country's institutional framework and economic policy. It also has the potential of being the regional distribution hub through its Free Trade Zones. Uruguay has a free-market economy characterized by an export-oriented agricultural sector, a well-educated workforce, and high levels of social spending (Index Mundi 2021).

2.2 Briefs on Uruguay's Cold War

This section is intended to capture the cold war in Uruguay between 1963 and 1976 and the roles the United States played during the hostilities.

According to Weinstein (1988), foreign diplomats in the early part of the 20th century captured the picture of Uruguay as that of democracy due largely to its unique politics of co-participation and power transitions void of violence. The political trajectory as captured by Morris (1976) however changed in the year 1976 with the emergence of a military regime and shutting down of nascent Uruguayan parliament. The military regime was described to have held the most political prisoners, per capita, in the world, and was the Amnesty International christened it as a regular practitioner of torture and human rights abuse. These conflict and abuses culminated in many Uruguayans going into exile from their home country.

Ford (2015) argued that activities of the United States' government mainly via the office of public safety (OPS) of USAID helped to destabilise the Uruguayan democracy and provided political, material, logistical and financial support to a repressive apparatus that tortured and brutalized the natives. The US changed the Uruguayan police force from an old-fashioned and underutilised institution into a major political actor with modern equipment and capabilities. The rise of the leftist Tupamaro insurgency rationalised the increased support for repressive apparatus in Uruguay which amplified the tempo of violence. The brutality of the police was met with an increase in guerrilla violence; this sank Uruguay into a bloody internal war that brought about the 1973 dictatorship. The spill over effect of the military dictatorship mentality persisted even after its return to democracy in 1985 (Lessa & LeGoff, 2013).

2.3 Major Economic Relationship With Other Countries of the World

2.3.1 Uruguay's Export

Uruguay's export in year 2020 is made of 20% beef with total value of US$1.6 billion, second is cellulose totaling US$1.1 billion in monetary volume. Soy and dairy products are Uruguay's third and fourth largest exports valued at US$748 million and US$648 million respectively. On the import side, the country imported a total of US$6.8 billion in goods (aside petroleum). The major components were vehicles, totaling US$519 million followed by agricultural chemicals with a value

Table 2. The main export destinations for Uruguay

Country	Percentage Trade (%)
China	27
Brazil	15
European Union	14
United States	7
Argentina	5
Mexico	3

Source: Trade agency, Uruguay XXI (2021)

Figure 2. Sectoral representation of export destinations for Uruguay
Source: *Trade agency, Uruguay XXI (2021), Authors' Design.*

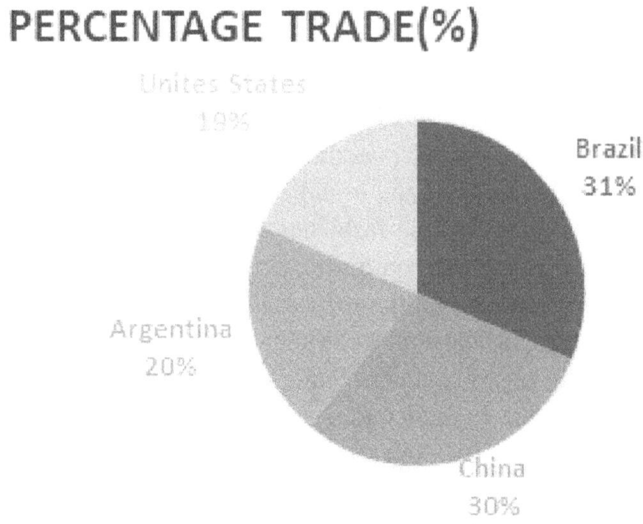

of US$392 million. Thirdly, clothing and footwear with monetary valuation of US$344 million, fourthly, US$318 million went into plastics. Food imports and pharmaceutical products were fifth and sixth which were valued at US$316 million and US$289 million respectively(source).

2.3.2 Uruguay's Export

Table 3. The main Imports of Uruguay

Country	Percentage Trade (%)
Brazil	20
China	19
Argentina	13
Unites States	12

Source: Trade agency, Uruguay XXI (2021)

Figure 3. Sectoral representation of imports for Uruguay
Source: *Trade agency, Uruguay XXI (2021), Authors' Design.*

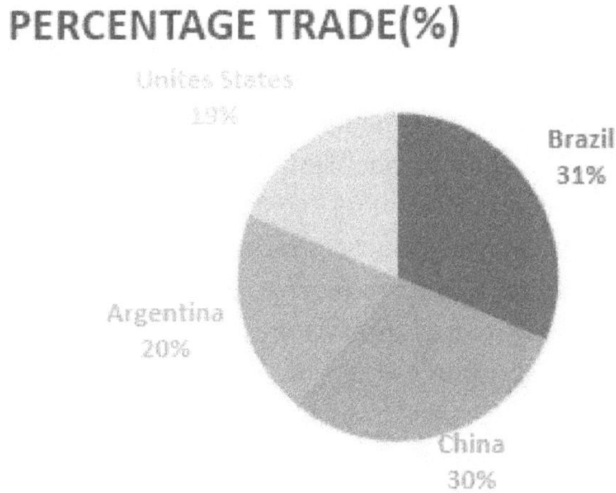

2.4 Key Economic Metrics

The key economic measures under consideration are gross fixed capital formation, exchange rate, real interest rate, import and export, foreign direct investment (FDI) and human development.

2.4.1 The Gross Domestic Product (GDP)

Gross domestic product (GDP) is the standard measure of the value of final goods and services produced by a country during a period, it is the most widely used indicator to capture economic performances, it is not a good measure of society's well-being and less important measure of people's material living standards (OECD, 2009). Simply put, GDP is the gross market value of aggregate of goods and services produced within the national boundary of a country over a period. Otherwise known as the national income total (Y). In terms of international trade, total imports and total exports are key estimators of the GDP. Quantitatively, GDP = C + I + G + X – M, where; C = Consumer expenditure, I = Investment expenditure, G = Government expenditure, X = Total exports and M = Total imports.

2.4.2 Gross Fixed Capital Formation

This is a very important factor of economic growth from both the theoretical and empirical points of view. For example, from the analysis of Solow (1957), physical capital accumulation contributes to increase the level of production. Further to this is the endogenous growth theory developed by Romer (1986), Lucas (1988), Romer (1990) develop and Barro (1990) re-evaluated this assertion with additional factors such as human capital, infrastructure, research and development, which are contributory to the acceleration of gross capital formation. Capital formation comprise of tangible goods like plants, tools and machinery and intangible goods like high standards of education, health and scientific knowhow, among others (Singer, 1950). Beyond tools and inventories, capital formation also includes capital expenditures (Kuznets, 1955). It depicts an investment of income or savings, mainly in real capital goods. In summary, capital formation requires that a country conservatively does not make use of the entire returns from its present productive efforts to satisfying immediate needs and desires but carves out or sets apart a portion of it in making capital goods. This is to increase the stock of capital goods towards an expansion of consumable output in the future (Ongo & Vukenkeng, 2014).

2.4.3 Import and Export

Imports depict goods and services residents, businesses, or government of a country buy from foreign countries instead of buying domestically produced items. On the other hand, goods and services made locally and sold to residents, businesses, or government of other countries are referred to as Exports. For the importing entity, he pays for the items and thus such is tracked as outflow while the exporting entity is paid for the goods and services and it is recorded as inflow. Imports and exports are essential in appraising the overall balance of trade of every country; a net positive balance of trade (positive net export) is critical to the growth of the country's economy. In other words, net exports are the estimation of the total value of a country's exports minus the total value of its imports; when positive or negative, it is regarded as a trade surplus or deficit respectively. It is important to state now that the developing economies' growth depend largely on the exportation of raw materials and commodities.

Imports and exports are phenomenal enablers and drivers of economic development in developing countries (Utonga and Dimoso, 2019). The neo-classical theory has it that the value of exports and imports plays a significant role in the determination of a country's economic and social development (Vijayasri, 2013). Thus, the importance of import and export in the measure of economic growth cannot be over emphasised because of the significant positive impacts of international exchange of goods on the economy. For example, Afaf (2015) investigated the impact of exports and imports on the economic growth of Tunisia for the period of 1977-2012 and confirmed that GDP, export and import are cointegrated and thus indicating an existence of long run equilibrium relationship between the variables. Similarly, Abugamea (2015) examined the both the long run and short run relationships between economic growth, exports and imports of Palestine for the time period 1968-2012 and confirmed a long run relationship between imports and economic growth, it further revealed exports and imports as main determinants of economic growth in the country.

2.4.4 Foreign Direct Investment (FDI)

Whether foreign direct investment (FDI) is going to be effective on the economic growth of a nation depends on how prepared the host nation is in terms of technological advancement, its investment policies, degree of openness, legal system and the overall economic stability, among others. Also, when viewed from the financing source, FDI could also affect capital formation. Zhang (1999) discovered a unidirectional causality also between FDI and economic growth in Hong-Kong. Furthermore, Moudatsou (2003) proposed a positive relationship between FDI inflows and economic growth in European Union countries through trade reinforcement between 1980 and 1996. FDI inflows have a positive effect on economic growth in European Union countries both directly and indirectly through trade reinforcement over the period 1980-1996. Lastly, Borenstein De Gegorio and Lee (1998) established the role of FDI as essential vehicle of economic growth when there is enough absorptive capability in the host country's economy, which is a function of human capital minimum threshold.

2.4.5 External Borrowings

External borrowings are funds lent to countries to finance capital or recurrent expenditures. With inadequate capital to fund their sustainable economic growth, developing countries (including Uruguay) depend on borrowings from external sources to bridge their resource gaps, (Getinet and Ersumo, 2020). In other words, developing economies with low capacity to mobilise funds locally depend much on external loans and grants (Tashome, 2015). Countries also engage in external borrowing to fund budget deficits or in the period of low investments (Gohar and Butt, 2012). All these are in tandem with the Keynesian macro-economic views that government borrowings are used to promote economic growth via financing government budget deficit expenditures, which stimulate aggregate demand and by extension encourage investments. In as much as external debt could be strategic in terms of bridging financial and infrastructural gap, governments should ensure that the level of country's outputs cover repayments in order not to overstretch or create a burden on the economy.

3. DATA AND METHODOLOGY

Theoretical Model

This study relies on Neoclassical theory (the Aggregate Production Function [APF]) of economic growth which was first propounded by Cobb-Douglas to achieve her objective. Cobb-Douglas production function is suitable for this study because it explains the long-term nexus between economic activities and factor inputs. This theory was also used by Agu & Nyatanga (2020); Al Kharusi & Mbah (2018) to examine the impacts of macroeconomic variables on economic growth. The model is specified thus:

$$Y_t = A_t K_t^{\alpha} L_t^{\beta} \tag{1}$$

Note that $0 < \alpha < 1; 0 < \beta < 1$

Where Y_t represents gross productivity in the economy as measured by the gross domestic product per capita (GDPPC), K represents stock of capital measured by gross fixed capital formation (GFCF). L stands for labour input measured by labour force, while A represents total factor productivity (TFP). $\alpha \, and \, \beta$ calculate the elasticities of the factor inputs. Cobb-Douglas production function adopts constant return to scale. This simply means that $\alpha + \beta = 1$. This indicates that if input factors (capital and labour) are increased, the output will as well increase in the same ratio Equation (1) is log-linearized as expressed in equation (2) as follows:

$$\log y_t = logA_t + \alpha logK_t + \beta logl_t + \mu_t \tag{2}$$

Where y, k and l signify output, capital and labour respectively. A represents other unconventional factor inputs which were not described by capital and labour. Agu & Nyatanga (2020) and Agu et al (2022) added the following variables amongst the determinants of economic growth viz, gross fixed capital formation, government capital expenditure, trade openness, total debt, real interest rate and human development index. However, labour variable was excluded due to unavailability of data.

Therefore, the study assumes that the variable A in the model (TFP) is a function of gross fixed capital formation (GFCF), government capital expenditure (GOV), trade openness (TRD), total debt (DEBT), real interest rate (RINTR) and human development index (HD). All the nominal variables are logged (except real interest

Table 4. Variables, labels, and sources of data

Labels	Variables	Data Sources
LNGDPPC	Log of Gross domestic product per capita	World bank and International Monetary Fund
RINTR	Real Interest Rate: a proxy for monetary policy	World bank and International Monetary Fund
LNGFCF	Log of gross fixed capital formation	World bank and International Monetary Fund
LNGOV	Log of Government capital expenditure: a proxy for fiscal policy	World bank and International Monetary Fund
LNOPEN	Log of degree of market openness	World bank and International Monetary Fund
LNDEBT	Log of debt	World bank and International Monetary Fund
LHHD	Log of human development	World bank and International Monetary Fund
Structural break DUMMY VARIABLES		
DM1 = dummy variable for 1997 DM2 = dummy variable for 2001 DM3 = dummy variable for 2003 DM4 = dummy variable for 2015 DM5 = dummy variable for 2019		

Source: Authors' 2023

rate [RINTR] variable, as it is already in rate) in order to convert the skewness of the data to approximately conform to normality. Put succinctly hence,

$$A_{it} = f\left(\text{logGFCF}_t, logGOV_t, logTRD_t, logDEBT_t, RINTR_t, logHD_t\right) \tag{3}$$

Consequently, plugging equation (3) into equation (2) and replacing $\log y_t \, with \, logGDPPC$ gives:

$$logGDPPC_t = logGFCF_t + logGOV_t + logTRD_t + logDEBT_t + RINTR_t + logHD_t + \sum_{j=1}^{n-s} \lambda_j D_{jt} + \mu_t \tag{4}$$

Where μ_t denotes stochastic error term. The notation $\sum_{j=1}^{n-s} \lambda_j D_{jt}$ is the structural break notation which corrects the structural instability of the model. Table 4 shows the variables and the sources of data.

Estimation Techniques

The study analysis follows these stages. The first stage was to check for the unit root of the series. Next, since all the series have unit root, that is they all are I(1) series, the study examined the challenge of estimating VECM that has $I(1)$ variables. The second stage was to test for the cointegrating nature of the series, the third was to test for causality by developing a vector error correction model (VECM). The study also tests for structural break Finally, the study considered the estimation of VECM when the short-run dynamics may differ within and between equations.

Stock and Watson (1989) noted that testing for causality largely depends on the stationarity nature of the data being examined, while Nelson and Plosser (1982) observed that many macroeconomic indicators have unit root. Therefore, in checking for the unit root of the series, the study utilized Augmented Dickey-Fuller (ADF), and Phillips Perron (PP) stationarity tests. The ADF and PP unit root result are contained in Table 5, showing that the stationarity result was I(1) series.

In order to determine the cointegration of the series, Johansen & Juselius (1990) suggested a VAR model of the following nature:

$$X_t = \mu + \vartheta_1 X_{t-1} + \vartheta_2 X_{t-2} + \ldots + \vartheta_p X_{t-p} + \varepsilon_t \tag{5}$$

where X is a (n x 1) matrix of variables, μ is a (n x 1) matric of constant terms, ϑ_1, ϑ_2, …, ϑ_p are (n x n) coefficient matrix and ε is a (n x 1) matrix of error terms with zero mean and constant variance. Reparameterizing equation (5) gives:

$$\Delta X_t = \mu + \in_{i=1} X_{t-1} + \grave{A}_2 X_{t-2} + \grave{A}_p X_{t-p} + \varepsilon_t \tag{6}$$

Table 5. Unit root result (augmented Dickey Fuller) and Phillip Peron

Augmented Dickey-Fuller (ADF)				Phillips Perron (PP)		
Variables	**At Level**	**First Difference**	**Results**	**At Level**	**First Difference**	**Results**
GDPPC	0.7236	0.0001	I(1)	0.4336	0.0000	I(1)
GFCF	0.7812	0.0000	I(1)	0.8812	0.0003	I(1)
GOV	0.6692	0.0000	I(1)	0.9292	0.0000	I(1)
OPEN	0.8687	0.0020	I(1)	0.9987	0.0004	I(1)
DEBT	0.9865	0.0001	I(I)	0.7564	0.0000	I(I)
RINTR	0.9245	0.0000	I(1)	0.3245	0.0002	I(1)
HD	0.4245	0.0002	I(1)	0.3245	0.0000	I(1)

Source: Author's 2023

where $\in_I = -I + \Pi_1 + \ldots + \Pi_i$ (i= 1, 2, …, p-1), and $\grave{A}_2 = -I + \Pi_1 + \ldots + \Pi_p$.

Johansen & Juselius (1990) noted two procedures to determine cointegrating vectors. First is the trace statistic which is employed to test for hypothesis that the cointegrating equation is at most *r as oppose to the* alternative. The second test is the maximum statistic which determines whether the alternative hypothesis is r + 1.

Trace statistic in Table 6 shows one cointegrating vector at 5% significance level using a linear trend in the series. The maximum statistic however, shows one cointegrating vector at 1% significance level employing the same modality. The implication is that is a cointegrating relationship between GDPPC and other macroeconomic indicators under consideration in Uruguay.

Engel and Granger (1987) observed that if there is cointegration between variables in the long-term, there is the likelihood of those variables having a unidirectional or a bidirectional Granger causality. Though, a finite sample size may not dictate this. Therefore, having cointegrated dependent (GDPPC) and independent (other macroeconomic) variables, there is need to employ a vector error correction model (VECM) estimating technique. Table 7 shows Granger causality result.

Table 6. Cointegration tests result

H_0	H_1	λ_{trace}	Critical values (95%)
$r = 0$	$r \geq 0$	34.365**	29.45
$r \leq 0$	$r \geq 2$	6.65431	19.26
H_0	H_1	λ_{max}	
$r = 0$	$r > 0$	25.3452*	21.14
$r \leq 1$	$r = 2$	7.4559	13.21

Table 7. VEC Granger causality/block exogeneity Wald tests dependent variable: D(LNGDPPC)

Excluded	Chi-sq	df	Prob.
D(LNDEBT)	0.312664	2	0.8553
D(LNGFCF)	0.373172	2	0.0008
D(LNGOV)	2.661975	2	0.0002
D(LNHD)	1.461185	2	0.4816
D(LNOPEN)	1.971185	2	0.3732
D(RINTR)	0.198586	2	0.9055
All	6.779509	12	0.8718

Within the ECM formulation, only two variables namely LNGFCF and LNGOV Granger cause LNGDPPC as their probability values are statistically significant while LNDEBT, LNHD, LNOPEN and RINTR do not Granger-cause GDPPC in Uruguay. The study went further to determine if the two variables that Granger cause GDPPC indicate short-run or long run causality, since VECM offers an opportunity to differentiate between the long-term and the short-term causality. The study achieved this by employing these three Granger causality models for the three variables thus:

$$\Delta LNGDPPC_t = \beta_0 + \sum_{j=1}^{M} \beta_{ij} \Delta LNGFCF_{t-j} + \sum_{j=1}^{M} \beta_{2j} \Delta LNOPEN_{t-j} + \alpha\varepsilon_{t-1} + \mu_{1t} \quad (7)$$

$$\Delta LNOPEN_t = \partial_0 + \sum_{j=1}^{M} \partial_{ij} \Delta LNGFCF_{t-j} + \sum_{j=1}^{M} \partial_{2j} \Delta LNGDPPC_{t-j} + \forall \propto_{t-1} + \mu_{2t} \quad (8)$$

$$\Delta LNGFCF_t = \gamma_0 + \sum_{j=1}^{M} \gamma_{ij} \Delta LNGFCF_{t-j} + \sum_{j=1}^{M} \gamma_{2j} \Delta LOPEN_{t-j} + \varphi\omega_{t-1} + \mu_{3t} \quad (9)$$

The F-tests of ΔLNOPEN, ΔLNGDPPC and ΔLNGFCF signify the short-run causality, while significant error correction terms α, $\forall$ and φ imply long-run causal relationship. ECM comprises the long-term information as far as it is formed from the association of long-run cointegration. It is noteworthy that the ECM term corrects long-term disequilibrium in the current period. The causality result amongst LNGDPPC, LNOPEN and LNGFCF obtained using ECMs in equations (7), (8) and (9) is reported in Table 8. The lag length was restricted to 1 as to preserve the degree of freedom.

The short-term causality result shows that there is a bidirectional causality flowing between LNGFCF and LNOPEN and that both LNGFCF and LNOPEN have unidirectional causality flowing from each to GDPPC. LNGDPPC does not Granger-cause LNOPEN. This implies that in the short-term, gross fixed capital formation and market openness enhance each other and both variables promote gross domestic product per capita in Uruguay.

In the long-run, there is a unidirectional causality flowing from LNGFCF to LNGDPPC and from LNOPEN to LNGFCF. The implication is that, in the long-term, other variables do not Granger-cause GDPPC except GFCF while LNOPEN

Table 8. Granger causality short-run and long-run estimates of ECMs

Equation 7		*Equation 8*		*Equation 9*	
Short-Run Estimates Using ECM					
Variables	**ΔLNGDPPC$_t$**	**Variables**	**ΔLNOPEN$_t$**	**Variables**	**ΔLNGFCF$_t$**
Constant	6.678* (4.328)	Constant	0.031 (1.316)	Constant	
ΔLNGFCF$_t$	0.324** (2.482)	ΔLNGDPPC$_t$	-0.024 (-0.061)	ΔLNGDPPC	0.0810 (0.460)
ΔLNOPEN$_t$	0.516* (3.230)	ΔLNGFCF$_t$	-0.268 (-0.321)	ΔLNOPEN	0.526** (2.663)
Long-Run Estimates Using ECM					
Equation 7		***Equation 8***		***Equation 9***	
Variables	**LNGDPPC$_t$**	**Variables**	**LNOPEN$_t$**	**Variables**	**LNGFCF$_t$**
LNGFCF$_t$	0.560* (3.361)	LNGDPPC$_t$	0.229 (0.591)	LNGDPPC$_t$	-0.003 (-0.137)
LNOPEN$_t$	0.027 (0.025)	LNGFCF$_t$	-0.042 (-0.251)	LNOPEN$_t$	-0.028** (-0.287)
E_{t-1}		-1.311* (-4.294)			
		Equation 7		***Equation 8***	***Equation 9***
R^2		0.83		0.02	0.73
Durbin-Watson statistic		2.05		1.88	1.98
Autoregressive Conditional Heteroscedasticity (2)		0.176		0.064	0.196
Autoregressive Conditional Heteroscedasticity (3)		0.034		0.043	0.053
Breusch-Godfrey test (2)		1.054		0.085	1.034
Breusch-Godfrey test (3)		1.745		0.212	1.545

The values in parenthesis are the t-stat. Lag lengths was obtained using AIC. *, ** and *** denote significant at 1%, 5% and 10% level respectively.

Source: Authors' 2023.

Granger-cause GFCF. This finding is in line with Agu & Nyatanga (2020) who noted that international trade and liberalization policy have the tendency of increasing the capital stock in the economy and this in turn, promote economic growth.

The Autoregressive Conditional Heteroscedasticity result shows that the errors are non-dependent on the independent variables. Therefore, homoscedastic. Breusch-Godfrey result shows the absence of serial correlation. The E_{t-1} which signifies the long-term changes in the model shows inverse relationship as expected and statistically significant. The coefficients of LNOPEN and LNGFCF in the model

Table 9. Error correction model estimates dependent variable: GDPPC

Variable	Coefficient	Std. Error	t-Statistic	Prob.	Results
D(LNDEBT)	-0.0098	0.0083	-1.1813	0.2482	NS
D(LNGFCF)	0.2783***	0.0363	7.6552	0.0000	S
D(LNGOV)	0.7516***	0.0764	9.8297	0.0000	S
D(LNHD)	0.7258	0.9348	0.7763	0.4445	NS
D(LNOPEN)	-0.7365***	0.0745	-9.8801	0.0000	S
D(RINTR)	0.0000	0.0003	0.0929	0.9267	NS
CointEq(-1)	-0.2714	0.1662	-1.6330	0.1145	NS

NS is non-significant, S is Significant. *, ** and *** denote significant at 1%, 5% and 10% level respectively.
Source: Author's 2023

are jointly significant at the 5% level, suggesting that the two variables have both long-term and short-term impacts on GDPPC in Uruguay.

Again, the study went ahead to test for the structural break in the series using Bai & Perron (2003) test. It was discovered that there were structural breaks in five years namely, in 1997, 2001, 2003, 2015 and in 2019. Consequently, the study introduced dummy variables in the model to correct the structural instability in the series. It was therefore noted earlier that the largest quantum leap in the country's economic trajectory happened between 2003 and 2019. This may account for the structural breaks in 2003, 2015 and 2019 (as observed in the result). However, the progress started slowing down in 2014 culminating in a decrease of 0.5% in 2019 alone; the downturn is attributable to recession in two of the country's trade partners (Argentina and Brazil).

From the error correction model estimates, LNGFCF, LNGOV and LNOPEN are statistically significant. While LNGFCF and LNGOV are positively related with LNGDPPC, LNOPEN has an inverse relationship with LNGDPPC.

Gross fixed capital formation (LNGFCF) shows a positive sign and statistically significant in relationship with gross domestic product per capita (LNGDPPC). A one dollar increase in GFCF increases GDPPC by 0.28 percent. The implication is that increase in capital stock in Uruguay affected GDPPC positively. This finding corroborates the study of (Index Mundi 2021) who observed that Uruguay is one of the most economically, socially and politically stable countries in the region, this has culminated in the growth in its foreign direct investment (FDI) from various countries in the past over 15 years largely due to the greater confidence in the country's institutional framework and economic policy. This also increased their capital formation and by extension, economic growth per capita. The study noted that Uruguay also has the potential of being the regional distribution hub through

Figure 4. Inverse root polynomial

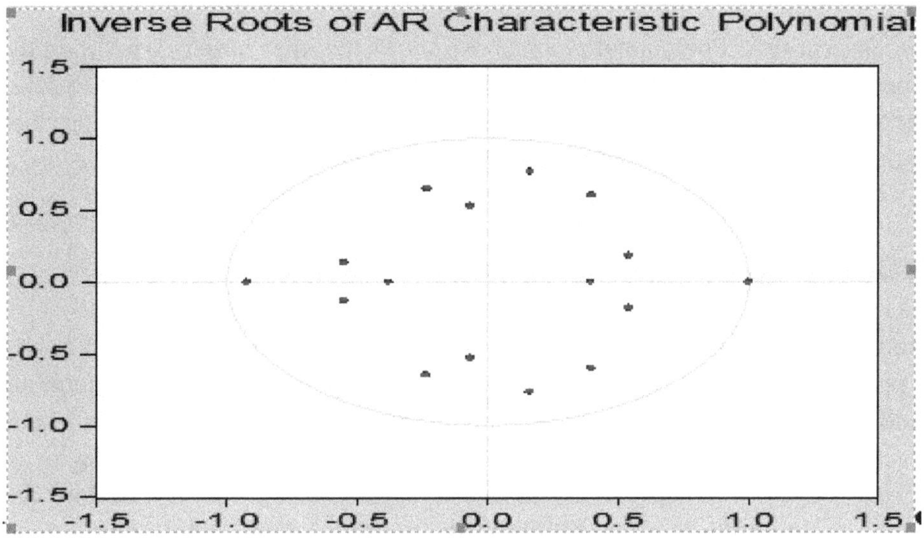

its Free Trade Zones. Uruguay has a free-market economy characterized by an export-oriented agricultural sector, a well-educated workforce, and high levels of social spending.

Government expenditure (LNGOV) exhibits a statistically significant and positive relationship with gross domestic product per capita (LNGDPPC). A one percent increase in government expenditure (LNGOV) increased gross domestic product per capita (LNGDPPC) by 0.75 percent. The implication is that the various government spendings such as capital and recurrent expenditure enhances welfare of the citizens in Uruguay. This study is in line with the studies of agu & Nyatanga (2020) who found that government provision of infrastructure and other necessities facilitated economic growth and by extension, economic wellbeing.

Finally, market openness (LNOPEN) shows a negative but statistically significant sign in relationship with gross domestic product per capita (LNGDPPC). A one percent change in LNOPEN negatively affected gross domestic product per capita (LNGDPPC) by 0.74 percent. The implication here is that, it seems that international trade does not favour Uruguay. It seems as if their net imports exceed their net exports, hence have an unfavourable balance of payment which affect was seen to have negative relationship with gross domestic product per capita (LNGDPPC).

POST ESTIMATION RESULT

The Inverse Root Polynomial graph above shows that the chosen variables in the model is fit and passed normality test, both individually and jointly. This shows that the residuals of the model are normally distributed, as the moduli of the eigenvalues of the dynamic matrix should falls within the unit circle.

5. CONCLUSION AND RECOMMENDATIONS

From the error correction model estimates, Gross fixed capital formation shows a positive sign and statistically significant in relationship with gross domestic product per capita. Government expenditure exhibits a statistically significant and positive relationship with gross domestic product per capita while the degree of openness exhibits a negative but statistically significant sign in relationship with gross domestic product per capita. The study therefore recommends that since gross capital formation and government expenditure influenced the economy of Uruguay the most, the Uruguay's government should focus on building more capacity in capital stock which is believed to attract more investment. They should also spend on real sectors of the economy, as to boost the economic growth and increase the gross domestic product per capita and by extension, welfare of the economy.

REFERENCES

Abugamea, G. (2015). External trade and economic growth relationship under Trouble: Time series evidence from Palestine, *Swift. Journal of Economics and International Finance*, *1*(2), 10–16.

Afaf, A. J. S., & Hussain, M. A. (2015). Impact of exports and imports on economic growth: Evidence from Tunisia. *Journal of Emerging Trends in Economics and Management Science*, *6*(1), 13–21.

Agu, O. C., & Asaolu, A. A. (2023). Can Nigeria Debt Be Sustained in the Face of Increasing Debt Profile? *EuroEconomica*, *42*(1), 108–123.

Agu, O. C., Nwosa, P. I & Ajoje O. I. (2022). Socio-economic Status, Savings and Income Inequality in Nigeria: The behavioral mechanism Approach. *Iranian Economic Review.*

Agu, O. C., & Nyatanga, P. (2020). An Investigation into the Crude Oil Price Pass-Through to Economic Growth in Nigeria. *Acta Universitatis Danubius. Œconomica, 16*(1).

Al Kharusi, S., & Mbah, S. A. (2018). External Debt and Economic Growth: The Case of Emerging Economy. *Journal of Economic Integration, 33*(1), 1141–1157. doi:10.11130/jei.2018.33.1.1141

Bai, E., & Perron, T. (2003). *Domestic petroleum product prices and subsidies: Recent developments and reform strategies*. International monetary fund working paper. Available from: Http://www.Ksri.Or.Kr/bbs/files/research02/ wp0771.Pdf.

Barro, R. (1990). Government Spending in a Simple Model of Endogenous Growth, *journal of Political Economy, 98*(5), 103-125.

Bayne, N. (1991). In the balance: The Uruguay round of interntional trade negotiations. *Government and Opposition, 26*(3), 302–315. doi:10.1111/j.1477-7053.1991.tb01142.x

Borenstein De Gegorio, J., & Lee, J. (1998). How does foreign direct investment affect economic growth? *Journal of International Economics, 45*(1), 115–135. doi:10.1016/S0022-1996(97)00033-0

Ford, M. (2015). *Subverting democracy, producing terror: the United States and the Uruguayan cold war, 1963-1976* [MA thesis]. California State University, Fresno, CA.

Galeano, E. (1996). *Open veins of Latin America* (C. Belfrage, Trans.). Monthly Review Press.

Getinet, B., & Ersumo, F. (2020). The impact of public external debt on economic growth in Ethiopia: the ARDL approach to con-integration. *Journal of Economic and Sustainable Development, 11*(11).

Gohar, M., & Butt, F. (2012). The impact of external debt servicing on the growth of low-income countries. Proceeding of International Conference on Business Management.

Gonzalez-Risotto, R., & Rodriguez, V. (1989). La importancia de las misiones jesuiticas en la formacion de la sociedad Uruguaya. *Estudo Ibero-Americanos, 15*(1), 191–214. doi:10.15448/1980-864X.1989.1.30514

IndexMundi. (2021). *Uruguay economy*. https://www.indexmundi.com/uruguay/economy_overview.html

International Trade Administration. (2021). *Uruguay – Country Commercial Guide (Uruguay Market Overview).* Author.

Johansen, S., & Juselius, K. (1990, March). Maximum Likelihood Estimation and Inference on Cointegration – With Applications to the Demand For Money. *Oxford Bulletin of Economics and Statistics, 52*(2), 169–210. doi:10.1111/j.1468-0084.1990.mp52002003.x

Kuznets, S. (1955). *International Differences in Capital Formation and Financing in: Capital Formation and Economic Growth.* National Bureau of Economic Research, Inc.

Lessa, F., & Pierre-Louis LeGoff, P. (2013). Skewed Priorities in Uruguay: Uruguay continues to Struggle With its Dictatorial Past. *Al Jazeera.* http://www.aljazeera.com/indepth/opinion/2013/ 11/skewed-priorities-uruguay-201311118133045296340.html

Lucas, R. Jr. (1988). On the mecanisme of economic development. *Journal of Monetary Economics, 22*(1), 2–42. doi:10.1016/0304-3932(88)90168-7

Martin Weinstein, M. (1988). Uruguay: Democracy at the Crossroads. Westview Press.

Morris, I. (1976, Mar. 8). Human Rights in Uruguay and Paraguay: Hearings Before the Subcommittee on International Organizations of the Committee on International Relations, House of Representatives, 64th Cong., 2d sess., June 17, July 27 and 28th and August 4, 1976, 37; "Torture in Uruguay." *New York Times.*

Moudatsou, A. (2003). Foreign direct investment and economic growth in the European Union. *Journal of Economic Integration, 18*(4), 689–707. doi:10.11130/jei.2003.18.4.689

Nelson, C. R., & Plosser, C. R. (1982). Trends and random walks in macroeconmic time series: some evidence and implications. *Journal of Monetary Economics, 10*(2), 139-162.

Ongo, E. N., & Vukenkeng, A. W. (2014). Does gross capital formation matter for economic growth in the CEMAC sub-region? *EuroEconomica, 2*(33).

Preston, E., Marvin, H., & Weistein. (2011). Antigas / Uruguay. *Encyclopedia Brittanica.* https://www.brittanica.com/place/antigas-uruguay

Romer, P. (1986). Increasing returns and long run growth. *Journal of Political Economy, 94*(5), 1002–1037. doi:10.1086/261420

Romer, P. (1990). Endogenous Technological Change. *Journal of Political Economy*, *98*(5, Part 2), 71–102. doi:10.1086/261725

Singer, H. W. (1950). Distribution of Gains between Investing and Borrowing Countries. *The American Economic Review*, *40*(May), 473–485.

Solow, R. (1957). A Contribution to the Theory of Economic Growth. *The Quarterly Journal of Economics*, *70*(1), 65–94. doi:10.2307/1884513

Stock, J. H., & Watson, M. W. (1989). New indexes of coincident and leading economic ` indicators. *NBER Macroeconomics Annual*, *4*, 351–394. doi:10.1086/654119

Tashome, A. (2015). *Development Finance and debt sustainability in Ethiopia: lesson to Sub-Saharan countries*. Academic Press.

Uruguay: Country Commercial Guide. (2022). International Trade Administration. https://www.trade.gov/country-commercial-guides/uruguay-market-overview

US Department of State, Foreign Relations of the United States, 1958-1960. (1960). In *American Republics. Volume V*. Washington DC: Government Printing Office.

Utonga, D., & Dimoso, R. L. (2019). The Nexus between Export and Economic Growth in Tanzania. *Journal of Business School*, *2*, 49–59. doi:10.26677/TR1010.2019.144

Vijayasri, G. V. (2013). The Importance of International Trade in the World. *International Journal of Marketing. Financial Services & Management Research*, *2*, 111–119.

Zhang, H. (1999). FDI and economic growth: Evidence from ten East Asian Economies. *Economia Internationale*, *7*(4), 517–535.

Chapter 5
Finance and Development in Vietnam Post Cold War

Henry Yua
https://orcid.org/0009-0000-4710-9757
Mewar International University, Nigeria

ABSTRACT

The study provides a deeper understanding of the current role of finance in improving economic development in Vietnam between 1981 and 2019. The study employed the autoregressive distributed lag (ARDL) modelling technique. Based on the long run model estimates, trade openness (TOP) and foreign direct investment (FDI) exert positive but insignificant impact of economic development in Vietnam, while gross capital formation (GFKF) is significant at 10%. Also, exchange rate was found to have negatively influenced economic development, while human development was also important to economic development. This study found that human development and external borrowing is seen to positively impact on economic development in Vietnam. It is recommended that external debt ratio at the threshold of 105% of annual GDP is manageable and beneficial; it is important to attract multinational corporations from developed countries; the government should strengthen and encourage the competitiveness of exports to maintain a sustainable balance with imports and improving the high-quality labor in Vietnam.

1. INTRODUCTION

After the conclusion of World War II, which followed by the collapse of Vietnam's empire and the plummet of Saigon (Ho Chi Minh City) in 1975, to the reunification in 1976 of the Northern and Southern Vietnam, the economy faced scores of challenges,

DOI: 10.4018/979-8-3693-1610-8.ch005

Figure 1. Vietnam map
Source: *New World Encyclopaedia (2021)*

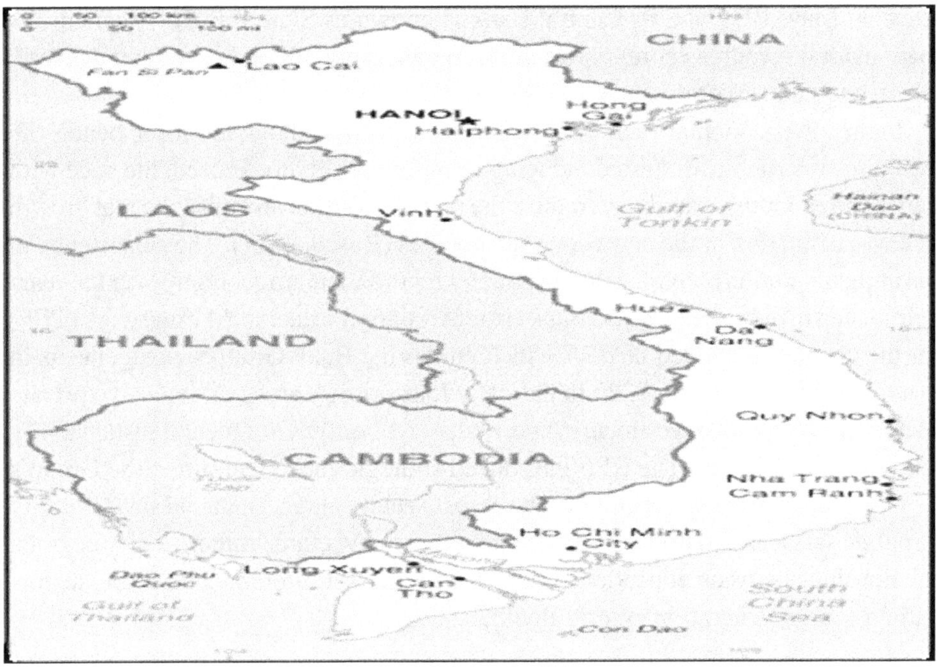

such as domestics repression and isolation from the global community as a result of existing cold war (American economic sanctions). The economic woes informed the decision of the Vietnam Communist Party in 1986 to commence a series of reforms in their economy through what was known as DOI MOI, which was an economic policy shift by a political movement led by Prime Minister Vo Van Kiet. Ever since the choice of market economy to planned economy and the successive reforms in the 1980s, Vietnam witness substantial economic prosperity (Liesbet & Kunal, 2008).

Southeast Asian nation of Vietnam is long and narrow, covering an area of 330,363 square kilometers, and is bordered by the Gulf of Thailand to the south, the South China Sea to the east, China to the north, Laos, and Cambodia to the west. See Figure 1.

On September 2, 1945, Vietnam formally proclaimed its independence from Japan and France. However, until the communist Viet Minh destroyed French forces at Dien Bien Phu in 1954, Vietnam was still governed by France. Tet or the Lunar New Year (movable dates in January or February), Liberation Day to commemorate the fall of Saigon on April 30, Labor Day on May 1, and Independence Day to mark Japan's retreat after losing the Second World War are all recognized holidays in Vietnam. II-September 2nd. (Library of Congress, 2005). It is with a population of

99,005,579 and expected to be 109,605,011 in 2050 with the current GDP of $310 billion. Vietnam currency is called Vietnamese Dong (VND), it has been in use since 3rd May, 1979 and its Central Bank is known as State Bank of Vietnam. Its main natural resources comprise of coal, copper, crude oil, gold, iron, manganese, silver, and zinc, (Worldometer 2022).

In the 1990s, Vietnam achieved both rapid growth and low inflation; hence, the economic restructuring started inducing economy positively. Indeed, the pace with which the economy was able to reduce the rate of inflation and raise the real growth rate was a function of the new economic policies (Busch, 2017). The consistency in the implementation of market driven policies for the Vietnam economy over the years culminated in the current World Bank Group Country Partnership Frame work (CPF) for the country, endorsed in 2017 which guides the Bank Group's engagements in the country from 2018 to 2022 in basically four priority areas of: inclusive private sector driven growth; investment in knowledge creation; environmental sustainability and good governance. The CPF introduced strategic move that direct the Group's work to: enhance private sector growth across sectors; attain financial sustainability of public services and transfers; lessen poverty among ethnic minorities; strengthen relationships between education and the labour market; promote and stimulate low carbon energy generation (World Bank 2022).

1.1 World Bank Interventions in Vietnam

As at April 14, 2022, the Bank had provided $25.27 billion in grants, concessional loans and credits to Vietnam via two hundred and fourteen (214) operations. Vietnam's existing portfolio consists of thirty one (31) active projects, with total net commitments of US$5.72 billion. Also, the World Bank Trung Son Hydropower Project increased rural area access to power (electricity) from 30 percent in 2015 to 97 percent in 2019. In spite of the preceding, nineteen (19) small hydropower plants were built with a total capacity of 320MW, which supplied an annual capacity of 1,260GWh. On ecological and natural capital, the World Bank get involved in the areas of: climate change and green growth development funding project; Mekong Delta Climate Resilience. The project intervene in the living conditions of about 625,000 direct beneficiaries and two million people indirectly benefited from city-wide infrastructure improvements, World Bank (2022).

Also, in the rural areas, between 2013 and 2019, more than a million citizens had their water supply linked to sustainable water systems, while 400,000 latest running water supply connections were constructed. In addition, about 1.4 million populace in two hundred and three (203) communities gained access to commune wide sanitation. Enhanced sanitary latrines were constructed in about 142,000 household and 1,500 schools. The World Bank has supported Vietnam in reforming the educational system at all levels using the instrumentality of the school readiness promotion project. In health, the North-east and Red River Delta Regions Health System Support Project improved the treatment capacity for 74 public hospitals at the district and provincial levels by investing in elevation of the medical infrastructure and training of health workers World Bank (2022).

Furthermore, the second poverty reduction project, benefited 192,000 households and resulted in a 16 percent-increase in incomes, provided good lessons for government to revise its poverty reduction policy and method. To enhance governance reforms, the World Bank facilitate the launching of National Public Services Portal and E-Cabinet in June 2019. In August 2020, the Vietnam's Open Budget Portal went live, making budget information for all government levels available for the public in one place, (World Bank 2022).

1.2 Religious Outlook in Vietnam

Many indigenous people practice a mixture of Mahayana Buddhism, Taoism, and Confucianism, also known as Vietnam's Triple Religion (Panuwatwanicha and Nguyen, 2016). The Vietnamese also practice spirit worship, a form of religious belief that was especially common among tribal peoples. Along with the aforementioned, Roman Catholics introduced Christianity to Vietnam in the 17th century. However, the spread of the Christian faith had major setbacks; as a result, the imperial court forbade Catholicism, which could only be practiced in secret. However, Christianity flourished throughout the 19th-century French conquest and occupation of Vietnam, and by the time the country regained its independence in 1954, there were more than two million Catholics living there; this number rose to between 6 and 7 million in 1998. Roman Catholics make around eight to ten percent of the population, according to estimates. (Dang, 2018).

About 65,000 Vietnamese people identify as Muslims, the most of whom are Sunnis, whereas 54,000 people identify as Hindu, the majority of whom are Cham. Approximately 8000 persons identify as members of the Baha'i Faith. The Hoa Hao and the Cao Dai have gained popularity in the Mekong Delta; the Cao Dai has about four million adherents. There are roughly one million three hundred thousand members of the Hoa Hao. Since the country's reunification in 1975, all religious organizations have been required to register with the appropriate government agency. This requirement was put in place by the government as a way to keep an eye on and regulate religious activity. (Office of Religious Affairs, 2021).

1.3 Succession of Political Leadership in Vietnam

Vietnam is a single party state, hence, the president is commonly considered to hold the second highest position in the political system, after the General Secretary of the Communist Party of Vietnam. The historical succession chart of Vietnam since 1945 is as follows:

The initiation of the 1986 reforms of Vietnam Communist Party and its eventual acceptance by successive governments triggered the transition from planned to market driven economy. Also, the deliberate implementation of policies and programmes by successive administrations stabilize the economy, set it on the path of sustainable growth and opened it up to international market, leading to the establishment of its capital market in the year 2000, (Hoan, 2019).

2. REVIEW OF RELATED LITERATURE

2.1 Economic Development and Management Philosophy

Vietnam has experienced tremendous economic growth since the Vietnamese Communist Party launched the Doi-Moi (policy shift from planned to market driven economy) during the party's 6th Congress in 1986. The innovative philosophy of the market focused economic restructuring influenced the International financial integration, which informed the investment environment in Vietnam to continuously improve and attract investment for development. The total social investment in proportion to Gross Domestic Product (GDP) have constantly increased and maintained high levels, of which those during the 1986-2021 periods increased from $43,009 million to $362.64 billion. The preceding put Vietnam on the of the highest investment countries in the world (World Data Atlas, 2022).

Vietnam has increasingly formed complete attachment with the regional and international markets. The goods and services market has gained the development and accomplishment in terms of scales. The financial market in Vietnam has consistently been growing and actively making contributions through diversifying investment capital sources. The insurance market has also been making positive contributions to the stabilization of production. The currency rate, prices of foreign currencies, and gold have been basically stabilized. The real estate market has gained certain development with rather synchronous technical & social infrastructure systems that have been making contributions to urbanization and the economic structure transformation toward industrialization and modernization of the country's socioeconomic development. The labour market has been formed with quite profuse

Table 1. Political leadership in Vietnam from 1945 to 2021

Democratic Republic of Vietnam (North Vietnam, 1945–76)					
S/N	**Name/Birth-Death**	**Political Affiliation**	**Took office**	**Left office**	**Period in Office**
1	Hồ Chí Minh (1890–1969)	Indochinese Communist Party	2-9- 1945	2-9- 1969	24 years
2	Tôn ứĐc Thắng (1888–1980	Workers'Party of Vietnam	2-9-1969	2-7-1976	6 years, 304 days
Republic of South Vietnam, (1969–76)					
3	Nguyễn Hữu Thọ (1910–1996)	Peoples Revolutionary Party of Vietnam	8-6-1969	2-7- 1976	7 years, 24 days
Socialist Republic of Vietnam (1976-Date)					
4	Tôn ứĐc Thắng (1888–1980	Communist Party of Vietnam	2-7-1976	30-3- 1980	3 years, 272 days
5	Nguyễn Hữu Thọ (1910–1996)	Communist Party of Vietnam	30-3- 1980	4-7-1981	1 year, 96 days (Acting President)
Chairman of the Council of State of the Socialist Republic of Vietnam					
6	Trờýng Chinh (1907–1988)	Communist Party of Vietnam	4-7-1981	18-6-1987	5 years, 349 days
7	Võ Chí Công (1912–2011)	Communist Party of Vietnam	18-6-1987	22-9-1992	5 years, 96 days
President of the Socialist Republic of Vietnam					
8	Army general Lê ứĐc Anh (1920–2019)	Communist Party of Vietnam	23-9-1992	24-9-1997	5 years, 1 day
9	Trần ứĐc L 睎ng (1937–date)	Communist Party of Vietnam	24-9-1997	27-6-2006 resignation	8 years, 276 days
10	Nguyễn Minh Triết (1942–Date)	Communist Party of Vietnam	27-6-2006	25-7-2011	5 years, 28 days
11	Tr睎ng Tấn Sang (1949–Date)	Communist Party of Vietnam	25-7-2011	2-4-2016	4 years, 252 days
12	Police general Trần aĐi Quang (1956–2018)	Communist Party of Vietnam	2-4-2016	21-9-2018	2 years, 172 days
13	ặĐng Thị Ngọc Thịnh (1959–Date)	Communist Party of Vietnam	21-9-2018	23-10-2018	32 days (Acting President)
14	Nguyễn Phú Trọng (1944–Date)	Communist Party of Vietnam	23-10-2018	5-4-2021	2 years, 164 days
15	Nguyễn Xuân Phúc (1954–Date)	Communist Party of Vietnam	5-4-2021	Incumbent	Over a year in Office

Source: Wikipedia

supply of labourer than before. The number of labourers has increased from 50.51 million in 2010 to 55.8 million in 2019. (Anh, 2020 and Hanh, 2021).

Human Capital Index (HCI) of Vietnam is ranks at 48th place out of 157 nations and territories while ranking at the 2nd place in ASEAN, behind Singapore only. Vietnam is a country with the highest HCI among the nations with average incomes (Vu-Thanh, 2017). Education in Vietnam has been good in the past 35 years of its reforms and has been an important historical factor in the developmental career of Vietnam. In that context, Vietnam's education has attracted many changes and development both in the scale and quality (Paquet, 2004).

The medical sector has also made copious progression; hence, the living standards have been further improved. According to the assessment by United Nations Development Program (UNDP), the country is listed as one of the country with exceptional medical achievements in relation to Gross Domestic Product. From 1986 to 2017, the mortality rate in children had reduced from 35.6 percent to 1.7 percent (out of 1,000 babies). The average longevity had increased from 71 to 76 years old from 1990 to 2020. The National Health Care Coverage Index stood at 73 percent, higher than the average rate in the region and the world, 87% of the population had gained medical insurance, (Hanh, 2021).

2.2 Vietnam Cold War

In literature, there is no consensus on the opening and ending points of Cold war, but the period is generally considered to span from the declaration of the Truman Doctrine on the 12th March, 1947 to the dissolution of the Soviet Union on 26th December, 1991 (Wikepia, 2021). Cold War in Vietnam was as a function of the intense rivalry for world domination between the USA and its allies on one hand and the Soviet Union and other communist countries on the other. While there were no direct military conflicts between the two superpowers, there were several armed clashes with military support by one side or the other or both (Vuving, 2021). There was no direct conflict between the two superpowers, but it was a part of the larger Cold War conflict and the American fight against the rise of Communism in the world. The domino hypothesis, according to which neighboring countries would definitely follow if one fell under the influence of Communism, was used by the US to justify its military intervention in Vietnam. The objective was to stop Communist takeover of South-East Asia. (CVCE, 2016).

At the very time Vietnamese nationalists were engaged in a bloody anti-colonial war with France, the cold war between the U.S. and the Soviet Union evolve into an ideological and power struggle with global proportions. As earlier stated, reasons related to the cold war why Americans attached great significance to Vietnam was to ensure that domino theory is rely upon to prevent loss of Indochina and then the rest of Southeast Asia, with economic and geopolitical repercussions spreading west to neutral India and east to key allies such as Japan and the Philippines (OAU, 2017).

Economic sanctions were an ongoing feature of USA foreign economic policy. In the context of the Cold War, specific sanctions were used against North Korea, China, Cuba, and North Vietnam. The primary U.S.A goals were among other issues to deter Communist, especially Chinese expansion and to maintain the credibility of U.S.A cold war commitments by preserving an independent, non-communist South Vietnam, (Cooper, 2008).

2.3 Economic Trade and Markets

Vietnam is one of the fastest growing economies in the world. The country's economic boom is attributed to the shift in labour allocation from agriculture to the manufacturing and services sector. Vietnam also received a boost from private investment, strong tourism, higher wages, and increased urbanisation (Forde, 2016). The rapid expansion of industries, such as textile, electronics, and seafood production, propelled export numbers to new heights. Vietnam recorded 10 year high GDP growth of 7.1 percent in 2018 and by 7.02 percent in 2019. Despite the Covid-19 outbreak in 2020, the country was one of the few economies that recorded positive growth with 2.91 percent. Its aggressive public health measures were able to minimise the impact of Covid-19 on Vietnam's economy. In 2021, the Southeast Asian country's GDP grew by 2.58 percent. The Vietnam economy is expected to recover fast and record GDP growth 6.6% in 2022 (IMF, 2022).

2.3.1 Vietnam Trade Partners

Vietnam had experienced a high rate of economic growth over the last three decades and that trade has been a major contributing factor in the structural transformation and development of the country's economy. Vietnam has earned its status as a country that has become an important-exporter in electronics, with electrical and electronic products being the top exporting goods surpassing coffee, textiles, footwear, and rice (Pincus, 2009). For instance, in terms of foreign direct investment, several U.S. businesses have invested into Vietnam, showing their commitment, and realizing the country's potential. Some of the major and noteworthy U.S. companies with manufacturers currently in Vietnam are Williams-Sonoma, Restoration Hardware, West Elm, Nike, Adidas, Puma, Lululemon, Gap, Apple, Intel, and Microsoft (Cindy, 2021).

Germany is the major E.U. trading partner with Vietnam and a German multinational automotive corporation, Daimler AG, is one of the world's leading car and truck manufacturers. Daimler AG currently has a factory in Ho Chi Minh

City that assembles various Mercedes-Benz models from CKD kits and in 1996; the first car assembled by Mercedes-Benz Vietnam was an E-Class (Turley, 1999). Peugeot is a French brand automotive company and opened a factory in 2019 in the central province of Quang Nam through joint venture with Truong Hai Auto Corporation (THACO). The powerhouse factory was designed with a total capacity to produce 20,000 Peugeot cars per year for domestic use as well as export and in 2013, also began exporting locally manufactured Mazda cars, accessories and spare parts, semi-trailers and special purpose vehicles to Columbia, South Korea, Malaysia, Russia, Kazakhstan, Laos, Myanmar, and Cambodia (Herr, Schweisshelm & Minh Vu, 2016).

It is no surprise that China is the biggest trade partner of Vietnam in Asia considering the fact that the country does rely on China for sourcing materials for the manufacturing of garment, footwear, and smart phones. Aside from imports, Vietnam main exports to China include smart phones, computers, machinery, wood, and cotton yarn, as well as Vietnamese fresh fruits and fish as China is the biggest export market of Vietnamese agricultural and seafood products (Quoc, & Thi, 2018).

2.3.2 Capital Market

The Vietnamese stock market in Ho Chi Minh City (formally, Saigon) made its milestone in the transitional process of Vietnam's economy. Five years later, another stock market was established in Hanoi. The two markets are playing a critical role of reflecting business investment decisions and considered an engine of both financial system and economy growth (Caporale, 2004). Since 1986, Vietnam has made many important changes to turn its economy into a market-oriented one, including reforming the banking system, adding more financial components, which had never been in place before the beginning of the reform, and most recently launching its first ever stock market as a bold move towards building a market-driven financial economy; called Ho Chi Minh City Securities Trading Center (HSTC). The birth of this early form of Vietnam's stock exchange had been nurtured for over seven years, marking a symbolic change to the Vietnamese contemporaneous financial system, (Hoan, 2019).

2.4 Macro-Economic Indicators

2.4.1 Gross Domestic Product

Gross Domestic Product is a monetary measure of the market value of all the final goods and services produced in a specific time period, usually a year by countries.

GDP growth rate is an important indicator of the economic performance of a country. Vietnam GDP is currently of $310 billion (Worldometer 2022).

2.4.2 Gross Fixed Capital Formation

Gross Fixed Capital Formation (GFCF) measures the value of acquisitions of new or existing fixed assets by the business sector, governments and households (excluding their unincorporated enterprises) less disposals fixed assets. GFCF is a component of the expenditure on Gross Domestic Product GDP), and thus shows something about how much of the new value added in the economy is invested rather than consumed. The value for Gross fixed capital formation in Vietnam was $66,063,160,000 as of 2020. Over the years, the value for this indicator has fluctuated between $66,063,160,000 in 2020 and $828,638,300 in 1989. (Wikipedia, 2022).

2.4.3 Government Capital Expenditure

Capital expenditure is refers to as a spending on assets, it is the purchase of items that will last and be used time and time again in the provision of good or service. In the case of government, it is the building of new hospital, the purchase of new computer equipment or net works, construction of new roads, schools among others, (IMF, 2010). In Vietnam, the Vietnamese Government is set to raise its spending on public investment projects by 8.3 percent year on year to VND516.7 trillion (US$22.7 billion), including VND35 trillion ($1.53 billion) from foreign sources, (Hanoi Times, 2021).

2.4.4 Import and Export

Imports are the goods and services that are purchased from the rest of the world by a country's residents, rather than buying domestically produced items. Imports lead to an outflow of funds from the country since import transactions involve payments to sellers residing in another country. Exports are goods and services that are produced domestically, but then sold to customers residing in other countries. Exports lead to an inflow of funds to the seller's country since export transactions involve selling domestic goods and services to foreign buyers.

Vietnam has followed an export-led growth model, combining trade liberalization and policies to attract foreign direct investment to spur exports. Vietnam's growth has also been accelerated in part due to the US-China trade war, which shows no sign of abating. Vietnam's exports to the US rose by 28.9 percent year-on-year in the first quarter of 2019, making the US the largest importer of Vietnamese goods, (Herr, Erwin & Vu, 2016).

2.4.5 Human Development Index

Human Development Index (HDI) is a composite index measuring average achievement in three basic dimensions of human development, a long and healthy life, knowledge and a decent standard of living. HDI ranks upper end of the Medium Human Development group of countries. With the HDI value of 0.693, Viet Nam ranks 118th out of 189 countries, and needs only an additional 0.007 points to join the High Human Development group (United Nations, 2019).

3. RESEARCH METHODOLOGY

The research design adopted in this study falls within the paradigm of an Ex-post facto design type which describes selected financial development variables in Vietnam between 1981 and 2019 and economic development (Real per capita income, YPK) to ascertain their trend and pattern over the period. Also, since it is not possible, due to paucity of data to execute review of all the financial development variables in Vietnam, the study is restricted to the financial development variables of $\ln FDI_t$ represents natural logarithm of foreign direct investment; $\ln TOP_t$ denotes natural logarithm of trade openness; $\ln EXDB_t$ is natural logarithm of external debt of government; $\ln GFKF_t$ is the natural logarithm of gross fixed capital formation; $\ln HDI_t$ indicates natural logarithm of human development index; and $\ln EXR_t$ also represents natural logarithm of exchange rate from 2009 to 2019. The data range are annual and sourced from the World Bank database.

3.1 Model Specification

The study adopted the neoclassical growth model which maintains that growth can arise when capital and labour are augmented by additional inputs in the production function. The Solow growth model explains economic growth as resulting from the combination of capital (K) and labour (L), that is:

$$Y_t = f\left(K_t,\ L_t\right)$$

Equation (1) gives rise to the question of how much of the increase in output can be attributed exclusively to changes in capital and labour exclusively. however, in contemporary times, it is possible for other factors to influence output. To resolve this problem, Solow (1956) disintegrates increase in output into three components:

physical capital accumulation (K_t), labour force (L_t) and total factor productivity (TFP). The TFP effect captures the increase in output that is not accounted for by an increase in labour and capital in the model. Thus, the TFP can be interpreted as the effect of exogenous technological progress that can also be reflected in increasing productive efficiency.

To account for this, Solow employed the Cobb-Douglas production function expressed in equation (2) below:

$$Y_t = f(A_t, K_t, L_t)$$

where Y_t is output or real GDP at time *t*, A_t is total factor productivity (TFP) at time *t*, K_t is capital stock at time *t*, L_t is labour stock at time *t*. Following Ofori-Abebrese, Pickson and Diabah (2017), the study specified the general finance-growth nexus but with modification such that K_t is gross fixed capital formation (GFKF), and exclude L_t due to data unavailability. For a developing country like Vietnam, with insufficient savings, foreign fund flows and external trading is seen as a source of economic growth, it means the factor of foreign direct investment (FDI), trade openness (TOP) and government external debt borrowing (EXDB) are important in capturing the TFP effect. This study will also adopt exchange rate (EXR), and human development index (HDI) as control variables, so that the growth model will be modified thus:

$$YK_t = f(FDI_t, TOP_t, EXDB_t, GFKF_t, HDI_t, EXR_t)$$

The economic model in Equation (1) above can be written as an log-linear econometric model specified as:

$$lnYK_t = \alpha + \beta_1 lnFDI_t + \beta_2 lnTOP_t + \beta_3 lnEXDB_t + \beta_4 lnGFKF_t + \beta_5 lnHDI_t + \beta_6 lnEXR_t + \mu$$

where, YK_t represents natural logarithm of real gross domestic product per capita; $lnFDI_t$ represents natural logarithm of foreign direct investment; $lnTOP_t$ denotes natural logarithm of trade openness; $lnEXDB_t$ is natural logarithm of external debt of government; $lnGFKF_t$ is the natural logarithm of gross fixed capital formation; $lnHDI_t$ indicates natural logarithm of human development index; and $lnEXR_t$ also represents natural logarithm of exchange rate. μ and t represent error term and time respectively.

3.2 Method of Data Analysis

The study adopted the Autoregressive Distributed Lag (ARDL) approach Pesaran, Shin and Smith (2001) developed a flexible model for the test of cointegration known as the bounds testing technique or the Autoregressive Distributed Lag (ARDL) approach based on three validations: first, the use of the ARDL model for the estimation of level relationships; second, the bounds test allows a mixture of I(1) and I(0) variables as regressors; and third, this technique is suitable for small or finite sample size (Pesaran, Shin & Smith, 2001).

The bounds testing approach involves estimating the following equation as postulated by Nwachukwu, Adebayo, Shettima, Anigwe and Udechukwu-Peterclaver (2016):

$$\Delta \ln YPK_t = \alpha_0 + \alpha_1 \ln YPK_{t-i} + \alpha_2 \ln FDI_{t-i} + \alpha_3 \ln TOP_{t-i} + \alpha_4 \ln EXDB_{t-i} + \alpha_5 \ln GFKF_{t-i}$$
$$+\alpha_6 \ln HDI_{t-i} + \alpha_7 \ln EXR_{t-i} + \sum_{i=1}^{a} \beta_i \Delta \ln YPK_{t-i} + \sum_{j}^{b} \partial_j \Delta \ln FDI_{t-j} + \sum_{k}^{c} \varphi_k \Delta \ln TOP_{t-k}$$
$$+\sum_{l}^{d} \theta_l \Delta \ln EXDB_{t-l} + \sum_{m}^{e} \pi_m \Delta \ln GFKF_{t-m} + \sum_{n}^{f} \rho_n \Delta \ln HDI_{t-n} + \sum_{r}^{g} \pi_r \Delta \ln EXR_{t-r} + \mu_t \quad (1)$$

After estimating obtaining the presence of long-run relationship from (1), Pesaran, Shin and Smith (2001) advocated that we obtain the short-run dynamic parameters by estimating an ARDL error correction model associated with the long-run estimates. This is specified as follows:

$$\Delta lnYPK_t = \alpha_0 + \sum_{i=1}^{a} \beta_i \Delta lnYPK_{t-i} + \sum_{j}^{b} \partial_j \Delta lnFDI_{t-j} + \sum_{k}^{c} \varphi_k \Delta lnTOP_{t-k}$$
$$+\sum_{l}^{d} \theta_l \Delta lnEXDB_{t-l} + \sum_{m}^{e} \pi_m \Delta lnGFKF_{t-m} + \omega ECT_{t-1} + \mu_t \quad (2)$$

where:

ECT = error correction term derived from equation (2)

Table 1. Descriptive statistics

	YPK	TOP	HDI	GFKF	FDI	EXR	EXDB
Mean	827.80	105.90	53.11	18.50	4.15	12465.57	105.88
Median	422.78	111.42	57.80	8.62	1.67	14167.75	48.87
Maximum	2715.28	210.40	71.20	63.33	16.10	23050.42	384.01
Minimum	94.56	13.21	17.40	1.02	0.06	8.07	27.53
Std. Dev.	795.09	59.94	15.33	19.26	4.91	7710.44	94.07
Skewness	1.06	-0.07	-0.94	0.86	1.09	-0.47	1.37
Kurtosis	2.73	1.94	2.72	2.34	2.87	2.01	3.91
Jarque-Bera	7.47	1.86	5.90	5.53	7.77	3.01	13.49
Probability	0.02	0.40	0.05	0.06	0.02	0.22	0.00
Sum	32284.11	4130.19	2071.20	721.64	161.67	486157.40	4129.49
Sum Sq. Dev.	24022661.00	136547.70	8933.67	14095.45	917.00	2260000000.00	336234.80
Observations	39.00	39.00	39.00	39.00	39.00	39.00	39.00

ω = the speed of adjustment

The error correction model shows the speed of adjustment needed to restore the long run equilibrium following a short run shock. The α_1 is the coefficient of the error correction term in the model and must be negative and significant for the return back to long-run equilibrium to hold (Pesara, Shin & Smith, 2001).

4. PRESENTATION AND DISCUSSION OF RESULTS

4.1. Data Presentation and Analysis

The data in this study was analyzed using descriptive statistics which involved calculating for the mean, median, skewness, kurtosis, and standard deviation. The inferential analysis involved estimating multiple regression models and the estimation technique was based on the unit root test and co-integration test.

Real output per capita (YPK) had a mean of $827.80 and a median of $422.78. The maximum value was $2715.28 while the minimum value was $94.56. Gross fixed capital formation (GFKF) had a mean of 18.50% of GDP and a median of 8.62% of GDP. The maximum value was 71.20% of GDP while the minimum value was 1.02% of GDP. The probability of the Jarque-Bera statistic shows that only Real output per capita (YPK), foreign direct investment (FDI) and external borrowing (EXDB), with probabilities less than 0.05, were not normally distributed. However,

Table 2. Stationarity tests

ADF Tests: Levels					ADF Tests First Difference				
Variables	Critical Values @ 5%	Test Statistic with intercept	p-values	Order of Integration	Variables	Critical Values @ 5%	Test Statistic with intercept	p-values	Order of Integration
LNYPK	-2.9571	0.848381	0.9934		Δ(LNYPK)	-2.9571	-3.3169	0.0224	*I(1)*
LNEXDB	-2.9411	-0.6179	0.8547		Δ(LNEXDB)	-2.9434	-4.4967	0.0009	*I(1)*
LNEXR	-2.9511	-4.3457	0.0016	*I(0)*	Δ(LNEXR)				*I(0)*
LNFDI	-2.9411	-1.1920	0.6679		Δ(LNFDI)	-2.9434	-4.5063	0.0009	*I(1)*
LNGFKF	-2.9434	-1.0602	0.7210		Δ(LNGFKF)	-2.9434	-3.8536	0.0055	*I(1)*
LNHDI	-2.9411	-11.7335	0.0000	*I(0)*	Δ(LNHDI)				*I(0)*
LNTOP	-2.9434	-1.9373	0.3123		Δ(LNTOP)	-2.9434	-5.8840	0.0000	*I(1)*

the over model normality will be determined with combined model variables. Again, exchange rate (EXR) is said to be more volatile with the highest standard deviation of 7710.44, which is clearly above the standard deviations of all the other variables.

4.2 Test for Stationarity Using the Augmented Dickey-Fuller Test

The stationarity tests level and first variables were estimated using the Augmented Dickey-fuller test. The result of the estimation is presented below.

From Table 2, only exchange rate (EXR) and human development index (HDI) were integrated at order zero, while the rest of the variables were integrated at order one. This makes the series to be integrated at different orders of integration, which satisfy one very important requirement of using ARDL.

4.3 Autoregressive Distributed Lag (ARDL) Bounds Test for Cointegration

The bound co-integration test conducted for the bank performance model which includes variables with I(0) and I(1) order of integration showed that there was cointegration among the variables.

The F-statistics of 30.20450 is greater than the critical values of the upper bound for all levels of significance. Therefore, the null hypothesis which states that there is no co-integration among the variables was rejected. There is therefore a long run relationship among the variables. The study proceeded to estimate both a long run and a short run model using the Auto-Regressive Distributed Lag (ARDL) method.

Table 3. ARDL bounds test

F-Bounds Test			Null Hypothesis: No levels relationship	
Test Statistic	Value	Signif.	I(0)	I(1)
			Asymptotic: n=1000	
F-statistic	30.20450	10%	1.99	2.94
k	6	5%	2.27	3.28
		2.5%	2.55	3.61
		1%	2.88	3.99

4.4 Autoregressive Distributed Lag (ARDL) Long-Run Estimation

The long run model is given as:

$$YPK = -13.3 + 0.2 * \ln TOP + 5.9 * \ln HDI + 0.5 * \ln GFKF$$
$$+0.08 * \ln FDI - 0.5 * \ln EXR + 0.3 * \ln EXDB$$

The long run model was estimated using the Auto-Regressive Distributed Lag (ARDL) method. The result is presented in Table 4.

Table 4. Long-run coefficient estimation

Variable	Coefficient	t-Statistic	Prob.	Results
LNTOP	0.2234	0.4377	0.6652	Positively insignificant
LNHDI	5.8864	4.1452	0.0003	Positively significant
LNGFKF	0.5214	1.7802	0.0867	Positively significant
LNFDI	0.0805	0.7717	0.4472	Positively insignificant
LNEXR	-0.8445	-4.4319	0.0002	Negatively insignificant
LNEXDB	0.3417	3.7990	0.0008	Positively significant
C	-13.3220	-2.9006	0.0075	

Based on the long run model estimates, trade openness (TOP) and foreign direct investment (FDI) exert positive but insignificant impact on economic development in Vietnam, while gross capital formation (GFKF) is significant at 10%. This means that, trade openness (TOP) and foreign direct investment (FDI) gross capital formation (GFKF) possess the ability to stimulate the needed change to transfer technology and effectively increase the allocation of resources. This is in agreement with the works of Le, Nguyen, Ho and Nguyen (2021) who showed that FDI, GFCF, and OPEN together influenced Vietnamese economic growth. From 1986, Vietnam opened her economy to attract foreign invest in order to accelerate economic growth. Vietnam Government also lifted restrictions on capital and profit repatriation gradually and opened up industrial sector for foreigners to participate investment. The government also regulated the preferred policies such as import duty exemptions for export processing industries, tax holiday schemes for undertaking investment in priority sectors and low development areas. This fundamental policy direction, if sustained and promoted, was capable of contributing more significantly to the development of Vietnam. As expected, exchange rate has been seen as negatively was found to negatively influence economic development. This is in variance with Huong (2019) who showed that a positive relationship exists between real exchange rates and economic growth. it should be noted that the high level of exchange volatility in Vietnam could be a good explanation for this and authorities need to review the monetary policy framework to reduce the negative impact of exchange rate. The state of human development is also important to economic development. this study found that human capital development positively impacts on economic development in Vietnam, this position agrees with the findings of Manh (2019) who found that gross capital formation, labour quantity, labour with different level of education and life expectancy positively and significantly impact on GDP in Vietnam. That means improving the quality of high-quality labour in Vietnam must become the most important factor in competition and development.

Finally, external borrowing is seen to positively impact on economic development in Vietnam. External debt seems to be beneficial to the Vietnamese economy considering the conscious management framework adopted to benefit from external borrowing. Vietnam's revamp 2021-2025 budget management strategy was expected to ensure national security and control public debt contained in it. This is aimed to mobilise, allocate, manage, and use in a more effective manner all resources, with internal resources considered a fundamental and long-term strategy in combination with important external resources. The strategy provides that ratio of mobilised sums in GDP will be not lower than 16 per cent, in which money from taxes and fees will occupy 13-14 per cent of GDP, and the ratio of domestic revenue will be about 85-86 per cent of the total state budget revenue. The average rate of state budget overspending will be at 3.7 per cent of GDP. In which, the average deficit of the central budget will sit at 3.4 per cent of GDP. Also, the country's annual public debt ceiling will not exceed 60 per cent of GDP, with the warning level of 55 per cent of GDP. The government's annual debt limit will not surpass 50 per cent, with the warning level of 45 per cent. The national foreign debt annually will be not over 50 per cent of GDP, with a warning level of 45 per cent of GDP.

Along with the sharp decrease in public debt, the debt structure has also changed positively. The proportion of domestic debt increased gradually, while the proportion of external debt gradually decreased. Domestic debt gradually increased from 60.1% in 2016 to 65.5% in 2020, while external debt gradually decreases from 39.9% in 2016 to 34.5% in 2020. At the same time, the structure of domestic/foreign loans was adjusted towards a more sustainable direction. For an observer from outside the country, it seems that Vietnam's debt policy so far has been characterised by a sense of proportion. Contrary to the global Keynesian trend, Vietnam has clearly reduced the public debt gap in the last four years. Consequently, the government has accumulated a considerable amount of cash reserves. In view of the economic crisis triggered by the Covid19 shock, Vietnam is benefiting from this careful fiscal policy now. There is enough space to counter the crisis. Together with the fiscal policy, another decisive positive factor was, that after a short period of lockdown and intervention, the Vietnamese economy is still running well.

Considering the short run dynamics in Table 5, the adjusted $R2$ shows a reasonable good fit of the model with a value of 93.39 percent. The Durbin Watson, with a value of 1.9092, which is approximately 2, shows that the model is free of first order

Table 5. ARDL short-run and error correction model estimate

ARDL Error Correction Regression				
Dependent Variable: D(LNYPK)				
Selected Model: ARDL(2, 1, 0, 0, 0, 0, 1)				
Variable	Coefficient	Std. Error	t-Statistic	Prob.
D(LNYPK(-1))	0.1237	0.0442	2.7976	0.0096
D(LNTOP)	-0.4961	0.0646	-7.6781	0.0000
D(LNEXDB)	-0.0276	0.0647	-0.4271	0.6728
ECT(-1)*	-0.4638	0.0265	-17.5126	0.0000
R-squared	0.9394			
Adjusted R-squared	0.9339			
Durbin-Watson stat	1.9092			

Table 6. Diagnostic Tests Estimates

	Prob. Chi-Square	Remark
Jarque Bera test for normality	0.0712	Normally Distributed
Breusch-Pagan-Godfrey Test for Heteroskedasticity	0.0624	Homoskedastic Distribution
Breusch-Godfrey Serial Correlation LM Tests	0.7855	No Autocorrelation

Source: Author's computation

autocorrelation. Table 5 also shows that the coefficient of ECM (-1) is significant at 1 percent level of significant. This indicates that the speed of adjustment for a short run to reach long run is significant. Furthermore, the error correction term is -0.4638 with the expected sign, suggesting that when the economic development model is above or below its equilibrium level, it adjusts by almost 46.38 per cent to converge to equilibrium.

Diagnostic Tests

Diagnostic tests show that residual series are normally distributed, homoskedastic and no serial correlation. The tests involved are Jacque Berra for normality, ARCH and Berusch-Godfrey for serial correlation as well as LM test.

Since the p-value of the probability values of the Chi-square in all the three tests were greater than 0.05, it means that the null hypotheses are accepted. Hence, we conclude that the data series are normally distributed, homoskedastic and not serially correlated.

Stability Tests

In the first instance, the absence of heteroscedasticity in the model is a kind of stability in its own sense because it indicates that the variances of the data series are stable with time.

However, further substantiation of our model stability can be done with the cumulative sum (CUSUM) and the cumulative sum of squares (CUSUMSQ) to test the stability of the long-run coefficients and short-run dynamics. Figure 2 and 3 show the graphical results of CUSUM and CUSUMSQ.

From figures 2 and 3, it can be seen that the plots of both the CUSUM fall within the 5% boundaries, and proving the stability of model coefficients of financial

Figure 2. CUMSUM test

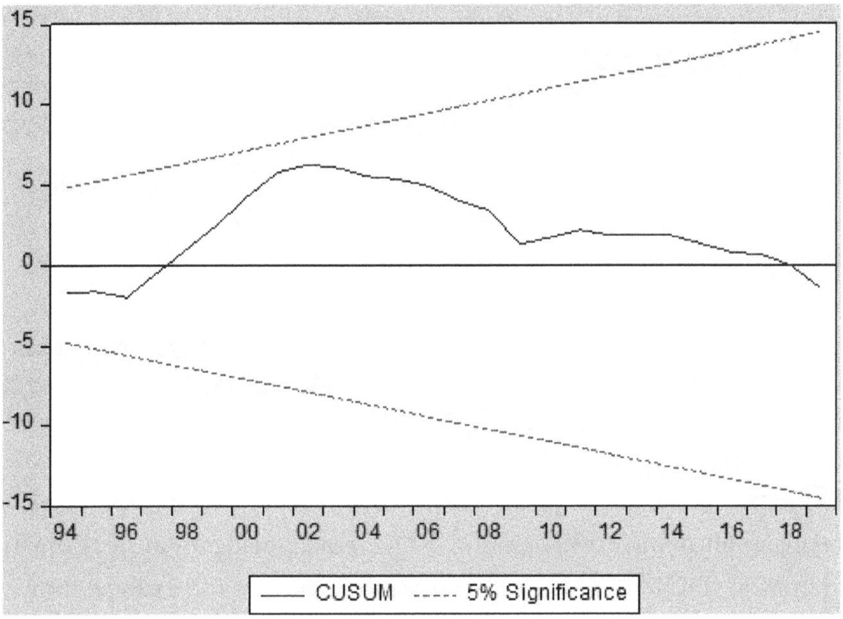

Figure 3. CUMSUM of square test

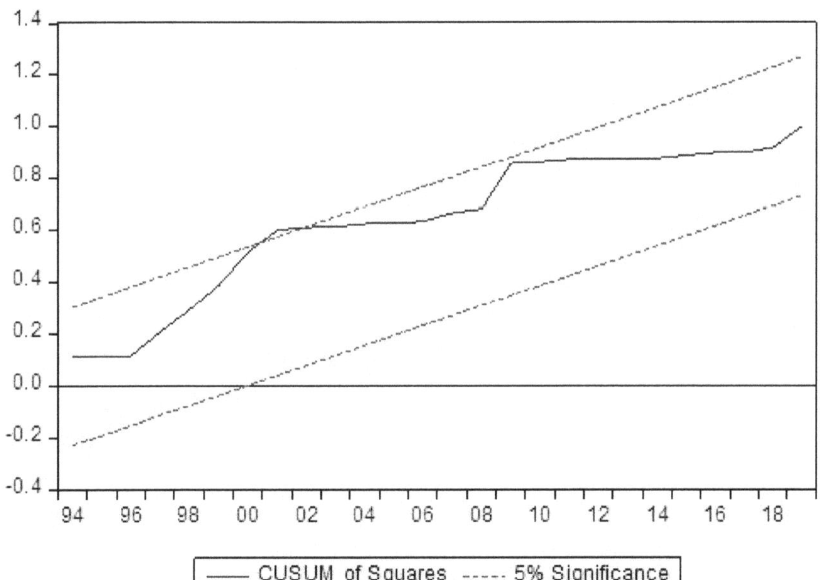

development have effect on economic development in Vietnam. Although, the CUSUMSQ plot showed that the model plot extended out of the 5 per cent boundary in 2002, it means that other economic variables that could have been included in the model were excluded due to data unavailability constraint. However, the overall model is stable and suitably specified since none of the two tests statistics deviated away from the 5 per cent bounds level.

SUMMARY AND CONCLUSION

The purpose of this study was to provide a deeper understanding of the current role of finance in improving economic development in Vietnam between 1981 and 2019. To ascertain their trend and pattern over the period. The study relied on and economic development (Real per capita income, YPK), financial development variables of $\ln FDI_t$ represents natural logarithm of foreign direct investment; $\ln TOP_t$ denotes natural logarithm of trade openness; $\ln EXDB_t$ is natural logarithm of external debt of government; $\ln GFKF_t$ is the natural logarithm of gross fixed capital formation; $\ln HDI_t$ indicates natural logarithm of human development index; and $\ln EXR_t$ also represents natural logarithm of exchange The study employed the Autoregressive Distributed Lag (ARDL) modelling technique. Based on the long run model estimates, trade openness (TOP) and foreign direct investment (FDI) exert positive but insignificant impact of economic development in Vietnam, while gross capital formation (GFKF) is significant at 10%. Also, exchange rate has been seen as negatively was found to negatively influence economic development, while human development is also important to economic development. this study found that human development and external borrowing is seen to positively impact on economic development in Vietnam.

RECOMMENDATIONS

On the basis of the findings of this study, the following recommendations are made:

i. For a given economic development target, the government should recognize appropriate external debt ratio around the threshold of 105% of annual GDP is seen as manageable and beneficial.
ii. In order for Vietnam's industries to wean themselves from their reliance on processing and assembly, it is crucial to entice multinational corporations

from developed nations and foster ties between foreign-invested enterprises and local businesses, as well as ties between production and the market.

iii. The government may improve, support, and encourage the competitiveness of exports to preserve a sustainable balance with imports and reverse the negative relationship between GDP and exchange rate.

iv. Enhancing high-quality labor in Vietnam must become a crucial component of competition and development.

REFERENCES

Chinh, H. Q., & Chi, D. T. (2018). Analysis of Foreign Direct Investment and Economic Growth in Vietnam, *International Journal of Business. Economics and Law*, *15*(5), 2289–1552.

Cindy L. (2021). *Vietnam Trade, an Overview, Part 2: The Doi Moi Reforms Modernizing Vietnam's Trade Economy*. Academic Press.

Era, A., & Vuving, L. (2021). *The Evolution of Vietnamese Foreign Policy in the Doi Moi*. Harvard University Press.

Fforde, A. (2016). Vietnam: Economic Strategy and Economic Reality. *Journal of Current Southeast Asian Affairs*, *35*(2), 3–30. doi:10.1177/186810341603500201

Hanoi Times. (2018). *Capital Expenditure in Vietnam*. Retrieved from https://hanoitimes.vn/vietnam-to-raise-capital-expenditure-t o-u227-billion-in-2022- 318651.html

Hansjörg, H., Erwin, S., & Truong-Minh V. (2016). *The Integration of Vietnam in the Global Economy and Its Effects for Vietnamese Economic Development*. The Digital Library of the Friedrich Ebert Foundation.

Huong, D. T. M. (2019). Real exchange rate and economic growth: An empirical assessment for Vietnam. *Asian Economic and Financial Review*, *9*(6), 680–690. doi:10.18488/journal.aefr.2019.96.680.690

James, R., & William, S. T. (1999). *The Politics and Economics of Transition to an Open Market Economy in Vietnam*. OECD Development Centre Working Paper No. 152.

Jonathan, P. (2009). Vietnam Sustaining Growth in Difficult Times. *ASEAN Economic Bulletin*, *26*(1), 11–24. doi:10.1355/AE26-1B

Koh, D. (2008). Leadership Changes at the 10th Congress of the Vietnamese Communist Party. *Asian Survey*, *48*(4), 650–672. doi:10.1525/as.2008.48.4.650

Le, T. D., Nguyen, P. H., Ho, Y. T. P., & Nguyen, T. N. (2021). The Influences of FDI, GFCF, OPEN on Vietnamese Economic Growth. *International Journal of Asian Business and Information Management*, *12*(3), 1–13. doi:10.4018/IJABIM.20210701.oa26

Manh, C. T. H. C. N. (2019). The Relationship Between the Human Capital and Economic Growth: A Case of Vietnam. *Industrial Engineering Letters*, *9*(5), 23–30.

Matthew B. (2017). *The missing middle: A political economy of economic restructuring in Vietnam: low institute*. Academic Press.

Minh, N. D. (2018). A New Decision Making Model based on the Made in Vietnam Lean Management Philosophy. *Economia e Sociologia*, *1*(3), 44–66.

Nwachukwu, N. E., Adebayo, R. O., Shettima, A. M., Anigwe, J. O., & Udechukwu-Peterclaver, C. T. (2016). Real effective exchange rate misalignment in Nigeria. *Central Bank of Nigeria Journal of Applied Statistics*, *7*(1), 71–91.

Ofori-Abebrese, G., Pickson, R. B., & Diabah, B. T. (2017). Financial Development and Economic Growth: Additional Evidence from Ghana. *Modern Economy*, *8*(2), 282–297. doi:10.4236/me.2017.82020

Pesaran, M. H., Shin, Y., & Smith, R. (2001). Bounds testing approaches to the analysis of level relationships. *Journal of Applied Econometrics*, *16*(3), 289–326. doi:10.1002/jae.616

Tu-Anh, V. (2017). *The Political Economy of Industrial Development in Vietnam: Impact of State-Business Relationships on Industrial Performance*. Oxford Scholarship.

Van, C. N., & Cooper, E. (1983). *Vietnam under Communism, 1975-1982*. Hoover Press.

Chapter 6
Finance and Economic Development in Brazil:
An Exposition of Policies and Economic Performance

Simon Okaja Epor
Nnamdi Azikiwe University, Awka, Nigeria

ABSTRACT

Ultimately, the study aimed to determine the significance of finance to the Brazilian economy from 1981 to 2019. On account of the nature of data stationarity, the study then adopted the autoregressive distributed lag (ARDL) modelling technique which possesses the ability to produce both long-run and short-run parameter estimates. The empirical outcome of the Brazilian growth model which has been achieved is the product of conscious and purposeful reforms to address financial and other macroeconomic deficiencies and crisis in the country. Given the theoretical assumptions and the empirical evidence, it could be concluded that credit, FDI, and human development were economically significant to the economic development of Brazil in the long-run. Although trade openness, gross capital formation, and external borrowing did not significantly account for the economic development of the Brazilian economy, they transmit the appropriate theoretical influence. However, the finance variables were seen to exert negative influence on economic growth in Brazil.

DOI: 10.4018/979-8-3693-1610-8.ch006

1. INTRODUCTION: A BRIEF BACKGROUND OF BRAZIL

Much of Brazil's history begins on Wednesday, April 22, 1500, the day the Portuguese explorer Pedro Álvares Cabral (c. 1467 - c. 1520) anchored his ship near Monte Pascoal in the present-day state of Bahia in north-eastern Brazil. Of course, the Portuguese were not the first to set foot in the country. Prior to their arrival, it was estimated that between two and four million indigenous peoples lived in some 2,000 countries and tribes of Brazil's wealthy coastal regions, from the present-day states of Maranana and Para in the north to Santa Catarina in the south. Currently, Brazil ranks fifth in the worldCurrently, Brazil ranks fifth in the world after Russia, Canada, China and the United States. With a total area of 3,287,612 square miles, it has the 7th largest population in the world, estimated at 215,313,498 by July 2022 (www.worldpopulationreview.com).

Brazil is the largest country in South America, covering 47% of the continent. The Atlantic coast spans 4,655 miles and has nearly 10,000 miles of inland borders with South American countries such as Uruguay to the south. Southwest Argentina, Paraguay and Bolivia; western Peru; northwest Colombia; Northern Venezuela, Guiana, Suriname, French Guiana. In fact, it borders all South American countries except Ecuador and Chile. In the Amazon, Brazil has unparalleled biodiversity, with more than a third of the world's species living in tropical rainforests. Brazil has five main types of climate: equatorial, tropical, semi-arid, tropical and subtropical plateaus, providing a diverse environment.

Although present-day Brazil is divided into 26 states and federal districts, the Brazilian National Institute of the Earth (Instituto Brasileiro de Geografia e Estatística) has divided the country into five main geographical divisions. The north consists

Figure 1. Geographical map of Brazil

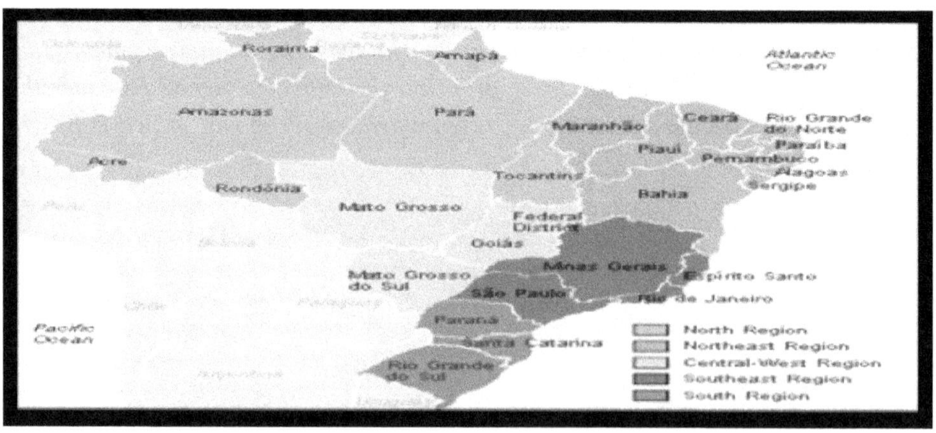

of the southern slopes of the mountains of Guyana and the mountains of northern Brazil and the Amazon basin. Considered the birthplace of Brazil, the northeast is known for its hot climate, beautiful beaches, and rich cultural traditions, including carnival. Of the 53.6 million population, about 15 million live in the dry interior or sertans, while the rest live in urban centers such as El Salvador, Recife and Fortaleza. Brasilia, the designated capital of Brazil in the Midwest, is located in an area known as the Federal District (Federal District). The other area is the lowlands of Mato Grosso and Mato Grosso do Sul, which consist mainly of the Pantanal, one of the largest tropical wetlands in the world. The Southeast Region of Brazil is the richest region in Brazil with a 60 per cent of its GDP. It contains São Paolo, Rio de Janeiro and Minas Gerais, the country's richest states.

2. HISTORICAL OVERVIEW OF THE ECONOMIC MANAGEMENT PHILOSOPHY OF BRAZIL

The global prominence of the Brazilian economy has been one of the most prominent features of the international economic landscape over the past two decades. Synonymous with growing economic instability and income inequality in the late 1970s and 1980s, Brazil represents a promising destination for sustainable growth, with increasingly favorable results in tackling entrenched poverty at the end of the last decade and narrowing the income gap between the rich. and poor. In doing so, Brazil has adopted and implemented several philosophies of structural change that are not only fertile ground for foreign direct investment but also raise international interest as an example of a country seeking to combine economic dynamism with poverty reduction and a social economy. righteousness. .

Undoubtedly, the development and implementation of the Plano Real Comprehensive Stabilization Plan was a decisive turning point in Brazil's economic recovery. Introduced between 1993 and 1994 by Finance Minister and then President Fernando Enrique Cardoso, this plan combines unorthodox and orthodox macroeconomic elements (Amann & Barrientos, 2014). Inflation in Brazil in 1970s was running at more than 1000 per cent and the economy had suffered huge contractions in output. It introduced a pegged exchange rate gradually and cleverly. Along with trade liberalization, this maintained an external check on domestic price formation.

As growth accelerated following stabilization it has proved feasible to combine fiscal rectitude with social spending, such as Bolsa Familía. It has been proven that the tax raising power of the various levels of government is impressive, accounting for over 30 per cent of GDP (Bernardi, Barreix, Marrenza & Projeta, 2007). As growth accelerated following stabilization, it has become possible for the federal government to combine fiscal rectitude with increased spending on social programs such as Bolsa Familia. The Real Plan is widely regarded as one of the most significant and lasting political achievements since the return to civilian rule in Portugal. One of the key reasons for its enduring success has been the manner in which it was able to secure a broad political consensus in its favour across political party divides, business, trade unions and civil society (Roett, 2010). The fall of these barriers to trade and investment led to a dramatic increase in foreign participation in some sectors (especially public utilities) and a thinning out of domestic industrial sector.

3. REFORMS IN BRAZIL: THE SOCIAL, POLITICAL, AND ECONOMIC PERSPECTIVES

The economic reforms of Brazil covers various economic reforms and changes and traces these changes in the Brazilian economy through historical course in the country. They are categorized by various reform philosophies that will be discussed in two categories: pre-1980s reforms and post-1980s reforms.

3.1 Reforms in Brazil: Pre-1980

Like the rest of Latin America, Brazil began its development journey haphazardly and in response to an economic crisis. Following the Great Depression, Brazil's then-president, Getulio Vargas (1930-45 and 1951-54), began to establish the institutions and policies that would later become the core instruments of state-led development: tariff protection and managed trade (1930s), state-owned steel firms (1940s and 1950s), a development bank (Banco Nacional de Desenvolvimento Econômico, BNDE, 1950s), a state-owned oil firm (Schneider, 2015).

Like many other states in "developing" nations, Brazil started actively promoting industrialization around the conclusion of World War II. There were apparently subsidies applied. The Brazilian state started to actively promote industrialisation by the end of World War II, along with many other states from "emerging" nations. Due to the "late comer" status of these countries' industries, subsidies were supposedly employed to make up for the lower productivity of industrial labour and to hasten the learning and catching-up process. Despite entering Brazil since the late 1940s, resources from outside the economy, such as credit capital, were not quantitatively important until the late 1960s. However, the notion that the funds utilized to subsidize the industrial sector were derived from the

Early in the 1960s, Brazil was neither politically nor economically stable. GDP stagnation in 1963 was caused by macroeconomic factors, including rising inflation, a substantial public deficit, and inefficiencies in the process of import substitution industrialization (ISI). After the military takeover in 1964, there was no significant shift in policy, but political and economic stability as well as a favorable situation in the outside markets prepared the ground for quick growth..

3.2 Reforms in Brazil: Post-2020

During the 1990s, the Brazilian economy underwent a series of structural as well as institutional reforms: trade liberalization, privatization and deregulation of economic activities; regional integration with neighbour countries of Latin America Southern Cone; financial liberalization, including controlled deregulation and aperture of domestic commercial banking sector to foreign banks; compliance to international trade rules and the establishment of a "market friendly" policy institutional framework (Buainain & da Silveira, 2002). These reforms have had deep and pervasive effects on both the functioning of the economy and the role of the State.

i. Stabilization

The Brazilian economy underwent a number of structural and institutional reforms in the 1990s, including trade liberalization, privatization, and deregulation of economic activities; regional integration with neighbouring countries in the Southern Cone of Latin America; financial liberalization, including controlled deregulation and opening of the domestic commercial banking sector to foreign banks; compliance with international trade rules; and the creation of a "market friendly" environment (Buainain & da Silveira, 2002). Both the state's role and the economy's ability to function have been significantly and widely impacted by these reforms.

Figure 2. Inflation in Brazil (annual %)

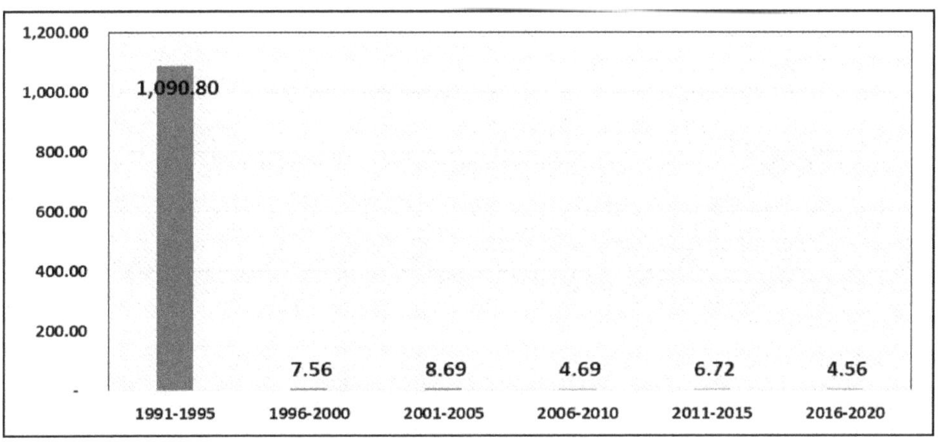

As we can see, the inflation rate, which remained low in comparison to previous records, is a beneficial indicator. The phenomenal success of the Real Stabilization Plan (launched in 1993–1994) was partially attributed to the strengthening of the Brazilian real, which was a result of high interest rates, which were crucial stabilization tools at the time (Amann & Baer, 2012). Since then, Brazil's inflation rates have consistently ranked among the lowest in the world, attracting significant amounts of foreign investment and boosting human development (see Figure 2).

ii. Trade Opening

The opening of the economy, in addition to stabilization, is the most significant component of the Brazilian reforms. Brazil's economy was very closed up until 1990. Due to the debt crisis in the 1980s and the drive to generate trade surpluses, this was the consequence of a planned import substitution strategy.

When the economic cycle in the heart of the capitalist world reverses, resources from international firms are sent back to their headquarters, which is another alarming aspect of the Brazilian economy. Foreign investments also cause profits and dividends to be sent home. Additionally, this has an immediate negative (large) influence on the income balance. Particularly in the second half of 2008, the global crisis that broke out in 2008 caused a rapid acceleration in interest, profit, and dividend remittances. The net remittance of profits and income from portfolio assets from 2008 to 2013 averaged US$ 7879 million annually. The average amount of profits and dividends paid out from direct investments (net of reinvested earnings)

Figure 3. Foreign debt, human development, and trade openness

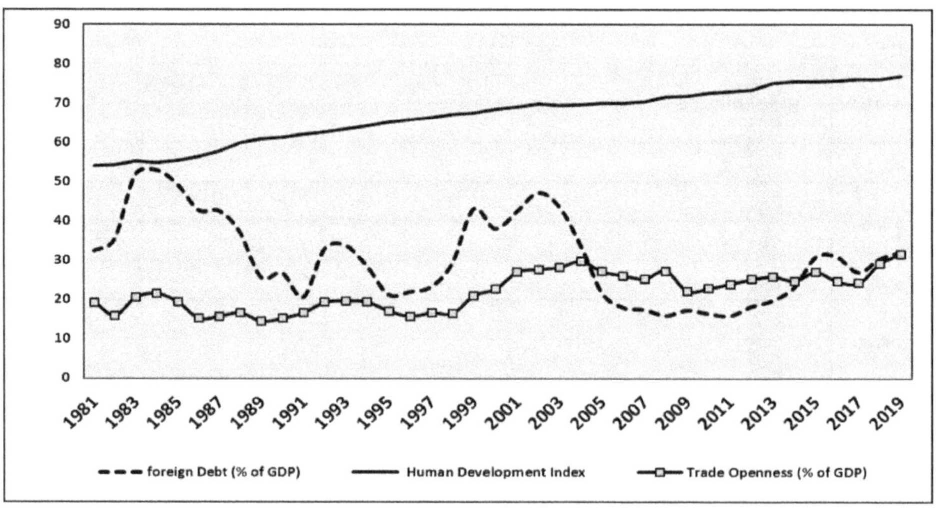

was US$ 21753.million per year. From this, one arrives to the conclusion that the growth strategy with foreign savings leads to a situation of growing vulnerability in the foreign accounts (Gomes, 2020).

From 1991 to between 2003 and 2010, when it averaged 17.01 percent of GNI, Figure 3 also demonstrates a declining trend in the stock of Brazil's external debt. The Brazilian state sector's net debt rose from 28.5 percent of GDP to 42.6 percent of GDP between 1995 and 1998. The country's present economic policies has come under fire for this astronomical growth, which has many people applauding.

iii. Financial Sector Reforms

About 15 years ago, Brazil's financial industry underwent significant improvements that greatly improved its stability and shock resistance. This evolution has been significantly influenced by policies and structural improvements. A significant barrier to the growth of robust financial markets in Brazil was the high and unstable inflation of the 1980s and early 1990s. Without a doubt, for the majority of the previous decade, these measures helped to significantly deepen financial intermediation. The 2008–2009 global financial crisis shocked the financial system, but it responded quite well. The expansion of the use of credit, particularly consumer borrowing, is a prominent aspect of Brazil's economy throughout the time period under consideration. The Table 4 will show that the ratio of bank credit to GDP has risen from 44.43% in 2006-2010 to 62.94% in 2016-2020. One result of the boom in consumer credit has been an acceleration in the sale of automobiles.

Figure 4. Brazilian banks' domestic credit to private sector (% of GDP)

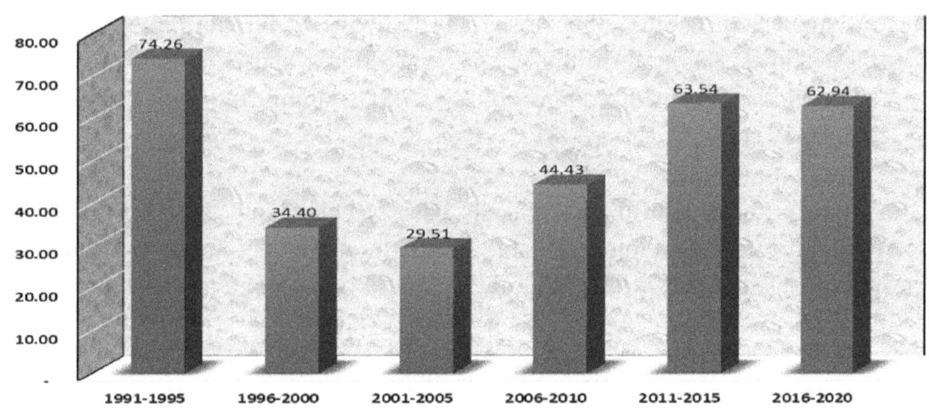

Other statutory and operational improvements are underway in Brazil in addition to the aforementioned structural reforms. The labor market and minimum wage policies include, but are not limited to, more flexible labor laws that allow for more room for negotiations between unions and employers, access to significant social benefits for undocumented workers, and an unemployment insurance system that encourages high turnover. Reducing regional inequities in the amount of resources allocated to basic (primary and secondary) education, expanding the scope of standardized achievement exams to cover more subjects, and enhancing the quality of instruction are the three main areas where education reforms will be concentrated. Once more, the privatization initiative was expanded to cover state-owned businesses and banks, as well as telecommunications, electricity, and oil and gas, as part of a country-wide debt restructuring plan (Mora & Giambiagi, 2005). Following this, strong anti-trust legislation and enforcement were developed, as well as the creation of reliable and open regulatory frameworks for the various industries. Other reforms include industrial and infrastructure policies, energy policies, and reforms to provide a reliable energy supply for the country's economy and people.

The necessarily summary review in the sections above of Brazil's record with structural macro, micro and social reforms points to very significant progress over the last two decades. In brief:

- The institutional framework for macroeconomic management.
- During the 1990s, significant progress was made towards liberalizing an economy historically characterized by a large presence of the public sector in key industrial and services sectors.
- On the social front, the decade of the 1990s saw important reforms in the health and education sectors.
- The financial system remains highly concentrated; lending spreads, especially for small and medium enterprises and individuals, remain quite high; and most domestic long term-financing to investment and exports continues to be provided (at subsidized rates) by BNDES, at significant fiscal and perhaps efficiency costs.

In essence, these reform policies may have produced substantial progress in the structural transformation of Brazil, unless the global economic environment deteriorates substantially where other reform initiatives will be needed.

5. DATA MODELING AND ANALYSIS

The study's research approach, known as an ex-post facto design type, describes specific financial development variables in Vietnam between 1981 and 2019 and economic development (Real per capita income, GDPK) to determine their trend and pattern during the period. The study is limited to the financial development variables of the lnCPS also represents natural logarithm of credit to the private sector; lnTOPN denotes natural logarithm of trade openness; lnGFCF is the natural logarithm of gross fixed capital formation; lnFDBT is natural logarithm of external debt of government; and lnHD t indicates natural logarithm of human development index; and represents natural logarithm of foreign direct investment from 2009 to 2019. The data range are annual and sourced from the World Bank database.

5.1 Model Estimation

Neo-classical growth model considered two factor production functions with capital and labour as determinants of output and the addition of exogenous determinant factor, technology. The neoclassical growth theory has a conviction that the collection of capital inside an economy and how the general population utilise the capital is imperative for the economic development. In this manner, the postulation of neoclassical theory is utilised to quantify the development and harmony of an economy and is written as:

$$Y = AF(K, L)$$

Where Y denotes an economy's GDP, k represents its share of capital, L describes the amount of labour in an economy and A denotes the determinant level of technology. As a result of the relationship between labour and technology, the production function of an economy will be written as:

$$Y = F(K, AL)$$

And subsequently,

$$GDPK = F(K, AL)$$

Where: GDPK = level of economic development of a country; K = investment in physical capital; L = labor force and human capital formation, *and A* denotes the determinant level of technology. This means that labour is augmenting and that workers' productivity depends on the level of technology.

Nweke, Odo and Anoke (2017) expanded K to include gross capital formation (GFCF) to output ratio, which include both private and public capital expenditures, so that we have:

$$GDPK = F\left(GFCF, AL\right)$$

Theory of endogenous development attempts to display innovation instead of expecting it to be exogenous. This position makes financial development an integral part of technological innovation. For the most part, financial development (FD) originates from innovative advancement (Orji, Nwagu, Ogbuabor & Anthony-Orji 2021).

Again, the two-gap model, which is an extension of the Harrod-Domar growth model, provides that developing countries like Brazil require to bridge the gap in inadequate domestic savings and foreign exchange earnings to make appreciable advancement. Both the savings and foreign exchange earnings can be bridged by foreign direct investment (FDI), external borrowings and trade (Davies & Quinlivan, 2006; Kharusi & Ada, 2018; Orji, Nwagu, Ogbuabor & Anthony-Orji, 2021). Because of the significance of human capital development (HKD) in the literatures, this study will replace labour (L) with human capital development (HKD). So, following these modifications, this study will state the econometric model thus:

$$GDPK = f\left(GFCF, CPS, FDBT, FDI, TOPN, HD\right)$$

Taking a natural logarithm of both sides produce

$$lnGDPK = f\left(lnGFCF, lnCPS, lnFDBT, lnFDI, lnTOPN, lnHD\right)$$

5.2 Method of Data Analysis

The study adopts autoregressive distributed lag approach to cointegration (ARDL) developed by Pesaran, Shin and Smith (2001). This method has the main advantage of being able to be applied applied irrespective of whether the series are I (0) or I (1). The technique is appropriate for small samples (Ahmed, Zhang & Cary, 2021). However, none of the variables is I (2) hence ARDL can be used to analyse data for this study. The bounds testing approach involves estimating the following equation as postulated by Ahmed, Zhang and Cary (2021):

$$\begin{aligned}\Delta(lnGDPK)_t =&\sigma_0 + \sum_{k=1}^{p}\beta_{ak}\Delta\left(lnGDPK\right)_{t-k} + \sum_{k=0}^{p}\beta_{bk}\Delta\left(lnCPS\right)_{t-k}\\ &+\sum_{k=0}^{p}\beta_{ck}\Delta\left(lnFDBT\right)_{t-k} + \sum_{k=0}^{p}\beta_{dk}\Delta\left(lnFDI\right)_{t-k}\\ &+\sum_{k=0}^{p}\beta_{ek}\Delta\left(lnGFCF\right)_{t-k} + \sum_{k=0}^{p}\beta_{gk}\Delta\left(lnHD\right)_{t-k}\\ &+\sum_{k=0}^{p}\beta_{ik}\Delta\left(lnTOPN\right)_{t-k} + \alpha_1(\ln GDPK)_{t-1} + \alpha_2(\ln CPS)_{t-1}\\ &+\alpha_3(\ln FDBT)_{t-1} + \alpha_4(\ln FDI)_{t-1} + \alpha_5(\ln GFCF)_{t-1}\\ &+\alpha_6(\ln HD)_{t-1} + \alpha_7(\ln TOPN)_{t-1} + \mu_t\end{aligned}$$

Where $\beta_{a, b, c, d, e, f, g, i}$ represent the short-run coefficients, $\alpha_{1, 2, 3, 4, 5, 6, 7}$ indicate the long-run coefficients, Δ refers to the first difference operator, and μ_t is the error term.

The null hypothesis for the ARDL bound test (H_0: $\alpha_1 = \alpha_2 = \alpha_3 = \alpha_4 = \alpha_5 = \alpha_6 = \alpha_7 = 0$) implies no cointegration between variables. The alternative hypothesis (H_0: $\alpha_1 \neq \alpha_2 \neq \alpha_3 \neq \alpha_4 \neq \alpha_5 \neq \alpha_6 \neq \alpha_7 \neq 0$) indicates the presence of cointegration.

As a result of the error correction model, the short-term dynamics were captured as follows:

$$\begin{aligned}\Delta(lnGDPK)_t =&\sigma_0 + \sum_{k=1}^{p}\beta_{ak}\Delta\left(lnGDPK\right)_{t-k} + \sum_{k=0}^{p}\beta_{bk}\Delta\left(lnCPS\right)_{t-k}\\ &+\sum_{k=0}^{p}\beta_{ck}\Delta\left(lnFDBT\right)_{t-k} + \sum_{k=0}^{p}\beta_{dk}\Delta\left(lnFDI\right)_{t-k}\\ &+\sum_{k=0}^{p}\beta_{ek}\Delta\left(lnGFCF\right)_{t-k} + \sum_{k=0}^{p}\beta_{gk}\Delta\left(lnHD\right)_{t-k}\\ &+\sum_{k=0}^{p}\beta_{ik}\Delta\left(lnTOPN\right)_{t-k} + \delta ECT_{t-1} + \mu_t\end{aligned}$$

Where, ECT = error correction term derived from equation (3.10), and δ = the speed of adjustment.

Table 1. Descriptive statistics

	GDPK	CPS	FDBT	FDI	GFCF	HD	TOPN
Mean	5556.539	51.06396	30.56256	30.99641	197.0085	66.75462	21.95000
Median	3975.390	45.65257	30.31000	18.18000	128.3300	68.40000	22.11000
Maximum	13245.61	134.1136	52.94000	102.4300	571.0200	76.90000	31.56000
Minimum	1570.540	0.000000	15.86000	0.990000	32.90000	53.90000	14.39000
Std. Dev.	3579.467	27.23129	10.77690	33.61475	155.9587	7.100186	4.864233
Skewness	0.750825	1.174386	0.412936	0.840229	1.099789	-0.391273	0.066772
Kurtosis	2.226302	5.295553	2.138728	2.205010	3.044602	1.998607	1.788295
Jarque-Bera	4.637036	17.52772	2.313761	5.615911	7.865211	2.624644	2.414851
Probability	0.098419	0.000156	0.314466	0.060328	0.019593	0.269194	0.298966
Sum	216705.0	1991.494	1191.940	1208.860	7683.330	2603.430	856.0500
Sum Sq. Dev.	4.87E+08	28178.65	4413.383	42938.16	924278.0	1915.681	899.1090
Observations	39	39	39	39	39	39	39

In the case where all variables remain the same as before, the coefficient for the speed of adjustment should normally be negative and significant to confirm the presence of a cointegrating relationship. Finally, ECM is the error correction term.

5.2 Empirical Results and Analysis

Real output per capita (YPK) had a mean of $5,556.539 and a median of $3,975.39. The maximum value was $13,245.61 while the minimum value was $1,570.54. As for foreign direct investment (FDI), had a mean of 30.996% of GDP, while credit to the private sector (CPS) averaged 51.06% of GDP as against 30.56% of GDP for foreign debt. Gross fixed capital formation (GFCF) had a mean of $197.0085 million and a median of $128.33 million. The maximum value was $571.02 million while the minimum value was $32.90 million. The probability of the Jarque-Bera statistic shows that only credit to the private sector (CPS) and Gross fixed capital formation (GFCF), with probabilities less than 0.05, were not normally distributed. However, the over model normality will be determined with combined model variables. Again, Real output per capita (YPK) is said to be more volatile with the highest standard deviation of 3579.47, which is clearly above the standard deviations of all the other variables.

Correlation Analysis

In determining whether or not a linear relationship exists between the variables employed in the model, the study made use of the Pearson correlation coefficient test. The test was also conducted to determine the possible existence of multicollinearity

Table 2. Correlation analysis test result

	GDPK	CPS	FDBT	FDI	GFCF	HD	TOPN
GDPK	1						
CPS	0.1398	1					
FDBT	-0.6874	-0.1883	1				
FDI	0.9346	0.1006	-0.4586	1			
GFCF	0.9833	0.1598	-0.6785	0.9059	1		
HD	0.8201	0.0619	-0.5253	0.8223	0.7602	1	
TOPN	0.4962	-0.0828	-0.0833	0.6064	0.4685	0.7333	1

Source: Author's computation

within the variables, which if present, can lead to errors in the coefficient estimates of the multiple regression.

In this regard, only the coefficients of FDI with GFCF as indicated in table 2 above was slightly above 0.9, which indicates possible existence of multicollinearity given that they are close to 1. This outcome entails that, reliance on the estimation results of a multiple regression will be done with extreme caution as multicollinearity could severely affect these results, hence further diagnostic tests will need to be carried out to empirically establish that core regression requirements and model stability tests will be a must before we accept the outcome of the parameter estimation of our model.

Test for Stationarity: Augmented Dickey-Fuller Test

To avoid problems of spurious regression, we first start by examining the stationarity properties of the data base. The Augmented Dickey-Fuller (ADF) test was applied to examine the stationarity of the variables used in the study. The results are shown in Table 3. Table 3 result reported that only credit to the private sector was stationary at the level, hence integrated of order zero; I(0), while the rest variables were adjudged stationary after first difference, meaning that they integrated of order one; I(1).

The study, then deemed it expedient to apply the ARDL Bounds test estimation technique, based on the order of integration of the data series, one and zero.

Table 3. Stationarity tests

ADF Tests: Levels				ADF Tests First Difference			
Variables	Test Statistic with intercept	p-values	Order of Integration	Variables	Test Statistic with intercept	p-values	Order of Integration
lnGDPK	-0.9086	0.7746		D(lnGDPK)	-5.0879	0.0002	*I(1)*
lnCPS	-3.1305	0.0361	*I(0)*	D(lnCPS)			*I(0)*
lnFDBT	-1.7180	0.4144		D(lnFDBT)	-4.7742	0.0004	*I(1)*
lnFDI	-0.6298	0.8504		D(lnFDI)	-3.0022	0.0457	*I(1)*
lnGFCF	-1.0487	0.7257		D(lnGFCF)	-5.5670	0.0000	*I(1)*
lnHD	-2.3716	0.1563		D(lnHD)	-4.8162	0.0004	*I(1)*
lnTOPN	-1.0971	0.7071		D(lnTOPN)	-6.1645	0.0000	*I(1)*

Source: Author's computation

The Autoregressive Distributed Lag (ARDL) Bounds Test for Cointegration

In order to determine the long-run relationship between the variables employed in the study, the ARDL Bounds test procedure was used. The results are presented in Table 4.

The results indicated that the F-statistic is 14.64466, and it turned out to be obviously larger than the 5% upper bound critical value of 3.28. The results suggest a long-run finance-growth nexus in Brazil.

4.4 Autoregressive Distributed Lag (ARDL) Long-Run Estimation

The long run model is given as:

Table 4. ARDL bounds test

Model Specification	F-statistic	5% Upper Bound Value	Decision
GDPK	14.64466	3.28	Reject H0

Source: Author's computation

$$\textit{lnGDPK} = 0.39 * \textit{lnCPS} - 0.39 * \textit{lnCPS} - 0.86 * \textit{lnFDBT} + 0.15 * \textit{lnFDI}$$
$$+0.17 * \textit{lnGFCF} + 0.93 * \textit{lnHD} + 0.32 * \textit{lnTOPN} + 3.6899$$

The long run model was estimated using the Auto-Regressive Distributed Lag (ARDL) method. The result is shown in Table 5. The information in table 5 demonstrates that domestic funding for the private sector has a large, beneficial impact on Brazil's economic growth over the long run. This shows that a 0.39 percent rise in real per capita income results from a 1% increase in the financial resources made available to private businesses. This suggests that over time, policies like credit rationing have increased the amount of credit available to the private sector, which has increased growth. of real per capita income in Brazil. This result corroborates the findings of Ofori-Abebrese, Pickson and Diabah (2017), and Adu, Marbuah and Mensah (2013). Brazil has undergone some significant changes in the past ten years, which account for the expansion of the credit market. Barbi (2014) claims that a number of fundamental microeconomic reforms that expanded creditors' property rights and created a market for credit portfolios increased the recycling of liquidity as part of the supply side adjustments. Four specific things need to be mentioned: The *Fundo de Investmento em Direitos Creditorios* was established as the first reform (FIDC). Small and medium banks can raise money using this financial instrument by selling their credit portfolios.

The legislation governing payroll-backed loans, which was passed in 2003 and permits lenders to automatically deduct principal and interest payments from borrowers' paychecks, was the second innovation. (thereby reducing the incidence of nonperforming loans) The current bankruptcy law, which was passed in 2005 to make it easier for creditors to recover assets, is the third change. As a result, the stock of personal credit equaled that of corporate credit, and the spreads between the two categories converged (Barbi, 2014).

In order to reduce social inequities and encourage consumption from the lowest socioeconomic groups, the government established a number of social transfer programs, a continual drop in unemployment, and a steady increase in real earnings. Formal employment was of the utmost importance for ensuring economic progress. Particular focus was placed on small businesses and labor-intensive industries like construction. Businesses received financial incentives in the form of payroll tax exemptions in order to retain employees; as a result, formal employment rates returned to their prior full employment levels. Despite these, the human development index (HD) in Brazil had only a positive significant effect on real output per capita with a coefficient of 0.9332. Although Brazil made appreciable progress in HDI (from 70.00 in 2005 to 76.9 in 2019), Brazil's human progress during the 1990s has not been balanced across all three dimensions that comprise the HDI. One dimension

Table 5. Long-run coefficient estimation

Variable	Coefficient	t-Statistic	Prob.	Decision
lnCPS	0.3951	4.9437	0.0003	Positively significant
lnFDBT	-0.8572	-3.1678	0.0081	Negatively significant
lnFDI	0.1537	3.0699	0.0097	Positively significant
lnGFCF	0.1685	1.0129	0.3311	Positively not significant
lnHD	0.9332	1.8305	0.0921	Positively significant
lnTOPN	0.3217	1.2931	0.2203	Positively not significant
C	3.6899	2.3667	0.0356	

Source: Author's computation

alone (access to knowledge) was responsible for about half the progress achieved. While the income and life expectancy components lagged behind in the country average (UNDP, 2004).

Another factor responsible for the significance of both supply and demand of credit to economic development in Brazil is the fact that the country gained credibility as it reached macroeconomic stability (Barbi, 2014). During the period when inflation converged to target, the Brazilian Central Bank (BCB) gained credibility and de facto independence to conduct monetary and regulatory policies. As a result of the BCB adopting a more transparent and predictable approach to policy-making, Brazil was granted investment grade status in 2008 (Standard & Poor's and Fitch) and in 2009 (Moody's). As domestic savings are below the necessary level to sustain investment, the inflow of funds supplemented the need for resources. Though we cannot ignore the role of FDI in economic development, but due to nature of domestic market in Brazil, there is empirical evidence that its effect is becoming less significant as domestic factors are contributing in higher to economic development compared to FDI. While domestic credit to the private sector accounted for 39.51% of variations in real per capita income, FDI's share was 15.37%, even though they both had statistically significant effect on economic development at 1%. This empirical position is in variance with that of Shahzad, Hussain, Qin and Muhamadi (2019) that FDI show insignificant response towards the gross domestic product of the Brazilian economy.

The FDI inflows was also expected to complement trade flows in any economy, but this was not the case with Brazil. The positive coefficient of trade openness (TOPN), 0.3217, was not enough to significantly account for changes in real per capita income. The insignificant impact of trade openness on real output per capita is in consonance with the position of Daumal and Özyurt (2011) and Chang, Kaltani, and Loayza (2009) revealed that the significance of trade openness is only under

Table 6. ARDL short-run and error correction model estimate

ARDL Error Correction Regression				
Dependent Variable: D(lnGDPK)				
Selected Model: ARDL(2, 3, 0, 3, 1, 2, 1)				
Variable	Coefficient	Std. Error	t-Statistic	Prob.
D(lnGDPK(-1))	-0.1726	0.0218	-7.9115	0.0000
D(lnCPS)	-0.0625	0.0208	-3.0022	0.0110
D(lnCPS(-1))	-0.1607	0.0125	-12.8304	0.0000
D(lnCPS(-2))	-0.0527	0.0193	-2.7296	0.0183
D(lnFDI)	0.0467	0.0102	4.5731	0.0006
D(lnFDI(-1))	0.0220	0.0081	2.7083	0.0190
D(lnFDI(-2))	-0.0264	0.0074	-3.5607	0.0039
D(lnGFCF)	0.4296	0.0247	17.4200	0.0000
D(lnHD)	-2.8542	0.4216	-6.7696	0.0000
D(lnHD(-1))	0.8304	0.3885	2.1375	0.0538
D(lnTOPN)	-0.0611	0.0425	-1.4381	0.1760
ECT(-1)*	-0.4100	0.0301	-13.6198	0.0000
R-squared	0.99519			
Adjusted R-squared	0.99240			
Durbin-Watson stat	2.11213			

Source: Author's computation

certain conditions, like human capital development and a flexible labour market, respectively. According to Barbi (2014), the Brazilian economy was susceptible to commodity price shocks being a big exporter of metals and food commodities which a side effect on the domestic currency. The outcome was not surprising as Brazil had favoured a non-liberal international trade framework until the 1990s. Trade liberalization, in earnest, took effect from 1991, after the removal of all the relevant nontariff barriers (NTBs) and the commencement of a four-year tariff reduction schedule and the phasing into its regional integration agreement with the other members of Mercosur (ie, a trade treaty of Asunción, signed in 1991 by Brazil, Argentina, Paraguay, and Uruguay) (Moreira, 2009).

Empirical results of Table 5 also revealed that gross fixed capital formation (GFCF) exert positive but insignificant impact on economic output. This is in variance with the findings of Kesar, Bandi, Jena and Yadav (2022), although in a panel study. Recall also that trade openness was insignificant to real output. This could be mean that is still exhibiting the traits of a closed merchandising economy, compared to its BRICS counterpart. The significant negative impact of external government borrowing means that the direct and indirect incidence of external government debt level in Brazil has reached the level where it is no longer supportive of economic development. This position was also revealed by Hsing (2003) that

Table 7. Diagnostic tests estimates

	Prob. Chi-Square	Remark
Jarque Bera test for normality	0.9057	Normally Distributed
Breusch-Pagan-Godfrey Test for Heteroskedasticity	0.7726	Homoskedastic Distribution
Breusch-Godfrey Serial Correlation LM Tests	0.7590	No Autocorrelation

Source: Author's computation

output reacts inversely to shocks to the external debt conditioned of money being considered as a monetary tool.

Table 6 also revealed that changes in credit to the private sector, foreign direct investment, gross fixed capital formation, and human development index and trade openness were significant in explaining the changes in output per capita. Although only immediate increases from foreign direct investment and gross fixed capital formation caused increases in real output per capita.

Diagnostic Tests

Diagnostic tests show that residual series are normally distributed, homoskedastic and no serial correlation. The tests involved are Jacque Berra for normality, ARCH and Berusch-Godfrey for serial correlation as well as LM test.

Since the p-value of the probability values of the Chi-square in all the three tests were greater than 0.05, it means that the null hypotheses are accepted. Hence, we conclude that the data series are normally distributed, homoskedastic and not serially correlated.

Stability Tests

Last but not least, a glance at the graphs of the cumulative sum (CUSUM) and cumulative sum of squares (CUSUMSQ) from the recursive estimation of the model (see Figures 1 and 2) demonstrates stability and the absence of any systematic change in the coefficient at the 5% significant level over the sample period. The plot of the stability test results (CUSUM and CUSUMSQ) of the model are given in Figures 1 and 2.

The CUSUM and CUSUMSQ plotted against the critical bound of the 5% significance level show that the model is stable over time; this can therefore be used for policy prescription. However, the overall model is stable and suitably specified since none of the two tests statistics deviated away from the 5 per cent bounds level.

Figure 5. CUMSUM and CUMSUM of square test
Source: Author's computation

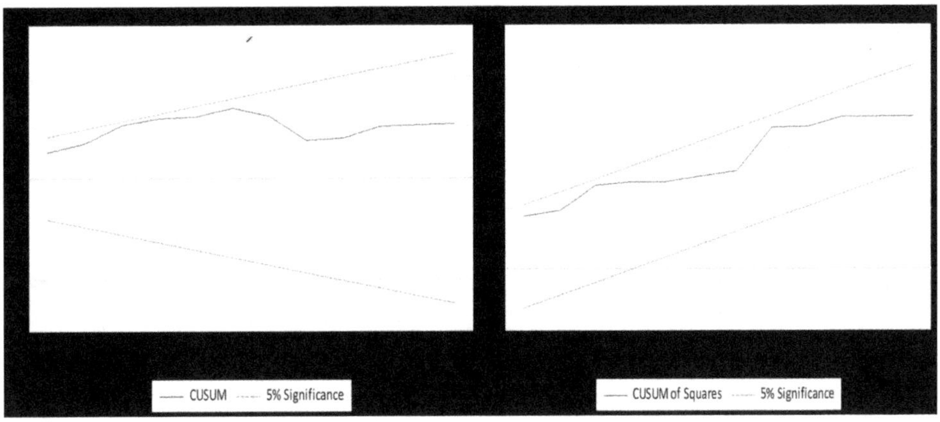

6. SUMMARY AND CONCLUSION

The ultimate goal of the study was determine the significance of finance to the Brazilian economy from 1981 to 2019. On account of the nature of data stationarity, the study then adopted the Autoregressive Distributed Lag (ARDL) modelling technique which posses the ability to produce both long-run and short-run parameter estimates. The empirical outcome of the Brazilian growth model which has been achieved is the product of conscious and purposeful reforms to address financial and other macroeconomic deficiencies and crisis in the country. Given the theoretical assumptions and the empirical evidence, it could be concluded that credit, FDI and human development were economically significant to the economic development of Brazil in the long-run. Although, trade openness, gross capital formation and external borrowing did not significantly account for the economic development of the Brazilian economy, they transmit the appropriate theoretical influence. However, the finance variables were seen to exert negative influence on economic growth in Brazil.

REFERENCES

Adu, G., Marbuah, G., & Mensah, J. T. (2013). Financial Development and Economic Growth in Ghana: Does the Measure of Financial Development Matter? *Review of Development Finance*, *3*(4), 192–203. doi:10.1016/j.rdf.2013.11.001

Ahmed, Z., Zhang, B., & Cary, M. (2021). *Linking economic globalization, economic growth, financial development, and ecological footprint: Evidence from symmetric and asymmetric*. Academic Press.

Amann, E., & Baer, W. (2012). Brazil as an emerging economy: A new economic miracle? *Revista de Economia Política, 32*(128), 412–423. doi:10.1590/S0101-31572012000300004

Amann, E., & Barrientos, A. (2014). *Is There a Brazilian Model of Development? Are There Lessons for Countries in Africa?* WIDER Working Paper 2014/134. Helsinki: UNU-WIDER. https://doi.org/ doi:10.35188/UNU-WIDER/2014/855-1

ARDL. (n.d.). *Ecological Indicators, 121*, 107060. doi:10.1016/j.ecolind.2020.107060

Barbi, F. C. (2014). *Determinants of Credit Expansion in Brazil.* Munich Personal RePEc Archive (MPRA) MPRA Paper No. 19535. Available online at https://mpra.ub.uni-muenchen.de/19535/

Bernardi, L., Barreix, A., Marrenza, A., & Projeta, P. (2007). *Tax Systems and Tax Reform in Latin America.* SIEP Working Paper 591. Parva: Societa Italiana di Economia Pubblica.

Buainain, A. M. & da Silveira, J. M. (2002). *Structural reforms and food security in Brazil.* Academic Press.

Chang, R., Kaltani, L., & Loayza, N. (2009). Openness can be Good for Growth: The Role of Policy Complementarities. *Journal of Development Economics, 90*(1), 33–49. doi:10.1016/j.jdeveco.2008.06.011

Daumal, M., & Özyurt, S. (2011). The Impact of International Trade Flows on Economic Growth in Brazilian States. *Revista de Economia Institucional, 2*(1), 5. Advance online publication. doi:10.5202/rei.v2i1.5

Davies, A., & Quinlivan, G. (2006). A panel data analysis of the impact of trade on human development. *Journal of Socio-Economics, 35*(5), 868–876. doi:10.1016/j.socec.2005.11.048

Gomes, L. (2020). *Brazil's economic growth strategy: the last two decades (1999-2019).* Munich Personal RePEc Archive (MPRA) Paper No. 104874. Available at https://mpra.ub.uni-muenchen.de/104874/

Hsing, Y. (2003). Impacts Of External Debt And Other Macroeconomic Policies On Output In Brazil: VAR Approach. *Revista de Análisis Económico, 18*(2), 97–108.

Kesar, A., Bandi, K., Jena, P. K., & Yadav, M. P. (2022). Dynamics of governance, gross capital formation, and growth: Evidence from Brazil, Russia, India, China, and South Africa. *Journal of Public Affairs*, *2022*(e2831), 1–14. doi:10.1002/pa.2831

Kharusi, S. A., & Ada, M. S. (2018). External debt and economic growth: The case of emerging economy. *Journal of Economic Integration*, *33*(1), 1141–1157. doi:10.11130/jei.2018.33.1.1141

Mora, M., & Giambiagi, F. (2005). *Federalismo e Endividamento Subnacional: Uma Discussão sobre a Sustentabilidade da Dívida Estadual e Municipal. TD 1142*. Instituto de Pesquisa Econômica Aplicada.

MoreiraM. M. (2009). Brazil's Trade Policy: Old and New Issues. Published by the Inter-American Development Bank. Available online at https://ssrn.com/abstract=1555947

Nweke, G. O., Odo, S. I., & Anoke, C. I. (2017). Effect of capital formation on economic growth in Nigeria. *Asian Journal of Economics. Business and Accounting*, *5*(1), 1–16. doi:10.9734/AJEBA/2017/36075

Ofori-Abebrese, G., Pickson, R. B., & Diabah, B. T. (2017). Financial Development and Economic Growth: Additional Evidence from Ghana. *Modern Economy*, *8*(2), 282–297. doi:10.4236/me.2017.82020

Orji, A., Nwagu, G. U., Ogbuabor, J. E., & Anthony-Orji, O. I. (2021). Foreign Direct Investment and Growth Nexus: Further Evidence from Africa's Largest Economy. *Journal of Infrastructure Development*, *13*(1), 65–78. doi:10.1177/09749306211024433

Pesaran, M. H., Shin, Y., & Smith, R. (2001). Bounds testing approaches to the analysis of level relationships. *Journal of Applied Econometrics*, *16*(3), 289–326. doi:10.1002/jae.616

Roett, R. (2010). *The New Brazil*. Brookings Institution Press.

Shahzad, U., Hussain, M., Qin, F., & Muhamadi, S. (2019). Role of FDI and Foreign Remittances in Boosting Economic Growth: Evidence from Brazil. *European Online Journal of Natural and Social Sciences*, *8*(1), 118–127.

Texto para Discussão. IE/UNICAMP n. 107, mar. 2002.

Chapter 7
Finance and Economic Development in Indonesia:
Post Cold War

Ukpabi Innocent Ogbu
University of Nigeria, Nsukka, Nigeria

ABSTRACT

The relationship between finance and economic development in Indonesia was assessed from 1980 to 2019 using the generalized least model. Indonesia witnessed significant improvement in the financial system and infrastructure, but this was not translated into development. Conventionally, the negative and nonsignificant relationship between the financial development index (FDI) and the human development index (HDI) and positive and nonsignificant relationship between FDI and gross fixed capital formation (GFCF). Private consumption (PRC) and GFCF/HDI revealed positive and statistically significant. Government capital expenditure (GCE) and external reserve (EXR) depict a negative and significant relationship on HDI and GFCF, respectively. A standardized corporate social responsibility was administered to financial institutions and markets to promote social welfare, and the introduction of special credit allocation was to fund infrastructural gaps and adequately monitor the special allocation fund projects. Regulation of luxuries via fiscal policy promote local production/consumption.

1. INTRODUCTION

Indonesia as an Archipelago country located off the coast of mainland, Southeast Asia and comprises 17,500 islands, 1,916,907 square kilometer and population of

DOI: 10.4018/979-8-3693-1610-8.ch007

275,400,000 people. Indonesia gained her independence from Dutch in 1945 and practices a presidential representative democracy, where the president is both head of state and government with a multi-party system. This pacific country goes to the poll to elect the president, members of the House of Representatives, regional representative council, members of provincial and district parliaments every five years, and also vote for governors, mayors, district leaders and village heads. The industrial sector dominates the Indonesian economy, with petroleum and natural gas, textiles and apparel, mining, footwear, plywood, garments, rubber and chemical fertilizers constituting major exports and the services sector contributing significantly to the economy. In 1999 the people of East Timor voted for independence from Indonesia, which was granted; after a period under UN supervision and achieved full sovereignty in 2002. In 2004 a large tsunami generated by an earthquake off the western coast of Sumatra caused widespread death and destruction in Indonesia. However, Indonesia is one of the emerging markets, member of MINT economic bloc and G20. Indonesia is the 17th largest economy in the world by nominal GDP and the 7th largest in terms of GDP (PPP), estimated at US$40 billion in 2019. This formerly Netherlands East Indies as the world's fourth most populous nation and predicted by Joko Widodo to be the 4th largest economy in the world by 2045 is expected to have a coordinated economic framework to harness and bridge the existing gap between developing financial architecture and macroeconomic development. Indonesian Law No. 33 of 2004 provides for special allocation fund in a large portion to education, health, and infrastructural sectors to assist in the funding of specific regional projects that conforms with the national priorities. But the relationship with economic development remains contentious especially in area of education, life expectancy at birth, gross national income (GNI) per capita and basic social amenities. Therefore, the study is a post cold war nexus between finance and economic development in Indonesia, 1980 to 2019.

1. LITERATURE REVIEW

2.1 Indonesia's Financial System Development

Conceptually, financial system is the improvement in the aggregated components of the financial sector, encompassing the regulatory authorities, the financial institutions and the financial markets in an economy. Financial system development is measured by relative ranking of countries on the depth, access, efficiency and stability of the financial institutions and financial markets (IMF, 2018). It is an aggregate of the financial institutions index (FI) and the financial markets index (FM). Tariq, Tariq, Khan and Rahman (2020) posit that financial development deals with the policies,

Figure 1. Indonesia's financial development index (actual) and the IMF benchmark for emerging markets (B.MARK), 1980-2019.

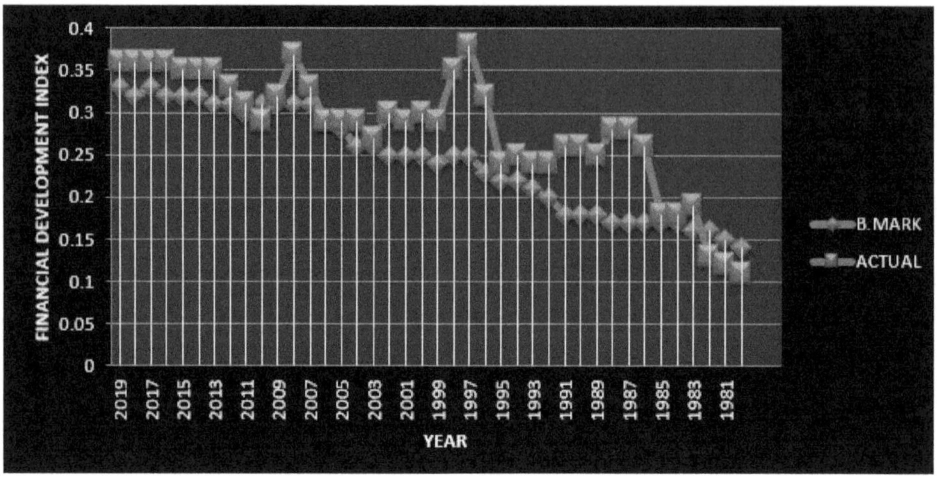

processes and strategies to enhance access, depth, and efficiency of the financial institutions and financial markets. Invariably, Indonesia as an emerging market is engulfed by a developing financial system as signified in chart 2.1.1 below. In recent years, the government has taken important steps to strengthen the financial sector, particularly the financial oversight and crisis management (Alfirman in Washington, 2020). However, Ismail (2015) asserts that the Indonesian financial sector remains small and far more dominated by banks than its regional peers attributed to fragmented regulatory structure, regulatory framework not in line with international best practices, and an enabling environment that is less conducive for financial sector development, including lack of diversity in capital market products.

Comparatively, the actual financial development index of Indonesia outweighs the International Monetary Fund (IMF) bench mark for emerging markets throughout the period of 1980 to 2019 except in 2010, 1982, 1981 and 1980 with the ratios of 31:29, 16:13, 15:12 and 14:11 respectively. The actual financial development index (FDI) slightly moved above the benchmark on forty year average of 0.28% and 0.24% respectively and reached equilibrium point of 0.29% in 2006. The Indonesia's FDI within the period under review climaxed in 1997 followed by 2008 with 0.38% and 0.37% respectively, and recorded 0.11% as the minimum in 1980 and consecutively dampened by 0.02% from 2010 to 2012. However, the FDI recorded a three year constant growth from 2004 to 2006, 2013 to 2015, and a four year unchanged development from 2016 to 2019 by 0.29%, 0.35% and 0.36% respectively. This affirmed Dewi et al (2018) submission that several multi-lateral agencies, including the World Bank, Asian Development Bank, and International Monetary Fund have long been supporting the development of the financial sector in Indonesia to attract foreign resources as part of broader efforts to develop the economy.

1.1. 2 Indonesia's Economic Development

Economic development is the phase of economic performance which measures how the living standard of the citizenry is been transformed or improved, including human and infrastructural development in an economy. Nugroho, Wicaksono and Reynald (2021) postulate that human development can be used as an indicator for the development of country, a country is categorized as a developed country based not only on the gross domestic product (GDP) but also on such aspects as life expectancy and education level of its citizens. Human development is an effort to enhance people's opportunity to achieve a decent life, which can be done through upgrading basic capacity and increasing purchasing power (Widodo, Waridin and Kodoatie 2011 in Nugroho, Wicaksono and Reynald, 2021). Kahkonen in Washington (2020) states that Indonesia's macroeconomic fundamentals continue to be strong, that the country's poverty rate has reached single digits, the lowest level ever. Chart 2.1.2 below shows the trends in human and infrastructural development in Indonesia, from 1980 to 2019. In this context the author utilized two measures of economic development, human development index (HDI) and gross fixed capital formation (GFCF). HDI is the index mean of years of schooling, expected years of schooling, life expectancy at birth and gross national income (GNI) per capita. GFCF presents the aggregate investment in infrastructure and social services. It's measured by the total value of a producer's acquisitions, less disposals of fixed assets in additions to the value of non- produced assets, including subsoil assets or major improvements in the quantity, quality or productivity of land realized by the productive activity of institutional units. However, Indonesian Law No. 33 of 2004 provides the special allocation funds in a large portion to education, health, and infrastructure sectors. (Nugroho, Wicaksono and Reynald, 2021).

Chart 2.1.2 above depicts inconsistent movements in Indonesia's GFCF and HDI. GFCF maintained positive trends throughout period with a forty year moving average of 7.5%, excluding the sharp decline in 1998, 1999 and a slight one in 1984 by -33%, -18.2 and -6% respectively. However, HDI recorded 1% on a forty moving average, with highest uptrend in 1982 (6.49%) followed by 1984 (5.86%). Positive trends were recorded in Indonesia's HDI throughout the period, except a sharp and slight decline witnessed in 1981 (-12.7%) and 1983 (-3%).

Figure 2. Indonesia's gross fixed capital formation (GFCF) and human development index (HDI), 1980-2019

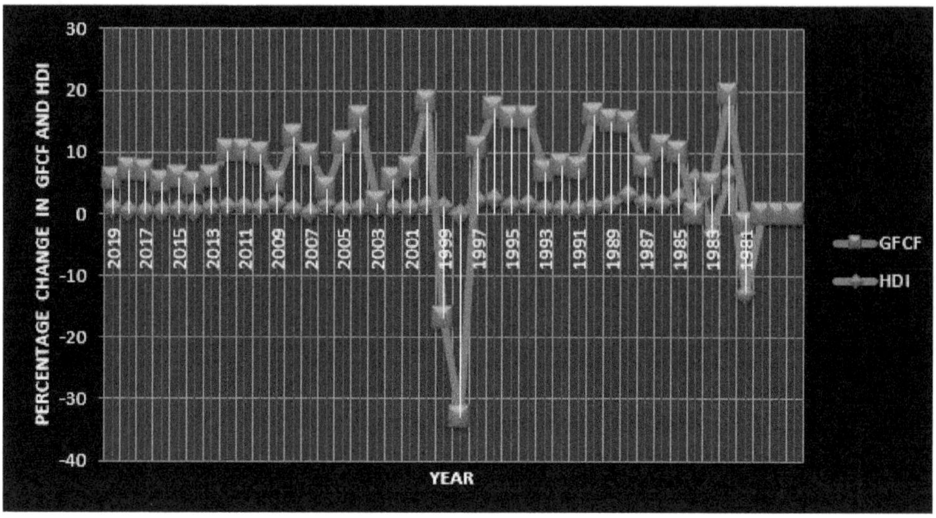

2.1.3 Indonesia's Finance and Infrastructural Development

The relationship between finance and infrastructural development in Indonesia posit as a surveying reference point marked with a pile of stones left by prospectors untapped. Alfirman in Washington (2020) asserts that accelerating of reforms that promote financial depth, access, efficiency and inclusion while not compromising stability is now needed to finance the infrastructure gap and broaden economic opportunities for individuals and firms in Indonesia" as the limited availability of financial services and lack of incentives for long-term savings creates further risks for individuals and restricts investment opportunities in critical sectors, such as infrastructure. Chart 2.1.3 above revealed that the aggregate financial system depth, access and efficiency portrayed by the actualized FDI in Indonesia surpasses the international standard for emerging markets, but how this development in finance is briskly accompanied by infrastructural development remains contemptuous. Therefore, the relationship between finance and infrastructural development in Indonesia was graphically presented in chart 1.3 below.

Chart 2.1.3 above shows uncorrelated relationship between the growth in FDI and GFCF. Whereas the FDI trends moved on a forty year average of 2.3%, GFCF recorded 7.5% average growth leaving a wide margin. FDI growth reached apex in 1983 with 31.58% followed by 1986 and 1996 respectively. Whereas GFCF maintained positive trends throughout the period excluding a sharp decline in 1998, 1999 and a slight one in 1984 by -33%, -18.2 and -6% respectively, FDI was

Figure 3. Trend of Indonesia's financial development index (FDI) and gross fixed capital formation (GFCF), 1980-2019

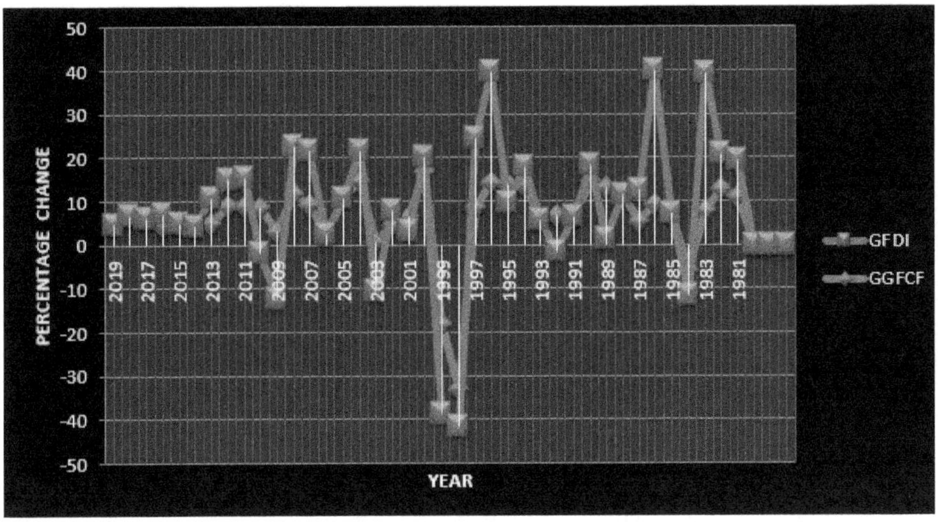

inconsecutively dampened in ten years with the highest rate in 1999 (- 20.69%) followed 2009 (-15.63%), others are 2010, 2003, 2001, 1998, 1995, 1992, 1989 and 1984 by -10.34%, -11.11%, -3.45%, -8.57%, -4.17%, -8.33%, -12% and -5.56% respectively. This uncorrelated trends in FDI and GFCF confirmed the submission of Wasiaturrahma, Rizal and Ajija (2019) that the role of financial intermediaries in Indonesia is mostly limited to saving and borrowing funds.

2.1.4 Indonesia's Finance and Human Development

Financial development is a veritable tool that plays catalytic role for sustainable economic development especially emerging economies. A sound and well-functioning financial sector is critical to sustain Indonesia's growth and to achieve the government's economic goals, particularly amidst the continued challenging global conditions (Kahkonen in Washington, 2020). Therefore, examining the relationship between financial sector performance and human development explores other phase of economic performance measures, dealing on how the economy affects the living standard of citizenry especially in area of social welfare. Chart 2.1.4 below presents the relationship between financial system performance and human development in Indonesia.

Comparatively, chart 2.1.4 depicts uncorrelated relationship between FDI and HDI throughout the period. Whereas the growth in FDI was 2.3% on a forty year average, HDI recorded 1% with highest uptrend in 1982 (6.49%) followed by 1984

Figure 4. Indonesia's financial development index (FDI) and human development index (HDI), and 1980-2019

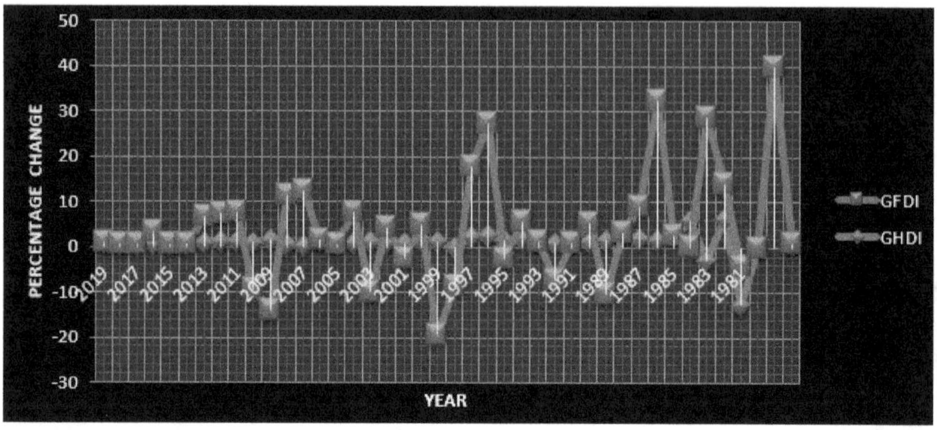

(5.86%). FDI trends apexed in 1983 with 31.58% followed by 1986 and 1996 respectively. Whereas FDI growth rates were lulled inconsistently in ten years with maximum decline in 1999 (-20.69%) followed 2009 (-15.63%), others negative trends were recorded in 2010, 2003, 2001, 1998, 1995, 1992, 1989 and 1984 by -10.34%, -11.11%, -3.45%, -8.57%, -4.17%, -8.33%, -12% and -5.56% respectively. HDI recorded positive trends throughout the period, except in 1981 and 1983 by -12.7% and -3% respectively. It could be deduced that financial system development in Indonesia did not significant influence human development as the state was unable to fully utilize the enormous benefits of financial development for the welfare of the people. This affirmed Basuki et al. (2020) assertion that strengthening the domestic economic cooperation becomes even more problematic when the state is unable to provide health insurance and decent quality of life for its citizens, failing in reducing inequality among regions and inequality of national income.

2.1.5 Significance of Finance on Economic Development

The economic importance of finance remains inexhaustible. Development of an economy requires its financial sector to be developed (Guru and Yadav, 2019). According to Levine (2005) in Dewi et al (2018), the financial sector plays six basic functions in the economy, namely: (i) mobilization of savings; (ii) management of risks; (iii) gathering of information about investment opportunities; (iv) exerting control for companies; (v) facilitating transactions; and (vi) promoting the exchange of goods and services. Adekunle, Salami and Adedipe (2013) in Idachaba, Olukotun and Elam (2019) avert that a well developed financial system plays several critical roles to boost the efficiency of intermediation through reduction of information, transaction and monitoring costs. It will also enhance investment by identifying and funding business opportunities, mobilize savings, encourage trading, hedging and diversification of risk, well as facilitates exchange of goods and services. All these results into efficient allocation of resources, accumulation of physical and human capital and faster technological progress, which in turn leads to economic growth and development. Imoagwu and Ezeanyeji (2019) stress that financial system play a vital role in economic development and acknowledged that financial development is a multidimensional concept which constitutes a potentially important mechanism for long run economic growth and development.

2.2 Theoretical Review

Theoretically, the financial sector has a strong link with the real economy through the provision of financial resources to the factors of production, stimulating the production of real output, increasing job opportunities, and reducing poverty levels. Ironically, in many cases, countries experiencing rapid financial development have exhibited greater income inequality, suggesting that efforts to reduce poverty may not have been realized despite rapid development in the financial sector (Dewi et al. 2018). The study was anchored on Legal Theory of Finance (LTF), which states that countries where legal systems enforce private property rights, support private contractual arrangements, and protect the legal right of investors, savers would be more willing to finance firms and financial system flourish. According to Pistor (2013) in Ukpabi, Iyodo and Abdul-Maliq (2021), the LTF postulates that financial markets are constructed legally and ensconced in a hybrid location between market and state, as confidence in the financial sector encourage investors to allocate her savings through financial system rather than to invest in non-productive assets in order to hedge against inflation or the risk of financial collapse (Chittedi, 2014).

LTF posits law as fundamental to modern finance, as it offers authority to private and public financial instruments; and validates financial instruments generated from private contracts if they are consistent with the law (Sarpong and Deodutt, 2019). Levine (2001) Avers that legal adaptability, channel of the law and finance theory holds that legal traditions differ in terms of their ability to adapt to changing commercial and financial circumstances and that legal systems that adapt more effectively to changing conditions will concomitantly support financial development more effectively. Arguably, significance of law to finance has increased with the transition from relational finance to entity and ultimately, market based finance. Financial instrument fungibility in anonymous markets depends on credible contractual commitments that can be legally enforced (Ukpabi, Iyodo and Abdul-Maliq, 2021). Laws and its enforcement influences the nexus of finance and economic development, as it affects acquisitions and utilization of financial resource for economic emancipations especially in developing economies bedeviled with bribery and corruption.

2.3 Empirical Review

Existing literature in this area of intellectual contests conducted in different countries, regions and economic blocs were approached with different techniques, variables and scopes. Jumono et al. (2021) examined the relation between the real sector and the financial sector in underdeveloped areas in Nusa Tenggara, Indonesia from 2008 to 2019. VAR/VECM analytical techniques were utilized, economic growth, inflation; liquidity and NPL at the provincial level were applied as variables. The study revealed a phenomenon of cost-push inflation in East Nusa Tenggara, negative relation between inflation and economic growth. Liquidity had positive impact on inflation and economic growth had negative impact on inflation. While, in West Nusa Tenggara, the impact of economic growth on inflation was positive, but the impact of liquidity and NPL on inflation and economic growth was negative. Basuki et al. (2020) analyzed the effect of public spending, macroeconomic variables, and BPK opinion on economic growth using dynamic panel regression model. Findings showed a short term population effect on regional economic growth, the economic growth was affected by the number of people, the poor in the long term. The long term general allocation fund became an obstacle to economic growth and fiscal policies carried out by local governments made small and ineffective contribution to promoting economic growth. Eko and Abdul (2021) explored the basic elements of macroeconomics and finance that are key to the transformation of China's economy and provided lessons for Indonesia's future economic transformation. The analysis of various studies and comparison of policy strategies between the two countries concluded that Indonesia needs to focus on fixing four critical elements for its successful economic transformation by promoting economic competitiveness focusing on aspects of infrastructure, human resources, technology, and institutions; boosting capacity and capability of the industry; optimizing the rapid growth of the digital economy and increasing the deepening of the financial sector for sources of financing.

However, Gupta (2021) determined the mechanisms and policies improve access to finance and encourage productivity growth through more effective matching of capital with labour, and the use of global best practices. Results indicated that the Indonesian economy could benefit substantially if the government allows a short-term trade deficit, as the potential gains for the Indonesian economy were shown using an extension of the global trade analysis project (GTAP) model, which covers possible changes in the cost of capital. Eko and Abdul (2021) investigated the need for Indonesia industrial upgrading, which is oriented towards high value added activities, utilizing medium and high technology. Findings revealed that increasing the capacity for innovation is an important supporting factor in providing a better impact on the industrial upgrading process. Dewi et al (2018) explored the inter linkages between financial sector development and poverty reduction in Indonesia from 1980 to 2015. The study adopted the autoregressive distributed lag (ARDL) cointegration approach to examine the long-run relationship between the variables. The study found a long-run relationship between financial development, economic growth, and poverty reduction in Indonesia. And revealed a unidirectional causality running from the financial sector to poverty reduction and a bidirectional causality between economic growth and poverty reduction. Nugroho, Wicaksono and Reynald (2021) examined the influence of the special allocation fund for education, health, and infrastructure on the poverty rate in Indonesia, using the poverty gap index (P1) as a proxy for the poverty rate. The study employed annual data from 33 Indonesian provinces from 2015 to 2018 and panel data regression analysis, utilizing the fixed effects model (FEM). Results revealed that the special allocation fund for education and health had a negative and significant impact on poverty, but the special allocation fund for infrastructure had a positive but not significant impact on poverty.

Erlando, Riyanto and Masakazu (2020) analyzed the contribution of the financial inclusion to economic growth, poverty alleviation and income inequality in Eastern Indonesia, using the Toda-Yamamoto VAR bivariate causality model and the dynamic panel vector autoregression (PVAR). Results of the bivariate causality model indicated a high relationship level between financial inclusion, economic growth, poverty and income distribution in Eastern Indonesia. The socio-economic growth had a positive impact on the level of financial inclusion, with a negative impact on poverty; financial inclusion had a positive effect on inequality, which leads to widespread income inequality in Eastern Indonesia. Hidayatinnisa et al. (2021) assessed the effect of financial literacy and financial inclusion on economic growth in Indonesia in 34 provinces, 2016 to 2019, using panel data regression. The results showed that financial literacy and financial inclusion had no significant effect on economic growth in Indonesia, neither partially or simultaneously. Dularif (2010) investigated the relationship between financial development and economic growth in Indonesia, from 1968 to 2009. A vector autoregressive was employed in analyzing the financial depth, role of commercial banks and credit to private sectors as three measurements of financial development. Results depicted that financial development in Indonesia does not have a significant positive impact on economic growth. Wasiaturrahma, Rizal and Ajija (2019) investigated the impact of financial deepening on economic growth in Indonesia, applying ARDL and error correction model (ECM). The results indicated that financial deepening had a significant negative impact on economic growth in Indonesia.

2. METHODOLOGY AND DATA ANALYSIS

The "ex-post facto" research design was adopted in this study to utilize secondary data that cannot be manipulated. A generalized linear model (GLM), precisely exponential regression as the most plausible technique to estimate the relationship between finance and economic development and the model was estimated at 5% level of significance. A GLM assumes independent random variables following a linear exponential family distribution with density and exponential regression model falls into this GLM framework with a log link and normal family. Models were specified thus:

$$HDI = f(\beta_0 + \beta_1 FDI_i + \beta_2 GCE_i + \beta_3 PR_i) + \epsilon_i \text{ .... (I)}$$

$$GFCF = f(\beta_0 + \beta_1 FDI_i + \beta_2 PRC_i + \beta_3 EXR_i) + \epsilon_i \text{ .... (II)}$$

Where: HDI is human development index, FDI is financial development index, GCE is government capital expenditure, PRC = Private consumption, GFCF is gross fixed capital formation and EXR is external reserve. β_0 is constant and ϵ is error term.

Preliminary Analysis

Econometrically, data that are not stationary produces spurious results. Consequently, Augmented Dickey-Fuller (ADF) unit root test was conducted to test the stationarity of the data to avoid wrong decisions due to unreliable results. Table 3.1 below presents the results of ADF unit root test of variables.

Table 1. Results of ADF unit root test

VARIABLE	ADF TEST STATISTIC	1% CRITICAL VALUE	5% CRITICAL VALUE	10% CRITICAL VALUE	TEST FOR UNIT	DURBIN WATSON STAT	PROBABILITY VALUE
FDI	-5.734118	-3.621023	-2.943427	-2.610263	1(1)	1.921002	0.0000
GFCF	-5.220034	-3.615588	-2.941145	-2.609066	1(0)	1.902675	0.0001
HDI	-3.852433	-3.626784	-2.945842	-2.611531	1(0)	1.634333	0.0056
GCE	-7.769246	-3.626784	-2.945842	-2.611531	1(2)	1.994220	0.0000
PRC	-4.368712	-3.621023	-2.943427	-2.610263	1(1)	1.962438	0.00014
EXR	-7.264879	-3.621023	-2.943427	-2.610263	1(1)	2.068562	0.0000

Source: Researcher's computation from E-Views results.

Table 2. ALM results

Dependent Variable: HDI				
Method: Generalized Linear Model (Newton-Raphson / Marquardt steps)				
Date: 06/02/22 Time: 08:32				
Sample (adjusted): 1981 2019				
Included observations: 39 after adjustments				
Family: Normal				
Link: Identity				
Dispersion computed using Pearson Chi-Square				
Convergence achieved after 0 iterations				
Coefficient covariance computed using observed Hessian				
Variable	Coefficient	Std. Error	z-Statistic	Prob.
C	46.73753	1.210910	38.59703	0.0000
FDI	-0.099655	0.174182	-0.572129	0.5672
GCE	-0.173707	0.042026	-4.133296	0.0000
PRC	0.150589	0.024776	6.078051	0.0000
Mean dependent var	59.10513	S.D. dependent var		8.576067
Sum squared resid	449.6474	Log likelihood		-103.1244
Akaike info criterion	5.493557	Schwarz criterion		5.664179
Hannan-Quinn criter.	5.554774	Deviance		449.6474
Deviance statistic	12.84707	Restr. deviance		2794.859
LR statistic	182.5484	Prob(LR statistic)		0.000000
Pearson SSR	449.6474	Pearson statistic		12.84707
Dispersion	12.84707			

HDI = 46.7375 - 0.09965FDI - 0.1737GCE + 0.15059PRC.

Table 3. GLM results

Dependent Variable: GFCF				
Method: Generalized Linear Model (Newton-Raphson / Marquardt steps)				
Date: 06/02/22 Time: 08:38				
Sample (adjusted): 1981 2019				
Included observations: 39 after adjustments				
Family: Normal				
Link: Identity				
Dispersion computed using Pearson Chi-Square				
Convergence achieved after 1 iteration				
Coefficient covariance computed using observed Hessian				
Variable	Coefficient	Std. Error	z-Statistic	Prob.
C	-13.58479	3.223538	-4.214249	0.0000
FDI	0.200318	0.576901	0.347231	0.7284
PRC	0.649316	0.034412	18.86862	0.0000
EXR	-0.003032	0.000759	-3.994411	0.0001
Mean dependent var	112.9259	S.D. dependent var		117.3321
Sum squared resid	4401.317	Log likelihood		-147.6077
Akaike info criterion	7.774752	Schwarz criterion		7.945374
Hannan-Quinn criter.	7.835970	Deviance		4401.317
Deviance statistic	125.7519	Restr. deviance		523139.2
LR statistic	4125.090	Prob(LR statistic)		0.000000
Pearson SSR	4401.317	Pearson statistic		125.7519
Dispersion	125.7519			

GFCF = -13.5848 + 0.2003FDI + 0.6493PRC - 0.0030EXR

The result of the unit root test in table 3.1 above reveals that the variables attained stationarity at 1%, 5% and 10% critical values for the independent, dependent and control variables. FDI, PRC and EXR variables were integrated in order one, by attaining stationarity at first difference 1(1). GFCF and HDI attained stationarity at level form, while GCE was integrated in order two by attaining stationarity at second difference. Obviously, the calculated ADF test Statistic values for all the variables were less than the critical values and the probability values less than one (1) for each of the variable tested. These further confirmed their stationarities. Moreover, to confirm the reliability of these results, the Durbin-Watson statistic values at each point were very significant at either 2.00 or approximately 2.00, indicating absence of the traits of serial autocorrelation in the time series data.

The coefficient estimates indicate that FDI is negatively related to the HDI and the relationship is statistically non significant at conventional level. The GCE dummy variable is negatively related to HDI, but the relationship is statistically significant. While the PRC dummy variable is positively related to HDI and the relationship is statistically significant. However, the deviance, deviance statistic, restricted deviance for this model is with only a constant, and the corresponding LR test statistic and probability, indicating that the FDI, GCE and PRC variables are jointly significant at roughly the 0% level. The sum of squared Pearson residuals and the estimate of the dispersion in this result is the Pearson statistic.

The coefficient estimates indicate that FDI and PRC is positively related to the GFCF, but only that of dummy variable (PRC) is statistically significant at conventional level. Whereas the EXR dummy variable is negatively related to GFCF, but the relationship is statistically significant. However, the deviance, deviance statistic, restricted deviance for this model is with only a constant, and the corresponding LR test statistic and probability indicating that the FDI, PRC and EXR variables are jointly significant at roughly the 0% level. The sum-of-squared Pearson residuals and the estimate of the dispersion in this result is the Pearson statistic.

3. CONCLUSION/IMPLICATION OF RESULTS AND RECOMMENDATIONS

Generally, the study assessed finance and economic development nexus in Indonesia, graphically analyzed their trends, explored the empirical evidence on its significance and specifically examined the relationship between finance system development and infrastructural/human development. Analytically, the interwoven of finance and economic development in Indonesia were practically despicable compared to its potency, this contempt needs vigorous mechanism to avert its exacerbation as finance pivots emerging markets potentials. The graphical analysis depicts that

Indonesia witnessed significant improvement in the financial system development and infrastructure, but such was not translated to social welfare. The negative and non significant relationship between financial development and human development at the conventional level implies that financial system development have not briskly impacted on social welfare, which is line with Wasiaturrahma, Rizal and Ajija (2019) results. The positive and non significant relationship between financial development and infrastructural depicts that financial system development in Indonesia impacted positively on her infrastructural development but at a slow pace compared to expectations, which corroborates Hidayatinnisa et al. (2021) . The positive and statistically significant relationship between private consumption dummy variable and endogenous variables implies that consumption of domestic products impact positively on economic development. The negative and significant relationship between government capital expenditure/external reserve dummy variables and human development/gross fixed capital formation posits that capital investments in Indonesia were not judiciously utilized across the priority sectors and that jeopardized the special allocation funds statute. Base on findings, the researcher recommends that a standardized corporate social responsibility should be administered to financial institutions and markets to promote social welfare of citizens, monetary authorities should introduce special credit allocation to fund infrastructural gap in Indonesia and adequately monitor the special allocation fund projects. Private consumption should be regulated via fiscal policy by increasing the rate of value added tax on imported/luxurious goods to promote local production/consumption.

REFERENCES

Basuki, A. T. (2020). Determinants of economic growth in Indonesia: A dynamic panel model. *Journal of Asian Finance, Economics and Business, 7*(11), 147-156. doi:10.13106/jafeb.2020.vol7.no11.147

Dewi, S. (2018). Dynamics of financial development,economic growth, and poverty alleviation: The Indonesian experience. *South East European Journal of Economics and Business, 13*(1), 17-30. doi:10.2478/jeb-2018-0002

Dularif, M. (2010). Financial development and economic growth: An empirical analysis of Indonesia. *Jurnal BPPK, 1*(4), 93–131.

Eko, L., & Abdul, M. P. (2021). Indonesia's macroeconomic and finance policy framework for structural transformation. United Nations conference on trade and development.

Erlando, A., Riyanto, F. D., & Masakazu, S. (2020). Financial inclusion, economic growth, and poverty alleviation: Evidence from eastern Indonesia. *Heliyon*, *6*(10), e05235. Advance online publication. doi:10.1016/j.heliyon.2020.e05235 PMID:33088971

Gupta, K. (2021). The importance of financial liberalisation for economic growth: The case of Indonesia. *Bulletin of Indonesian Economic Studies*, *57*(2), 175–201. doi:10.1080/00074918.2020.1747596

Guru, B. K., & Yadav, I. S. (2019). Financial development and economic growth: Panel evidence from BRICS. *Journal of Economics, Finance and Administrative Science*, *24*(47), 113–126. doi:10.1108/JEFAS-12-2017-0125

Hidayatinnisa. (2021). The effect of financial literacy and financial inclusion on economic growth in Indonesia. *Jurnal Bisnis, Manajemen dan Perbankan, 7*(2), 339-359. doi:10.21070/jbmp.v7vi2.1539

Imoagwu, C. P., & Ezeanyeji, C. I. (2019). Financial Development and Economic Growth Nexus in Nigeria. *International Journal of Business and Management Invention*, *8*(3), 50–63. www.ijbmi.org

Ismail, M. S. (2015). *Indonesia finance sector assessment*. Asian Development Bank.

Jumono, S. (2021). Bank liquidity and economic development in underdeveloped regions: An empirical study in Indonesia. *Journal of Asian Finance, Economics and Business, 8*(7), 31-42. doi:10.13106/jafeb.2021.vol8.no7.0031

Nugroho, D. F., Wicaksono, B. R., & Reynald, M. R. (2021). Special allocation fund and poverty rate in Indonesia. *Economics and Finance in Indonesia, 67*(2), 257-269.

Tariq, R., Khan, M. A., & Rahman, A. (2020). How does financial development impact economic growth in Pakistan? New Evidence from Threshold Model. *Journal of Asian Finance, Economics and Business, 7*(8), 161-173. doi:10.13106/jafeb.2020.vol7.no8.161

Ukpabi, Iyodo, & Abdul-Maliq. (2021). Financial system development in emerging economies: An array of mint economic bloc. *International Journal of Science and Technoledge*, *9*(6), 39-46. doi:10.24940/theijst/2021/v9/i6/ST2106-003

Washington. (2020). *Reforms in Indonesia's financial sector open new economic opportunities.* Press release no: 2020/141/EAP.

Wasiaturrahma, R. M., & Ajija, S. R. (2019). Financial deepening and economic growth in Indonesia. *Media Trend*, *14*(1), 24-32. doi:10.21107/mediatrend.v14i1.455225

Chapter 8
Finance and Economic Development Post Cold War:
The Case of Mexico

Yekeen Oku Abdul-Maliq
University of Abuja, Nigeria

ABSTRACT

This chapter is a detailed and critical study of Mexico, from the Mayan period to the arrival of the conquistadors in 1521. It also reviewed the country's political and economic development policies from independence in 1821/24 to date. Thirty-nine years (1981–1999) time series multivariate data were analyzed using an ARDL model. Results show that the independent variables, especially export, and private consumption expenditure accounted for as much as 95% variation in the dependent variable. The study discovered that Mexico's economic performance could have been much better but for low total factor productivity, large informal sector, and less than desirable level of domestic savings and investment. Addressing these and sustaining the drive towards FDI flows, export expansion, and increase in ease of doing business are suggested policy focus for Mexico going forward.

1.0 INTRODUCTION

Mexico: officially called, the United Mexican States, is one of the three largest countries that make up the continent of North America; the others being the United States of America, (the USA), to the immediate North of Mexico; and Canada further North.

DOI: 10.4018/979-8-3693-1610-8.ch008

With a population of approximately one hundred and twenty-eight million and six hundred thousand; (128.6 million; 2022 est.); (predominantly Catholics), Mexico operates a federal presidential system of government with a bi-cameral Legislature: Congress of the Union; the Upper House and the Chamber of Deputies, (the Lower House), at the Federal level; and similar legislative structures at the state level; thirty-one in number; each of which is sovereign in status. At the head of the Executive at the Federal level is an elected president while each state is equally headed by an elected Governor. (Alonso, 2004; Ramirez, 2021) among others.

The aborigines of Mexico were the Maya tribe; (Mesoamerican) who inhabited the land from about 250 to 900 AD. They were displaced by the Astecs from about 250AD, (Maiolo 2014). The Astecs settled and dominated the land until February 1519, when Spanish explolers/colonizers, invaded and quickly took over Mexico in the name of the Spanish Crown. Mexico thus became a vice royalty of Spain thus began Spanish colonization of Mexico by the conquerors (conquistadores), (Macnutt, 1909).

Neither Spaniards nor the conquistadores hid their intention; they were in New Spain, as in the Americas (the New World, in quest of Eldorado; (Gold) Oziah (2011).

Figure 1. Map of Mexico

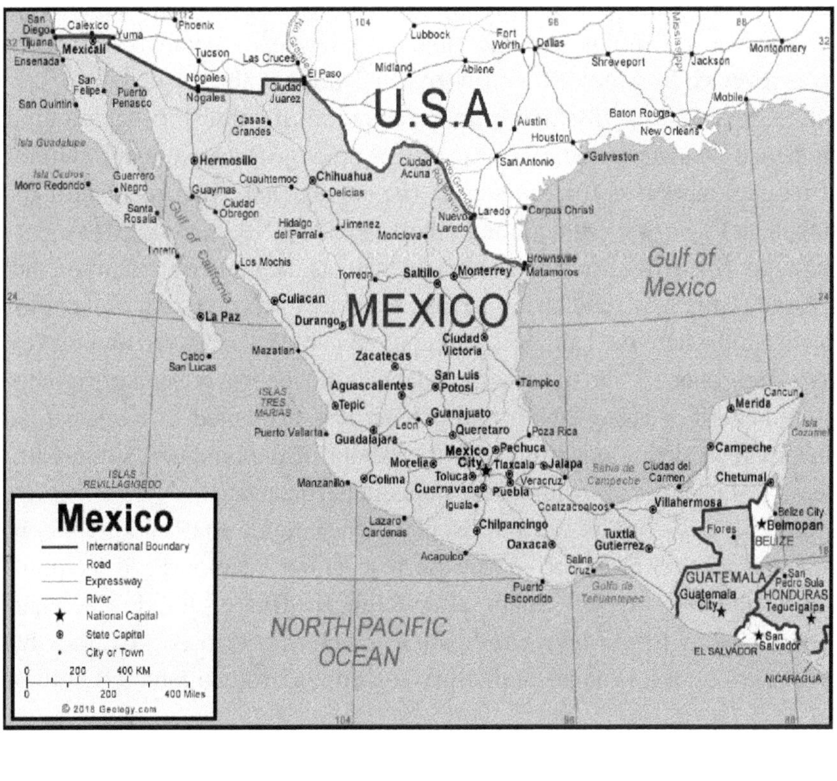

After establishing themselves as 'overlords', the *conquestatores* quickly established; or better still, perfected a seven-strata social class in Mexico. These were the *Peninsulaies*; people of Spaniard blood born in Spain and their uprisings and the *Cleoles*; also, of Spanish blood but born in Mexico or elsewhere other than Spain. Others were *mestioze* and *mullatoes;* people of mixed blood. Then came still below these, the Indian native Americans, Africans, and slaves in descending order of status or superiority; and with little or no difference between the last two (Hackle, 1997; Mecaa, Schwatz & Gubesic, 2009; & Flores and Telles, 2012).

2.0 MEXICO: THE COLONIAL/ERA

Spanish colonization of Mexico is a classic case of European colonial exploits; characterized by three major *modus operandi* (i) a firm and enforced master-slave class stratification; a *caste* system, as described above; (ii) a conscious and vicious enforcement of the 'capture of the mind', a systematic enforcement of the colonial masters' language, religion and culture in general on the colonized at the peril of severe and sometimes, dehumanizing punishment, (including death), for any sign of resistance, and (iii) politico-economic integration of the colony's economy into that of the 'home country'; in which the colony is a mere appendage of the home country and the colony is economically 'milked' to feed the home country. In the case of new-Mexico, things were the same if not worse, especially in the economic sphere as revealed by Meza, 2019; Ecker, 2022 among others.

In the case of Spanish-Mexico, colonial economic relationship, exploitation was accomplished by many principles or practices among which were agricultural and industrial exploitation via (i) *hacienda*: (ii) *encomienda*, (iii) mercantilism, (iv) bullionism, (v) *repartimiento,* among others (Meza, 2019; Anaya, 2023).

Although, Spain did not find gold in Mexico as they had dreamt, they did find silver, large fertile land, and cheap labour. Hacienda was a system of right to pure land ownership where the land of the conquered people was shared among key role players in the conquest. On the other hand, encomienda was a grant of right to land for use to benefit or enjoy labour and tribute. It is explained as a Spanish labour system that rewarded conquerors with the labour of the conquered non-Christian people; like Hacienda; but with lower status in permanence.

Mercantilism *per se* is the philosophy which holds that nations' economic development depends on export expansion, restrictions on import and accumulation of gold. In the case of New Spain, after failing to find el-dorado, mercantilism involved exporting from Mexico to Spain as much as possible and at rock-bottom prices, of agricultural produce and silver, mined with forced labour. On the other hand, imports from Spain to New Spain were at as high a price as possible, being determined, often, by the buyer rather than the seller.

Bullionism was another instrument of economic exploitation: a policy of mining silver at near-zero cost and shipping to Spain, the result of which was that silver miners had to work under conditions of near slavery (Hackle, 1997; Dobado & Morero, 2011).

Repartimiento was another economic policy or method by which Spain sapped Mexico. Repartimiento involved force farm labour of forty-five days each year by every Indian adult in large agricultural farm estates such as *haciendas* or encomienda held by individuals especially the peninsulies on which to grow corn, wheat, and rear cattles and sheeps.

From all indications, it will appear that these economic exploitative mechanisms were employed concurrently, and each emphasized or intensified as leaders and or conditions in Spain dictated.

2.1 Religion, Catholicism, and Colonization in Mexico

The role of Christianity; (Catholicism especially); in the economic and political lives of New Spain is well documented. According to various sources, for Spain, Catholicism was much more than just a religious institution. Spain, like all other colonialists deployed or employed religion to not only legitimize conquest and colonialism but also to justify subjugation and exploitation. As common with European colonizers, perhaps, from their Roman Empire reminiscences; the *Conquestaldors* were on a mission for Gold, Glory, and God.

Religion thus allowed Spain to justify its conquest and mis[rule]. To the Spaniards, like other colonialists, colonization was a mission to save souls, to continually transform, mold hearts and minds of the conquered people.

The role of the Virgin of Guadalupe among others, did not only help to introduce and indoctrinate Mexicans into Catholism, but it also helped to justify and cement whatever Spain did, in the eyes of Spainard, (Tuck, 2005; Yeh & Olagnibel (2011).

3.0 MEXICO'S ROUGH ROAD TO INDEPENDENCE

3.1 Decolonization of Mexico and the Mexican Revolution

As usual in colonial history, and in most Master-servant relationship; as time went on in Mexico, the colonized people became aware of their state of dishonor, deprivation, and exploitation, giving them courage, experiences and sometimes, direct, or indirect encouragement to revolt against their masters. In addition, social classes began to merge or at least, interact better, forge alliances and soon identified the colonialists as a common enemy and therefore began to unite in resistance.

In Mexico, this was exactly what happened. Drawing experience and courage, perhaps, from the American Revolution 1775-1783; French Revolution 1789 and Haitian Revolution 1789-1804 gave the Mexicans some impetus to agitate for freedom. After a long time, some forms of resistance, demands and even audacious anti-colonial actions, especially from 1808 or thereabout, became prevalent. Things came to a head on September 16th, 1810, when Father Miguel Hidaldo issued his Crito de Dolores and declared that Mexico was not Span. This inspired a huge uprising that became unstoppable. Leading to why that date is often recognized in Spanish-Mexican history as declaration of independence. Although, Father Miguel was tried, convicted, and eventually executed in Spain in 1811; the fire of independence struggle had been ignited. The Mexican war of independence lasted more than a decade (1810-1821) and eventually via the Treaty of Cordoba 4th October 1824; and finally based on the August 24th, 1824, *Constitution Federal de los Estados Unidos Mexicanos de* (Spanish) or the Federal Constitution of the United Mexican States. Mexico became independent of Spain (English). (Gueclea, 2000; Maiolo, 2014; Beeley & MacLachlan, 2009).

3.2 Post-Independence Mexico

Unfortunately, for Mexico, independence did not bring internal unity, peace, cohesion, and integration. In Mexico, immediately post-independence, personal crashes, intra as well as inter-group crises began, or better still, persisted. Things were so turbulent that Meza (2019) described it as a 'troubled start'.

So troubled was Mexico that the first President of the newly independent Mexico, Victoria Guadalupe's regime was so uneasy that his Vice tried twice (unsuccessfully, though) to overthrow him. Meza (2019) also, reports that between 1821 and 1850; a thirty-year period; Mexico experienced up to fifty changes in government.

Apart from these, Mexico faced two powerful foreign aggressions, (i) from Spain who tried unsuccessfully too, to recolonize her and (ii) Mexico's powerful neighbor to the North; the United State of America, which sooner disputed possession of large parts of Mexican territory. During this period, Mexico was either at war internally, at war with Spain or at war with the USA. (Archer, 2011; Beeley & MacLachlan, 2009).

The Mexico-Spanish wars of 1821-1825 was against Spain's attempt to recolonize Mexico; the Mexico-Spanish war of 1826-28 was Mexico's attempt to reposes her land while the Mexican-Spanish war of 1829 was a Mexican expedition, led by General Issidro Barrados to assert Mexico's sovereignty.

Worse still, Mexico had hardly settled down from her domestic squabbles and the Spanish intimidation than Mexico's giant neighbour to the North; the United State of America laid claims to Texas and some other hitherto Mexican territories. So, in a gruesome three-year war; between 1846 and 1848; Mexico was again at war; this time, with the USA. At the battle of Capitulation Castle in 1948, the USA defeated Mexico; and by the Treaty of Guadalupe Hidalgo, ('Treaty of Peace, Friendship, and Limits'), February 2nd 1848; Mexico lost up to fifty-five percent of its territory comprising of present day States of California, Nevada, Utah, New Mexico, most part of Arizona and Colorado as well as part of Oklahoma, Kansas and Wyoming to the US (Hepler & Lutz, 2021).

With the enemy or enemies within; the Satan from afar and the Jackals at the backyard; it can be understood what Meza (2019) meant by a troubled start.

In addition, other smaller nations, Guatemala, Honduras, El-Salvador, Costa Rica, Nicaragua, and others also 'escaped' from the Mexican territory.

In view of the above, it is not surprising that Mexico did not play any noticeable role in global economy and or politics; being dwarfed by the US on the one hand and saddled down by persistent domestic maneuverings on the other. In addition, the whole of North America did not play much role in global politics until World War II; and even then, except for the United State of America's late entry and more poignantly; Hiroshima and Nagasaki; the Americas did not come into the forefront of global politics and or economy until after WWII.

Although Mexico joined WWII *de facto* in 1942; one major connection she had with WWII was the *Brakoro* programme: a migrant labour scheme involving Mexicans going to work in farms, factories, or railroad construction in the US due to shortage of labor because of American citizens joining the war.

3.3 Mexico: Macroeconomic Management and Outcomes Post-World War II

The best place to start the empirical review of Mexico's political and economic history is perhaps with the work of Kirkwood Burton. (Burton, 2005). Although not an empirical study per se, but a historical account of Mexico from as far back as the commonly cited Mayan era, the Olmec era before then and even beyond.

The book then treats Mexico's history from the Spanish conquest to the three hundred years of colonization, 1521-1821. Kirkwood confirm that the Mexican struggle for independence started in earnest in 1808 and lasted till 1821; with Father Miguel Hidalgo's croites Doroles being a major catalyst in the struggle.

Kirkwood (2005) The book divided the history of Mexico's post-independence into six major phases: (i) the immediate post-independent period 1821-1876 (ii) the period of intense internal crises as well as external confrontations with Spain, the USA, France, and other smaller countries of the Spanish-Mexican empire and (iii) The era of porfiriato 1870-1911. According to Kirkwood, the Mexican revolution can be said to span three phases: the revolution per se, 1910-1920; the period of the consolidation of the revolution; 1920-1940 and the third phase being what the book described as when the revolution moved right: 1940-1970; what others describe as the era of liberalization, market reforms, opening and internationalization. The period between 1970 and 1999 is described as the era of searching for stability. The often-cited 2017 Mexican Constitution may therefore be adjudged as the beginning of political stability and economic prosperity in Mexico.

As said earlier, the above exposition is not an empirical review in the same light as what follows next, it provides a good timeline within which the empirical overviews that follow can be undertaken.

Empirical studies on the economic history of Mexico, from after WWII and even from the 1990s to date; are enormous. We shall therefore review only a few in this chapter, just to provide a glimpse into Mexico in the last six to eight decades.

Ros (1993) took a long-range view of the Mexican economy: from 1960-1990. The study broke down Mexican economic history into three broad phases. According to the author, 1960-70 was a period of import substitution, fixed exchange rate regime among other controls. The second phase; 1970-80, was export oriented while the last phase, 1980-1990 and beyond was geared towards policy reforms, entry into the global economy, trade liberalization and what not.

The study also reveals that history of Mexico between 1990 and 2017 has been that of economic (i) greater political stability, better national unity and cohesion (ii) steadier economic growth due to major reforms and global integration and (iii) a much-improved good neighborliness between her and the US. Mexico's admission into the organisation for Economic Cooperation and Development (OECD) in 1994 as an observer nation and the renewal of NAFTA and the major constitutional changes that resulted into the oft-referenced Mexico's Constitution of 2017 all point to Mexico's improved relation with the USA and the resultant benefits as well as internationalization of her economy.

However, the studies by Carstens and Wener (1999), Hanson (2012); among many others reached similar conclusions: that the Mexican economy did not benefit from its over three decades of modernization and reforms as much as expected. Factors accounting for this underperformance include financial crisis, especially, of 1994-1995, (Carsten and Werner, 1999); faulty credit *modus*, low credit to the private sector, financial instability, high informal sector, and what Hanson, (2012) described as perverse incentives, among others.

Kose, Meredith & Towe (2004) assessed the performance of the Mexican economy vis-à-vis her entry into NAFTA; especially as it relates to export. The study summarized the findings of several studies which reveal among other things, that Mexico's export to US and Canada doubled between 1993 and 2002: increasing from twenty-five percent in 1993 to about fifty-one percent in 2000. The study, however, observed that there were some sort of cyclical growth trend including periods of very slow growth resulting from declining total factor productivity (TFP).

Moreno-Brid, Valdivia & Santamaria (2005) assessed Mexico's industrial performance post NAFTA. According to the paper, for Mexico, NAFTA was more than a mere trade-boosting vehicle: it was a culmination of a radical change in the country's development strategy. The strategy was non-inflationary, export-led growth path driven by sales of manufactured goods. The paper also reported that NAFTA increased FDI flows as well as triggered export boom. The paper however noted that irrespective of the above, the Mexican economy did not seem to have grown as much as her growth capacity seem to portend. According to the author, GDP growth was marked by sharp short-lived growth. The paper attributed this to pressure on trade balances, exchange rate instability, low fixed capital formation twenty-one percent as against minimum of twenty-five percent recommended by UNCTAD, among others.

Kehoe and Ruhl (2010) examined the impact of the several reforms undertaken by Mexico since the 1980s, especially opening up, trade liberalization and others. The study observed that, not only did the Mexican reforms occasion significant foreign direct investment inflows but that FDI inflows also impacted economic growth to a great extent. The study: based on standard theory, however, noted that these performances were not as impressive as China's in the same respect given that China also undertook similar reforms at about the same period, and considering the Special and cultural proximity of Mexico to the USA which rose to become major export destination for both countries in the period under review.

The study by Wilson (2017) reviewed Mexico's economic growth in relation to USA 'on growing together bases' 26 years after entry into NAFTA. Due to Mexico's geographical proximity to the USA, as well as the cultural ties between the two; as against China; the study opined that Mexico was expected to have benefited more from trade relation with US than China. In view of the relative success of NAFTA, the United State-Mexico-Canada Agreement (USMCA) was signed in 2022, thus the paper canvased continued reforms and more transparency in the management of the economy.

The study of Iniguez-Montiel and Kurosaki (2018) reviewed Mexico's economic management based on 1992-2014 time series data using cross sectional analysis. The study revealed that while the Mexican economy grew in the period under study, poverty and inequality were still very much present in the economy. The study opined that the high level of the informal sector, and less transparency in public sector management corruption, may have contributed to this poor results.

OECD's (2019) study was a survey of the Mexican economy. The study examined Mexico's microeconomic management, especially with respect to monetary, fiscal and exchange rate policies. The study confirmed that strong macroeconomic framework, commitment to fiscal targets, sound debt management, flexible exchange rate, among others, accounted for some degree of moderate growth in the Mexican economy since the 1980s. The study however noted that low productivity growth accounted for Mexica's inability to achieve convergence of living standards between the more productive, more modern north and central Mexico compared to those of the more traditional south.

The work by Ukpabi, Iyodo and Abdul-Maliq (2022), was an assessment of the impact of financial system development on the economies Mexico, Indonesia, Nigeria and Turkey; the (MINT) countries. Based on 2000-2020 time series data and via a VAR regression analysis technique, the study revealed that financial sector development indicators like financial institution depth, financial institution access, market efficiency among others, were instrumental to growth in these emerging economies.

With the foregoing, it appears that at the turn of the 20th century, Mexico had risen from the ashes of colonialism, internal disharmony, and enemy-clad nation to a focused country on growth and development trajectory; only hoping to sustain this into the 21st century.

4.0 ECONOMETRIC ANALYSIS OF MEXICO'S ECONOMIC MANAGEMENT 1991-2020

4.1 Data and Methodology

Thirty-nine annual time series data, 1981 – 2019 were sourced from IMF/World Bank data bases. GDP per capita was used as the dependent variable while FDI, GFCF, export, government capital expenditure, human development index, economic openness among others were used as independent variables.

4.2 Model Specification

The time series data utilized in this study were subjected to stationarity and Cointegration Tests. Thereafter the Augmented Dickey-Fuller version was adopted for Stationarity test, while, on the basis of the mix level of stationarity among variables, the Autoregressive Distributed Lag (ARDL) Model alternative to cointegration test was implemented.

The empirical model of the study is specified below:

$$\text{GDPPERCAPITA} = \beta_0 + \beta_1 EXPO + \beta_2 \text{EXR} + \beta_3 \text{FDI} + \beta_4 \text{GCFC} + \beta_5 GOVTCAP + \beta_6 \text{HD} + \beta_7 OPENNESS + \beta_8 + \beta_9 \text{PRCONS} + \beta_{10} RINR + \text{E}_t$$

Where GDPPERCAPITAL is Gross Domestic Product Per Capital, EXPO is value of Export, EXR is Exchange rate, FDI is Foreign Direct Investment, GFCF is Gross Fixed Capital Formation, GOVTCAP is government capital expenditure, HD is Human Development index, OPPENNESS is as known, PRCONS is private Consumption Expenditure, RINR is Real interest rate, and E_t is the error term of the model.

A general ARDL model is also specified as follows:

$$yt = a0 + a1t + \sum_{i=1}^{p} \psi_i y_{t-i} + \sum_{j=1}^{p} \sum_{lj=0}^{qj} {}^{2}{}_{j,}\ \text{lj}xj, t - \text{lj} + \epsilon t$$

where ϵt are the usual innovations, a0 is a constant term, and a1,ψi, and βj,lj are respectively the coefficients associated with a linear trend, lags of yt, and lags of the k regressors xj, t for j=1,…k.

The time series properties of the variables were investigated for stationarity, under the null hypothesis that the series were individually not stationary at level. The p value for all the series indicates that the variables are stationary both at level and after being cointegrated to certain degrees, with two of them (FORDEBT and IMP) being stationary after seventh and eight difference respectively. Because most of the variables were stationary at both level and after first difference, cointegration test is better conducted following the Bound test procedure, by allowing the variables that were stationary after first difference not to enter the long run model specification.

5.0 DATA ANALYSIS

5.1 Diagnostic Analysis of the ARDL Model

The appropriate ARDL (2, 2, 2, 0, 2, 2, 2, 2, 2, 2) model that was estimated for the study (see appendix I) to test whether there is a long-run relationship between the variables yields two time periods lag for all the variables, with the exception of FDI which entered the model at level. The model was further subjected to serial correlation and heteroscedasticity test for robustness, and the results presented as follows:

Table 1. Augmented Dickey-Fuller stationarity test of the time series variables

Series	Prob.	Lag	Max Lag	Obs
D(EXPO)	0.0000	0	9	37
D(EXR)	0.0002	0	9	37
D(FDI)	0.0000	1	9	36
D(FORDEBT)	0.8646	8	9	29
D(GDPPERCAPITAL)	0.0000	1	9	36
D(GFCF)	0.0000	0	9	37
D(GOVTCAP)	0.0000	0	9	37
D(HD)	0.0000	0	9	37
D(IMP)	0.1900	7	9	30
D(OPENNESS)	0.0001	1	9	36
D(PRCONS)	0.0000	1	9	36
D(RINTR)	0.0000	1	9	36

Table 2. Serial correlation test

Breusch-Godfrey Serial Correlation LM Test			
F-statistic	3.316203	Prob. F(2,5)	0.1211
Obs*R-squared	21.09615	Prob. Chi-Square(2)	0.0000

Table 3. Heteroscedasticity test: Breusch-Pagan-Godfrey

F-statistic	1.169576	Prob. F(29,7)	0.4475
Obs*R-squared	30.67022	Prob. Chi-Square(29)	0.3811
Scaled explained SS	1.196038	Prob. Chi-Square(29)	1.0000

Since the null hypothesis is that the residuals are **serially uncorrelated**, the F-statistic p-value of 0.1211 indicates that we will **fail** to reject this null. We therefore

Table 4. Bound test for cointegration

F-Bounds Test		Null Hypothesis: No Levels Relationship		
Test Statistic	Value	Signif.	I(0)	I(1)
			Asymptotic: n=1000	
F-statistic	3.752437	10%	1.8	2.8
K	9	5%	2.04	2.08
		2.5%	2.24	3.35

conclude that the residuals are serially uncorrelated.

Since the null hypothesis is that the residuals are **homoscedastic**, the F-statistic p-value of 0.4475 indicates that we will **fail** to reject this null even for a significance level of 10\%. We therefore conclude that the residuals are homoscedastic at 10\% significance.

Since the estimated ARLD model has no serial correlation and heteroscedasticity problem, we proceed to test for cointegrating relationship between the variables as follows:

Since the f-statistic value 3.7524379 is evidently above the I(1) critical value bound even at the 2.5% level, we therefore reject the null hypothesis that there is no equilibrating relationship, and conclude that there is a level relationship between the variables.

5.2 Findings

The results of the ARDL, (long-run form), as presented above show that only export, human development index and private consumption expenditures were significantly impactful, at 5% level, in explaining the growth of the Mexican economy over the period of investigation. While the influence of export on growth was negative, that of Human development index and private consumption expenditures were positive. In all, the estimated model is robust as about 99.7% of the total variation in the real GDP *per capita* was explained by the estimated model.

Table 5. Estimation of the relevant long-run model form

Dependent Variable: GDPPERCAPITAL				
Method: Least Squares				
Date: 08/25/22 Time: 11:37				
Sample: 1981 2019				
Included observations: 39				
Variable	Coefficient	Std. Error	t-Statistic	Prob.
EXPO	-7.154225	1.490972	-4.798363	0.0000
EXR	-6.901650	29.62352	-0.232979	0.8174
FDI	-8.755153	7.928723	-1.104232	0.2783
GFCF	14.39623	9.148453	1.573625	0.1261
GOVTCAP	-4.106017	10.02819	-0.409447	0.6851
HD	15.98361	6.206725	2.575208	0.0152
OPENNESS	-2.737007	13.14160	-0.208271	0.8364
PRCONS	12.22398	1.529943	7.989827	0.0000
RINTR	18.63061	8.837160	2.108212	0.0435
R-squared	0.996639	Mean dependent var		6417.095
Adjusted R-squared	0.995743	S.D. dependent var		3010.449
S.E. of regression	196.4108	Akaike info criterion		13.59747
Sum squared resid	1157316.	Schwarz criterion		13.98137
Log likelihood	-256.1506	Hannan-Quinn criter.		13.73521
Durbin-Watson stat	1.016824			

6.0 SUMMARY, CONCLUSION, AND RECOMMENDATION

This chapter examined the politico-economic history of Mexico in four phases: (i) 250-900 described as the 'classical Maya City states (ii) Mexico (New Spain) as vice royalty of Spain; that is, the colonial era, 1521-1821; (iii) period of Mexican war of independence or the Mexican revolution, 1810-1821 and (iv) post-independent Mexico, from 1824 to date.

Approximately forty-year data: thirty-nine; 1991-2019 were sourced from IMF/WB data bases. A dynamic growth model was adopted for the study via ARDL technique. Results show that the Mexican economy witnessed many fundamental, some, radical changes in macroeconomic management philosophies and paradigms. The results show that only export, human development index and consumption expenditures were significant in explaining the modest growth in the Mexican economy for the period under review.

More worrisome is that export; a common enabler of economic growth, had significant but negative impact on economic growth in Mexico in the period under study. These findings are quite similar to earlier works like Rose, 1993, Kose *et al* (2004) and even more recent ones like Iniguez-Montiel and Kurosaki (2018), Belhia & Techiko 2019; OECD 2019 among others.

The conclusion that can be drawn from these findings are like the above-referenced studies have observed: (i) reforms and seeming changes in economic management paradigms have not engendered enough desirable or warranted growth results in the Mexican economy, and (ii) that persistent evidence of high level of informality, low level of factor productivity, want of transparency in government as well as less than desirable level of investment domestic and foreign are causative factors in holding down the Mexican economy from growing according to its domestic as well as global potentials suggest. The chapter therefore recommends that factors or policies that improve or increase domestic savings, attract productive FDI, expands export, reduce informality as well inequality all of which will help to productivity are still needed to enable Mexico grow faster and better.

REFERENCES

Alonso, A. G. (2004). *The Parliament System, and the Mexican Service.* Paper presented at the AGDS, Mexico 2004 SRE (nd) Colonial Mexico, SRE, Embassy of Mexico, United Kingdom.

Anaya, A. R. (2023). Mexico: colonial and early post-colonial state creation: A political Marxist account. *America Latino el la historian economical, 30*(1), 1-16.

Archer, C. I. (2011). Mexican War of Independence (1810-1821). The Encyclopedia of war. Wiley. doi:10.1002/9781444338232.wbeow399

Beeley, W. H., & MacLachlan, C. M. (2009). *Mexicans in Revolution, 1910-1956.* University of Nebraska Press-Sample Books. doi:10.2307/j.ctt1dgn3xj

Carstens, A. G., & Werner, A. (1999). *Mexico's Monetary Policy Framework Under A Floating Exchange Rate Regime.* Banco de Mexico Research Paper No. 9905.

Dobado, R., & Marrero, G. A. (2011). The role of Spanish imperial state in the mining led growth of bourbon Mexico's economy. *The Economic History Review, 64*(3), 855–884. doi:10.1111/j.1468-0289.2010.00555.x

Eckler, C. R. L. (2000). *Prevailing facets and Spanish colonialism the root of exploitation and in equality* [Latin American Honors Thesis]. University of Tennessee at Chattanooga.

Faal, E. (2005). *GDP Growth, Potential, Output and Output Gaps in Mexico.* IMF Working Paper; Western Hemisphere Department WP/05/93.

Flores, R., & Telles, E. R. (2012). Social Stratification in Mexico: Disentangling Color, Ethnicity, and Class. *American Sociological Review, 77*(3), 486–494. doi:10.1177/0003122412444720 PMID:25382861

Guedea, V. (2000). The process of Mexican independence. *The American Historical Review, 105*(1), 116–130. doi:10.2307/2652439

Hackle, S. W. (1997). Land, Labor, and Production: The Colonial Economy of Spanish and México California. *California History (San Francisco), 76*(2-3), 111–146. doi:10.2307/25161664

Hanson, G. H. (2012). *Understanding Mexico's Economic Under-Performance.* The Regional Migration Study Group. Woodrow Wilson International Center for Scholars Migration Policy Institute.

Hepler, R. & Lutz, A. (2021). *Mexican-American War & Treaty of Guadalupe Hidalgo.* Academic Press.

Iniguez-Montiel, A. J. & Kurosaki, T. (2018). Growth inequality and poverty dynamics in Mexico. *Latin America Economic Review, 27*(12), 1.

Kehoe, T. J., & Ruhl, K. J. (2010). *Why Have Economic Reforms in Mexico not Generated Growth?* Federal Reserve Bank of Minneapolis, Research Department Staff Report No. 453.

Knight, A. (2004). Mexico: The Colonial Era. Cambridge University Press.

Kose, A. M., Guy, M., Meredith, G. M., & Christophe, M. T. (2004). *How has NAFTA Affected the Mexican Economy? Review and Evidence.* IMF working paper wp 04/59.

Kose, M. A., Meredeth, G. M., & Towe, C. M. (2004). *How Has NAFTA Affected Mexican Economy? Review and evidence.* IMF Working Paper. WP/04/59

Macnutt, F. A. (1909). *Fernando Cortse and the conquest of Mexico 1485-1547.* The Knickerbocker Press.

Maiolo, S. (2014). *A Brief History of Mexico: The Classic Period to the Present.* Treaty of Guadalupe Hidalgo.

Mecaa, R., Schwartz, S. B. & Grubesic, A. (2009) Race and Class in Colonial Latin American. *A critique, Comparative Studies in Society and History, 21*(3). doi:10.1017/500/0417500013074

Meza, F. (2019). *The Case of Mexico. Working Paper, Macro Finance Research Program: Wp.* A Program of Becker Friedman Institute.

Meza, F. (2019). *The monetary and fiscal history of Mexico, 1960-2017.* Macro Finance Research Programe, Making Paper. https://ssu.com/abstract=3238181

Moreno-Brid, J. C., Santamaria, J. & Valdira, J. C. R. (2005). *Mexico: economic growth export and industrial performance after NAFTA united nation publication.* CEPAL: Economic Development Unit.

OECD. (2019). Economic Surveys: Mexico. *Online (Bergheim).* Advance online publication. doi:10.1787/9536dooe-en

Oziah, K. (2011). *God, Gold and Glory: Causes of expansion into the new world.* American Military University. AMUID4226500.

Phelan, L. (2018). *Pan-Latinism, French intervention in Mexico (1861-1867) and the genesis of the idea of Latin America Historicas Digital.* https://www.historicas.unam.mx/publicacines/publicdigital/li bros/114/canciencia.autenticidad/html

Ramirez, E. G. (2021). *Mexico's parliament and other political institutions, emperies.* European Parliamentary Research Services.

Ref-Kirkwood, B. (2005). *The History of Mexico New York.* Palgrave McMillian Press.

Ros, J. (1993). *Mexico's Trade and Industrialization Experience Since 1960: A Reconsideration of Past Policies and Assessment of Current Reforms.* Kellogg Institute for International Studies, Working Paper No. 186/January 1993.

Topik, S. (2004). The Revolution, the State and Economic Development in Mexico. *History Compass, 2*(2004), 1-36.

Tuck, J. (2005). History of Mexico-Miguel Hidalgo: The Father who Fathered a Country 1999, Mexconnect. *World History: Don Miguel Hildalgo Reading.*

Ukpabi, I. O., Iyado, B. Y., & Abdul-Maliq, Y. (2021). Financial System Development in Emerging Economies: An Array of MINT Economic Bloc. *International Journal of Science and Technoledge*, *9*(6), 39–46. doi:10.24940/theijst/2021/v9/i6/ST2106-003

Wilson, C. (2017). *Growing Together: Economic Ties between US and Mexico*. Development Bank of Latin America and Wilson Center Mexico Institute. Woodrow Wilson International Centre for Scholars.

Yeh, A., & Olagnibel, G. (2011). The Virgin of Guadeloupe: A Study of Socio-Religious Identity. *International Journal of Frontier Missiology*, *28*(4), 169–177.

APPENDIX

Dependent Variable: GDPPERCAPITAL				
Method: ARDL				
Date: 08/25/22 Time: 10:09				
Sample (adjusted): 1983 2019				
Included observations: 37 after adjustments				
Maximum dependent lags: 2 (Automatic selection)				
Model selection method: Akaike info criterion (AIC)				
Dynamic regressors (2 lags, automatic): EXPO EXR FDI GFCF GOVTCAP				
HD OPENNESS PRCONS RINTR				
Fixed regressors: FORDEBT IMP C				
Number of models evalulated: 39366				
Selected Model: ARDL(2, 2, 2, 0, 2, 2, 2, 2, 2)				
Variable	Coefficient	Std. Error	t-Statistic	Prob.*
GDPPERCAPITAL(-1)	0.175569	0.253401	0.692853	0.5107
GDPPERCAPITAL(-2)	-0.484024	0.239599	-2.020144	0.0831
EXPO	10.90960	3.999813	2.727527	0.0294
EXPO(-1)	-2.603464	3.102376	-0.839184	0.4291
EXPO(-2)	-5.797300	6.116992	-0.947737	0.3748
EXR	90.33722	60.56489	1.491577	0.1794
EXR(-1)	-74.54894	86.37478	-0.863087	0.4167
EXR(-2)	80.24363	96.43431	0.832107	0.4328
FDI	-6.549541	4.309587	-1.519761	0.1724
GFCF	16.66102	5.605039	2.972508	0.0207
GFCF(-1)	8.517821	8.405215	1.013397	0.3446
GFCF(-2)	-33.14075	8.398965	-3.945814	0.0056
GOVTCAP	-11.52775	8.176874	-1.409800	0.2014
GOVTCAP(-1)	-1.462137	7.419196	-0.197075	0.8494
GOVTCAP(-2)	24.24820	8.251957	2.938479	0.0218
HD	-30.28297	70.79828	-0.427736	0.6817
HD(-1)	-294.9470	142.3976	-2.071291	0.0771
HD(-2)	109.7416	85.71698	1.280279	0.2412
OPENNESS	-2.807091	17.44080	-0.160950	0.8767
OPENNESS(-1)	9.093523	14.79402	0.614676	0.5582
OPENNESS(-2)	18.94626	28.57127	0.663123	0.5285
PRCONS	17.01651	2.324014	7.322036	0.0002

PRCONS(-1)	-5.694573	3.352027	-1.698845	0.1332
PRCONS(-2)	11.66425	5.399021	2.160437	0.0676
RINTR	10.65322	7.111037	1.498125	0.1778
RINTR(-1)	4.235328	8.585873	0.493290	0.6369
RINTR(-2)	-8.090274	6.222549	-1.300154	0.2347
FORDEBT	-0.135850	5.914296	-0.022970	0.9823
IMP	-16.46631	6.385548	-2.578684	0.0365
C	13264.00	5605.281	2.366340	0.0499
R-squared	0.999922	Mean dependent var		6590.964
Adjusted R-squared	0.999596	S.D. dependent var		2990.025
S.E. of regression	60.07050	Akaike info criterion		10.98553
Sum squared resid	25259.25	Schwarz criterion		12.29168
Log likelihood	-173.2323	Hannan-Quinn criter.		11.44601
F-statistic	3075.371	Durbin-Watson stat		2.546654
Prob(F-statistic)	0.000000			
*Note: p-values and any subsequent tests do not account for model				
selection.				

Chapter 9
Finance and Economic Development Post Cold War:
The Case of Ethiopia

Osmond Agu
Federal University, Oye-Ekiti, Nigeria

Adepoju Adeoba Asaolu
Federal University, Oye-Ekiti, Nigeria

ABSTRACT

This chapter examined the effect of finance in the development of the Ethiopian economy post-Cold War. The result of the autoregressive distributed lag (ARDL) estimates shows that human development is positive and statistically significant both in the short-run and in the long-run while GDPPC, real interest rate, GDPPC, and exchange rates had significant but negative impacts on the Ethiopian economy. Finally, the result also shows that the gross fixed capital formation (GFCF) is statistically significant but negative in the short-run and positive in the long-run. The study therefore recommended that real interest rate in Ethiopia should be stabilized by the monetary authority in order to enhance private investment and by extension improve the GDPPC. Ethiopian authorities should improve on the capital accumulation to enhance total factor productivity.

1. INTRODUCTION

Ethiopia's historiography reveals a number of uniqueness in its history, physical formation, economic trajectory and politics, among others. It is regarded as the oldest

DOI: 10.4018/979-8-3693-1610-8.ch009

Figure 1. Map of Ethiopia
Source: *Encyclopedia Britannica (2011)*

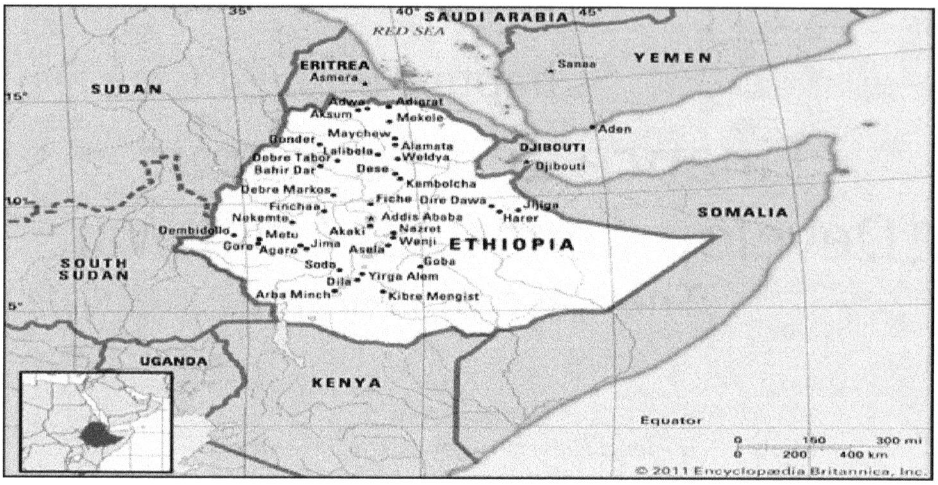

independent country in Africa. Aside the five-year occupation by Mussolini's Italy, it has not been colonised (Encyclopedia Britannica). It is a country situated on the horn of Africa sharing borders with Eritrea, Sudan, Kenya, Somalia and Djibouti. Ethiopia's topography is broadly classified into five namely, the Western Highlands, the Western Lowlands, the Eastern Highlands, the Eastern Lowlands, and the Rift Valley. It is noteworthy that the Western Highlands are the most widespread and rough of the five. Ethiopia occupies 1,127,127km^2 mass land.

History has it that Ethiopia's formation was influenced from the Middle East and Africa (mainly Egypt). It is also on record that the Queen of Sheba, who reigned in the Northern City of Ethiopia, Aksum, had a son with King Solomon. The son was later pronounced as King Menelik I. Ethiopia was also ruled by other descendants of King Menelik I until the end of Kaiser Haile Selassie reign as a fall out of the communist seizure of power in 1974.

Ethiopia underwent massive modernization between late 19th and early 20th century; the period witnessed the creation of Addis Ababa as the capital by Emperor Menelik II. Reputed as one of the original members of the United Nations, it hosts the headquarters of the African Union (AU) and United Nation's Economic Commission for Africa; the unique roles played in Africa has culminated in many referring to Ethiopia as the capital of Africa. The table below summarises the political history of Ethiopia:

Ministry of Foreign Affairs in Ethiopia describe Ethiopia as the 'cradle of humanity' which connotes that human beings are likely to have their root in Ethiopia with a

Table 1. Political history of Ethiopia at a glance

S/N	Event	Date
1	Reign of King Haile Selassie	1930 -1974
2	Occupation of Ethiopia by Italian troops	1935 /36
3	Liberation of Ethiopia by the British troops	1941
4	Ousting of King Haile Selassie by Communist Military Council	1974
5	Reign of Mengistu Haile Mariam (Leader of Military council & Government	1977 - 1991
6	Overthrow of Mengistu Haile Mariam by guerrilla forces led by the Tigray Peoples Liberation Front	1991
7	Formation of Ethiopian People's Revolutionary Democratic Front (by a coalition of guerilla group) led by Former Prime Minister Meles Zenawi	1991
8	Formation of Ethiopian's Constitution (country described as ethnic-based federal system and formation into 10 regions)	1994
9	Election History	1995, 2000, 2005, 2010 & 2015
10	Reign of Meles Zenawi (terminated by death)	1991 - 2012
11	Hailemariam Desalegn became acting Prime Minister	2012
12	Hailemariam Desalegn re-elected as the Prime Minister	2015

Source: Author's Compilation.

claim that Lucy, the best-preserved version of the predecessor to man is approximately 3.5 million years old and has been found in part of the Great Rift Valley.

In terms of religion. Ethiopia is regarded as one of the oldest Christian nations on earth. It is on record that Christianity dates back to 300 AD when the then capital of Ethiopia, Aksum was converted to Christianity making the Orthodox Church in the country one of the oldest in the world. Christianity is deeply rooted in Ethiopian history, but Islam also has roots in Ethiopia.

It is pertinent to state that the Ethiopian government is raising the bar in its efforts to attract foreign investors, particularly in the textile sector which encourages importation of machines free of customs duties, tax exemptions, below market price rents, cheaper labour and huge concessions in water and electricity supplies. The trade pacts between Ethiopia and the European Union allow them to export duty-free.

Table 2. Economic history of Ethiopia at a glance

Date	Event
Late 1940s to 1950s	a. Static economy remained unchanged. b. Expansion of the bureaucratic structure and ancillary services. c. Most farmers cultivated small plots of land or herded cattle. d. Dependence on traditional and primitive methods of farming. e. Nomadic people raised livestock and engaged in transhumance. f. Mild growth in Agricultural and the industrial sector was negligible on the overall economy.
Early 1950s	a. Transition from a subsistence economy to an agro-industrial economy via infrastructure to exploit resources, a material base to improve living conditions, and better health, education, communications, and other services. b. Adoption of centrally administered development plans.
1957 - 1961	Five-Year Plan, sought to develop a strong infrastructure, particularly in transportation, construction, and communications, to link isolated regions.
1962 -1967	The Second Five-Year Plan signaled the start of a 20-year program to change Ethiopia's predominantly agricultural economy to an agro-industrial type.
1968 - 1973	a. The Third Five-Year Plan sought to facilitate Ethiopia's economic well-being via increase in manufacturing and agro-industrial performance. b. Expansion of educational opportunities and c. Improvement on peasant agriculture.
1960/61 - 1973/74	Achievement of sustainable economic growth.
Early 1970s	a. Growth in the economy and diversification into areas such as manufacturing and services. b. No improvement in standard of living.
1974 Revolution	Revolution of Ethiopia's economy.
1974 -1978 Revolution	Fall out of four phases. Internal political upheaval, armed conflict, and radical institutional reform.
1978 - 1980	Recovery of economy through government's consolidated power and implemented institutional reforms. " Security conditions improved as internal and external threats reduced
1980 -1985	Economic Set back
1985 - 1990	Economic Stagnation
1991 - Date	a. Massive program of economic reform (privatization of state enterprises and rationalization of government regulation) b. These reforms have attracted much-needed foreign direct investment (FDI)

Source: **Author's Compilation, 2023.** (Wubneh, 1993)

2. LITERATURE REVIEW

2.1 Economic Strategy and Management Philosophy

The country's growth strategy is skewed towards industrial development and agriculture with an aggressive and strong public infrastructural drive. Contributors

Figure 2. Most prominent sectors in Ethiopia's economy

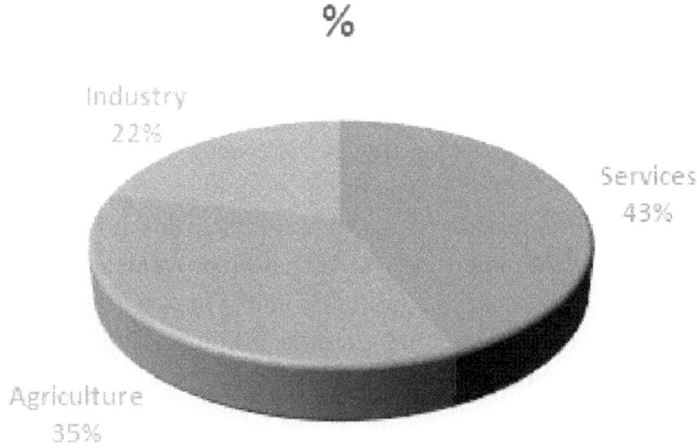

to the growth witnessed in Ethiopia are largely traceable to service and agricultural sectors, this is not unconnected with government's huge investments in energy, transport, communications and social sectors, among others. (World Bank, 2015).

Ethiopia is reputed as one of the fastest-growing economies in the world and occupies the second position in terms of population in Africa (IFC, 2012). Its population as at 2022 is 120,812,698 (Macrotrend, 2022). About half of the country's population is under the age of 18 years, although the education enrolments at primary and tertiary level witness significant increase, job creation has not matched up with the increasing number of graduates. Therefore, the country is advised to create hundreds of thousands of jobs every year to keep up with the growth in population (The Economist, 2007).

From time immemorial traders in the country operated under the barter system trading in ivory, musks, gold, agricultural products and wild animal skins for salt and luxury goods (clothing materials). As at the 19th century, most trades were carried out along two major routes both terminating in the far south west (Kefa-Jema region); one of the routes was towards the north (Mitsiwa) via Gonda and Adwa and the other route along Awash river valley to Harer, then to Berbera or Zeila (on the red sea) (Wubneh, 1993).

Ethiopia's economy is a mixed and a transitional one (dynamic) with the public sector having a large chunk of it. It is noteworthy that government-owned companies mainly control telecommunications, banking and transportation sectors (Maasho, 2015). In its strategy, the government has commenced the privatisation of a number of government-owned enterprises as it gravitates towards a market economy (Sanchez, 2017). This is evidenced in the fact that many government's properties in the successive previous regimes are either presently privatised or undergoing the process of privatisation (Reuters, 2012). Despite the quest for privatisation, certain sectors considered being key to the government such as financial, air and land transport services and retail and insurance are expected to remain under the grip of the government due to their strategic importance.

Ethiopia has transited from its robust economic recovery of the 1990s to a swiftly growing one since early 2000s (Manyazewal and Shiferaw, 2019). The genesis of Ethiopia's economic progression is traceable to 1992, this further accelerated in 2004 resulting to reduction in poverty index with improvement in life expectancy and reduction in child and maternal mortality rates. The report also suggested the following three policy recommendations to assist Ethiopia achieve the desired status of becoming a lower middle-income nation by 2025:

i. Continued infrastructure investment with sustainable financing.
ii. Supporting the private sector through credit markets
iii. Tapping into the growth potential of the country's structural reforms (Moller, 2015).

2.2 Political Alignments of Ethiopia During the Cold War

Cold war represents the period devoid of large scale fighting as obtained when superpowers were involved; however, they each gave backing to major regional conflicts otherwise called proxy wars. Globally, it lasted for about 45 years (that is, 1946 - 1991) without direct military operations between the major antagonists namely the United States of America and Soviet Union(Wikipedia).

Ethiopia has its own share of the cold war. Broich (2017) better captures this as follows:

(a) Ethiopia and Somalia became classic examples of pawns in cold war politics. The antagonists (United States and the Soviet Union) above swap sides to support countries they had hitherto assisted at the height of the cold war.
(b) The governments of Ethiopia are able to use international development assistance as the instrument to implement their policies. The imperial government of Ethiopia (1941-1974) and Ethiopian communist government (1974-1990) targeted the optimization of the external financial resources over the policy agenda to sustain its sovereignty.
(c) The famine that spread across the horn of Africa between 1984 and 1986 underscores the moral problem international donor governments encountered when helping recipient states that are not democratic.

Figure 3. Cold War foreign military aid to Ethiopia (US$' Millions)
Source: SIPRI Arms Transfer Database

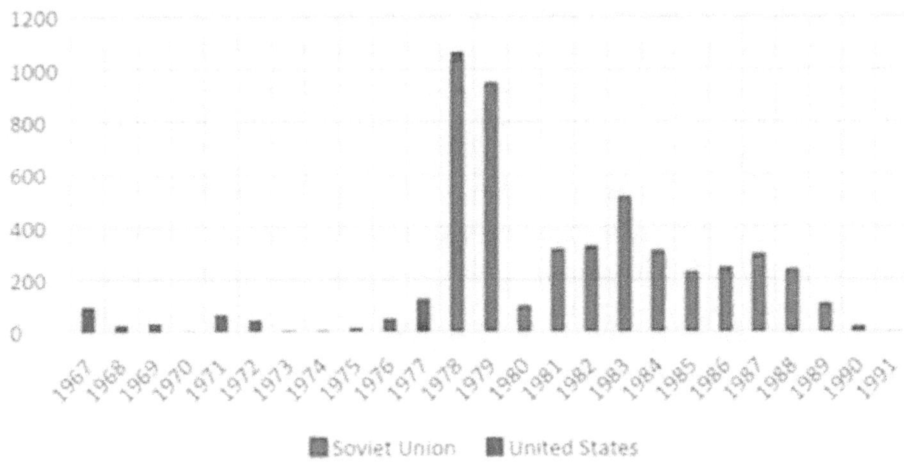

He concluded by highlighting the valuable lessons this history lent the subsequent Ethiopian Government during the post-Cold War era:

1. Magnitude of lack of economic development coupled with the pervasive fatalities caused by famine during the cold war added to the collapse of the two Ethiopian governments.
2. The degree of both governments on large financial and military dependence on the US and Soviet Union during the cold war added to the overthrow of both governments.

2.3 Relationship With Other Countries on the Horn of Africa

The current government in Ethiopia came with vast opportunities of social, political and economic reforms in the country that is expected to cut across the entire region. This transformational integration of countries in the horn of Africa region (Ethiopia, Eritrea, Somalia and Djibouti) is a firm method towards ending the longstanding hostility, unhealthy competition and various wars among nations in the region. In other words, in view of religious, societal, ethnic and cultural sensitivities of the people, this could culminate in political stability and economic prosperity in the region. This is expected to be achieved through a multidimensional process that would factor in changes and alignment of governance structure, harmonization of laws and its regulatory institutions, among others (SIDRA, 2018).

Ethiopia remains one of the most stable countries and appears to be the safest in Africa. This is evidence in the number of tourists visiting the country yearly and its strategic position as the headquarters of African regional organisations and other diplomatic missions earlier mentioned. The renewed drive towards the regional integration would have positive impacts on the less stable areas especially those in the neighborhood such as Somalia, Sudan, South Sudan and Eritrea, among others (Manyazewal and Shiferaw, 2019).

Ethiopia is strategically located in the horn of Africa; close to the Middle East and its markets. It is landlocked with borders around Somalia, Kenya, Eritrea, Djibouti, South Sudan and Sudan. In particular, it has been using the Djibouti's main port for its international trade. A good addition to this is the proposed resumption of trade activities through the Eritrean's Assab and Massawa ports with the peace agreement between the two countries. It is also tapping into the opportunities offered by Berbera, Port Sudan, Lamu and the possibility of developing its southern corridor to Djibouti via Dewele (World Bank Report, 2021).

2.4 Relationship With Other Countries of the World

History has it that the Greek, Armenian and Arab traders eventually became the economic intermediaries between Ethiopia and the outside world, this also culminated in the Arabs dominating major commercial activities. As at 1941 after the Italian occupation, the country's economy had been static, that is, no net economic improvements by the Italian occupants. For this period, there were minor improvements in road construction, emergence of small industries, commercial farming. Wage labour was limited, economic units were independent· Arabs were also established in the country and eventually dominated all commercial activity except petty trade, foreign and manufactured goods were negligible (Wubneh, 1993).

It is important to state now that Ethiopia is a key associate of Western countries, especially the United States, which considers it an important regional security partner in the global war on terror in Africa. This differs from its more complicated role in the horn of Africa region (Manyazewal and Shiferaw, 2019).

Table 3. Ethiopia's trade with the United States (2009 – 2020)

Year	U.S. Exports to Ethiopia (US$)	U.S. Imports From Ethiopia (US$)
2009	266,866,655	112,911,249
2010	773,159,838	127,946,985
2011	689,890,633	144,417,834
2012	1,274,672,068	183,126,469
2013	688,507,736	193,566,884
2014	1,668,912,927	207,209,040
2015	1,555,249,376	310,269,077
2016	826,095,277	236,229,022
2017	877,154,121	291,458,720
2018	1,308,252,189	444,834,941
2019	1,010,790,000	571,540,000
2020	910,940,000	524,530,000

Source: Department of Commerce, Trade Policy Information Systems, Global trade Atlas and National Bank of Ethiopia

2.5 Ethiopia's Major Export Destinations

Table 4. Major export destinations

S/N	Country	Percentage of Export
1	Netherlands	7.90%
2	United States	7.30%
3	Saudi Arabia	6.90%
4	China	5.50%
5	United Arab Emirate	5.00%
6	Djibouti	4.90%
7	Japan	4.60%
8	Others	57.90%

Author's Design

Figure 4. Major export destinations
Source: Encyclopaedia Britannica

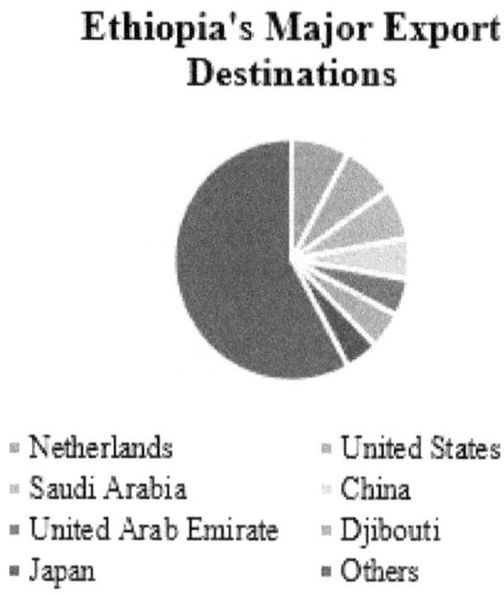

2.6 Ethiopia's Major Import Sources

Table 5. Major import sources

S/N	Country	Percentage of Import
1	China	25.90%
2	United States	9.00%
3	United Arab Emirate	3.60%
4	Japan	2.50%
5	Italy	2.30%
6	United Kingdom	2.20%
7	Germany	2.10%
8	Others	52.40%

Source: Authors' design

Figure 5. Major import sources
Source: Encyclopaedia Britannica

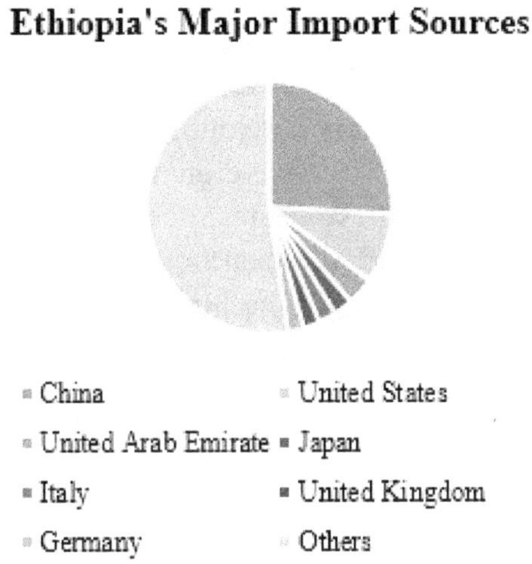

2.7 Key Economic Metrics

The key economic measures under consideration are gross fixed capital formation, exchange rate real interest rate, import and export, foreign direct investment (FDI) and human development.

2.7.1 The Gross Domestic Product (GDP)

Gross domestic product (GDP) is the standard measure of the value of final goods and services produced by a country during a period. Although it is the most widely used indicator to capture economic performances, it is not a good measure of society's well-being and less important measure of people's material living standards (OECD, 2009). Simply put, GDP is the gross market value of aggregate of goods and services produced within the national boundary of a country over a period. Otherwise known as the national income total (Y). In terms of international trade, total imports and total exports are key estimators of the GDP. Quantitatively, GDP = C + I + G + X – M, where; C = Consumer expenditure, I = Investment expenditure, G = Government expenditure, X = Total exports and M = Total imports.

2.7.2 Gross Fixed Capital Formation

This is a very important factor of economic growth from both the theoretical and empirical points of view. For example, from the analysis of Solow (1957), physical capital accumulation contributes to increase the level of production. Further to this is the endogenous growth theory developed by Romer (1986), Lucas (1988), Romer (1990) develop and Barro (1990) re-evaluated this assertion with additional factors such as human capital, infrastructure, research and development, which are contributory to the acceleration of gross capital formation. Capital formation comprise of tangible goods like plants, tools and machinery and intangible goods like high standards of education, health and scientific knowhow, among others (Singer, 1950). Beyond tools and inventories, capital formation also includes capital expenditures (Kuznets, 1955). It depicts an investment of income or savings, mainly in real capital goods. In summary, capital formation requires that a country conservatively does not make use of the entire returns from its present productive efforts to satisfying immediate needs and desires but carves out or sets apart a portion of it in making capital goods. This is to increase the stock of capital goods towards an expansion of consumable output in the future (Ongo & Vukenkeng, 2014).

2.7.3 Import and Export

Imports depict goods and services residents, businesses, or government of a country buy from foreign countries instead of buying domestically produced items. On the other hand, goods and services made locally and sold to residents, businesses, or government of other countries are referred to as Exports. For the importing entity, he pays for the items and thus such is tracked as outflow while the exporting entity is paid for the goods and services and it is recorded as inflow. Imports and exports are essential in appraising the overall balance of trade of every country; a net positive balance of trade (positive net export) is critical to the growth of the country's economy. In other words, net exports are the estimation of the total value of a country's exports minus the total value of its imports; when positive or negative, it is regarded as a trade surplus or deficit respectively. It is important to state now that the developing economies' growth depend largely on the exportation of raw materials and commodities.

Imports and exports are phenomenal enablers and drivers of economic development in developing countries (Utonga and Dimoso, 2019). The neo-classical theory has it that the amount of exports and imports plays a significant role in the determination of a country's economic and social development (Vijayasri, 2013). Thus, the importance of import and export in the measure of economic growth cannot be over emphasised because of the significant positive impacts of international exchange of goods on the economy. For example, Afaf (2015) investigated the impact of exports and imports on the economic growth of Tunisia for the period of 1977-2012 and confirmed that GDP, export and import are cointegrated and thus indicating an existence of long run equilibrium relationship between the variables. Similarly, Abugamea (2015) examined the both the long run and short run relationships between economic growth, exports and imports of Palestine for the time period 1968-2012 and confirmed a long run relationship between imports and economic growth, it further revealed exports and imports as main determinants of economic growth in the country.

2.7.4 Foreign Direct Investment (FDI)

Whether foreign direct investment (FDI) is going to be effective on the economic growth of a nation depends on how prepared the host nation is in terms of technological advancement, its investment policies, degree of openness, legal system and the overall economic stability, among others. Also, when viewed from the financing source, FDI could also affect capital formation. Zhang (1999) discovered a unidirectional causality also between FDI and economic growth in Hong-Kong. Furthermore, Moudatsou (2003) proposed a positive relationship between FDI inflows and economic growth in European Union countries through trade reinforcement between 1980 and 1996 FDI inflows have a positive effect on economic growth in European Union countries both directly and indirectly through trade reinforcement over the period 1980-1996. Lastly, Borenstein De Gegorio and Lee (1998) established the role of FDI as essential vehicle of economic growth when there is enough absorptive capability in the host country's economy, which is a function of human capital minimum threshold.

2.7.5 External Borrowings

External borrowings are funds lent to countries to finance capital or recurrent expenditures. With inadequate capital to fund their sustainable economic growth, developing countries (including Ethiopia) depend on borrowings from external sources to bridge their resource gaps, (Getinet and Ersumo, 2020). In other words, developing economies with low capacity to mobilise funds locally depend much on external loans and grants, (Tashome, 2015). Countries also engage in external borrowing to fund budget deficits or in the period of low investments. (Gohar and Butt, 2012). All these are in tandem with the Keynesian macro-economic views that government borrowings are used to promote economic growth via financing government budget deficit expenditures, which stimulate aggregate demand and by extension encourage investments. In as much as external debt could be strategic in terms of bridging financial and infrastructural gap, governments should ensure that the level of country's outputs cover repayments in order not to overstretch or create a burden on the economy.

3. ECONOMY, POLITICS, AND SOCIAL REFORMS OF ETHIOPIA (WRAP UP)

Tables 1 and 2 above capture the summary of economic (1940 – date) and political (1930 -2015) trend of Ethiopia's history. According to the World Bank report (2021), Ethiopia's economy in the past 15 years has been among the fastest growing in the world at an annual average of 9.5 percent. This growth is largely attributable to investments in public infrastructure. It is important to state also that due to the devastating covid-19, the country's gross domestic product (GDP) growth slowed down between 2019 and 2021 to single digits in industry and services. However, the agricultural sector was immune to the pandemic especially between 2020 and 2021 with slight improvements in contribution to GDP over 2019 figures. The growth experienced in Ethiopia, especially, pre covid-19 period brought about reduction in poverty for both rural and urban settlements; that is, the proportion of the population living below the national poverty line reduced from 30% to 24% between 2011 and 2016. Furthermore, human development index also improved (within the country's measure and not global). However, the level of inequality is increasing (World Bank report, 2021).

As part of the renewed drive towards improving the country's economic fortunes, the government has launched a decade-plan development (2020/2021 – 2029/2030) agenda based on the year 2019 home-grown economic reform agenda. The aims of the agenda are among others to:

a. Sustainability of the growth achieved under the growth and transformation plan of the previous years.
b. Facilitate the swing towards more private-sector-driven economy.
c. To foster efficiency and introduce competition in key growth-enabling sectors, such as energy and telecommunications, among others.
d. Create an improved business environment and
e. To address issues around macroeconomic imbalances World Bank report (2021)

Furthermore, Tada (2001) has aptly captured economic reforms of Ethiopia in the 1990s to date as follows:

a. That Ethiopia has successfully sprung economic reforms in the earlier part of 1990s, proceeded with the privatisation in the early part of the millennium, and marked progress achieved so far. This report also captured that agricultural sector has recorded increases in the volume of food grains output and per capita food production. There is also an increase in the value of agricultural exports during 1993-1996.

b. In addition, there has been a remarkable growth of GDP after the introduction of 1992/1993 reform program.
c. There is also an improvement in saving and investment since 1992.
d. Very high rate of inflation (21%) occurred between 1990 and 1992. Nevertheless, tight fiscal and monetary policy, good performance of the economy (with the exception of few years) market integration and transport deregulation, the accelerated inflation has been contained.
e. The excessive government expenditure over revenue in the 1980s were reversed after 1992 /1993. This has culminated in the fact that the average government revenue has been growing faster than government expenditure fully covering the recurrent expenditure and a significant part of the capital outlay.
f. Although deficit level is still high because of growing size of capital budget, the financing of the deficit has been non-inflationary.
g. Money supply that grew at higher rates until the end of 1994-95 has slowed down since then conforming to the objective of stabilizing the economy.

Meanwhile, the border disputes with Eritrea slowed down the pace of reforms implementation and lack of funds impeded the process of developmental programmes between 1999 and 2000. However, the renewed economic drive by the present administration in harnessing the country's potentials would put it back on the right track of economic prosperity.

4. METHODOLOGY AND DATA

This study used time series data from 1980 - 2019 which were sourced from International Monetary Fund (IMF) and World Bank (WB) data bases. It employed Solow-Swan (1957) Growth theory as the theoretical framework. Solow-Swan growth theory is an exogenous model of economic growth which centres on the long-run economic model. This model analyses changes in the level of output in an economy over time as a result of changes in socio-economic characteristics and demographic factors. It looks at capital accumulation, labour or population growth and technological advancements as key factors of economic growth. Simply put, the theory believes that capital investment increases growth rate.

Building on the above premise, Solow-Swan growth model specified output as a linear function of labour (L), capital (K) and index of technology (T), expressed as:

Where: Y is output, K is capital accumulation, L is labour force and T is an index of technology or efficiency parameter.

According to Lucas (1988), the Solow-Swan theory argues that it is technological progression that triggers growth because other factors (such as labour & capital) adjust according to the technology progression.

Model Specification

The model used in this study derived substantially from the theoretical framework and it is in line with the model used by Agu & Nyatanga, 2020; Ikenna *et.al (*2018) and Agu etal (2022) who augmented Solow growth model by adding some variables other than the ones specified in the theoretical framework (Equation 1). In their studies, economic growth was specified as a function of gross fixed capital formation, government capital expenditure and human development. However, this study augmented the model by adding such variables as exchange rate as used by Getinet & Ersumo (2020), foreign direct investment as used by Nunnenkamp (2002) and real interest rate as used by Borio & Zabai (2018).

The model for the study is therefore shown thus:

Table 6. Definition of variables

Labels	Variables	Data Sources	
LNGDPPC	Log of Gross domestic product per capita	World bank and International Monetary Fund	
RINTR	Real Interest Rate: a proxy for monetary policy	World bank and International Monetary Fund	
LNGFCF	Log of gross fixed capital formation	World bank and International Monetary Fund	
LNGOVEX	Log of Government capital expenditure: a proxy for fiscal policy	World bank and International Monetary Fund	
LNFDI	Log of foreign direct investment	World bank and International Monetary Fund	
LNHD	Log of human development	World bank and International Monetary Fund	
EXCHR	Exchange rate	World bank and International Monetary Fund	
Structural break DUMMY VARIABLES			
DM1 = dummy variable for 1994 **DM2 = dummy variable for 1999** **DM3 = dummy variable for 2004** **DM4 = dummy variable for 2014**			

Source: Authors' 2021

Table 6 below shows the variables, labels and sources of data

It is noteworthy that all the variables are logged because they are in nominal values except exchange rate and real interest rate which are in rates. Therefore, the econometrics model for the equation (2) becomes:

Where μt =Stochastic disturbance or error term and t stands for the time variant variable. β_0, β_1, β_2, β_3, β_4, β_5 and β_6 are the parameters to be estimated.

Since the study used time series data, there was the need to subject the data to some preliminary tests. Such tests are stationarity test, cointegration test, causality test and structural break test. Stationarity test sought to know if the relationship between the variables stationary in levels or after the first difference, as non-stationary variables may give a spurious relationship. Dickey and Fuller, 1981 test was used to achieve this. Table 7 below shows that there is a mixed series in the variable. That is a mixture of I(0) and I(1). Cointegration test on the other hand intends to know whether the variables have long run equilibrium. ARDL bound testing approach was used achieve this. The advantages of using this approach instead of the conventional Johansen (1998) approach is that while the conventional cointegration method estimates the long-run relationships within a context of a system of equations, the ARDL method employs only a single reduced form equation (Pesaran et al., 2001). In addition, different optimal lags can be used for the different variables, which is not applicable in the standard cointegration test. Table 8 below shows the that there is cointegration amongst the variables. This is evident from the F-statistic which is greater than the upper bound result at 5% significant critical value. Causality test was used to establish the direction of causation between variables. Table 9 shows that there is unidirectional causality running from GDP per capita to FDI and from GDP per capita to government capital expenditure. Finally, the structural break test

Table 7. Unit root result (augmented Dickey-Fuller)

Variables	At Level	First Difference	Results
GDPPC	0.9236	0.0001	I(1)
GFCF	0.9812	0.0000	I(1)
FDI	0.6292	0.0000	I(1)
EXCHR	0.9987	0.0050	I(1)
RINTR	0.0002	0.0000	I(0)
GOVEX	0.3245	0.0000	I(1)
HD	0.3245	0.0000	I(1)

Source: Authors' 2023

Table 8. Cointegration test

Test Statistic	Value	K
F-statistic	5.307050	6
Critical Value Bounds		
Significance	I0 Bound	I1 Bound
10%	2.12	3.23
5%	2.45	3.61
2.5%	2.75	3.99

Source: Authors' 2023

Table 9. Causality test

LNFDI does not Granger Cause LNGDPPC LNGDPPC does not Granger Cause LNFDI	37	0.69674 3.52777	0.5056 0.0413
LNGOVEX does not Granger Cause LNGDPPC LNGDPPC does not Granger Cause LNGOVEX	37	0.71581 4.43359	0.4965 0.0200

Source: Authors' 2023

was employed. In order to test for structural breaks, the study used the Bai and Perron (2003) test and identified four structural breaks in the series (1994, 1999, 2004 and 2014). These breaks matched with the years preceding the election years in Ethiopia. It seems that economic activities increase in the years prior to the election years. Therefore, dummy variables were used to control for these fluctuations.

Drawing from the various tests done in this study, Autoregressive distributed lag (ARDL) estimating technique is found to be the most appropriate technique for this study. This is because (i)ARDL handles a mixed series conveniently (ii) ARDL technique handles times series with limited years (in this case 37 years). Therefore, the study specified the ARDL dynamic model from the econometric model in Equation (3) thus:

A typical ARDL dynamic model has the lags of both the dependent and the independent variables in both sides of the model. $n = (n1, n2, \ldots, n4)$ represents the number of lags which was obtained using sequential modified LR test statistic (LR), Hannan-Quinn information criterion (HQ), Final prediction error (FPE) and the Akaike (1974) information criterion (AIC). $\beta_1 \ldots\ldots \beta_4$ stands for the short run dynamics while $\lambda_1 \ldots \lambda_7$ stand for the long-run relationship of the variables, i stands for the lag length while Δ stands for the first difference operator. The notation

Table 10. Lag length

Lag	LogL	LR	FPE	AIC	SC	HQ
0	-212.2566	NA	0.000460	12.18092	12.48883	12.28839
1	18.18647*	358.4670*	2.03e-08	2.100752*	4.564003*	2.960493
2	83.42034	76.10618	1.14e-08	1.198870	5.817467	2.810884
3	162.0455	61.15290	6.08e-09	-0.446972	6.326970	1.917315*

Source: Authors' 2023

$\sum_{j=1}^{n-s} \lambda_j D_{jt}$ is the structural break notation which corrects the structural instability of the model.

Having chosen ARDL as the most appropriate technique, the study conducted a lag length selection as to know how many lags to adopt in the study. Table 10 shows that the automatically selected lag length was one (1), as (*) was selected by most of the criteria.

5. PRESENTATION AND DISCUSSION OF FINDINGS

Table 11 below showcases the short-run and the Long-run results of the study. The estimation result shows that in the short-run, the variables that showed a statistically significant relationship with the GDPPC are exchange rate (EXR), real interest rate (RINTR), Gross fixed capital formation (GFCF) and human development variables.

Table 11. Short run and long run estimates

Short-Run Estimates			Long-Run Estimates		
Variable	**Coefficient**	**Prob.**	**Variable**	**Coefficient**	**Prob.**
D(EXR)	-0.078173	0.0043	**EXR**	-0.423078	0.0050
D(EXR(-1))	-0.051388	0.0339	**RINTR**	0.103328	0.4542
D(RINTR)	-0.002065	0.0062	**LNFDI**	1.164079	0.3390
D(LNFDI)	-0.059590	0.0973	**LNGFCF**	1.351051	0.0008
D(LNGFCF)	-0.069161	0.0027	**LNGOVEX**	1.721703	0.0019
D(LNGOVEX)	-0.088135	0.5178	**LNHD**	0.002378	0.0367
D(LNHD)	0.967287	0.0316	**C**	21.695973	0.1290
ECT	0.051191	0.0001			

Source: Authors' 2023

In the long-run, exchange rate (EXR), gross fixed capital formation(GFCF), government capital expenditure (GOVEX) and human development. In the short-run, all the variables have negative relationship with the GDPPC except human development variable (LNHD), whereas in the long-run, all the variables possess positive relationship with the GDPPC except exchange rate (EXR). In other words, it seems that majority of the macroeconomic indicators in Ethiopia only affect gross domestic product per capita (GDPPC) in the log-run. This may point to the fact that Ethiopia authority make policies that focus mainly on the long-run sustainable economic growth.

Specifically, human development (HD) is positive and statistically significant both in the short-run and in the long-run. In the short-run a one per cent dollar increase in human development improves GDPPC by 0.05 percent while in the long-run, a one percent dollar change in human development brings about 0.037 percentage increase in GDPPC. It therefore implies that Ethiopia expenditure in education and health for her populace improves their wellbeing. This finding is in line with the study of Moudatsou (2003) who also found a positive relationship between HD and GDPPC.

The estimation result shows that RINTR is negatively and statistically significant in relationship with GDPPC in the short-run but in the long-run, it is positive though statistically non-significant. In the short-run, a one percentage increase in RINTR reduced GDPPC by 0.002 percent. This is in line with the studies of Agu & Nyatanga (2020) and Agu & Asaolu, (2023) who also found the same negative result. The implication is that high interest rate discourages private investment which in turn spirally increase unemployment rate and GDPPC and finally affects living standards.

The estimated result also shows that in the short-run and in the long-run, exchange rate variable is negative and statistically significant in relation to GDPPC. A one percent increase in exchange rate negatively influences GDPPC by 0.004 percent and by 0.01 percent in the short-run and in the long-run respectively. Historical data shows that in Ethiopia, exchange rate increased from 2.07 to 27.43 within the study period. It seems therefore that in Ethiopia, the increase and unstable exchange rate negatively affected and made macroeconomic indicators unstable that the economy found it difficult to plan endogenously to improve on the GDPPC of the populace.

Government capital expenditure (GOVEX) shows a positive and statistical significant result in the long-run but negative and non-significant result in the short-run. A one percent increase in GOVEX brings about 1.72 percent increase in GDPPC. This implies that the impact of government expenditure on capital is only felt in the long-run. Finally, the estimation result shows that the GFCF is statistically significant in both short-and in the long-run. Whereas it is negative in the former, it is positive in the later. In the short-run, a one percent increase in GFCF reduces GDPPC by 0.07 percent in the short-run but increases GDPPC by 1.35 percent in the long-run.

The Error correction term (ECT) is the variable for the speed of adjustment in the model. The value of ECT indicates that 51 percent of the short-run disequilibrium in the economy can be corrected in the current period.

Post-Estimation Results

Figure 6 below shows the normality test, the Jarque-Bera statistic (0.095) is not less than 0.05 significant level. The implication is that the model used is stable.

Figure 6. Stability test

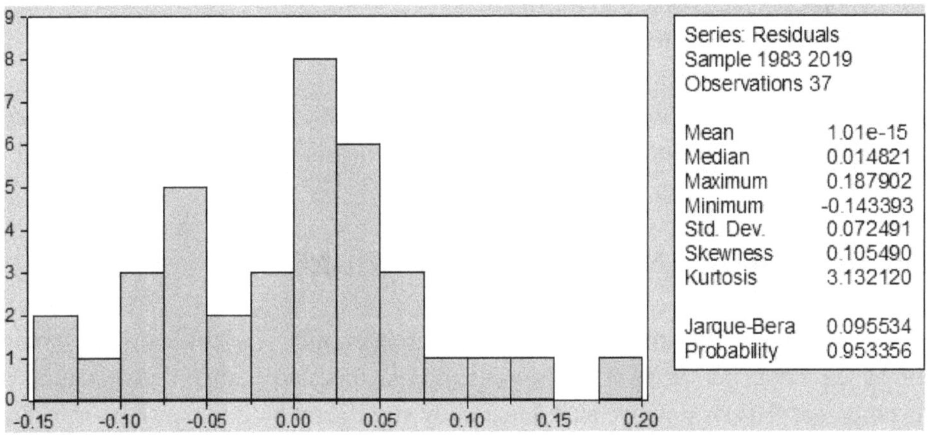

Table 12. Breusch-Godfrey serial correlation LM result

F-Statistic	1.022706	Prob. F(2,23)	0.3754
Obs*R-squared	3.021722	Prob. Chi-Square(2)	0.2207

Source: Authors' 2023

Table 13. Heteroskedasticity test: Breusch-Pagan-Godfrey

F-statistic	1.323460	Prob. F(11,25)	0.2691
Obs*R-squared	13.61665	Prob. Chi-Square(11)	0.2549
Scaled explained SS	6.627176	Prob. Chi-Square(11)	0.8284

Source: Authors' 2023

Serial Correlation Test

The hypothesis that was tested is thus:

H_0: There is serial correlation in the model

H_1: There is no serial correlation in the model

Since the F-statistic and Chi-square probability are greater than 0.05 significant level. The study rejected the null hypothesis and accepted the alternative hypothesis, showing there is no serial correlation in the model.

Heteroskedasticity Test

The hypothesis that was tested for this was:

H_0: There is autocorrelation in the model

H_1: There is no autocorrelation in the model

Since the probability values of both F-statistic and Chi-square are greater than 0.05 significant level. The study accepted that there is no autocorrelation in the model.

6. CONCLUSION AND RECOMMENDATIONS

Having discussed the impacts of some macroeconomic variables on the gross domestic product per capita (GDPPC) of Ethiopia, this study concluded that human development (HD) is positive and statistically significant both in the short-run and in the long-run. RINTR is negatively and statistically significant in relationship with GDPPC in the short-run but in the long-run, it is positive though statistically non-significant. The estimated result also shows that in the short-run and in the long-run, exchange rate variable is negative and statistically significant in relation to GDPPC. Government capital expenditure (GOVEX) shows a positive and statistical significant result in the long-run but negative and non-significant result in the short-run. Finally, the estimation result shows that the GFCF is negative and statistically significant in the short-and but the long-run, it is positive statistically significant. The speed of adjustment is about 51 percent for the economy to revert to equilibrium. The study therefore recommended that real interest rate in Ethiopia should be stabilized by the monetary authority so as to enhance private investment and by extension improve the GDPPC. Since the GFCF had a negative relationship with GDPPC in the short-run, Ethiopia government should improve on the capital accumulation in the economy as to enhance productivity per capita of the economy.

REFERENCES

Abugamea, G. (2015). External trade and economic growth relationship under Trouble: Time series evidence from Palestine, *Swift. Journal of Economics and International Finance*, *1*(2), 10–16.

Afaf, A. J. S., & Hussain, M. A. (2015). Impact of exports and imports on economic growth: Evidence from Tunisia. *Journal of Emerging Trends in Economics and Management Science*, *6*(1), 13–21.

Agu, O. C., & Asaolu, A. A. (2023). Can Nigeria Debt Be Sustained in the Face of Increasing Debt Profile? *EuroEconomica*, *42*(1), 108–123.

Agu, O. C., Nwosa, P. I., & Ajoje O. I. (2022). Socio-economic Status, Savings and Income Inequality in Nigeria: The behavioral mechanism Approach. *Iranian Economic Review.*

Agu, O. C., & Nyatanga, P. (2020). An Investigation into the Crude Oil Price Pass-Through to Economic Growth in Nigeria. *Acta Universitatis Danubius. Œconomica, 16*(1).

Bai, E., & Perron, T. (2003). *Domestic petroleum product prices and subsidies: Recent developments and reform strategies*. International Monetary Fund Working Paper. Available from: http://www.ksri.or.kr/bbs/files/research02/ wp0771.pdf

Barro, R. (1990). Government Spending in a Simple Model of Endogenous Growth. *Journal of Political Economy*, *98*(5), 103-125.

Borenstein De Gegorio, J., & Lee, J. (1998). How does foreign direct investment affect economic growth? *Journal of International Economics*, *45*(1), 115–135. doi:10.1016/S0022-1996(97)00033-0

Borio, C., & Zabai, A. (2018). Unconventional monetary policies: a re-appraisal. In *Research Handbook on Central Banking*. Edward Elgar Publishing. doi:10.4337/9781784719227.00026

Broich, T. (2017). *US and Soviet foreign aid during the cold war: a case study of Ethiopia*. United Nations University (UNU-MERIT) Working Papers #2017-010.

Dana, S. (2017). Ethiopia moves towards privatisation. It's not about money, it's about tech. *AFKInsider*.

Getinet, B., & Ersumo, F. (2020). The impact of public external debt on economic growth in Ethiopia: the ARDL approach to con-integration. *Journal of Economic and Sustainable Development, 11*(11).

Gohar, M., & Butt, F. (2012). The impact of external debt servicing on the growth of low-income countries. Proceeding of International Conference on Business Management.

Ikenna, A. A., Penzin, D. J., Nkang, N. M., & Golit, P. (2018). Impact of Oil Price Volatility on Selected Macroeconomic Indicators in Nigeria. *Editorial Committee*, *56*(1), 1.

Johansen, S. (1998). Determination of cointegration rank in the presence of a linear trend. *Oxford Bulletin of Economics and Statistics*, *54*(3), 383–397. doi:10.1111/j.1468-0084.1992.tb00008.x

Kuznets, S. (1955). *International Differences in Capital Formation and Financing in: Capital Formation and Economic Growth*. National Bureau of Economic Research, Inc.

Lucas, R. Jr. (1988). On the mecanisme of economic development. *Journal of Monetary Economics*, *22*(1), 2–42. doi:10.1016/0304-3932(88)90168-7

Maasho, A. (2015). *Ethiopia launches 4G mobile service in the capital*. Reuters.

Maasho, A. (2015). *Ethiopia sells off seven state firms, to offer more*. Reuters.

Macrotrends. (2022). https:www.macrotrends.net

Manyazewal, M., & Shiferaw, A. (2019). Economic Policy and Structural Transformation in Ethiopia. Institute of Political Science and International Relations, Jagiellonian University and Jagiellonian Research Center for African Studies.

Ministry of Foreign Affairs. (2020). *Ethiopian history*. https://etiopien.um.dk/en/about-etiopia/ethiopia-history

Moller, L. C. (2015). *To continue the impressive run, Ethiopia needs to modernize the policy framework to further strengthen the foundations of its economy*. World Bank Report on Ethiopia. https://www.worldbank.org/en/news/press-release/2015/11/23/wbethiopia-a-unique-economic-strategy-delivering-high-growth

Moudatsou, A. (2003). Foreign direct investment and economic growth in the European Union. *Journal of Economic Integration*, *18*(4), 689–707. doi:10.11130/jei.2003.18.4.689

Nunnenkamp, P. (2002). *Determinants of FDI in developing countries: has globalization changed the rules of the game?* (No. 1122). Kiel Working Paper.

OECD. (2009). National accounting of OECD countries 2009, Vol.1, main aggregates. OECD Publishing. http://dx.doi.org/ doi:10.1787/data-00001-en

Ongo, E. N., & Vukenkeng, A. W. (2014). Does gross capital formation matter for economic growth in the CEMAC sub-region? *EuroEconomica, 2*(33).

Pesaran, M., Shin, Y., & Smith, R. (2001). Bound testing approaches to the analysis of level`relationship. *Journal of Applied Econometrics, 16*(3), 289–326. doi:10.1002/jae.616

Reuters. (2012). https://www.reuters.com

Romer, P. (1986). Increasing returns and long run growth. *Journal of Political Economy, 94*(5), 1002–1037. doi:10.1086/261420

Romer, P. (1990). Endogenous Technological Change. *Journal of Political Economy, 98*(5, Part 2), 71–102. doi:10.1086/261725

Sanchez, D. (2017). *Ethiopia moves towards privatization. It's not about money, it's about tech.* Retrieved from Moguldom Nahon: https://moguldom.com/136888/

SIDRA. (2018). *Regional integration in the horn of Africa: is prime minister Abiy's initiative an institution ahead of its time?* Somali Institute for Development Research and Analysis, SIDRA policy brief 08, 2018. www.sidrainstitute.org /

Singer, H. W. (1950). Distribution of Gains between Investing and Borrowing Countries. *The American Economic Review, 40*(May), 473–485.

Solow, R. (1957). A Contribution to the Theory of Economic Growth. *The Quarterly Journal of Economics, 70*(1), 65–94. doi:10.2307/1884513

Tada, P. R. (2001). Economic Reforms and Structural Changes in Ethiopia since 1992; An Inquiry. *International Conference on African Development.* https://scholarworks.wmich.edu/africancenter_icad_archive/18

Tashome, A. (2015). *Development Finance and debt sustainability in Ethiopia: lesson to Sub-Saharan countries.* Academic Press.

The Economist. (2007). https://www.economist.com

Utonga, D., & Dimoso, R. L. (2019). The Nexus between Export and Economic Growth in Tanzania. *Journal of Business School, 2*, 49–59. doi:10.26677/TR1010.2019.144

Vijayasri, G. V. (2013). The Importance of International Trade in the World. *International Journal of Marketing. Financial Services & Management Research, 2*, 111–119.

World Bank. (2015). Ethiopia's Great Run: The Growth Acceleration and How to Pace It. *World Bank Report: A Unique Economic Strategy Delivering High Growth.*

World Bank Report. (2021). Africa CAN. *The World Bank in Ethiopia Special Report.*

Wubneh, M. (1993). The Economy. Ethiopia: a country study (4th ed.). Federal Research Division, Library of Congress. OCLC 25869403.

Zhang, H. (1999). FDI and economic growth: Evidence from ten East Asian Economies. *Economia Internationale*, *7*(4), 517–535.

Chapter 10
Finance and Nigeria's Economic Development Post First Cold War

Yekeen Oku Abdul-Maliq
University of Abuja, Nigeria

ABSTRACT

This chapter x-rayed Nigeria's political and economic history from independence to date. Nigeria has been managed under four different paradigms: free market 1960-1972; socialist inclined; mixed economy, posture, structural adjustment, 1986-1994; and quasi-capitalist approach. Based on 39 multivariate time series data, econometric analyses reveal that foreign direct investment, domestic savings (GFCF) capital expenditure, private consumption, and economic openness made a positive and significant impact on the Nigerian economy. On the other hand, import, exchange rate, foreign debt, monetary management indicators, and reinterest rates had negative and significant impacts on the Nigerian economy during the period. The study therefore recommends that Nigeria adopt export focused policy, institute FDI-friendly policies, and improve on her good governance image. In summary, the study concluded that the Nigerian economy could have done better.

1. INTRODUCTION

The Federal Republic of Nigeria, more commonly called, Nigeria, is a country in West African; bounded by the Republics of Tchard and Niger to the north, by Cameroon to the east, to the west by Benin Republic and to the south by the Atlantic Ocean. With a landmass of 923,770km^2; (World Bank), and a population of two

DOI: 10.4018/979-8-3693-1610-8.ch010

hundred and six million people, (206 million) (2022 estimate), Nigeria is Africa's largest economy by population as well as by nominal GDP and is; therefore, often romanticized as the 'Giant of Africa'.

Nigeria obtained independence from Great Britain on October 1st, 1960, and inherited the British West Minister Parliamentary system of government with three regions: Western, Eastern, and Northern regions; with a fourth region; the Mid-Western Region, added in 1963.

Nigeria's Judiciary is also a brought forward of the British Judicial system. The existence of Customary Laws and Courts, in the South and Central parts of Nigeria; and Sharia Law (in the North), are complementary to the Nigerian Legal system occasioned by Nigeria's demographic and multi-religious composition. The official language in Nigeria is English. There are however over five hundred different languages spoken in Nigeria, three of which Hausa, Yoruba, and Igbo, are the most prominent.

After a shaky but prosperous start in 1960, Nigeria's polity witnessed series of crises that culminated into a military coup *d'état* on January 15th, 1966, which snow-balled into a thirty-month civil war, (June 1967 to January 1970). Nigeria, a multi-ethnic and multi-religious country adopted the unitary system of government after the said military coup but couldn't be sustained.

Nigeria is currently a federation, operating the American-styled presidential system of government with an elected Executive President. There are thirty-six states and an autonomous Federal Capital Territory. There is a bi-camera Legislature at the federal level: the Senate and the House of Representatives; called the Red (Upper) Chamber and the Green (Lower) Chamber respectively. Each state is headed by an elected executive governor with a uni-camera legislature: the State House of Assembly. (Adamolekun & Ayo, 1989; Falola & Heuton, 2008).

Nigeria's political and economic narrative can be undertaken in three phases: (i) Before Nigeria: that is, before the influx of non-Africans, especially Europeans, into the hinterland of Nigeria and West Africa; up to the beginning of colonization in 1914 when the name Nigeria is said to have been coined; (ii) the colonial period; 1914-1960 and (iii) 1961-date.

To the extent that there was no country called Nigeria before 1914, the history of Nigeria, as a nation, can only start from after that date. Secondly, before then, the area called Nigeria was not, (in fact, had never been) inhabited by a consistent and in any way homogenous aborigines. Rather, a number of empires and kingdoms, made up of different tribes and peoples of different ethnic and racial backgrounds inhabited the land at different times. Prominent among these ancient West African empires and kingdoms were the Songai, Ghana, Benin, Oyo, Borno, Kwararafa, Kanuri; Kanem, Nupe, Junkun, Hausa, Fulbe, Zazzau, the Sokoto Caliphate among others. In the Southeast and the Niger Delta regions also existed some rather autonomous

Figure 1. Map of Nigeria

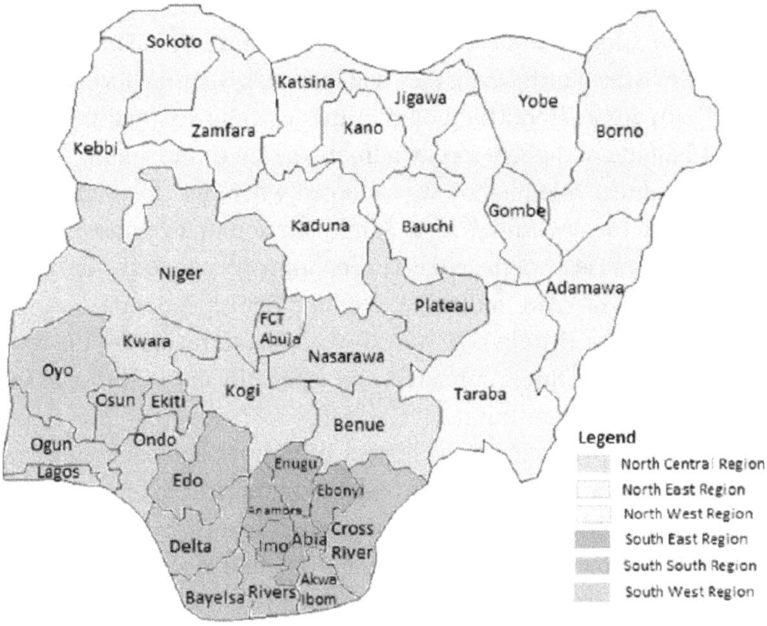

or republican kingdoms like the Okpobo, Istshekiri, Calabaries kingdoms among others (Green, (nd); Atmore, 2008).

It is a generally accepted historical fact that the final collapse of the Oyo empire somewhere in 1935, marked the beginning of sixty or more years, of instability and rivalry among the Yorubas of Western Nigeria and their kins across the West African region (Falola & Heaton, 2008). On the other hand, although the Sokoto Caliphate Jihadists had defeated most other northern kingdoms and empires and appeared to reign over the region before the Europeans come into the Nigerian hinterland; the later were not only able to halt the Caliphate's advance to the south but also to defeat it and establish the northern protectorate in 1903. (Atmore, 2008; Ochonu, 2008).

Under such a state of affairs, it was not difficult for the colonial masters to take over the political and governance structures (where there were) and replace them with theirs. For this text, this era for the aforementioned reasons, is hardly relevant and is therefore not discussed any further in this text.

1.1 Nigeria: The Colonial Era 1914-1960

Nigeria was under effective colonial rule from 1914 to 1960. During this period, Nigeria, like all other European colonies, was administered as an appendage of

Britain and the British economy. Nigeria was essentially self-financing but in which political power was exercised from 'Home'; that is, from London.

In Nigeria, the colonial masters adopted two different administrative techniques: the Indirect Rule in the North where they had met a fairly strong form of centralized governmental structure. Here, the colonial masters allowed native or traditional rulers greater latitude in the day-to-day administration of the region. In the South, (West and East), direct rule method was adopted where the colonial masters were engaged directly in the day-to-day local administration to a greater extent.

Like everywhere else also, the Nigerian economy was not only tied to the apron string of Britain but was also 'milked' to feed the British economy.

It may not be fair to Britain however, if we failed to recognize the remarkable development in infrastructure, commerce, and especially the educational and health sectors occasioned by colonization.

The rest of this paper includes the history of politics and economics pattern in Nigeria, literature review section discusses a comprehensive empirical review of the previous interrelated, follow by the methodology, data presentation and analysis section justify for empirical analysis of the dataset; and lastly, conclusions section clarifies the overall conclusion drawn from the study.

2. POLITICS AND ECONOMICS: 1960-1967/72

In the immediate post-independence era, Nigeria maintained the political structure as well as the macro-economic management principle of free market. There was a high degree of Central Bank autonomy over monetary and exchange rate policies. It should be added though, that during this period, Nigeria and most other countries were on the fixed exchange rate regime. During this era, agriculture (anchored on the operations of the Nigerian Marketing Board), was the mainstay of the economy. Export of cocoa, coffee, groundnut, palm produce, and a few other agricultural produces provided the bulk of the Nigerian government's revenue and foreign exchange earnings.

The Nigerian economy grew fairly well, including during the thirty-month civil war period. The Nigerian Marketing Board was vibrant and although, there was fixed exchange rate policy, Nigeria's currency; the Nigerian pound, was strong enough to sustain domestic price stability, thus fiscal policy also had an ordered stance. Domestic output was high, import component of Nigeria's life was relatively low and inflation did not spiral.

Nigeria was already on her second National plan when the January 15th, 1966, *coup d'état* occurred. That was the beginning of a forty-three minus four period of military rule in Nigeria; but that did not affect the economic management philosophy until 1972 when two major policy initiatives were undertaken that in the opinion of Abdul-Maliq & Abubakar (2021) seems to have affected (and is still affecting) the Nigerian economy (and polity) negatively: the Udoji Award-cum-Arears and the Nigerian Enterprise Promotion Decree (NEPD); (FGN 1972).

On religion, the colonists seemed in the 19th Century; and beyond; (at least in West Africa) to have become more honest in their quest for 'Gold'; (treasure) and glory with only sublime concern for God unlike in the 15th and 16th Century in the New World; (the Americas),. Thus, although Christianization was pursed vigorously in the Eastern and Western regions, it was more by peaceful and persuasive methods rather than force. Schools 'Sunday schools' scholarships; education in general, became instrumental in the propagation of Christianity. On the other hand, the Islamic religion, haven taken root in the North because of the Uthman Dan-Fodio Jihad, was left to flourish although efforts to penetrate the region with Christianity was intense but not confrontational; at least, then there were no known serious Christian-Muslim crises as Nigeria was to witness in the 1980s and beyond.

2.1 Era of Indigenization: 1973-1985

By indigenization, the Federal Military Government nationalized all foreign companies, took over direct control and management of the companies; placed some in the capital market and encouraged, enthused, and even granted civil servants' loans to acquire shares in the quoted ones. The intention of indigenization was to fast-track Nigeria's economic growth. With the Udoji award and areas, there was much money with which government wished to stimulate consumption and or production. Perhaps, because of the manner it was prosecuted, it was a near fiasco: the principal architect of the Udoji award; the Chairman of the Udoji Committee, Sir Jerome Udoji, confirmed that the Committee's Report was a 'cache' of recommendations, but the FMGN chose to implement the salary review and areas payment, whether as a starting point or as the only accepted recommendation, it has remained difficult to determine.

Thus, the Udoji award and the arears payment had three immediate deritorious impacts on the Nigerian economy: (i) since it could not and did stimulate production but hyper-stimulated demand, it created immediate disequilibrium between money supply, price level and output. The effect was spiral inflation in the late 1970s to the early 1980s. (ii) it stimulated excessive import and therefore foreignized Nigerians' taste and consumption. In fact, between 1973 and 1979; importation of beverages and other grocery items, textiles, furniture, among others, increased in quanta and variety and (iii) it introduced into Nigeria the most cancerous ailment known to economics: 'money illusion'. Since then, the only way to cushion the effect of economic hardship; as far as Nigerians are concerned, is to increase salaries, notwithstanding the obvious and acknowledged fact that, in real-time, such salary increases always have contrary welfare and wellbeing effect on living standards.

This era saw what can be described as the most flippant and ridiculous trivialization of macro-economic management. To reduce inflation, all that Nigerian federal military government did was to resort to direct importation and physical distribution of essential commodities; being Rice, Sugar, Milk and the likes. If a nation was at war for thirty months and did not need "salvation-Army" relief; it will be difficult to accept that essential commodities was necessary in 1976-1978. More ridiculous; how can rice, sugar and milk become essential in a nation that produced yam, beans, maize, guinea-corn, cassava, etc.?

However, it must be mentioned that, during this era, especially from 1972-1983, government's policy was focused on industrialization may be, in the spirit of industrialization through indigenization. Four important automobile assembly plants: Volkswagen (VON), Peugeot (PAN), Mercedes Benz (ANAMCO) and Styre assembly plants were established by the Federal Military Government. At state levels, textile companies and other low and middle-technology industries were established. Import substitution was the central policy framework of the governments.

The civilian government of 1979 to 1983 continued this industrialization spree and crowned it with the development of an Iron and Steel Industry. Policies to accelerate the rate of industrialization included import restriction, import license and other forms of controls. Unfortunately, with increasing import dependency declining FDI inflow as general holding-back tendencies of multi-national corporation in the face of free flow of petro-dollar of the oil boom era, the industrialization efforts were ineffectual.

In the area of finance, (fiscal as well as monetary policies) came under direct control of government. Sectorial credit allocation, fixed interest and exchange rates etc. were the order of the day. With the NEPD's schedule I & II companies reserved for local industrialists; companies sprang up in lips and bounds to take advantage. Unfortunately, this era saw more of portfolio chairmen, chief executives or (CEOs) Managing Directors (MDs) than true industrialist businessmen or entrepreneurs. Almost every company was an Importer and Exporter. Most actually imported even if it was powder-milk, stock-fish heads, and the likes. Manufacturing in this era could mean as ridiculous as importing liquid perfume, bottling it, labelling it with imported papers, ink, and other materials; and call it 'made in Nigeria'. The forever doomed slogan, 'Buy made in Nigeria' was born in this era. Thus, financial resources: bank loans, foreign exchange allocation, among others went to so-called manufacturers, industrialists, importers, and exporters amidst reports of consistent decline in total installed capacity as well as capacity utilization.

The folly of the indigenization (NEPD) policy was apparent as early as 1974/76 when the Nigerian government had to concession the management of the Nigerian

Railway Corporation which they hardly taken over from foreigners back to foreigners, to Rail India Technical and Economical Services (RITES), specifically; which was described as 'how not to indigenize' (The President, 1982; Ayoola, 2008).

The civilian government of 1979-1983, thus inherited this burden; and tried to reestablish a modicum of credibility in public sector management and reduction in uncertainty in the Nigerian business ecosystem, but its life was cut short once again by the military on December 31st, 1983.

One prominent project or programme undertaken by the military regime was the Operation Feed the Nation (OFN), which failed calamitously, perhaps not for want of good faith or honest intention but because it's *modus operandi* was inconsistent with agricultural economic theories in a populace that was copiously capitalist in mindset.

Other major projects or achievements of the miliary government during indigenization includes the Shiroro and Kanji hydroelectric projects; created by military, which were up and running. Nigeria joined, (or would have joined) the world's 'Iron and Steel' economy 1981/1983 with the Itakpe, Ajaokuta, Katsina and Aladja Steel projects but the Federal Military Government (haven overthrown the democratically elected civilian government on December 31st, 1983) terminated the Nigerian-Russian Pact on Ajaokuta Iron and Steel development in 1984. Others include refineries manufacturing companies' development banks among other, almost all these failed.

It may be instructive to note that today, forty years after, the Ajaokuta steel project remains moribund with successive governments at loss as to how to salvage it. The civilian government was far gone into negotiation with IMF and World Bank for a restructuring facility when the said December 31st, 1983, overthrow occurred.

By way of assessment of the military in government in Nigeria, it is obvious that each of the military government in Nigeria since 1966 did not do much better than the civilians it overthrew. For instance, only one or two of the first twelve Nigerian military governors were found free of corruption and embezzlement during the Muritala Muhammed's 'great purge'. The story was similar even among the Federal executive and military brass. That the purge itself was not in good faith and not sufficiently transparent is also no longer discussed in secrete. And, that the military regimes left the civil service far worse than they met it; with respect to corruption, commitment to probity, transparency, accountability, professionalism, dedication to duty and patriotism is also now public knowledge. (Salisu, 2001; Ogunode, 2021; Odetola, 2008; Ladan-Baki, 2016; Igewereme, 2015; Iyanowua, 2014; Etebon, 2021; Olaopa, 2012) among others.

The four most insidious damages the 1983-1985 Buhari-Idiagbon military regime did to the Nigerian economy and polity were: (i) unilateral cancellation of the Nigeria-Russia Pact on the Ajaokuta project (ii) the hamstringing and liquidation of the Nigerian Marketing Board (iii) the politicization of the civil service and destruction of the principle of 'stability of tenure' in the Nigerian civil service; and (iv) the change or redesign of the nation's currency within a fortnight in 1984. The cumulative effect of the Udoji award, NEPD and the Buharism, is that; the Nigerian economy has been fully unhanged from any economic theoretic anchor hence the ineffectiveness of all economic reforms in Nigeria; even the ones that seem correct, articulate and apparently well managed. That is why too; as at 2020, most efforts or policy provisions to woo foreign investors back to Nigeria do not seem to have yielded or be yielding much results. Unfortunately, many Nigerians, some in the economic and financial professional spheres, excuse this by what Abdul-Maliq & Abubakar (2021) described as Nigeria's unique species hypothesis.

The fact that the military regimes' anti-corruption crusades, including the so-called war against indiscipline (WAI), were necessitated is not denied. Under WAI and anti-corruption war in general, many people, especially politicians and civil servants, were sent to jail following legal procedures 'unknown' to intelligent and civilized societies hence such jail terms as "100, 200 and 300-year concurrent" jail terms became more of slogans than indictment for corruption. The 'ban and unban' policy of the succeeding military regimes were neither substantiated in law nor in morality; and were therefore unsustainable. To that extent, the guilty and the innocent were thrown back at the society. The most 'criminalized' of the civil servants and politicians became the building blocks of subsequent military as well as civilian governments; and like wounded lions or scotched snakes, these 'returnee' politician-civil-servants became more hardened than ever before. That the military as an entity itself, is not absorbed of corruption too, is a fact now so obvious to the world. (Ogunode, 2021; Odetola, 2002).

Throughout the military era, especially from 1970s to 1980s, there were always loud cries of 'removing bad eggs from the civil service'. The more bad eggs that were removed, the more bad eggs there were because the bad cocks and the bad hens that mated to produce bad eggs were also the ones in charge of removing bad eggs. The more they removed, the more they laid. While it is true corruption in Nigeria did not start with the military regimes, it is a generally accepted fact that corruption ossified and became more or less a culture in Nigeria; progressively during successive military regimes especially in the public sector.

2.2 The Reforms Era: 1986-1999

That economic reform in Nigeria was desirable, in fact, inevitable since 1976; to undo the ills of indigenization, is not contestable. According to Adeyemi (1996); there was a consensus pre-SAP, that Nigeria needed an economic reform. But, from 1986, when the structural adjustment program (SAP) was introduced, Nigeria has operated an economic management policy that cannot be regarded as still capitalist, nor can it be denied as such.

That SAP did not achieve its stated objectives is equally documented. That SAP was ill-conceived and or badly managed is not deniable. There are many factors accounting for this. Very strong among these is the IMF/World Bank conspiracy theory. Apologists of conspiracy theory argue that as a follow up from colonialism and neo-colonialism, the Western world did not want Africa to develop. These group will not hear counterargument; for instance, that India, Malysia, South Korea, Taiwan etc. were also colonies; in fact, of the self-same Britain.

Another common argument is that of tribal and religious differences. But these have not stopped excellent raporshmour among Nigerians from different tribes and opposing religions divides in their private endeavours, in politics and in governmental institutions. A third and more generally accepted argument in this regard is the poor or unconducive business and investment climate. However, the causes of the non-conduciveness and unattractiveness of the Nigerian economy to high impact domestic and foreign investment often generate another string of arguments. A nation in which electricity, petroleum, oil and gas among other things are still under the ownership and management of the President or the Presidency *de jure or de facto* cannot be transparent and friction-free enough to generate a free enterprise or free market philosophy that most global investors cherish: the eclectic, (Ownership, Location and Internalization; OLI) paradigm (Dunning & Lundan, 2008; de Crus, Floriani & Anal, 2020) say it all.

2.3 Return to Democracy or Quasi-Military Government: 1999-2020

Nigeria returned to civil rule in 1999. Since then to date, each of the presidents that emerged through the electoral process in Nigeria admitted technical flaws in the electoral processes that brought him into power. But not only is it that none of them has attempted to address or redress the problems but also that elections in Nigeria degenerate further and further, because more and more rancour, after every presidential electoral circle. State Governors don't hide their ability to install and control state legislatures; the above have therefore given rise to what we can describe as democratic-dictatorship or dictatorial-democracy. Under such a cloudy political environment, it is difficult to expect a very hygienic economic and investment climate.

Despite all these, the Nigerian economy grew to become Africa's number one economy by nominal GDP in the year 2014. Also, in the political arena, sit-tight syndrome, at president level, has not manifested (or not been allowed to manifest) itself in Nigeria like in some other African countries, not because it has not been attempted but because it has been strongly resisted. It is in light of the foregoing that the Nigerian economy has been described as resilient, irrespective of the less than desirable outcomes that are frequently reported.

3. LITERATURE REVIEW

Empirical studies on Nigeria's politico-economic management since independence are enormous; more so, since the 1986 structural adjustment. In this section, only a few of such works are selected and reviewed.

The work of Adeyemi (1996) as well as Soludo (1996), did some critical appraisals of the Nigeria economy, and highlighted why the SAP reforms of 1986 became inevitable. They also critiqued the objectives and implementation of the reforms as to whether the reform was honestly and correctly prosecuted.

According to Adeyemi (1996), the fundamental premise of SAP was that long-term goal of self-sustaining economic development was better achieved with adequate participation of the private sector. As noted earlier, power and energy sectors, the most important pedestals of development are still under government control even as of 2020. Apart from this, the paper noted that Nigeria seemed to have contracted more external debt than before SAP.

In a similar vein, Soludo (1996) re-echoed World Bank's (1994) observation that African was more or less on the slow growth part of the 1960s and 1970s due to fragile, incoherent and incomplete reform efforts.

The works of Okonjo-Iweala, Soludo & Mukhar, 2003; Adesola 2009, are in relation to Nigeria's external debt management since the reforms. They, among others confirm that Nigeria's external debt stock which underscored the need for reforms in the 1980s did not seem to have been addressed.

Okonjo-Iweala & Osafo-Kwaako's (2007) study was an in-depth assessment of Nigeria's development programmes, especially the National Economic Empowerment and Development Strategy (NEEDS). The study gave the four objectives of NEEDS as (i) streamlining public expenditure framework, (ii) improving macroeconomic performance, (iii) agricultural reforms and (iv) institutional and governance reforms. It may be noted that it was in this vein that public sector procurement, public sector remuneration structure and downsizing were undertaken. The extent to which these objectives have been achieved, calls for investigation. How well the supposed changes in the institutional structures have impacted governance and the economy is open to argument.

Owunmere, Ibe & Okpara's (2012) work was on foreign capital inflows vis-à-vis Nigeria's economic growth against the backdrop of the objectives of economic reforms in Nigeria. The work reinforced previous research findings like Asiedu (2004); that the reforms were more of absolute progress but little or no improvement. The study further confirmed that capital inflows were not impactful on the Nigerian economy.

Ogunmike & Salisu (2012), used 1975-2005 data, via bound test and other econometric tests to examine the relationship between financial development and economic growth in Nigeria. Based on the VAR granger causality tests, the study reported that there was a positive long-run but a negative short-run relationships between financial development and economic growth.

Magaji & Abdul-Maliq (2013) among others, submitted that the Nigerian economy was dollarized *de-facto* since 2000, even though Nigerians argue to the contrary.

Bamgboye (2014), assessed the role of the military in Nigerian government from 1983-1999 and concluded that they made little or no positive overall impact on the Nigerian economy. The study suggested direct budgetary allocation to the military as well as professionalization to ensure that they live politics and focus on their primary assignment.

Ikhide (2015) studied the impact of financial sector reforms and monetary policy in Nigeria. The paper reported that the impact was weak; almost, non-existent. According to author, this was due to the inability of the economy to meet certain necessary conditions. In the view of the author, continued direct control a midst claim of liberalization compromised the successful implementation of the reform programs.

Nwanosike, Kalu, Ogbuabor, Uzochina and Ebenyi (2016), undertook a 100-year review of Nigeria's economic management. The paper reports that most economic management policies in Nigeria's 100-year existence (1914-2014) including the vision 20-20-20 programme did not seem to achieve their stated objectives because, according to the authors, political expediencies, most of the times, override economic reasoning.

Abdul-Maliq & Magaji (2017) compared the forex policies of the four (4) Anglophone west African countries to those of eleven non-Anglophone countries. Based on a 15-year pooled regression data (2001-2015), the study revealed that the non-Anglophone currency anchor to French franc, and later to the euro, impacted economic performance better than the flexible exchange rate policy practiced by the Anglo-phone countries.

Abdul-Maliq (2018) assessed the responsiveness of the Nigerian economy to foreign capital flows from 1973-2015. The study reported that there was positive and significant response from the Nigerian economy to aggregate foreign capital inflows but FDI, FPI, and oversees development assistance made no positive impact on the Nigerian economy in the period under study.

Based on data for 1980-2017, Abiola, Lawal, Adetiloye, Bede and Akinjare (2021), investigated the impact of financial sector reforms on the Nigerian economy. The study adopted human development index (HDI), as dependent variable and savings/GDP ratio and other financial sector variables as independent variables. The study found negative long run impact of financial reforms on HDI. The study further reported that although was positive short-run improvement in HDI; this was not attributable to financial sector reform.

The work of Ukpabi, Onu & Abdul-Maliq (2021) examined financial system development in Nigeria from 1990 to 2020. The study which adopted the ARDL model reported that money supply exerted negative but insignificant impacts on the Nigeria's real GDP in the period of the study.

Abdul-Maliq & Abubakar's (2021) study was on Nigeria's policy makers' dispositions to economic theories in relation to the free-fall fate that befell the Nigerian currency, the naira, since 1986. Based on econometric analysis of 1981 data (2020), the study revealed that import; (private and public; government consumption), external debt and poor FDI flows accounted for about 84% of the decline in value of the naira vis-à-vis the US$ in the period under study. The paper opined that why most macroeconomic policies and programmes, including exchange rate management; were unsuccessful was because of Nigeria's unique species hypothesis. According to the authors, Nigerian policy makers are more inclined to believe that economic theories cannot work or do not in Nigeria. That seems to explain why they are likely to change policies midway failing to acknowledge and allow for policy lags and gestation periods.

From the foregoing, it may be concluded that macroeconomic management in Nigeria; for as long into the past, till date has not meet their expectation. It is however worth nothing that irrespective of the above rather unsatisfactory picture, Nigeria's economy has witnessed some reasonable growth; intermittent, may be, in the period 1999 to 2020 with Nigeria rising to become Africa's biggest economy by nominal GDP since 2014. The issue however has been weather Nigeria could not have done as well as India, Malaysia, Singapore and other developing economies given Nigeria and these countries had rather similar starting points at independence.

4. METHODOLOGY

This study modified the model specified by Tariq, Khan, & Rahman (2020), they examine how financial development impact economic growth in Pakistan. As such the model for this study is specified thus:

GDPPC = f(GOV_CAP, PRCONS, IMP, FDI, RINTR, GFCF, HD, OPENNESS, EXR, FOR_DEBT, EXP, LF, TRO) (1)

The choice of the model specification is borne out of the fact that it covers some of the strategic variables that are prevailing in the economic setting of Nigeria.

expressing Equ. (1) in econometrics form

$$GDPPC = a_0 + a_1GFCF_t + a_2GOV.\ CAP_t + a_3HD_t + a_4IMP_t + a_5OPENNESS_t + a_5PR\_CONS_t + a_6EXR_t + a_7FDI_t + a_8FOR\_DEBT_t + a_9EXP_t + a_{10}RINTR_t + u_t \quad (6)$$

Where:

GDPPC = Gross Domestic Product per capita; GFCF = Gross Fixed Capital Formation; GOV_CAP = Government Capital Expenditure; IMP = Import; HD = Human Development; OPENNESS = Trade Openness; PR_CONS = Private Consumption; EXR = Exchange Rate; FDI = Foreign Direct Investment; FOR_DEBT = Foreign Debt; EXP = Export; RINTR = Real Interest Rate. a_1-a_{10} = parameters; u = error term.

5. DATA PRESENTATION, ANALYSIS AND DISCUSSION OF FINDINGS

5.1 Descriptive Statistics

In Table 5.1, the descriptive statistics are presented, and it shows that all the variables under consideration contained 39 observations. As can be seen the mean, median and other descriptive statistics, especially of government capital expenditure (GOV_CAP), private consumption (PR_CONS), import (IMP) and foreign direct investment (FDI) show swings that are not very impressive. Others includes Gross Domestic Product per capita (GDP), Real Interest Rate (RINTR), Gross Fixed Capital Formation (GFCF) Human Development (HD), OPENNESS, the Exchange rate (EXR), Foreign Debt (FOR_DEBT), Export (EXP), Labor Force (LF), and Trade Openness (TRO). The mean of about 2.60 for FDI against import, government expenditure already indicates poor flow of FDI, high import content among other things.

Additionally, GDP has the highest mean value followed by PR_CONS, EXR, Gov. Cap, and so on. Further, Table 5.1 also revealed that only EXR and HD are negatively skewed. Moreover, only the distribution of foreign debt and foreign direct investment is mesokurtic given that the kurtosis values. Finally, the Jarque-Bera probability of GDP, HD, IMP, OPENNESS, and FOR_DEBT series shows normal distribution as their probability values pass the normality test at a 5 percent significance level.

Table 1. Descriptive statistics are presented

	GDP_ PER_ CAP_	RINTR	GFCF	GOV__ CAP	HD	IMP	OPENNESS	PR__ CONS	FOR_ DEBT	FDI	EXR	EXP01
Mean	1312.415	0.293077	47.07897	48.22077	41.52821	26.82154	32.39333	121.9497	34.91846	2.598974	95.84744	36.68821
Median	902.2200	4.310000	35.55000	36.99000	43.10000	15.76000	34.18000	35.30000	25.65000	1.870000	101.7000	20.91000
Maximum	3222.690	18.18000	147.0200	147.0100	57.20000	88.88000	53.28000	414.7800	120.8400	8.840000	360.2200	144.9200
Minimum	270.2200	-65.86000	12.34000	12.35000	25.30000	2.130000	9.140000	13.03000	4.080000	0.190000	2.730000	2.880000
Std. Dev.	887.5848	14.59720	30.11309	30.70514	9.003916	26.18295	12.42702	131.5949	30.92607	2.602664	96.02441	37.37467
Skewness	0.548815	-2.637153	1.283379	1.154238	-0.162164	0.798096	-0.386780	0.928402	0.844093	1.065824	0.965065	1.291995
Kurtosis	1.908813	12.27281	4.803855	4.324424	1.799266	2.176272	2.245845	2.325251	3.008255	2.909118	3.348976	3.808167
Jarque-Bera	3.892654	184.9304	15.99347	11.51014	2.513796	5.242826	1.896611	6.342390	4.631312	7.397294	6.251675	11.91147
Probability	0.142798	0.000000	0.000337	0.003167	0.284535	0.072700	0.387397	0.041953	0.098701	0.024757	0.043900	0.002591
Sum	51184.20	11.43000	1836.080	1880.610	1619.600	1046.040	1263.340	4756.040	1361.820	101.3600	3738.050	1430.840
Sum Sq. Dev.	29936658	8096.974	34458.33	35826.61	3080.679	26050.78	5868.369	658054.6	36344.02	257.4068	350386.1	53080.92
Observations	39	39	39	39	39	39	39	39	39	39	39	39

Source: Eviews Results Output 2022

Table 2. Augmented Dickey-Fuller test

Variable	ADF-Test	t-Critical Value @5%	Order of Integration	Interpretation
GDP_PER CAP.	-3.83	-3.53	I(1)	Stationary @1st diff.
GFCF	-6.27	-3.53	I(0)	Stationary @ Level
GOV_CAP	-6.11	-3.53	I(1)	Stationary @1st diff
HD	-4.57	-3.53	I(1)	Stationary @1st diff.
IMP	-5.23	-3.57	I(1)	Stationary @1st diff
OPENNESS	-4.55	-3.57	I(1)	Stationary @1st diff
PR_CONS	-5.28	-3.56	I(0)	Stationary @ Level
EXR	-4.81	-3.53	I(1)	Stationary @1st diff
FDI	-7.3	-3.53	I(1)	Stationary @1st diff
FOR_DEBT	-5.87	-3.53	I(1)	Stationary @1st diff
EXP	-6.79	-3.53	I(1)	Stationary @1st diff
RINTR	-7.47	-3.53	I(0)	Stationary @ Level

Source: Authors computation, 2022.

5.2 Unit Root Test

The Augmented Dickey-Fuller Test unit root test result from Table 5.2 established that at a 5 percent level of significance, the data series of Gross Domestic Product (GDP) per capita, Gov. Cap, Human Development (HD), Import (IMP), OPENNESS, the Exchange rate (EXR), Foreign Direct Investment (FDI), Foreign Debt (FOR_DEBT) and Export (EXP) were all stationary at first difference i.e. integrated of order one, I(1). While GFCF, PR_CONS, and Real interest rate (RINTR) were stationary at level i.e. integrated of order zero, I(0).

After establishing the stationarity level of the variables, we proceed to estimate the parameters of the specified model to determine their impact on the dependent variable.

5.3 Data Analysis

The results from Table 5.3 shows that GFCF has a positive relationship with the GDP per capita income because a unit change leads to a 20-unit increase in GDP per capita income. This result shows that the GFCF directly influences the current income level of Nigeria. The findings reveal that there exists a negative relationship between government capital spending and the level of income in the economy. A

Table 3. Ordinary least squared regression

Variable	Coeff.	Std. Err	t-Stat	Prob.**
C	30.74	6.52	4.71	0.00
GFCF	20.2	9.36	2.16	0.04
GOV_CAP	8.55	3.80	2.25	0.03
HD	1.07	5.86	0.18	0.85
IMP	-6.03	1.77	-3.40	0.02
OPENNESS	0.70	0.31	2.25	0.03
PR_CONS	4.53	0.36	12.31	0.00
EXR	-1.43	0.345	-4.10	0.00
FDI	30.86	7.95	3.87	0.00
FOR_DEBT	-2.91	0.61	-4.72	0.00
EXP	5.74	0.69	8.26	0.00
RINTR	-1.10	0.80	-1.38	0.17
R2		0.99		
AD. R2		0.99		
F-STATS		1167.3		
Prob(F-STAT)		0.00		
D.W		2.23		

Source: Eviews Results Output, 2022

1-unit change in the GOV_CAP will cause the GDP per capita to increase significantly by approximately 8.5 units. When government spending causes the unemployed to gain jobs then they will have more income to spend leading to a further increase in aggregate demand. In these situations of spare capacity in the economy, government spending may cause a bigger final increase in GDP per capita than the initial injection.

Human development (HD) was also found to positively affect the GDP per capita in Nigeria since a 1-unit increment leads to a 1.07 improvement in the economy. Human capital and economic growth have a strong correlation. Human capital affects economic growth and can help to develop an economy by expanding the knowledge and skills of its people. Human capital refers to the knowledge, skill sets, and experience that workers have in an economy. In this situation, there will be an advancement in the economy.

Likewise, PR_CONS, OPENNESS, FDI, and, EXP which are the measure of cross-border transactions, have impacted GDP per capita positively, i.e., a 1-unit change in PR_CONS, foreign direct investment, and export will significantly increase

GDP per capita by 4.5, 0.7, 30.8, and 5.7 units respectively. This implies that in the short and long run if there is a higher inflow of capital stock into the economy, the gross domestic product per capita income of Nigeria will be higher. When FDI and EXP are rising, businesses, importers, and exporters will enjoy the benefits attached to them. Also, trade openness will cause earnings to rise and boom in the stock markets, implying that the increase in the rate of EXPORT and FDI can accelerate and ensure sustainable development. Accordingly, the level of exportation in the country has helped in stimulating the level of income.

Conversely, the import level has negatively influenced the GDP per capita, i.e., a unit change in the level of import will subject the development level of GDP per capita to deteriorate by 6.03 units. Import substitution is popular in economies with a large domestic market. For large economies, promoting local industries provided several advantages: employment creation, import reduction, and saving in foreign currency that reduced the pressure on foreign reserves. The analysis also shows that EXR, FOR_DEBT, and RINTR affected the GDP per capita inversely. The result, as observed above depicts that a 1-unit change in EXR, FOR_DEBT, and RINTR will cause the GDP per capita to reduce by 1.4, 2.9, and 1.1 units respectively. This implies that the interest rate and exchange rate push or shatter Nigeria's economic development in some ways. The Keynesian liquidity preference theory can be attributed to this evaluation. This indicates that the lower rate of interest discourages savings, which will eventually affect the level of investment, and ultimately decrease the productivity and output of the economy. Likewise, the exchange rate affects the development of the economy most directly through changes in the demand for exports and imports. A bad exchange rate policy of the domestic currency makes exports less competitive abroad and imports more competitive domestically, thereby increasing demand for foreign-produced goods. High public debt can negatively affect capital stock accumulation and economic development via heightened long-term interest rates, higher distortionary tax rates, inflation, and a general constraint on countercyclical fiscal policies, which may lead to increased volatility and lower growth rates.

The coefficient of determination and its adjusted version is 99%. The t-statistics and f-statistics values validate the worthiness of the explanatory power of the independent variables.

The evaluated model of the Durbin-Watson test is 2.2 indicating the absence of serial correlation, implying that the residual estimates of the estimated econometric model are uncorrelated. The fitness of the model is confirmed by the coefficient of determination and its adjusted value which are 98% and 96% respectively.

5.4 Discussion

The results above analyses reveal long-run relationships among the dependent and independent variables. The results also confirm the robustness of the research model as well as the estimation technique.

From the results, it is revealed that the combined independent variables account for as much as 99.9% of total variation in the dependent variable. Result also show FDI, GFCF, government capital expenditure, export, private consumption, and economic openness as the independent variables having positive significant impacts on Nigeria's economic development in the approximately forty years under investigation.

It is however revealed that import, foreign debt, and exchange rate had negative impact on the Nigeria economy in the period under study. These findings are quite in line with many previous works on financial development and the Nigeria economy, some of which were reviewed in the chapter.

Although the long-run impact of finance on the Nigeria economy can be described as fair or even impressive; it can actually be argued, anecdotally, though as far as this study is concerned, that the Nigerian economy could have or ought to have done as well as India, South Korea, Malaysia and Singapore among others.

6. SUMMARY, CONCLUSION, AND RECOMMENDATION

This chapter x-rayed Nigeria's politico-economic history from independence in 1960 to date, with greater emphasizes on the last 40 years 1981-2020. The chapter divided the economic history of Niger into three different period from; 1960-1972, 1973-1998 and 1999-2020; during which Nigeria can be said to have been under a free-market macroeconomic management paradigm, the period of leftist inclination and the post adjustment era and period of return to democratic (or quasi-military) rule respectively.

Both literature review and data analyses show that the Nigeria economy witnessed some remarkable growth; intermittently though, within the period under study. Empirical literature reveals that those basic drivers of growth in modern economy, especially foreign capital inflows; especially FDI, was neither as impress nor as impactful as it could or should be. Export was also reported to be unimpressive while import and external debt seem to have impacted Nigeria's economic growth negatively in the period under review.

The study also revealed that, notwithstanding the not-so-impressive performance of the Nigeria economy, the country's human and material resources endowment seem to have helped her keep ahead of most other countries in the sub-region. Among the most germaine observations as to why the Nigerian economy may not have performed as well as expected include: (i) the copious absence of a long-term coherent, holistic, and consistent development plan as seen in most developed and even developing countries (ii) the less than desirable of transparency and accountability in governance since government official are still largely influential in what are otherwise private sector business; the issue of case of doing business, and (iii) the nations apparent unpreparedness to undertake genuine socio-political and economic reform with long-term focus as well as stick to it through its gestation and through its expected duration.

It is also advisable that domestic policy and regulatory climate be made more investor friendly. This is especially critical in view of divergence of FDI and export performance as revealed by several empirical studies before and including this.

REFERENCES

Abdul-Maliq, Y. O. (2018). *Responsive of the Nigerian economic to foreign capital inflows: 1973-2015.* University of Nigeria, Unpublish Banking Thesis.

Abdul-Maliq, Y. O., & Abubakar, D. I. (2021). Nigeria's Unique Species Hypothesis and the Fate of the Naira: Why Not, If Not? *International Journal of Business and Management*, *9*(2), 381–390. doi:10.24940/theijbm/2021/v9/BM2102-033

Abdul-Maliq, Y. O., & Magaji, S. (2017). *Does exchange rate policy matter for economic growth? Evidence from Economic Community of West Africa States.* Paper presented at the 2nd Nigerian Turkish Nile University's 2nd International Conference on Social Science and Law.

Adamolekun, L., & Ayo, S. B. (1989). The Evolution of the Nigerian Federal Administration System. *Publius*, *19*(1), 157–176. doi:10.1093/oxfordjournals.pubjof.a037761

Adesola, W. A. (2009). Debt Servicing and Economic Growth in Nigeria: An Empirical Investigation. *Global Journal of Social Sciences*, *8*(2), 1–11.

Adeyemi, J. O. (1996). Beyond Structural Adjustment: A Policy Framework. In A. Ekpo (Ed.), Beyond Adjustment: Management of the Nigerian Economy (pp. 133–142). Academic Press.

Asiedu, E. (2004). Policy reform and foreign direct investment to Africa: Absolute progress but relative decline. *Development Policy Review*, *22*(1), 41–48. doi:10.1111/j.1467-8659.2004.00237.x

Atmore, A. E. (2008). Africa on the Eve of Partition. Cambridge History of Africa.

Ayoola, T. (2008). Colonial Inheritance, Post-Colonial neglect and Management of Nigerian Railway by Rail India Technical and Economic Services (RITES). *African Journal,* (14). Advance online publication. doi:10.4134/Inrv1411.46493

Bamgboye, P. (2014). The Military and Social-Economic Development in Nigeria (1983-1999): A Critical Appraisal. *Mediterranean Journal of Social Sciences.* Advance online publication. doi:10.5901/mjss.2014.v5n23p2340

de Cruz, C. B. B., Floriani, D. E. & Anal, M. (2020). The OLI Paradigm as a Comprehensive Model of FDI determinants: a sub-national approach. *International Journal of Emerging Markets.* doi:10.1108/IJOEM-07-2019-0517

Dunning, J. H., & Lundan, M. (2008). Instituting and the OLI paradigm of Multinational enterprise. *Asia Pacific Journal of Management, 25*(4), 573–593. doi:10.1007/s10490-007-9074-z

Etebon, J. M. (2021). The Long years of Military rule in Nigeria: A Blessing or a Course. *Journal of Public Administration and Government, 11*(2), 71–84.

Falola, T., & Heaton, M. M. (2008). Africa, Empire and Globalization: Essays in honour of A. G. Hopkins. Academic Press.

FGN. (1972, February). Nigeria Enterprise Promotion Decree, 1972, No. 4. *Gazette, 59*(10), 28.

Green, T. (2008). *African Kingdoms: A guide to the Kingdoms of Songhay.* Oxford Cambridge & RSA A-Level.

Igewereme, O. B. (2015). Anatomy of Corruption in the Nigerian Public Sector: Theoretical Perceptiveness and some Empirical Explanation. *SAGE Open, 5*(2). Advance online publication. doi:10.1177/2158244015581188

Iyaniwura, W. (2014). Corruption and Military Rule in Nigeria: An Overview 1966-1999. *Global Journal of Human Social Sciences for Political Science., 14*(4), 1–7.

Ladan-Baki, I. S. (2016). Arms procurement mirage; corruption and insurgency in Nigeria. *International Journal of Politics and Good Governance, 7*(3), 1-7.

Magaji, S., & Abdul-Maliq, Y. O. (2013). Dollarization of Exchange Rate Management in Nigeria: Issues, Wishes and Realities. *Proceedings of the 3rd AFRA International Conference on Critical Accounting and Finance Issues in Developing Economies.*

Nwanosike, D. U., Kalu, U. I., Ogbuabor, J. E., Uzoechina, B., & Ebenyi, G. O. (2016). *Economic Development Dynamics in Nigeria: Evidence from 1914- 2014.* Saudi Journal of Business and Management Studies. doi:10.21276/sjbms.2016.1.4.1

Ochonu, M. (2008). Colonialist within Colonialism: The Hausa-Caliphate Imaginary and the British Colonial Administration of the Nigeria Middle Belt. *African Studies Quantory*, *10*(2&3), 95–127.

Odetola, T. O. (2008). Military Politics in Nigeria: Economic Development and Political Stability in the Developing Economics. Cambridge University Press.

Ogunmike, O. F., & Salisu, A. A. (2012). Financial Development and Economic Growth in Nigeria. *Journal of Monetary Economics Integration*, *12*(2), 91–119.

Ogunode, S. A. (2021). The Military Foray into Nigerian Politics and Nation-Building: Historical Reflections on Murtala/Obasanjo Military Regime. *West Bohemian Historical Review*, *X1*(2), 273–281.

Okojo-Iweala, N., Soludo, C. C., & Mukhtar, M. (2003) The Debt Trap in Nigeria: Towards a Sustainable Debt Strategy, Africa World Press, Inc.

Okonjo-Iweala, N., & Osafo-Kwaako, P. (2007). *Nigeria's Economic Reforms: Progress and Challenges*. The Brookings Institution.

Olaopa, T. (2012, Apr. 10). Nigeria: Public Service and Udoji Reform – A Review. *Daily Trust*.

Onwumere, J. U. J., Ibe, I. G. & Okpara, G. C. (2012). Foreign Private Capital Inflows and Real Sector Growth: Evidence from Nigeria. *International Journal of Finance Management*, *43*, 6724-6729.

Salisu, M. (2001). *Incentive structure, Civil Service Efficiency and the Hidden Economy in Nigeria*. United Nation University/WIDER Discussion paper No. 2001/86.

Soludo, C. C. (1996). Theoretical Framework of SAPs in Africa: Some better ideas from dead economists. In A. H. Akpo (Ed.), Beyond Adjustment: Management of the Nigerian Economy (pp. 107-132). Multi-Media Publishers Ltd. Nigerian Economic Society.

Tariq, R., Khan, M. A., & Rahman, A. (2020). How does financial development impact economic growth in Pakistan? New evidence from threshold model. *The Journal of Asian Finance, Economics and Business*, *7*(8), 161–173.

The President. (1982). The unacceptable face of indigenization. *The President, 2*.

Ukpabi, I. O., Onu, C., & Abdul-Maliq, Y. O. (2021). Economic Growth in The Wake of Nigerian Financial System Development: A Model of ARDL Bounds Test. *IRE Journals.*, *5*(4), 2456–8880.

World Bank. (1994). *Adjustment in Africa: Reforms, Results and the Road Ahead*. University Press.

World Bank. (1996). *Nigeria and the World Bank: Learning from the Past, Looking into the Future*. World Bank Washington D.C.

APPENDIX

EXP AT 1ST DIFF.

Null Hypothesis: D(EXP01) has a unit root				
Exogenous: Constant, Linear Trend				
Lag Length: 0 (Automatic - based on SIC, maxlag=9)				
			t-Statistic	Prob.*
Augmented Dickey-Fuller test statistic			-6.792792	0.0000
Test critical values:	1% level		-4.226815	
	5% level		-3.536601	
	10% level		-3.200320	
*MacKinnon (1996) one-sided p-values.				
Augmented Dickey-Fuller Test Equation				
Dependent Variable: D(EXP01,2)				
Method: Least Squares				
Date: 09/13/22 Time: 16:52				
Sample (adjusted): 1983 2019				
Included observations: 37 after adjustments				
Variable	Coefficient	Std. Error	t-Statistic	Prob.
D(EXP01(-1))	-1.150158	0.169320	-6.792792	0.0000
C	1.736774	6.641808	0.261491	0.7953
@TREND("1981")	-0.004352	0.292886	-0.014857	0.9882
R-squared	0.575787	Mean dependent var		0.175676
Adjusted R-squared	0.550834	S.D. dependent var		28.38101
S.E. of regression	19.02092	Akaike info criterion		8.806560
Sum squared resid	12301.04	Schwarz criterion		8.937175
Log likelihood	-159.9214	Hannan-Quinn criter.		8.852608
F-statistic	23.07425	Durbin-Watson stat		1.970735
Prob(F-statistic)	0.000000			

EXR AT 1ST DIFF.

Null Hypothesis: D(EXR) has a unit root				
Exogenous: Constant, Linear Trend				
Lag Length: 0 (Automatic - based on SIC, maxlag=9)				
			t-Statistic	Prob.*
Augmented Dickey-Fuller test statistic			-4.814240	0.0022
Test critical values:	1% level		-4.226815	
	5% level		-3.536601	
	10% level		-3.200320	
*MacKinnon (1996) one-sided p-values.				
Augmented Dickey-Fuller Test Equation				
Dependent Variable: D(EXR,2)				
Method: Least Squares				
Date: 09/13/22 Time: 16:55				
Sample (adjusted): 1983 2019				
Included observations: 37 after adjustments				
Variable	Coefficient	Std. Error	t-Statistic	Prob.
D(EXR(-1))	-0.860410	0.178722	-4.814240	0.0000
C	-4.839208	6.297656	-0.768414	0.4475
@TREND("1981")	0.667630	0.295770	2.257263	0.0305
R-squared	0.408812	Mean dependent var		1.459189
Adjusted R-squared	0.374036	S.D. dependent var		22.68247
S.E. of regression	17.94588	Akaike info criterion		8.690203
Sum squared resid	10949.86	Schwarz criterion		8.820818
Log likelihood	-157.7688	Hannan-Quinn criter.		8.736251
F-statistic	11.75567	Durbin-Watson stat		1.906491
Prob(F-statistic)	0.000132			

FDI AT 1ST DIFF.

Null Hypothesis: D(FDI) has a unit root				
Exogenous: Constant, Linear Trend				
Lag Length: 0 (Automatic - based on SIC, maxlag=9)				
			t-Statistic	Prob.*
Augmented Dickey-Fuller test statistic			-7.366449	0.0000
Test critical values:	1% level		-4.226815	
	5% level		-3.536601	
	10% level		-3.200320	
*MacKinnon (1996) one-sided p-values.				
Augmented Dickey-Fuller Test Equation				
Dependent Variable: D(FDI,2)				
Method: Least Squares				
Date: 09/13/22 Time: 16:56				
Sample (adjusted): 1983 2019				
Included observations: 37 after adjustments				
Variable	Coefficient	Std. Error	t-Statistic	Prob.
D(FDI(-1))	-1.230146	0.166993	-7.366449	0.0000
C	0.349083	0.423245	0.824778	0.4152
@TREND("1981")	-0.014514	0.018663	-0.777680	0.4421
R-squared	0.614796	Mean dependent var		0.010270
Adjusted R-squared	0.592137	S.D. dependent var		1.886819
S.E. of regression	1.205002	Akaike info criterion		3.288444
Sum squared resid	49.36897	Schwarz criterion		3.419058
Log likelihood	-57.83620	Hannan-Quinn criter.		3.334491
F-statistic	27.13243	Durbin-Watson stat		2.006256
Prob(F-statistic)	0.000000			

FOR. DEBT AT 1ST DIFF.

Null Hypothesis: D(FOR_DEBT) has a unit root				
Exogenous: Constant, Linear Trend				
Lag Length: 0 (Automatic - based on SIC, maxlag=9)				
			t-Statistic	Prob.*
Augmented Dickey-Fuller test statistic			-5.875365	0.0001
Test critical values:	1% level		-4.226815	
	5% level		-3.536601	
	10% level		-3.200320	
*MacKinnon (1996) one-sided p-values.				
Augmented Dickey-Fuller Test Equation				
Dependent Variable: D(FOR_DEBT,2)				
Method: Least Squares				
Date: 09/13/22 Time: 16:57				
Sample (adjusted): 1983 2019				
Included observations: 37 after adjustments				
Variable	Coefficient	Std. Error	t-Statistic	Prob.
D(FOR_DEBT(-1))	-1.010076	0.171917	-5.875365	0.0000
C	4.568070	4.607647	0.991411	0.3285
@TREND("1981")	-0.220195	0.203906	-1.079885	0.2878
R-squared	0.503829	Mean dependent var		0.017027
Adjusted R-squared	0.474643	S.D. dependent var		17.91837
S.E. of regression	12.98751	Akaike info criterion		8.043458
Sum squared resid	5734.963	Schwarz criterion		8.174073
Log likelihood	-145.8040	Hannan-Quinn criter.		8.089506
F-statistic	17.26239	Durbin-Watson stat		1.982447
Prob(F-statistic)	0.000007			

GDP PER CAP. AT 1ST DIFF.

Null Hypothesis: D(GDP_PER_CAP_) has a unit root				
Exogenous: Constant, Linear Trend				
Lag Length: 0 (Automatic - based on SIC, maxlag=9)				
			t-Statistic	Prob.*
Augmented Dickey-Fuller test statistic			-3.834291	0.0257
Test critical values:	1% level		-4.226815	
	5% level		-3.536601	
	10% level		-3.200320	
*MacKinnon (1996) one-sided p-values.				
Augmented Dickey-Fuller Test Equation				
Dependent Variable: D(GDP_PER_CAP_,2)				
Method: Least Squares				
Date: 09/13/22 Time: 16:57				
Sample (adjusted): 1983 2019				
Included observations: 37 after adjustments				
Variable	Coefficient	Std. Error	t-Statistic	Prob.
D(GDP_PER_CAP_(-1))	-0.593265	0.154726	-3.834291	0.0005
C	-55.19936	81.45062	-0.677703	0.5025
@TREND("1981")	3.198119	3.624195	0.882436	0.3837
R-squared	0.303457	Mean dependent var		11.20054
Adjusted R-squared	0.262484	S.D. dependent var		260.3485
S.E. of regression	223.5841	Akaike info criterion		13.73506
Sum squared resid	1699655.	Schwarz criterion		13.86567
Log likelihood	-251.0986	Hannan-Quinn criter.		13.78111
F-statistic	7.406238	Durbin-Watson stat		2.045192
Prob(F-statistic)	0.002139			

GFCF AT LEVEL

Null Hypothesis: GFCF has a unit root				
Exogenous: Constant, Linear Trend				
Lag Length: 0 (Automatic - based on SIC, maxlag=9)				
			t-Statistic	Prob.*
Augmented Dickey-Fuller test statistic			-6.279100	0.0000
Test critical values:	1% level		-4.219126	
	5% level		-3.533083	
	10% level		-3.198312	
*MacKinnon (1996) one-sided p-values.				
Augmented Dickey-Fuller Test Equation				
Dependent Variable: D(GFCF)				
Method: Least Squares				
Date: 09/13/22 Time: 16:58				
Sample (adjusted): 1982 2019				
Included observations: 38 after adjustments				
Variable	Coefficient	Std. Error	t-Statistic	Prob.
GFCF(-1)	-0.262725	0.041841	-6.279100	0.0000
C	-2.670242	2.964374	-0.900777	0.3739
@TREND("1981")	0.665744	0.113397	5.870903	0.0000
R-squared	0.645688	Mean dependent var		-1.852895
Adjusted R-squared	0.625441	S.D. dependent var		12.36559
S.E. of regression	7.567886	Akaike info criterion		6.961361
Sum squared resid	2004.552	Schwarz criterion		7.090644
Log likelihood	-129.2659	Hannan-Quinn criter.		7.007359
F-statistic	31.89147	Durbin-Watson stat		1.806329
Prob(F-statistic)	0.000000			

GOV_CAP AT 1ST DIFF.

Null Hypothesis: GOV__CAP has a unit root				
Exogenous: Constant, Linear Trend				
Lag Length: 0 (Automatic - based on SIC, maxlag=9)				
			t-Statistic	Prob.*
Augmented Dickey-Fuller test statistic			-6.115922	0.0001
Test critical values:	1% level		-4.219126	
	5% level		-3.533083	
	10% level		-3.198312	
*MacKinnon (1996) one-sided p-values.				
Augmented Dickey-Fuller Test Equation				
Dependent Variable: D(GOV__CAP)				
Method: Least Squares				
Date: 09/13/22 Time: 16:59				
Sample (adjusted): 1982 2019				
Included observations: 38 after adjustments				
Variable	Coefficient	Std. Error	t-Statistic	Prob.
GOV__CAP(-1)	-0.264457	0.043241	-6.115922	0.0000
C	-2.491161	3.076123	-0.809838	0.4235
@TREND("1981")	0.673074	0.120000	5.608929	0.0000
R-squared	0.621742	Mean dependent var		-1.945526
Adjusted R-squared	0.600128	S.D. dependent var		12.57362
S.E. of regression	7.950985	Akaike info criterion		7.060125
Sum squared resid	2212.636	Schwarz criterion		7.189408
Log likelihood	-131.1424	Hannan-Quinn criter.		7.106123
F-statistic	28.76476	Durbin-Watson stat		1.851869
Prob(F-statistic)	0.000000			

HD AT 1ST DIFF.

Null Hypothesis: D(HD) has a unit root				
Exogenous: Constant, Linear Trend				
Lag Length: 0 (Automatic - based on SIC, maxlag=9)				
			t-Statistic	Prob.*
Augmented Dickey-Fuller test statistic			-4.573045	0.0041
Test critical values:	1% level		-4.226815	
	5% level		-3.536601	
	10% level		-3.200320	
*MacKinnon (1996) one-sided p-values.				
Augmented Dickey-Fuller Test Equation				
Dependent Variable: D(HD,2)				
Method: Least Squares				
Date: 09/13/22 Time: 22:14				
Sample (adjusted): 1983 2019				
Included observations: 37 after adjustments				
Variable	Coefficient	Std. Error	t-Statistic	Prob.
D(HD(-1))	-1.200189	0.262448	-4.573045	0.0001
C	1.111270	0.375418	2.960086	0.0056
@TREND("1981")	-0.005935	0.011663	-0.508872	0.6141
R-squared	0.396871	Mean dependent var		0.081081
Adjusted R-squared	0.361393	S.D. dependent var		0.885010
S.E. of regression	0.707237	Akaike info criterion		2.222703
Sum squared resid	17.00627	Schwarz criterion		2.353318
Log likelihood	-38.12001	Hannan-Quinn criter.		2.268751
F-statistic	11.18636	Durbin-Watson stat		1.453134
Prob(F-statistic)	0.000185			

IMP AT 1ST DIFF.

Null Hypothesis: D(IMP) has a unit root				
Exogenous: Constant, Linear Trend				
Lag Length: 8 (Automatic - based on SIC, maxlag=9)				
			t-Statistic	Prob.*
Augmented Dickey-Fuller test statistic			-5.231568	0.0011
Test critical values:	1% level		-4.309824	
	5% level		-3.574244	
	10% level		-3.221728	
*MacKinnon (1996) one-sided p-values.				
Augmented Dickey-Fuller Test Equation				
Dependent Variable: D(IMP,2)				
Method: Least Squares				
Date: 09/13/22 Time: 22:15				
Sample (adjusted): 1991 2019				
Included observations: 29 after adjustments				
Variable	Coefficient	Std. Error	t-Statistic	Prob.
D(IMP(-1))	-5.997161	1.146341	-5.231568	0.0001
D(IMP(-1),2)	4.535927	1.068100	4.246723	0.0005
D(IMP(-2),2)	4.019020	1.002811	4.007754	0.0008
D(IMP(-3),2)	4.187004	0.972516	4.305333	0.0004
D(IMP(-4),2)	4.234587	0.959932	4.411341	0.0003
D(IMP(-5),2)	4.221167	0.932359	4.527407	0.0003
D(IMP(-6),2)	3.409032	0.795914	4.283168	0.0004
D(IMP(-7),2)	2.342689	0.581472	4.028891	0.0008
D(IMP(-8),2)	1.751202	0.428305	4.088679	0.0007
C	-20.39663	6.575512	-3.101907	0.0062
@TREND("1981")	1.360496	0.345976	3.932341	0.0010
R-squared	0.850806	Mean dependent var		0.045172
Adjusted R-squared	0.767921	S.D. dependent var		15.68254
S.E. of regression	7.555005	Akaike info criterion		7.163994
Sum squared resid	1027.406	Schwarz criterion		7.682624
Log likelihood	-92.87792	Hannan-Quinn criter.		7.326422
F-statistic	10.26483	Durbin-Watson stat		1.855367
Prob(F-statistic)	0.000015			

OPENNESS AT 1ST DIFF.

Null Hypothesis: D(OPENNESS) has a unit root				
Exogenous: Constant, Linear Trend				
Lag Length: 8 (Automatic - based on SIC, maxlag=9)				
			t-Statistic	Prob.*
Augmented Dickey-Fuller test statistic			-4.559959	0.0056
Test critical values:	1% level		-4.309824	
	5% level		-3.574244	
	10% level		-3.221728	
*MacKinnon (1996) one-sided p-values.				
Augmented Dickey-Fuller Test Equation				
Dependent Variable: D(OPENNESS,2)				
Method: Least Squares				
Date: 09/13/22 Time: 22:16				
Sample (adjusted): 1991 2019				
Included observations: 29 after adjustments				
Variable	Coefficient	Std. Error	t-Statistic	Prob.
D(OPENNESS(-1))	-6.960518	1.526443	-4.559959	0.0002
D(OPENNESS(-1),2)	5.589876	1.428272	3.913734	0.0010
D(OPENNESS(-2),2)	4.731487	1.274012	3.713848	0.0016
D(OPENNESS(-3),2)	4.045663	1.127463	3.588290	0.0021
D(OPENNESS(-4),2)	3.181204	0.941227	3.379848	0.0033
D(OPENNESS(-5),2)	2.380414	0.737650	3.227025	0.0047
D(OPENNESS(-6),2)	1.710952	0.539252	3.172824	0.0053
D(OPENNESS(-7),2)	0.827983	0.361363	2.291277	0.0342
D(OPENNESS(-8),2)	0.563061	0.200203	2.812452	0.0115
C	30.73475	8.286925	3.708825	0.0016
@TREND("1981")	-1.120111	0.306745	-3.651607	0.0018
R-squared	0.848306	Mean dependent var		0.267931
Adjusted R-squared	0.764032	S.D. dependent var		13.58459
S.E. of regression	6.598928	Akaike info criterion		6.893388
Sum squared resid	783.8254	Schwarz criterion		7.412018
Log likelihood	-88.95413	Hannan-Quinn criter.		7.055816
F-statistic	10.06600	Durbin-Watson stat		2.140274
Prob(F-statistic)	0.000017			

PR_CONS AT LEVEL

Null Hypothesis: PR__CONS has a unit root				
Exogenous: Constant, Linear Trend				
Lag Length: 8 (Automatic - based on SIC, maxlag=9)				
			t-Statistic	Prob.*
Augmented Dickey-Fuller test statistic			-5.282502	0.0009
Test critical values:	1% level		-4.296729	
	5% level		-3.568379	
	10% level		-3.218382	
*MacKinnon (1996) one-sided p-values.				
Augmented Dickey-Fuller Test Equation				
Dependent Variable: D(PR__CONS)				
Method: Least Squares				
Date: 09/13/22 Time: 22:17				
Sample (adjusted): 1990 2019				
Included observations: 30 after adjustments				
Variable	Coefficient	Std. Error	t-Statistic	Prob.
PR__CONS(-1)	-0.882443	0.167050	-5.282502	0.0000
D(PR__CONS(-1))	0.693737	0.185694	3.735926	0.0014
D(PR__CONS(-2))	0.408620	0.200651	2.036473	0.0559
D(PR__CONS(-3))	0.902612	0.231550	3.898125	0.0010
D(PR__CONS(-4))	0.872065	0.361068	2.415236	0.0260
D(PR__CONS(-5))	1.040008	0.361440	2.877399	0.0096
D(PR__CONS(-6))	2.008294	0.441305	4.550808	0.0002
D(PR__CONS(-7))	1.639195	0.503931	3.252817	0.0042
D(PR__CONS(-8))	1.662786	0.563326	2.951729	0.0082
C	-5.444337	20.74696	-0.262416	0.7958
@TREND("1981")	1.905317	1.299468	1.466229	0.1589
R-squared	0.669587	Mean dependent var		9.933333
Adjusted R-squared	0.495685	S.D. dependent var		28.70525
S.E. of regression	20.38508	Akaike info criterion		9.144059
Sum squared resid	7895.479	Schwarz criterion		9.657831
Log likelihood	-126.1609	Hannan-Quinn criter.		9.308419
F-statistic	3.850370	Durbin-Watson stat		1.864254
Prob(F-statistic)	0.005591			

RINT AT LEVEL

Null Hypothesis: RINTR has a unit root				
Exogenous: Constant, Linear Trend				
Lag Length: 0 (Automatic - based on SIC, maxlag=9)				
			t-Statistic	Prob.*
Augmented Dickey-Fuller test statistic			-7.476432	0.0000
Test critical values:	1% level		-4.219126	
	5% level		-3.533083	
	10% level		-3.198312	
*MacKinnon (1996) one-sided p-values.				
Augmented Dickey-Fuller Test Equation				
Dependent Variable: D(RINTR)				
Method: Least Squares				
Date: 09/13/22 Time: 22:18				
Sample (adjusted): 1982 2019				
Included observations: 38 after adjustments				
Variable	Coefficient	Std. Error	t-Statistic	Prob.
RINTR(-1)	-0.852824	0.114068	-7.476432	0.0000
C	-3.465696	3.288780	-1.053794	0.2992
@TREND("1981")	0.280661	0.151670	1.850467	0.0727
R-squared	0.630975	Mean dependent var		1.852105
Adjusted R-squared	0.609888	S.D. dependent var		14.39533
S.E. of regression	8.991174	Akaike info criterion		7.306021
Sum squared resid	2829.442	Schwarz criterion		7.435304
Log likelihood	-135.8144	Hannan-Quinn criter.		7.352019
F-statistic	29.92224	Durbin-Watson stat		1.624735
Prob(F-statistic)	0.000000			

DESCRIPTIVE STAT.

	GDP_PER_ CAP_	RINTR	GFCF	GOV__ CAP	HD	IMP	OPENNESS	PR__ CONS	FOR_ DEBT	FDI	EXR	EXP01
Mean	1312.415	0.293077	47.07897	48.22077	41.52821	26.82154	32.39333	121.9497	34.91846	2.598974	95.84744	36.68821
Median	902.2200	4.310000	35.55000	36.99000	43.10000	15.76000	34.18000	35.30000	25.65000	1.870000	101.7000	20.91000
Maximum	3222.690	18.18000	147.0200	147.0100	57.20000	88.88000	53.28000	414.7800	120.8400	8.840000	360.2200	144.9200
Minimum	270.2200	-65.86000	12.34000	12.35000	25.30000	2.130000	9.140000	13.03000	4.080000	0.190000	2.730000	2.880000
Std. Dev.	887.5848	14.59720	30.11309	30.70514	9.003916	26.18295	12.42702	131.5949	30.92607	2.602664	96.02441	37.37467
Skewness	0.548815	-2.637153	1.283379	1.154238	-0.162164	0.798096	-0.386780	0.928402	0.844093	1.065824	0.965065	1.291995
Kurtosis	1.908813	12.27281	4.803855	4.324424	1.799266	2.176272	2.245845	2.325251	3.008255	2.909118	3.348976	3.808167
Jarque-Bera	3.892654	184.9304	15.99347	11.51014	2.513796	5.242826	1.896611	6.342390	4.631312	7.397294	6.251675	11.91147
Probability	0.142798	0.000000	0.000337	0.003167	0.284535	0.072700	0.387397	0.041953	0.098701	0.024757	0.043900	0.002591
Sum	51184.20	11.43000	1836.080	1880.610	1619.600	1046.040	1263.340	4756.040	1361.820	101.3600	3738.050	1430.840
Sum Sq. Dev.	29936658	8096.974	34458.33	35826.61	3080.679	26050.78	5868.369	658054.6	36344.02	257.4068	350386.1	53080.92
Observations	39	39	39	39	39	39	39	39	39	39	39	39

REGRESSION ANALYSIS

Dependent Variable: GDP_PER_CAP_				
Method: Least Squares				
Date: 09/14/22 Time: 09:27				
Sample: 1981 2019				
Included observations: 39				

Chapter 11
Post-Cold War and Economic Development:
The Indian 40 Years of Post-Cold War Experience

Friday Edwin Nkwede
Ebonyi State University, Nigeria

Maria-Friday Chinonye Nkwede
Ebonyi State University, Nigeria

ABSTRACT

War in any form and at any point in time in human existence is horrific. Among all the expectations of human race and nation, war is not one, including cold war. No doubt, cold war has always been with humanity. The author in this study set out to explore the effect of the post-cold war on the Indian economic growth and development. Due to the nature of the variables of the study, a quantitative econometric model formed the research methodology. The data scope covered the period of 39 years. The overall empirical results show that some macroeconomic variables have significant effect and positive relationship with the Indian economic development. The implication is that these factors in the long run are statistically significant and positively related to the Indian economic development. It is concluded from the study that long run relationships exist among the variables though the speed of adjustment differs.

DOI: 10.4018/979-8-3693-1610-8.ch011

INTRODUCTION

Cold war is not a phrase, it is a threat. War in any form and any point in time, in human existence poses giant danger to humanity and peace. Among all the expectations of human race and nation, war is not one, including cold war. It constitute the biggest security challenges and breach to peace, just like the current Russia and Ukraine war characterizes the biggest threat to peace in the entire Europe and other parts of the world ever since the end of the cold war. No doubt, cold war has always been with humanity; such that humanity have always suffered cold war between nations and the global regions.

In the global perspective, nations often lead and sponsor cold war between one region and another. For instance, cold war between Western nations such as USA, Britain, France, among other others. There are various forms of cold war emanating from ideological differences for various economic and religious gains. The complicating issues in a cold war and post cold war is often conflict driving, empire acquisition dominance struggle, secession, freedom among others.

On the other hands, socialism and capitalism struggle and dominance among nations manifest greatly most cold war experiences. Western and Eastern influence, neocolonialism and imperialisms induce cold war among nations of the world. There is rarely any nation that has not directly or indirectly suffered from cold and post cold war. In this study and in this chapter, we shall focus on India as a state in the Asian continent. The rest of the introductory part of this study is discussed along the Indian geographical, political and economic history. Section two shall focus on economic philosophy and management of India while sections three will periscope the major economic political reforms and programme in India from 1900 to 1980 and 1981-2020. Section five shall concentrate on the study methodology and data analysis while section six concludes the study.

a) The geographical and political history of India

Geographically, India as a state/country is located at the southern part of Asia. India is one of the countries in the Asia continent. It occupies the largest part of the southern Asia. By geographical mass, India measures 3,214km (from North to South) to 2933KM from East India to West part of India (FXTM, 2020). It also has a "land frontier of 15,200km and coastline of 7,516.6km" (FXTM, 2020). The 'total land mass of India is s3,287,263km^2 with 91% land space and 9% occupied by water'. The capital of India is located at New Delhi which was built around 20th century. New Delhi serves as the administrative centre of India. The demographic history of India posits that India has the second largest population in the world. Thus, after China, India is among "the most populous country in the world with diverse ethnic groups and hundreds of diverse languages". Historically, India has one-sixth of the total world population. The archaeological fact shows that inspite of her large population, India has a deeply sophisticated culture that is urban based. Such that by "26000 BCE, the Indus civilization had already prominently dominating the major parts of the North Western part". This Indus dominance and civilization principally cumulated into Hinduism as a distinctive tradition in India till date.

Due to the manner the Indus civilizations overwhelmy dominated the Northwest part of the Indian subcontinent, other religious organization such as Jainism and Buddhism historically traced their origin to subcontinent (Isaac, 1983). The entire India is surrounded by many notable countries both North and South. Simply put, the Northwest part of India is surrounded by Pakistan while the North is bounded by China, Bhutan and Nepal, (Isaac, 1983).

The Eastern part of India is bounded by Myanmar. In the southeast coast of India, there is an Island country called Sri Lanka that is situated "40 miles off the southeast coast, across the pack strait and the Gulf of Mannar". It is worthy of note that major parts Indian's present territory biologically lies around the Reninsula which is geologically 'bounded by the Arabian Sea in the west and the Bay of Bengal in the East', then the 'Cape Comorin, the southernmost point of the Indian mainland" which "marks the dividing line between those two bodies of water" (Schwartzberg, 1988). According to him, India as a country has two joint territories that is composed entirely of Island namely Lakschadweep situated in the Arabian Sea and the Andamanand Nicobar Islands, that is situated between the "Bay of Bengal and the Andaman Sea"(Isaac, 2013).

The geographical stance of India cannot be complete without the mention of Himalays which are divided into three basic longitudinal belts namely the outer Himalays, the lesser Himalays and the great Himalays. The Himalays of India originated from the Sanskrit word- "Hima" (meaning snow) and "alays" (meaning abode). It constitute the loftiest mountain system in the world, with the great geological young mountain arc which measures about 1,550 miles "stretching from the peak of Nanga Parbat in the Patkistani- administered portion of the Kashnir region to the Namecha Barwa Peak in the Tibet autonomous region of China". (Cubilt, 2013).

b) Demographic Trends in India

It is on record that Indian population is young. The general life expectancy of India is about 68 for men and 70 for women (Isaac, 2013). The trend in the population explosion in India started during the great "influenza epidemic of 1918-1919 such that, as at 1961, the population of India had hit 251 million people. According to the last India census of 2011 total population was 1, 210, 193, 422 (over 1 billion population), while the interpolation projection of India population for 2022 is 1,406,174,950 (World Population Review, 2022).

The climate condition of India has been adjudged as the world model of a "monsoon climate". The type of climate has both wet and dry seasons system. Its annual temperature fluctuates and produces about three universal climatic periods in the country. These include- hot wet weather from June to September, cold dry weather from early October to February and the hot-dry weather from Britch to mid-June.

The political history of India started with the Mauryan Empire, this empire was the first government and political Administration formed in the year 321 B.C.E. As a political structure, it ended in the year 185 BCE as the first pan- India Empire that spanned across major part of India.

c). Synoptic Indian Political History

The Indian political historical facts hold that India got her independent on 15 August 1947. During the struggle for her independent, some sections of the country were carved out and a new country-Pakistan was created. This was the making of the former Mgual Empire by dividing the nation of India into India and Pakistan.

Indian independent was the government of India Act of 1935 that envisioned the India self government as an entity of its own. Though the constituent Assembly of India deliberation of the future India, the constitution of India was promulgated and India became a Republic on 26 January 1950. The political struggle for the independent of India lasted for decades of resistance. It was difficult for Britain to accept Indian independence, save for the self-rule that had earlier been announced during the World War II. The India government from the beginning of her republic is fashioned in line with the British style of government. It consists of president, the head of state. His powers are mostly ceremonial except on emergency; an executive headed by the prime minister, a legislature that consist of parliament and the Judiciary (Price, 1982). The Indian government structure also has the lower and the upper house in the parliament and the Supreme Court structure. The Indian political structure is bravely set by the Indian constitution with federal structure, government powers and freedom of the citizenry. The Indian constitution which set the political code of Indian democracy is also very complicated by the India "Caste system which permits a "hierarchical social structure that divides the Hindu majority" into Brahmin group and Dalits group (Price, 1982). About 543 members are elected to the "Lok Sabah" via a "first-past-the-post-general election" that are held every five years. In the political history of India, the Indian government was initially dominated by the first popular political party known as India National Congress Party, generally addressed as "congress". The dominance was a result of the role the leader of the party played for independent of India- the Late Mahatina Gandhi who was assassinated by the Hindu Nationalist in 1948.

Perhaps, the developments of democracy in India to the present stage have suffered some challenges. Some of the challenges include but not limited to the failure of India demography to hatch a sustainable economic development that will lift Indians from extreme poverty that are currently inherent in the country, as apparently enjoyed by the neighboring countries like China.

Again, even though there is a considerable development in India since independence, such developments have recorded even spread across sections. For instance, an educated citizen of India in a more developed cities like Delhi and Mumbai no doubt live a more comfortable life than the whelming poorest citizens in India. Therefore, the Indian democracy has not been to eliminate the abject poverty in the country. Low-wage and low-skilled jobs have dominated millions of young citizens of India especially in the states like Uttar, Pradesh which brings about disenchanted voters.

There is also a challenge of the fed off of the popular Indian nationalism and the populism which gave way for increasing the arrogant of the many Hindus. The nationalism was regarded as the National movement for Indian democratic development with the political ideology of Hindutua-arguing that India should be the homeland for South Asia and Hindus just as can be observed in Pakistan for its Muslims dominance. To this effect, since the take of BJB, his government have being pushing the stability Indian democracy but the Hindus nationalism are not so much concerned. It is hoped the challenges will grow less and the India democracy grows stronger.

c) Economic History of India

The economic account of India is partly watershed. Notwithstanding, the economic history of India is also linked to "Maurya Empire". As at two Millennia ending about 500BC, India was already recorded among the top largest economies of the world (Bairoch, 1995). It is on record, that by "500 BC the Mahajanapades of India had minted punch-marked silver coins for effective trade activities".

Between the interval of 1st century and 18th century, and even until 1000 AD, India had a subsistence economy with the GDP per capital slightly above subsistence level. But within the medieval era, India experienced high GDP growth rate. This was as a result of uniting the Indian subcontinent under the "Mughal Empire". The unification also help the economy as India became the largest economy and manufacturing power in the world; producing about one quarter of the global GDP then. It was not long, and India was conquered and her economy became fragmented, such that by 18th century, serious economic programmes had started for the purpose of ambitious economic development. This led to the establishment of "Kingdom Mysore as the major India economic power" (Prasannan, 2011).

The economy of India suffered deindustrialization and cession under Pritish rule which brought about India economic decline. This resulted in 24.4% down fall of the India economy up till 1950. India being a capitalist economy, and due to its ancient history, used its trading zone and its colonial status, integrated her economy with the whole world, and with such economic integration launched an economic reforms.

The "India economic reforms" means the fundamental changes that were 'launched around 1991 with the sole purpose of liberating the economic challenges in India and attain high growth rate economically'.

Again, the 'India economic reforms aims to achieve economic stabilization and macroeconomic stability'. However, there was serious economic policy thinking that started in early 1980s in India. Because of the poor performance of India public sector, adverse balance of payment; decline in foreign exchange reserve, huge debts on India government, inflationary pressure, terms and conditions of World Bank and IMF among others. It was a complete economic structure reforms. The economic history of India cannot be complete, if the major issues of the India economic reforms are not highlighted in this chapter. Such major issues are as follows:

i. **Fiscal Consolidation Reform**: The fiscal deficit of India was dreadfully high. The economic reform policy was targeted on reducing the fiscal deficit of the country as a prospective for crowding out the requirement of the stress on interest rate, enterprise sector, and the then rising interest payment on government debts. Before the reform, 'the fiscal deficit of the central government was 8.3% of the GDP in the 1990/91 fiscal year'. But through the reform it was brought to 5.9 percent of the GDP, the next fiscal year-1992. Since the reform, the India fiscal deficit has witnessed a steady and gradual decline. The major fiscal consolidation reforms were done on the India revenue deficit; as government increase savings culture, Central government of India capital expenditure, and general government fiscal surplus. As Bajpai (2002) put it, "the Indian economy was able to accomplish higher economic growth in the post reform years irrespective of inadequate investment infrastructure because there was some slack in the scheme of things".

ii. **Tax Reforms:** Though the reform brought about a significant progress in the tax system, apparently the tax system in India is still relatively multifarious with some level of high tax rate. The success of the reform in tax system/ structure of India was recorded in establishing the regime of moderate tax rates which can be compared to other countries in Asia. From the beginning of the reform, 'the maximum personal income tax was reduced from 56% to 30%'. The corporation tax also varies but has reduced too.

The steady percentage increase in tax revenue as a ratio of GDP is an indication that the strategic reforms in that area is working well and therefore required to be broadened especially the income tax payers. It is only an excise duty that is the major indirect tax in India. Thus, India had introduced a mortified value added tax known as "modvat". In 'modvat', "credit is duly given for excise taxes paid on input against excise taxes due on output", thereby avoiding dropping down of excise duties. This practice has been extended and generally rationalized the economic reform. 'Modvat' is not applied to all products but it is currently a universal coverage on all products.

iii. **Inflation Control**: Within the first four years of economic reform in India, (ie from 1990s and above), the country experienced "double-digit inflation" regarding the wholesale price index with a peak of 13.6%. According to Bajpai and Sachs (2000), "from 1995/96, there has been an increase and the average inflation for the period of 1996-2011". It was observed that the 'point-to-point average inflation rate in India' is the lowest since the reforms in 1990.

iv. **Reforms in Trade & Investment:** The reforms on the area of trade and investment took the form of a deliberate policies on external sector of the Indian economy such as devaluation of the Indian currency (Rupee), ensuring that rupee is highly "convertible on current account", the liberalization of the trade regime, granting import of gold to India, allowing "foreign direct investmen"t including "technology inflows", opening up of the Indian "capital market" for huge 'portfolio investment' by institutions and blue cheep investors, granting the Indian domestic companies access to foreign capital market among others. There is no gain saying that reformative approach in India foreign direct investment greatly brought a steady progress and stability in her balance of payment. For instance, the Indian export-import ratio improved, the merchandize export and non-oil import had a dramatic turn around.

v. **Industrial Policy Reforms:** The major area of the industrial policy reforms was on two areas. First, is the Central government industry licensing practices and permission. On this reform, government permission was granted for substantial expansion in both existing industries and the new ones while central government abolished licensing in seven industries namely such as 'beverages, electronics, defense, chemicals and pharmaceuticals. However, unique permission was given under "Monopolies and Restrictive Trade Practice Act" (MRTP) (SIA, 2001). Second, is the opening of the Indian economy technology industries. This industry was regarded as the biggest beneficiary of the industries reform policies. For example, available records show that between 1995 and 2000, information and telecommunication industry in India improved to a level greater than '42.4%', and 'software' have constantly continued to make great contributions to the India IT industry's revenue. After the September 11 incident, India made a frank market penetration in software industry with massive software giant and steady exportation around the globe.

vi. **Financial Sector Reforms:** Before the financial reforms, India financial sector had suffered inadequate capacity to mobilize savings, inadequate manpower, externally induced constraints on banks' and insurance company. This is because, the profitability of Indian banks and financial institutions were very weak.

Thus, the reforms in this sector were made to address these challenges. For instance, the reform addressed the 'high statutory cash requirements in which most banks were compelled to make compulsory investment in government of India securities'. The very high requirement was reduced for the banks such that some government financial papers carry "market-clearing rates". Again, the reform removed the restrictions on interest rate and freed interest rate on money market related instruments.

In line with various institutions, many agencies were basically adjusted to trade in money and long term debt instruments. The reform also established a strong prudential regime about capital adequacy, income recognition, loan-loss provision and transparency of account for the purpose of improving the efficiency and the workability of the banks. The banks were to embrace technology and ensure massive computerization across board. Again, the reforms brought about a healthy competition among the banks as many new private banks were encouraged and allowed entry into the market. All banks' supervision were strengthened and over the years, the Indian capital market, in terms of capital-base, listed companies, trading volumes, market capitalization and investor's base have grown and the number and diversity of market intermediaries such as merchant banks, transfer agents, mutual fund, share registrars, rating agencies, underwriters among others-have all grown with high expectations.

INDIA POLITICAL AND INTERNATIONAL ASSOCIATION DURING THE COLD WAR ERA OF 1947-1980

The cold war in India is almost as old as the independent state of Indian nation. India was directly administered by the British in since 1855. This British administration affected the India economic and political unity and this made India a nation to face many crisis and violence related political experiences. For example, Indian was with faced religious crisis, terrorism crisis, violence, naxalism and separatist insurgencies. Additionally, India has "an unresolved terrorist dispute with China" that escalated into the 'Sino-Indian war in 1962' as well as the 'India-Pakistan war or 1965, 1971 and 1999'. Although India was initially neutral in the cold-war, but she had an alliance with the Soviet Union because of the Pakistan alliance with United States of America and China. The involvement of India into the cold war was as a result of the Soviet Union dissolution; in which before the dissolution there was a strong and strategic, military, economic and diplomatic relationship between the two countries. But Russia, even after the USSR dissolution, diplomatic alliance with India and both nations began to share a special relationship.

This relationship, alliance and economic association between the two countries have been judged the best any country has in the world. This alliance gave birth to the "India and Russia treaty of peace, friendship and cooperation enclosed on August 9th, 1971". This treaty led to massive assistance which India received from Russia during the India war of 1971.

Meanwhile, other countries apart from Russia that also had international and political association with India are the United Arab Emirate, Israel, Afghanistan, France, Bhutan Bangladesh and United States. Outside these countries, other countries also like India such as Republic of Korea among others. India-Japan Association was established in 1903, and presently it stands as the oldest international alliance between the two countries.

RESEARCH METHODOLOGY

On the basis of the variable of the study in this chapter a quantitative economic model forms the research method of the study. This is anchored on multiple regression models. The research variables utilized in the study are completely out of the control of the researcher coupled with the fact that they share characteristics of observation or influence that have taken place for a long time. The variables of the study include the foreign direct investment, exchanges rate, trade openness, foreign debt ratio, export ratio, real interest rate, import ratio, private consumption, government capital expenditure, human development index, gross fixed capital formation and real gross domestic product per capital income serving as the endogenous variable of the study. The choice of these variables is as a result of their roles in economic development of any nation of the world. The scope of the data covered the period of 39 years spanning from 1981 to 2019.

Model Specification

The study adopted a sample linear regression model specified as follows:

$$GDPCap = \infty + BGFCF_t + \beta_{12}FD1_t + \beta_3 FDEBT_t + \beta_4 EXR_t + \beta_5 PCONS_t + \beta_6 GOVCAP_t + \beta_7 IMP_t + \beta_8 EXP_t + \beta_9 BHD_t + \beta_{10} OPeness_t + \varepsilon \quad (1)$$

Although the model appears addictive but was ignored due to the nature of the data that were used in the model and other controlled measures that was applied.

Empirical Results

Table 1 presents the summary of all the basic variables used in the study. Due to the numerous nature of the variables, it is only major one that are highlighted and discussed here. For instance, the average exchange rate in India within the period under study is 37.93. But between 2019 and 2014, the exchange rates were relatively high ranging from 69.33 and 61.03. Meanwhile the maximum exchange rate recorded in India since 1981 was 69.33 in 2019 while the minimum rate was 8.66 in the year 1981. The GDP growth rate of India maintained an average growth rate of 778.0546. Although, India economic growth had her picked in 2018 with GDP capitalization. This is expected as the country had maintained steady growth due to deliberate economic policies aimed at improving the entire economy of India. In terms of human

Table 1. Summary of descriptive statistics

	GDPCAP_	GFCF	FDI	FDEBT	EXR	EXP01	PCONS	GOVCAP	IMP	HD	OPNES
Mean	778.0546	272.6426	13.81103	21.00487	37.92718	172.6782	552.4577	302.4479	202.7497	50.60513	30.46590
Median	443.3100	126.3400	3.580000	20.16000	43.06000	60.88000	298.5500	129.4100	65.12000	49.70000	25.99000
Maximum	2104.660	789.2400	45.37000	33.16000	69.33000	559.0700	1833.410	869.0900	674.6200	66.10000	55.79000
Minimum	270.4700	38.44000	0.140000	11.62000	8.660000	11.49000	147.3300	40.30000	16.34000	36.50000	12.22000
Std. Dev.	584.0813	254.2117	16.96685	4.939649	18.66592	190.4334	481.6878	287.2754	226.2676	8.673400	14.77946
Skewness	0.970751	0.791727	0.806447	0.661902	-0.088221	0.823567	1.185086	0.746008	0.839939	0.171018	0.302021
Kurtosis	2.489271	2.042373	1.938702	3.268977	1.934357	2.025952	3.176265	1.911200	2.068565	1.841435	1.593562
Jarque-Bera	6.549197	5.564609	6.057647	2.965305	1.895931	5.950453	9.179273	5.543846	5.995539	2.371300	3.807269
Probability	0.037832	0.061896	0.048373	0.227035	0.387529	0.051036	0.010157	0.062542	0.049898	0.305548	0.149026
Sum	30344.13	10633.06	538.6300	819.1900	1479.160	6734.450	21545.85	11795.47	7907.240	1973.600	1188.170
Sum Sq. Dev.	12963736	2455696.	10939.21	927.2052	13239.83	1378066.	8816880.	3136032.	1945486.	2858.659	8300.433
Observations	39	39	39	39	39	39	39	39	39	39	39

and economic development in India, the average Human Development (HD) index was 50.606, with maximum of 66.1 in 2019. The India lowest HD index was in 1982 with a record of HD index of 36.5. In the same vein, the private consumption rate in India has maximum of 1833.410 which is relatively high in relation to the poverty level of other Asian countries. From the available records, the private consumption (pcons) have remained steady and progressive in India.

Moreso, the India government, capital expenditure (GovCAP) on average is $302.4479 billion, with a maximum expenditure of $869.0900 billion. The highest foreign direct (FDI) investment in India is $45.3700 billion while the lowest rate is $0.1400 billion.

From the table, all the Skeweness in the statistics and the Kurtosis were observed; and they all have the expected signs and benchmarks. The hypothesis of normality test using Jarque-Bera (JB) statistics at 5% level was accepted with the conclusion that the structure of statistical data used in the study and their residuals are well distributed.

Correlation Output

From table 2, the correlation coefficient between the indicators of economic development and other macroeconomic factors outside Federal debt (0.138%) are higher than 50%. For instance, correlations between all other variables range from 99% to 82% at both esteems. The negative relationship between foreign direct investment and Gross domestic product in India perhaps suggest a response of foreign investment in India due to various economic reforms arising from the cold war effect. It shows the degree of the relationship connecting all the factors. It can be observed that some variable have positive correlation as they change together in the same direction as can be seen from diagonal. Such variables include GFCF-Gross Fixed capital formation, government capital expenditure (GOVCAP), trade openness (OPNES). The implication of these variables that proved positively correlated is that as the economic growth and development of India increases, those economic factors also increase in line with growth of the economy.

Empirical Results and Discussion

The empirical result arising from the study is presented in table 3. On the discovery of the co-integrating equation see appendix 2, the researcher proceeded to generate a system equation to run for vector error correction model (VCEM) to ascertain the speed of the adjustment since long run effect have been established among the exogenous variables.

Table 2. Correlation result

	GDPCAP_	GFCF	FDI	FDEBT	EXR	PCONS	GOVCAP	IMP	EXP01	HD	OPNES
GDPCAP	1										
GFCF	0.9944633326386426	1									
FDI	0.94672375267502	0.9546372541923084	1								
FDEBT	-0.1387776633869125	-0.1495290857164405	-0.1601369756172804	1							
EXR	0.8377521538201058	0.8415044478085151	0.7936276709085	0.06127526457392143	1						
PCONS	0.9949422309495074	0.980667404586744	0.9311782001264473	-0.1208165579897289	0.8370857980723089	1					
GOVCAP	0.9894731890868376	0.9984009013484659	0.9515895748155223	-0.1572833420889734	0.8308669571493629	0.971830177881797	1				
IMP	0.9854883887596011	0.994168220919062	0.9424680565699694	-0.1470925655622882	0.8140903427252593	0.9701731968901755	0.9936506060947235	1			
EXP01	0.9895807351168634	0.9952712022658466	0.9454036392404212	-0.1362132735939442	0.8302494696459841	0.9756945602396064	0.993185143682968	0.9978056418892519	1		
HD	0.9298946611414542	0.9416422975648293	0.9003682727389194	-0.02375163744447589	0.9615161286526113	0.9165283309690719	0.9381181258832684	0.9213271976158096	0.9304787180776216	1	
OPNES	0.8248666828595191	0.8731835445213084	0.8487132649979595	-0.1605189507390461	0.8270755287502904	0.7815605132158609	0.8839947056509283	0.8786980555343036	0.8754299306884811	0.9097053711464236	1

Source: Author's compilation

Table 3. Empirical results

Dependent Variable: D(GDPCAP				
Method: Least Squares (Gauss-Newton / Marquardt steps)				
Sample (adjusted): 1984 2019				
Included observations: 36 after adjustments				
D(GDPCAP_) = C(1)*(GDPCAP_(-1) + 4.93476095408*GFCF(-1) -				
2107.60967075) + C(2)*D(GDPCAP_(-1)) + C(3)*D(GDPCAP_(-2)) +				
C(4)*D(GFCF(-1)) + C(5)*D(GFCF(-2)) + C(6) + C(7)*FDI + C(8)*FDEBT				
+ C(9)*EXR + C(10)*PCONS + C(11)*GOVCAP + C(12)*IMP + C(13)				
*EXP01 + C(14)*HD + C(15)*OPNES				
	Coefficient	Std. Error	t-Statistic	Prob.
C(1)	-0.306848	0.025262	-12.14640	0.0000
C(2)	-0.572199	0.133968	-4.271152	0.0003
C(3)	-0.112299	0.135927	-0.826175	0.4180
C(4)	0.923771	0.310360	2.976449	0.0072
C(5)	0.055520	0.252409	0.219960	0.8280
C(6)	-1105.998	187.9113	-5.885746	0.0000
C(7)	1.945253	0.576284	3.375510	0.0029
C(8)	-1.846337	0.640081	-2.884538	0.0089
C(9)	-1.700282	1.020966	-1.665365	0.1107
C(10)	0.065011	0.082970	0.783555	0.4420
C(11)	0.865193	0.140661	6.150925	0.0000
C(12)	0.055503	0.336480	0.164953	0.8706
C(13)	1.204010	0.448647	2.683649	0.0139
C(14)	17.28553	5.157004	3.351856	0.0030
C(15)	-6.272265	1.817601	-3.450849	0.0024
R-squared	0.983323	Mean dependent var		50.37278
Adjusted R-squared	0.972205	S.D. dependent var		73.75335
S.E. of regression	12.29596	Akaike info criterion		8.150755
Sum squared resid	3175.003	Schwarz criterion		8.810555
Log likelihood	-131.7136	Hannan-Quinn criter.		8.381043
F-statistic	88.44535	Durbin-Watson stat		1.849892
Prob(F-statistic)	0.000000			
Breusch-Godfrey Serial Correlation LM Test:				
F-statistic	2.092283	Prob. F(2,19)		0.1509
Obs*R-squared	6.497614	Prob. Chi-Square(2)		0.0388

Source: Author compilation

The overall empirical results show that gross fixed capital formation, foreign direct investment, exchange rate, export, private consumption, trade openness, human index, government capital expenditure, foreign debt, export have significant effect and relationship with the Indian economic growth as represented by the real GDP CAP. These results arise from judging by the probability values of the exogenous variables. In specific terms, the implication of the results is as follows: for trade openness in India, in the long run, one period lag of GDP as the dependent variable are statistically significant and positively related to the current trade openness at 1% significant level. This means that in concrete terms, unit change (increase) in one period lag of trade openness with induce about 6.27 units decrease in the level of trade openness in the current period, indicating an increase in the long run in India economy. Similarly, a unit increase human development index among the citizens of India cause about 17.28 unit increase in the overall economic development in India. This shows that the level of significant increase in standard of leaving in the country within the period under study. This result is expected because, all these years, India has maintained steady development while fighting the poverty in the country. All these explanations apply to other major development indicators that proved significant in the study.

Further, among the macroeconomic factors/indicators studied, it is only exchange that was empirically established to have significant negative effect economic growth in India. Although it is at 10% level significant but the researcher accepted it because it pass 90% level of confidence. To this effect exchange rate has significance effect in economic growth and development in India. It is also empirically established that a unit in the long run, one period lag of the dependent variable and the exchange rate are negatively related at 10% level as. Meaning that a unit increase in one period lag or regime of exchange rate in India will bring about 1.7% unit decrease in the exchange rate of the current period, which means that previous increase in exchange rate leads to more exchange rate increase in India economy.

On the other hands, other exogenous factors such as importation (IMP), price consumption (PIONS) gross-capital formation (GFCF) were found to have significant influence on India economic growth and development within the period under study. In the cause of the analysis, inflation rate as macroeconomic factors was removed because of noticed incident multicorreleanity in the model.

Other econometric model diagnostics that worth discussing are the adequacy of the estimated long run and short run impact of the exogenous variables of the study on Indian economy in the post cold war. These diagnostic results have become necessary due to the basic assumptions ordinary least square model:

Unit Root Test

The unit root of the variables was checked using the popular augmented Dicky-Fuller (ADF) and Philips-Perron (PP) unit root test techniques. The major purpose was to determine the order of integration of the variables and the procedure applied was by accommodating a constant term with constant trend. See table appendix 1.

Serial-correlation: This occurs when the error in one period is correlated with error in other periods of the study. The negative resultant effect of this problem is that it makes variance estimation deceptive, leading to inferences. Thus, the null hypothesis tested, up to 2 lags. In this regards, the respective results are obtained shows an evidence that there is no serial correlation leading to accepting the null hypothesis. Therefore, there is a strong evidence to conclude that the estimated model is free from the error of serial correlation. Again, the issue of autocorrelation was also ruled out using Durham Walton. This assumption arises if the disturbance term grows to influence the dependent variables. The conventional rule is that the closer the value of DW to 2, the less likelihood of the problem of autocorrelation. Meanwhile, from our result, the value of DW is 1.85.

Heteroskedasticity: It occurs when the error term fails to maintain a constant variance. This assumption is tested using Preusch-Pegan-Godfrey method. The conventional benchmark and its hypothesis is that Error is Homoskedastic and it can be accepted when the probability values of F. statistics and the Obs.R. squared statistics are higher than ten (10).

Other assumption such as normality distribution, multicorrilearity among other were all in food standing. Finally, R-square (R^2) and the adjusted R-Squared were also checked. The outcome indicates that the explanatory error correlation model (ECM) altogether explained about 98% variation of the entire economy of India within the period under study. Even when the model is adjusted, it still captured 97%.

SUMMARY AND CONCLUSION

Succinctly put, this chapter primarily focused on assessing the effect of the post cold war experience in India on her economic development over the period of 40 years. It was also set out to examine the relationship between the major macroeconomic factors in India and the economic development bearing in mind the dichotomy that occurred between communism, socialism, capitalism arising from the ideological differences and the political strife of India and other nations. For the purpose of achieving the set goal of the study, many issues surrounding India and her neighboring countries were highlighted in the study- such as the economic, political and geographical history of India.

Additionally, an economic model was developed in the research methodology for the purpose of establishing the expected nexus between the India economy within the post cost war period and the major macroeconomic variables. As such, the model developed in the course of the study was analyzed using econometric tools to explore empirical evidence of the relationship and/or effect on the India economic development.

In the light above, results were generated and via the results it is concluded that the post cold war experience in India arising from the differences in economic ideology and the struggle for dominance and power control share a strong relationship with India economic development. It is thusly accomplished that among the major macroeconomic variables including some moderating or controlled factors that were selected for the study; gross 'fixed capital formation', 'foreign direct investment', private consumption index, 'exchange rate', trade openness, human index, government capital expenditure proved to have statistical significant effect on India economic development. It is also concluded from the study that long run relationship exist among the variables though the speed of adjustment differs. Again, other variables such import, price consumption and exchange rate share no significant relationship and have no effects on the India economy during the post cold war period. The implication of these conclusion are that economic reforms in India cum her political and economic ideologies and her perceptions in economic development have greatly influence the overall economic management of India as an independent state in the post cold war era.

REFERENCES

Bairoch, P. (1995). *Economic and world History Myths and Paradoxes*. Harvester Publishers.

Bajpai, N. (2001). *Sustaining high rates of economic growth in India.* CID working paper No 65, Center for International Development, Harvard University.

Bajpai, N. (2002). *A decade of economic reforms in India: The unfinished Agenda.* CID working paper 67, Center for International Development, Harvard University.

Bajpai, N., & Saches, J. (2000). *Indians Decades of Development.* Working paper No.46, Center for International Development, Harvard University.

Cubit, G. (2013). *Economic History and Practice Working Paper*. Academic Press.

Gujarati, D. N. (2003). *Basic Econometrics McGrow*. Hill Publishing Ltd.

Isaac, J. (2013). *Indian Geographical History*. Available online at www. encydopediaBritanica.com

Isaac, J. E. (1983). *Realism and Social Scientific Theory*. Available online www. onlinelibrary.com

Koutsoyiannis, A. (2001). Theory of Econometrics. Palgrave Publishers St. Martin's Press.

Pomesh, D. L. E. (1902). *The economic history of India*. Trench Publishing.

Sharma, B. S., & Jha, D. N. (2015). *The economic history or India up to AD 1200: Trends and prospects*. Available online from www.jstor.org

Singh, K., & Kumer, A. (2020). Empirical analysis of India and foreign trade and economic growth. *International Journal of Research*, *8*(10), 105–111.

Srinivasan, T. N. (1996). *Indian economic reforms: Background, Rationale, Achievements and future prospects*. Sage Publishers.

Chapter 12
Post-Cold War Finance and Economic Development in Uruguay:
Perceptions, Paradigms, and Outcomes

Adekunle Alexander Balogun
https://orcid.org/0000-0001-9683-8964
University of Ibadan, Nigeria

Oladapo Fapetu
Federal University Oye-Ekiti, Nigeria

Gbenga Olorunmade
Federal University Oye-Ekiti, Nigeria

ABSTRACT

This chapter examines the post-Cold War Uruguayan finance and economic development. It explores both the theoretical and empirical structure of the country concerning the socio-economic philosophy and economic performance. The study uses the data collected from the World Bank from 1981-2019. The results of the study show that a significant short-run relationship exists between the dependent and the independent variables with deviation in the long-run equilibrium being offset in the present at a 62.84% speed in the short-run. It is recommended that Uruguay continue to make the country competitive to attract FDIs and also provide regulations to the financial system, both the money and capital markets, to enhance its gross fixed capital formation for local investments and savings and strengthen the currency.

DOI: 10.4018/979-8-3693-1610-8.ch012

1. INTRODUCTION

The Uruguayan financial and economic performance in the 1970s during the Cold War was adjudged to be relatively modest. According to the World Bank (1978), the Uruguayan economy achieved high rate of urbanization at 53%, relative even income distribution, high literacy rate with adult literacy at 94% and relatively low poverty index, as at 1975. Nevertheless, as a result of policy of transitioning from agro-based economy to an industrial state through import substitution industrialization (ISI), the economy of Uruguay suffered stagnation, which led to economic difficulties and increase in poverty. A comprehensive change in a country that can be ascribed to activities in an industry or economic policy/system is known as economic contribution (Watson, Wilson et al, 2007).

The Cold War saw the United States and its allies pitted against the defunct Union of Soviet Socialist Republic (USSR or the Soviet Union) and its own allies for more than 4 decades since the end of World War II till the collapse of the Soviet Union in 1991. Countries in Eastern Europe and Latin America were largely aligned with the USSR. These alliances were in the economic cooperation and financial integration. Technologically, both sides had relative cooperation, which assisted the transfer of technology and knowledge continuously, nevertheless, embargo on technology transfer by the United States and its Western allies dominated (Autio-Sarasmo, 2018).

Countries in some part of Asia, Africa and Latin America had employed ISI to attempt to leapfrog to industrialized societies from agro-based primary product nations, with limited success (Segal, 2021). ISI is primarily aimed at using fiscal instruments, like tariffs, subsidized credit to the productive sector, protection of infant industries and import quotas to safeguard and build up local manufacturing output. The economic policies were implemented side by side with social reforms – social security financing, income distribution and market efficiency borrowing from examples of social reforms in other countries (Mitchell, 1996). These reforms were of liberal structure.

Accordingly, government workers qualified for earnings-related benefits only after 10 years of employment, while retirement age was pegged at 45 for women and 50 for men. However, these inward-based state control policies were largely unsuccessful. The model did not lead to expected economic growth – the majority remained in poverty (Franko, 2018). As a result, a change in economic course began with the phased implementation of the market economy – financial liberalization and trade linearization.

The Cold War effectively ended with the collapse of the Soviet Union in 1991. At the end of the Cold War, Uruguay entered the trade liberalization phase of its socio-economic life. Collaboration with other Latin American countries (*Mercosur*) in a broad customs union agreement was integrated with a steady reduction in tariffs

(Barrios et al., 2010). These initiatives resulted in reduction in inflation from a decade-long high rate as well as the rise in the value of the peso in relation with currencies of countries outside the *Mercosur* agreement.

Uruguay is a Latin American country bounded by the Pacific Ocean in the south, Brazil in the north and west as well as Argentina in the east. The economy is small compared to the surrounding countries; however, the country has remained politically stable and has outperformed its neighbours in spite of the economic volatility experienced in the region (The Economist, cited in Lanzilotta et al., 2018).

In this study, an evaluation of the dynamics of post Cold War finance and economic development of Uruguay would be undertaken. The assessment covers the period between 1991-2019; cutting across the various global events covering geo-political, socio-economic and financial dynamics.

2. REVIEW OF LITERATURE

2.1 Theoretical Review

2.1.1 Import Substitution Industrialization

Import substitution industrialization connotes an economic strategy by import dependent developing countries in Latin America, Asia and Africa - that are reliant on primary products - to achieve economic growth and socio-economic modernization. These countries depend majorly on export of agricultural goods and unprocessed raw materials for industries. By employing ISI, countries hope to set up their own industrial systems to manufacture goods that are being imported. The choice of ISI was owing to the notion that industrialized Europe went through a stage where investments were strategically targeted at industries to replace imports (Baer, 1972), and invariably the protection of the their infant industries with subsidies before turning their economy to free markets (Bear, 1972; Change, 2002).

The theoretical underpinning of ISI is attributed to Fredrich List (1844). According to Irwin (2020), latter proponent of the theory was Raul Prebisch who, as the Secretary General of the United Nations Economic Commission for Latin America (ECLA) from 1949-1963, made the case that the Smithsonian principle of comparative cost advantage did not benefit developing countries of Latin America. The theory advocated that backward countries that are arriving to industrialization at late stage should strengthen their economies with internal production through engagement of their local industries. An important necessity for ISI to succeed is for nations to build knowledge and skills that would transform the production process through innovation in different fields (Bruton, 1989). The enormous economic achievements of the four Asian Tigers (Hong-Kong, Singapore, Taiwan and South Korea) were ascribed to ISI and the role played by education and innovation. In particular, the knowledge and skills amassed by Taiwan and South Korea as colonies of Japan were responsible for the higher economic growth recorded in latter years (Wade, 1990).

ISI was the preferred economic policy of most Latin American countries post Cold War era, Uruguay inclusive. It was thought to be the best policy to achieve industrialization of the region, given the low productivity of the agro-based systems which performance had been disappointingly low. However, the ISI policy also proved to have performed below optimal level. State controlled industries did not promote excellence and competence rather; they led the economies into rent systems. Also, high inflation was rife, which resulted in reduced competitive advantage of the domestic products against imported goods they were meant to replace (Dosman, 2017).

2.1.2 Washington Consensus

In 1990, John Williamson came up with a set of policies that could be deployed to effectively change the economic structure of the Latin American countries in replacement of the centrally control economic system or *statism* that had failed to yield good results for decades. He opined that these policies would have broad acceptability in the major economic and political institutions, namely; the World Bank, the International Monetary Fund (IMF), the United States government, the United States' Federal Reserve Board, the Inter-American Development Bank, and the various *Think Tanks* (expert groups working on economic policies), hence the term Washington Consensus (Marangos, 2009). Therefore, Washington Consensus comprises fiscal discipline, international economic outlook (liberalized trade and foreign investment or globalization) and removal of restrictions in national economic productive functions as the *laissez faire* economic policies

In the view of Stiglitz (2002) and Kolodko, (1999), the deployment of these structural adjustment policies are believed to be responsible for the turnaround of some depressed economies in Eastern and Central Europe, some developing economies in the Commonwealth Independent States as well some developed economies in Europe that experienced severe economic downturn.

However, the adoption of the Washington Consensus in Uruguay as well as other developing countries where it has been embraced did not yield the desired goals. According to Jaglinska and Motyovszki (2010), the main causes of failure lie with the free market and financial liberalization ideas. The principles of *laissez-faire* is found deficient in the efficient allocation of resources in the economy, which leads to volatility in the system, hence, the argument for greater government participation in the production process in line with Keynesian theory. In particular, the banking crises that occurred in the Latin American countries, Argentina, Mexico and Venezuela in the late 1990s confirmed the believe that countries with weak regulations and authorities cannot develop adequate capacity to supervise the monetary/financial system to prevent financial crisis (Marangos, 2009).

2.1.3 Democratic Changes and Capitalism

Uruguay, like most the countries in South America was engulfed with the plague of military dictatorship for the most part of the decade from mid 1970s to mid '80s. The advent of the democratic governance saw a shift from state control economic policies to building of financial and economic institutions and reforms that saw the implementations of liberalized economic system targeted at reduction in inflation and raising revenue through taxes as well as reforming the inefficient public financial system (Acerenza & Barrios, 2016).

According to Hall and Soskice (2001), the practice of capitalism can be classified into: Liberal Market – where labour laws and union activities are weak, corporate objectives are basically on short-term profit maximization, deregulation of production functions, high education standard characterized by possession of general skills and high competitive among the competing productive units; and the Coordinated Market Economies – featuring strong labour laws and unionization of workers, long term financing aimed at corporate sustenance and strong employment generation, emphases on vocational education and crafts (Acerenza & Barrios, 2016).

The Uruguayan experience has tended to mirror the Liberal Market Economies (LME) than Coordinated Market Economies in the post-Cold War era with the various reforms in the financial, industrial and public utility sectors. Banks and insurance ownership was transferred to the private sector while the dominance of monopolies in the sector was broken with taxes and industrial relations significantly liberalized – collaborations between the labour unions and the industrial sectors were not encouraged or promoted.

2.2 Empirical Studies

Literature on the Uruguayan economic growth is diverse and extensive; based on the effects of certain factors and circumstances by various authors. The effect of several contributory factors and phenomenon on the economy of Uruguay have been examined by scholars ranging from political, to socio economic reforms and global environmental crises.

Using data for the period 1980-2018, Awosusi et al (2022) investigated the effect of a set of variables; trade globalization, natural resources rents, economic growth and financial development on carbon emission in Uruguay. The study found that trade liberalization exerts positive effect on CO_2 emissions in the long and short run which is indicative that environmental deterioration is increased in the long and short run by the abundance of natural resources. The result of the causality test indicates that carbon emissions are predicted by international business, economic growth and natural resources, but not financial development.

Morales-Olmos and Pienika (2022) studied the evolution, distribution and contribution of the forest sector in the economy of Uruguay between 1997 and 2018. The study employed macroeconomic data from the Central Bank of Uruguay to evaluate the contribution of the production in the forest sector to the economy. Findings reveal that the forest sector outperformed the economy in growth with 7.6 percent growth and peaks in 2007-2008 and 2013-2015 while the economy grew by 2.6 percent. The study also found that forest production was responsible for 10.5 percent of the total country's exports while export allocation for forest production was 46.76 percent. The study concludes that the forest sector has contributed greatly to the Uruguayan economy in the past decades.

Piaggio, Alcantara and Padilla (2012) examined the effect of atmospheric pollution on the economic production of Uruguay using input-output analysis. Results of the study indicated that key polluting sectors were connected to the different determinants analysed, as a result of emissions excluding motor vehicles and oil retail trade that have both forward and backward links to CO_2 emissions. Conclusively, the study identified the best policy for reducing and limiting atmospheric emission and compered it with the national plans. Using panel data from several South American countries,

Lanzilotta et al (2018) investigated the effect of local and global economic policy uncertainty on the Uruguayan economic volatility using the composite index, future expectations of the exchange rate and the uncertainty measures appropriate economic-world as proxies for policy uncertainty, local and external uncertainty measures and regional and global shocks respectively. The findings of the study revealed that whilst the measures of uncertainty appear to be appropriate to forecast changes for the whole period, the predictable power waned in the latter years.

Scholars have evaluated the development policies being executed in Uruguay. Barrios, Gandelman and Michelin (2010) assessed the economic strategies carried out in the 2010s consisting of both horizontal and vertical policies; including innovation, industrial promotion and directives for industrial; and, technological development, and forestry law, meat traceability and the agricultural sustainable production projects; respectively. In examining the economic growth, Che (2021) analysed the causes of boom and burst economic cycle in Uruguay - which particularly experienced a historic boom between 2004-2014, and has steadily declined since then. The study employed a range of structural indicators for comparison between the high-growth nations to identify priority sector reform for a sustainable growth prospect.

Rius (2015) investigated the determinants of Uruguayan tax reform success following years of failures with other social and financial reforms in the country and around the Latin American sub-regional economic region. The important factor is found to be the political ascendancy of the fiscal left (progressives) who started afresh the effort of income distribution, around 2006, through a reintroduction of a gamut of progressive taxation (including tax exemption for the very low income earners). Fiscally, the reform did not have any consequences on the total income accrued to the state. This change in the direction of power and the policy changes it brought resulted in the rich paying more taxes while the poor are either exempted or pay far less, to accommodate their household needs.

3. METHODOLOGY

The economic and financial development of Uruguay was examined with data from the World Bank and World Development Indicators for the period of 1981-2019. This interval covers the period when the Cold War was already winding down and much of the post-Cold War developments. The variables employed include Gross Domestic Product Per Capita (GDPPC) as the dependent variable, while exchange rate (EXR), foreign direct investment (FDI), foreign debt (FOR_DEBT), gross capital formation (GCFC), trade openness (OPENNESS) and real interest rate (RINTR) are the explanatory variables.

The study analyses the data with descriptive statistics for the distribution of the series, and correlation analysis for correlation between the variables. The study employed Augmented Dickey Fuller unit root test and Johansen cointegration model to determine the stationarity and the cointegration between the variables. Estimation was carried out using Vector Error Correction Model (VECM) normalized cointegrating equation to determine the existence and nature of short-run relationship between the variables to capture the long run effect between the dependent and independent variables.

3.1 Model Specification

The functional relationship between the variables is expressed mathematically as:

$$GDPPCt = f(EXRt, FDIt, FOR\_DEBTt, GFCFt, OPPENNESSt, INTR) \quad (3.1)$$

Where: GDPPC = Gross Domestic Product Per Capita; EXR = Exchange Rate; FDI = Foreign Direct Investment; FOR_DEBT = Foreign Debt; GFCF = Gross Fixed Capital Formation; RINTR = Real Interest Rate.

Table 1. Descriptive statistics

	GDPPC	EXR	FDI	FOR_DEBT	GFCF	OPENNESS	RINTR
Mean	7580.758	13.79128	0.840000	0.199487	4.437436	44.97231	22.53538
Std. Dev.	5264.540	11.42168	1.294982	0.169068	3.783323	8.687298	19.59684
Skewness	0.764341	0.146848	2.193145	1.553709	0.883455	0.682581	1.280362
Kurtosis	2.135950	1.555649	8.209329	4.834969	2.329782	2.486851	5.426561
Jarque-Bera	5.010603	3.530161	75.36206	21.16264	5.803140	3.456361	20.22394
Probability	0.081651	0.171173	0.000000	0.000025	0.054937	0.177607	0.000041
Observations	39	39	39	39	39	39	39

Source: Authors' Computation (2022)

The VECM estimation is expressed as:

$$\Delta GDPt = a_0 + \Sigma^p_{i=1} a_{1i}\, \Delta GDP_{t-i} + \Sigma^q_{i=1} a_{2i}\, \Delta GDP\_PER\_CAP_{t-1} + \Sigma^q_{i=1} a_{3i}\, \Delta EXR_{t-1} + \Sigma^q_{i=1} a_{3i} \Delta FDI_{t-1} + \Sigma^q_{i=1} a_{4i} \Delta FOR\_DEBT_{t-i} + \Sigma^q_{i=1} a_{5i}\, \Delta GFCF_{t-1} + \Sigma^q_{i=1} a_{6i}\, \Delta OPENNESS_{t-1} + \Sigma^q_{i=1} a_{7i}\, \Delta RINTR_{t-1} + \lambda ECM_{t-1} + e_t \quad (3.2)$$

4. DATA ANALYSIS AND INTERPRETATION

Table 1 presents the descriptive statistics for the variables. The average of GDPPC, EXR, FDI, FOR_DEBT, GCFC, OPENNESS, and RINTR is 7580.758, 13.79128, 0.8400, 0.199487, 4.437436, 44.97231, and 22.53538 respectively. The standard deviation measures dispersion, from the table GDPPC, has the highest dispersion while FOR_DEBT has the lowest dispersion. The skewness shows that all the variables are skewed to the right. While the kurtosis coefficients show that most of the variables are platykurtic except for FDI, FOR_DEBT, and RINTR. The Jarque-Bera probability shows that GDPPC, EXR, GCFC, and OPENNESS all follow a normal distribution, while FDI, FOR_DEBT, and RINTR do not follow a normal distribution.

The correlation among the variables is presented in table 2. The correlations between GDPPC and EXR; GDPPC and FDI; GDPPC and GCFC; and GDPPC and OPENNESS, all show a positive correlation while the correlations between GDPPC and FOR_DEBT, GDPPC and RINTR both show a negative correlation. The table also shows the correlation between the independent variables.

Figure 1. Trend of the variables
Source: Authors' Computation (2022)

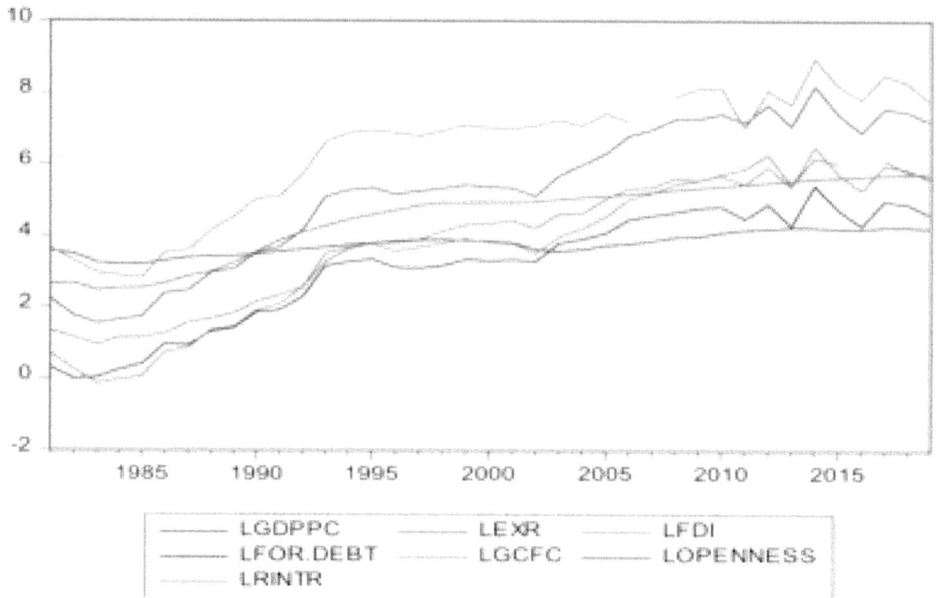

Table 2. Correlation matrix

	LGDPPC	LEXR	LFDI	LFOR_ DEBT	LGCFC	LOPENNESS	LRINTR
LGDPPC	1						
LEXR	0.81	1					
LFDI	0.86	0.82	1				
LFOR_DEBT	-0.53	-0.37	-0.60	1			
LGCFC	0.99	0.78	0.86	-0.57	1		
LOPENNESS	0.13	0.33	0.52	-0.18	0.16	1	
LRINTR	-0.53	-0.33	-0.69	0.46	-0.55	-0.65	1

Source: Authors' Computation (2022)

Table 3 presents the unit root test using ADF test statistics. None of the variables are stationary at levels. However, all the variables are stationary at first difference due to the random nature of the data. They were logged differenced once before they could attain stationarity. Therefore, the variables are all integrated at I(1). Based on the foregoing, the result obtained from the unit root test analysis provides a good

Table 3. Unit root test results (ADF)

Null Hypothesis: The Variable Has a Unit Root							
At Level							
	LGDPPC	**LEXR**	**LFDI**	**LFOR_ DEBT**	**LGCFC**	**LOPENNESS**	**LRINTR**
t-Statistic	0.8494	-0.1238	-1.5650	-0.7529	-0.4068	0.1676	-1.0810
Prob.	***0.8897***	***0.6344***	***0.1091***	***0.3836***	***0.5301***	***0.7292***	***0.2479***
	n0	n0	n0	n0	n0	n0	n0
At First Difference							
t-Statistic	-3.3939	-1.9827	-8.8110	-5.3600	-3.4161	-6.1049	-5.5357
Prob.	***0.0012***	***0.0466***	***0.0000***	***0.0000***	***0.0012***	***0.0000***	***0.0000***
	***	**	***	***	***	***	***

Notes:
a: (*)Significant at the 10%; (**) Significant at the 5%; (***) Significant at the 1% and (no) Not Significant
b: Lag Length based on SIC
c: Probability based on MacKinnon (1996) one-sided p-values.
Source: Authors' Computation (2022)

Table 4. Johansen cointegration test-trace test

Unrestricted Cointegration Rank Test (Trace)				
Hypothesized		**Trace**	**0.05**	
No. of CE(s)	**Eigenvalue**	**Statistic**	**Critical Value**	**Prob.****
None *	0.858070	178.1379	125.6154	0.0000
At most 1 *	0.726581	117.6129	95.75366	0.0007
At most 2 *	0.595043	77.41363	69.81889	0.0109
At most 3 *	0.535290	49.39044	47.85613	0.0356
At most 4	0.382665	25.63388	29.79707	0.1400
At most 5	0.197044	10.68123	15.49471	0.2319
At most 6 *	0.117592	3.878113	3.841466	0.0489

Trace test indicates 4 cointegrating eqn(s) at the 0.05 level
*denotes rejection of the hypothesis at the 0.05 level
**MacKinnon-Haug-Michelis (1999) p-values
Source: Authors' Computation (2022)

justification for employing the Johansen cointegration and Vector Error Correction Model (VECM) to capture the long and short-run coefficients.

Table 5. Johansen cointegration test-Eigen test

Unrestricted Cointegration Rank Test (Maximum Eigenvalue)				
Hypothesized		**Max-Eigen**	**0.05**	
No. of CE(s)	**Eigenvalue**	**Statistic**	**Critical Value**	**Prob.****
None *	0.858070	60.52497	46.23142	0.0008
At most 1 *	0.726581	40.19927	40.07757	0.0484
At most 2	0.595043	28.02319	33.87687	0.2124
At most 3	0.535290	23.75656	27.58434	0.1435
At most 4	0.382665	14.95266	21.13162	0.2922
At most 5	0.197044	6.803112	14.26460	0.5127
At most 6 *	0.117592	3.878113	3.841466	0.0489

Max-eigenvalue test indicates 2 cointegrating eqn(s) at the 0.05 level
*denotes rejection of the hypothesis at the 0.05 level
**MacKinnon-Haug-Michelis (1999) p-values
Source: Authors' Computation (2022)

Table 6. Normalize cointegrating equation

1 Cointegrating Equation(s): Log-Likelihood 281.3529						
Normalized Cointegrating Coefficients (Standard Error in Parentheses)						
LGDPPC	**LEXR**	**LFDI**	**LFOR_ DEBT**	**LGCFC**	**LOPENNESS**	**LRINTR**
1.000000	0.014824	-0.099399	-0.029484	-0.691481	0.616519	-0.028493
	(0.01658)	(0.02266)	(0.02030)	(0.02582)	(0.09666)	(0.02605)

Source: Authors' Computation (2022)

The Johansen cointegration test consists of trace and max-eigen tests to confirm the existence of long-run prelateship between the dependent variable and independent variables. Tables 4 and 5 present the Johansen cointegration tests. The results confirm the existence of a long-run relationship between the variables. The result of the trace test in table 4 confirms the existence of at least one cointegration equation among the variables with a probability value of 0.0000, this result is confirmed by the result of the Max-Eigen test in table 5, which found that there is at least one cointegration equation between the variables at a probability value of 0.0008. Hence, based on the Johansen cointegration test, this study confirms the existence of a long-run relationship between GDP per capita and the independent variables (exchange rate, foreign direct investment, foreign debt, gross fixed capital formation, trade openness,

Table 7. Vector error correction model

Error Correction:	D(LGDPPC)
CointEq1	-0.628413 (0.19031) [-3.30197]
D(LGDPPC(-1))	0.778974 (0.54931) [1.41810]
D(LEXR(-1))	0.095539 (0.12058) [0.79230]
D(LFDI(-1))	0.056125 (0.03861) [1.45379]
D(LFOR_DEBT(-1))	0.031574 (0.05001) [0.63140]
D(LGCFC(-1))	-0.141881 (0.30343) [-0.46759]
D(LOPENNESS(-1))	0.452669 (0.31014) [1.45958]
D(LRINTR(-1))	0.067234 (0.04775) [1.40799]
C	-0.004392 (0.01416) [-0.31018]
R-squared	0.685988
Adj. R-squared	0.571802
Sum sq. resids	0.057595
S.E. equation	0.051166
F-statistic	6.007631
Log-likelihood	53.48173
Akaike AIC	-2.869789
Schwarz SC	-2.453470
Mean dependent	0.015074
S.D. dependent	0.078191

Source: Authors' Computation (2022)

and real interest rate). To capture the individual effect of each of the variables on GDP per capita, the study employs the normalized cointegrating equation.

Table 6 presents the normalized cointegrating equation. The normalized cointegrating equation captures the long-run effect of the independent variables on the dependent variable, the output is interpreted in the opposite sign. Exchange rate exerts a negative and insignificant effect of 0.014824 on GDP per capita, which implies that a unit increase in the exchange rate will cause a statistically insignificant decrease of 0.014824 in GDP per capita in the long run. Foreign direct investment is found to have a positive and significant effect of 0.099399 on GDP per capita, which indicates that a unit increase in foreign direct investment will cause a statistically significant increase of 0.099399 in GDP per capita in the long run. The result also shows that foreign debt exerts a positive but insignificant effect of 0.029484 on GDP per capita, which implies that a unit increase in foreign debt will cause a statistically insignificant increase of 0.029484 in GDP per capita in the long run. Also, gross fixed capital formation has a positive and significant effect of 0.691481, which implies that a unit increase in gross fixed capital formation will cause a statistically significant increase of 0.691484 in GDP per capita in the long run. Furthermore, trade openness exerts a negative and significant effect of 0.616519 on GDP per capita, which implies that a unit increase in trade openness will cause a statistically significant decrease of 0.0616519 in GDP per capita in the long run. The result also shows that the real interest rate exerts a positive but insignificant effect of 0.028493 on GDP per capita, which implies that a unit increase in real interest rate will cause a statistically insignificant increase of 0.028493 in GDP per capita in the long run.

Table 7 presents the result of the Vector Error Correction Model, which captures the short-run relationship between the variables. The CoinEq1 shows that there is a short-run relationship between the GDP per capita and the independent variables, the relationship is also significant. The coefficient indicates that deviation in the long-run equilibrium is corrected in the current at an adjustment speed of 62.84% in the short run. The result in table 7 indicates that those changes in the GDP per capita in the short has a positive and insignificant effect on GDP per capita at present. Similarly, exchange rate, foreign direct investment, foreign debt, trade openness, and real interest rate all exert a positive and insignificant effect on GDP per capita in the short run. While gross fixed capital formation exerts a negative and insignificant effect on GDP per capita in the short run.

All diagnostic testing on the model was successful. The test statistic f-statistic = 1.154237 in the VEC residual serial correlation tests is not significant under the null hypothesis of "no serial correlation," with a p-value of 0.3074. This suggests that serial correlation in the residual's lags is not present in the calculated model. Similar to this, homoskedasticity is used as the null hypothesis for the VEC residual heteroskedasticity test. The residual of the calculated model is homoscedastic in this

Table 8. Diagnostic tests

VEC Residual Serial Correlation Tests	
F-statistic	1.154237
p-values	0.3074
VEC Residual Heteroskedasticity Test	
Chi-sq	466.0474
p-values	0.2685
Jarque-Bera Test for Normality of Residual	
Jarque-Bera	17.90332
p-values	0.2112

Source: Authors' Computation (2022)

instance with Chi-sq = 466.0474 and a p-value of 0.2685. Finally, the Jarque-Bera test for residual normality carried out under the null hypothesis of "normality," reveals that the residual of the estimated model is normally distributed, with Jarque-Bera = 17.90332, which is insignificant and has a p-value of 0.2112.

4.1 Discussion of Findings

The study evaluates the post Cold War finance and economic development of Uruguay. It examines data covering the period various global phenomena during the 1991-2019. Empirical results indicate a significant short-run relationship between the GDP per capita and all the explanatory variables of exchange rate, foreign direct investments, foreign debt, trade openness and real interest rate with the exception of gross fixed capital formation, which exerts positive and insignificant effect on per capita GDP in the short-run. These results indicate that the economy of Uruguay, as proxied by GDP per capita, responded to the liberal economic reforms positive in the short-run.

In the long run, both foreign direct investment and gross fixed capital formation exert positive and significant effect on Gross Domestic Product per capita by 0.099399 and 0.691481 respectively. This is an indication that the globalization policies of the Uruguayan government over the years have impacted the economy positively, a very strong testament to the favorable argument of the adoption of Washington Consensus by the Latin American country. Similarly, foreign debt and real exerts positive, but insignificant effect on the economy in the post Cold War period in Uruguay with 0.029484 and 0.024849 respectively. This symbolizes better debt management and monetary policies implementation of the Central Bank of Uruguay. Indebtedness to foreign financial institutions and governmental agencies as well as real interest rates management have resulted in the insignificant but positive impact on the per capita GDP.

However, both exchange rate and trade openness have impacted the economy negatively. While, exchange rate has an insignificant negative impact of 0.014824, trade openness has impacted the economy significantly negatively by 0.616519 in the post Cold War period in Uruguay. The findings are in agreement with Lanzilotta et al (2018), which found that the predictive power of measures of uncertainty was strong in the short-run and appears to wane in the longer term. Similarly, the results agree with Che (2021), which found that the Uruguayan economic boom circle, which started in 2000 and climaxed in 2014, has since declined. The study supports the work of Awosusi et al (2022), which found that carbon emissions (economic productivity) are predicted by international business, economic growth and natural resources. However, the results of the study is contrary to the findings of Rius (2015), which found that tax reforms in Uruguay exerts no effect on the national income and exerts negative effect on the income of the poor.

5. CONCLUSION

Uruguay occupies a prominent place in the economy of Latin America because of its strong, transparent, well regulated financial system: both banking and the capital market. The country's economic system has evolved in the last three decades after the Cold War through both extremes of the leftist nationalism and the neo liberal globalism with mixed results. The study approaches the financial and economic development in Uruguay by examining the effects of macroeconomic variables on the per capita GDP since end of the Cold War. It concludes that there exist short-run and long run relationships between the dependent variables and the independent variables. The results of the study indicate that the measures taken by the economic managers of the country have seen positive outcomes, albeit in the short-run. The country's GDP per capita has witnessed positive impact of the macroeconomic variables, except for gross fixed capital formation. The long run effects of the variables employed are mixed. Two variables, foreign direct investments and gross fixed capital formation have positive and significant impact on the dependent variable; another two, foreign debt and real interest rate exert positive but insignificant effect on per capita GDP, while both exchange rate and trade openness exert negative effect, the former insignificant and the latter significant.

In view of the above, it is recommended that Uruguay continue to make the country competitive to attract FDIs and also provide regulations to the financial system, both the money and capital markets, to enhance its gross fixed capital formation for local investments and savings. In the same vein, local production should be aggressively pursued to increase exports in order to strengthen the currency. Also, the fiscal authorities in Uruguay should ensure that a review of the trade openness policy is carried out to engender innovations and technology growth of the country.

REFERENCES

Acerenza, S., & Barrios, J. J. (2016). *Capitalism in Uruguay* (Documento de Investigación, Nro. 107). Universidad ORT Uruguay.

Autio-Sarasmo, S. (2018). Transferring western knowledge to a centrally planned economy: Finland and the scientific-technical cooperation with the Soviet Union. In M. Christian, S. Kott, & O. Matějka (Eds.), Planning in Cold War Europe: Competition, cooperation, circulations (1950s-1970s) (1st ed., pp. 143–164). De Gruyter. doi:10.1515/9783110534696-008

Awosusi, A. A., Xulu, N. G., Ahmadi, M., Rjoub, H., Altuntaş, M., Uhunamure, S. E., Akadiri, S. S., & Kirikkaleli, D. (2022). The sustainable environment in Uruguay: The roles of financial development, natural resources and trade globalization. *Frontiers in Environmental Science*, *10*, 1–13. doi:10.3389/fenvs.2022.875577

Baer, W. (1972). Import substitution and industrialization in Latin America: Experiences and expectations. *Latin American Research Review*, *7*(1), 99–122. doi:10.1017/S0023879100041224

Baker, A., & Green, K. F. (2011). The Latin American left's mandate: Free-market policies and issue voting in new democracies. *World Politics*, *63*(1), 43–77. doi:10.1017/S0043887110000286

Barrios, J. J., Gandelman, N., & Michelin, G. (2010). *Analysis of several productive development policies in Uruguay* (IDB Working Paper Series No. IDB-WP-130). Washington, DC: Inter-American Development Bank.

Bruton, H. (1989). *Handbook of development economics*. Elsevier.

Chang, H. J. (2002). *Kicking away the ladder: Development strategy in historical perspective*. Anthem Press.

Che, N. (2021). *Dissecting economic growth in Uruguay* (IMF Working Paper WP/21/2). IMF.

Dosman, J. D. (2017). *Raul Prebisch and the XXIst century development challenges*. United Nations – ECLAC.

Franko, P. (2018). *Puzzle of Latin American economic development* (7th ed.). Rowman and Littlefield Publishers.

Hall, P., & Soskice, D. (2001). *Varieties of capitalism: The institutional foundations of comparative advantage*. Oxford University Press. doi:10.1093/0199247757.001.0001

Irwin, D. A. (2020). *The rise and fall of import substitution* (Working paper WP 20-10). Peterson Institute for International Economics.

Jaglinska, D., & Motyovszki, G. (2010). *The Washington Consensus: A post Keynesian perspective* (Unpublished manuscript). Universiteit Van Amsterdam, Amsterdam.

Kolodko, G. W. (1999). *Ten years of post-socialist transition: The lessons for policy reform*. The World Bank. doi:10.1596/1813-9450-2095

Lanzilotta, B., Mordecki, G., & Umpiérrez, V. (2018). Political economic uncertainty in a small and open economy: The case of Uruguay (Serie Documentos de Trabajo DT 05/2018). Instituto de Economía, Uruguay.

List, F. (1977). *The national system of political economy*. (Original work published 1844)

Marangos, J. (2009). The evolution of the term 'Washington Consensus'. *Journal of Economic Surveys*, *23*(2), 350–383. doi:10.1111/j.1467-6419.2008.00565.x

Mitchell, O. S. (1996). *Social security reform in Uruguay: An economic assessment* (Wharton Pension Research Council Working Papers. 527). https://repository.upenn.edu/prc_papers/527

Morales-Olmos, V., & Pienika, E. (2022). Contribution of the forest sector to the Uruguayan economy: A first approach with National Accounts. *Journal of Forest Science*, *68*(3), 116–119. doi:10.17221/149/2021-JFS

Piaggio, M., Alcantara, V., & Padilla, E. (2012). *Economic structure and key sector analysis of greenhouse gas emissions in Uruguay* (Documente de Treball 12.04). Universitat Autonomia de Barcelona.

Rius, A. (2015). The Uruguayan tax reform 2016: Why did it not fail? In J. E. Mahon Jr, M. Bergman, & C. Arnson (Eds.), *Progressive tax reform and equality in Latin America*. Woodrow Wilson International Center for Scholars.

Segal, T. (2021). *Import substitution industrialization-ISI*. https://tinyurl.com/2p9h4cku

Stiglitz, J. (2002). *Globalization and its discontents*. W. W. Norton.

Watson, P., Wilson, J., Thilmany, D., & Winter, S. (2007). Determining economic contributions and impacts: What is the difference and why do we care? *The Journal of Regional Analysis & Policy*, *37*, 140–146.

World Bank. (1978). *Uruguay: Staff appraisal report on a vocational training and technological development project* (Report No. 1928b-UR). World Bank.

Compilation of References

Abdullahi, Y. Z., Aliero, H. M., & Yusuf, M. A. (2012). Does FDI cause economic growth? Evidence from selected countries in Africa and Asia. *African Journal of Social Sciences*, *2*(4), 114–124.

Abdul-Maliq, Y. O. (2018). *Responsive of the Nigerian economic to foreign capital inflows: 1973-2015*. University of Nigeria, Unpublish Banking Thesis.

Abdul-Maliq, Y. O., & Magaji, S. (2017). *Does exchange rate policy matter for economic growth? Evidence from Economic Community of West Africa States*. Paper presented at the 2nd Nigerian Turkish Nile University's 2nd International Conference on Social Science and Law.

Abdul-Maliq, Y. O., & Abubakar, D. I. (2021). Nigeria's Unique Species Hypothesis and the Fate of the Naira: Why Not, If Not? *International Journal of Business and Management*, *9*(2), 381–390. doi:10.24940/theijbm/2021/v9/BM2102-033

Abiad, A., Detragiache, E., & Tressel, T. (2008). *A New Database of Financial Reforms. mimeo*. International Monetary Fund.

Abugamea, G. (2015). External trade and economic growth relationship under Trouble: Time series evidence from Palestine, *Swift. Journal of Economics and International Finance*, *1*(2), 10–16.

Acerenza, S., & Barrios, J. J. (2016). *Capitalism in Uruguay* (Documento de Investigación, Nro. 107). Universidad ORT Uruguay.

Adamolekun, L., & Ayo, S. B. (1989). The Evolution of the Nigerian Federal Administration System. *Publius*, *19*(1), 157–176. doi:10.1093/oxfordjournals.pubjof.a037761

Adediran, O. S. (2020). Autoregressive distributed lag approach to external credit and economic growth in Nigeria. In P. O. Alege (Ed.), *Applied Econometric Analysis: Emerging Research and Opportunities*. Covenant University. doi:10.4018/978-1-7998-1093-3.ch003

Adesola, W. A. (2009). Debt Servicing and Economic Growth in Nigeria: An Empirical Investigation. *Global Journal of Social Sciences*, *8*(2), 1–11.

Adeyemi, J. O. (1996). Beyond Structural Adjustment: A Policy Framework. In A. Ekpo (Ed.), Beyond Adjustment: Management of the Nigerian Economy (pp. 133–142). Academic Press.

Adhikary, B. K. (2015). Dynamic Effects of FDI, Trade Openness, Capital Formation and Human Capital on the Economic Growth Rate in the Least Developed Economies: Evidence from Nepal, *International Journal of Trade. Economics and Finance*, *6*(1), 1–7.

Adu, G., Marbuah, G., & Mensah, J. T. (2013). Financial Development and Economic Growth in Ghana: Does the Measure of Financial Development Matter? *Review of Development Finance*, *3*(4), 192–203. doi:10.1016/j.rdf.2013.11.001

Afaf, A. J. S., & Hussain, M. A. (2015). Impact of exports and imports on economic growth: Evidence from Tunisia. *Journal of Emerging Trends in Economics and Management Science*, *6*(1), 13–21.

Agu, O. C., & Nyatanga, P. (2020). An Investigation into the Crude Oil Price Pass-Through to Economic Growth in Nigeria. *Acta Universitatis Danubius. Œconomica, 16*(1).

Agu, O. C., Nwosa, P. I & Ajoje O. I. (2022). Socio-economic Status, Savings and Income Inequality in Nigeria: The behavioral mechanism Approach. *Iranian Economic Review.*

Agu, O. C., Nwosa, P. I., & Ajoje O. I. (2022). Socio-economic Status, Savings and Income Inequality in Nigeria: The behavioral mechanism Approach. *Iranian Economic Review.*

Agu, O. C., & Asaolu, A. A. (2023). Can Nigeria Debt Be Sustained in the Face of Increasing Debt Profile? *EuroEconomica*, *42*(1), 108–123.

Ahamad, M. H. (2018). Impact of international trade on economic growth in Bangladesh. *International Journal of Scientific Research*, *7*(11), 1624–1627.

Ahluwalia, I. J., & Mahmud, W. (2004). Economic transformation and social development in Bangladesh. *Economic and Political Weekly*, *39*(36), 4009–4011. https://www.jstor.org/stable/4415501

Ahmed, H. A., & Uddin, Md. G. S. (2009). Export, imports, remittance and growth in Bangladesh: An empirical analysis. *Trade and Development Review,* 2(2), 79-92. http://www.tdrju.net

Ahmed, K. S. (2011). *Economical development of Bangladesh- Problems & solutions.* Arcada University of Applied Sciences. https://www.theseus.fi/bitstream/handle/10024/38338/Ahmed_Kazi%20Siam.pdf

Ahmed, Z., Zhang, B., & Cary, M. (2021). *Linking economic globalization, economic growth, financial development, and ecological footprint: Evidence from symmetric and asymmetric.* Academic Press.

Ahmed, S. (2005). Development performance and policy reforms since independence. In S. Ahmed (Ed.), *Transforming Bangladesh into a middle-income economy*. Macmillan India Ltd. for the World Bank.

Ajose, K. (2018). Capital formation and economic growth in Nigeria. *International Accounting and Taxation Research*, *2*(2), 131–142.

Akhter, M. (2015). The impact of export and import on economic growth in Bangladesh. *World Vision, 9*(1), 66–81.

Ali, G. (2015). Gross fixed capital formation and economic growth of Pakistan. *IMPACT Journal of Research in Humanities. Arts and Literature, 1*(2), 21–30.

Ali, M. A., Saifullah, M. K., & Kari, F. B. (2015). The impact of key macroeconomic factors on economic growth of Bangladesh: A VAR Co-integration analysis. *International Journal of Management Excellence, 6*(1), 667–673. doi:10.17722/ijme.v6i1.820

Ali, R., & Mustafa, U. (2012). External debt accumulation and its impact on economic growth in Pakistan. *Pakistan Development Review, 51*(4), 79–96. doi:10.30541/v51i4IIpp.79-96

Alonso, A. G. (2004). *The Parliament System, and the Mexican Service*. Paper presented at the AGDS, Mexico 2004 SRE (nd) Colonial Mexico, SRE, Embassy of Mexico, United Kingdom.

Amann, E., & Barrientos, A. (2014). *Is There a Brazilian Model of Development? Are There Lessons for Countries in Africa?* WIDER Working Paper 2014/134. Helsinki: UNU-WIDER. https://doi.org/ doi:10.35188/UNU-WIDER/2014/855-1

Amann, E., & Baer, W. (2012). Brazil as an emerging economy: A new economic miracle? *Revista de Economia Política, 32*(128), 412–423. doi:10.1590/S0101-31572012000300004

Anaya, A. R. (2023). Mexico: colonial and early post-colonial state creation: A political Marxist account. *America Latino el la historian economical, 30*(1), 1-16.

Archer, C. I. (2011). Mexican War of Independence (1810-1821). The Encyclopedia of war. Wiley. doi:10.1002/9781444338232.wbeow399

ARDL. (n.d.). *Ecological Indicators, 121*, 107060. doi:10.1016/j.ecolind.2020.107060

Arnone, M., & Luca, B. (2015). *External debt sustainability: Theory and empiricalevidence*. http://www3.unicatt.it/unicattolica/Dipartmenti/DISES/allegati/ArnoneBandiera Presbiter033.pdf

Asaduzzaman Md. (2019). *FDI an opportunity for economic growth of Bangladesh: A VECM analysis*. MPRA Paper No. 110328, 1-28.

Asiedu, E. (2004). Policy reform and foreign direct investment to Africa: Absolute progress but relative decline. *Development Policy Review, 22*(1), 41–48. doi:10.1111/j.1467-8659.2004.00237.x

Asteriou, D., & Monastiriotis, V. (2004). What do unions do at the large scale? Macro-economic evidence from a panel of OECD countries. *Journal of Applied Econometrics, 7*(1), 2746.

Atiku, S. D., & Nwala, M. N. (2021). Analysis of the Effect of External Public Debt on Economic growth in Nigeria. *International Journal of Innovative Research in Accounting and Sustainability, 6*(4), 68–82.

Atmore, A. E. (2008). Africa on the Eve of Partition. Cambridge History of Africa.

Autio-Sarasmo, S. (2018). Transferring western knowledge to a centrally planned economy: Finland and the scientific-technical cooperation with the Soviet Union. In M. Christian, S. Kott, & O. Matějka (Eds.), Planning in Cold War Europe: Competition, cooperation, circulations (1950s-1970s) (1st ed., pp. 143–164). De Gruyter. doi:10.1515/9783110534696-008

Awokuse, T. O. (2007). Causality between exports, imports, and economic growth: Evidence from Transition economies. *Economics Letters*, *94*(3), 389–395. doi:10.1016/j.econlet.2006.08.025

Awosusi, A. A., Xulu, N. G., Ahmadi, M., Rjoub, H., Altuntaş, M., Uhunamure, S. E., Akadiri, S. S., & Kirikkaleli, D. (2022). The sustainable environment in Uruguay: The roles of financial development, natural resources and trade globalization. *Frontiers in Environmental Science*, *10*, 1–13. doi:10.3389/fenvs.2022.875577

Ayoola, T. (2008). Colonial Inheritance, Post-Colonial neglect and Management of Nigerian Railway by Rail India Technical and Economic Services (RITES). *African Journal,* (14). Advance online publication. doi:10.4134/Inrv1411.46493

Baer, W. (1972). Import substitution and industrialization in Latin America: Experiences and expectations. *Latin American Research Review*, *7*(1), 99–122. doi:10.1017/S0023879100041224

Bahname, M. (2012). Foreign direct investment and economic growth: Evidence from Southern Asia. *Atlantic Review of Economics*, *2*(2), 34–48.

Bai, E., & Perron, T. (2003). *Domestic petroleum product prices and subsidies: Recent developments and reform strategies*. International Monetary Fund Working Paper. Available from: http://www.ksri.or.kr/bbs/files/research02/ wp0771.pdf

Bai, E., & Perron, T. (2003). *Domestic petroleum product prices and subsidies: Recent developments and reform strategies*. International monetary fund working paper. Available from: Http://www.Ksri.Or.Kr/bbs/files/research02/ wp0771.Pdf.

Bairoch, P. (1995). *Economic and world History Myths and Paradoxes*. Harvester Publishers.

Bajpai, N. (2001). *Sustaining high rates of economic growth in India.* CID working paper No 65, Center for International Development, Harvard University.

Bajpai, N. (2002). *A decade of economic reforms in India: The unfinished Agenda.* CID working paper 67, Center for International Development, Harvard University.

Bajpai, N., & Saches, J. (2000). *Indians Decades of Development.* Working paper No.46, Center for International Development, Harvard University.

Baker, A., & Green, K. F. (2011). The Latin American left's mandate: Free-market policies and issue voting in new democracies. *World Politics*, *63*(1), 43–77. doi:10.1017/S0043887110000286

Balassa, B. (1989). Financial liberalization in developing countries. *Policy Research Working Paper Series 55*, The World Bank.

Bamgboye, P. (2014). The Military and Social-Economic Development in Nigeria (1983-1999): A Critical Appraisal. *Mediterranean Journal of Social Sciences*. Advance online publication. doi:10.5901/mjss.2014.v5n23p2340

Banerjee, A., Dolado, J., & Mestre, R. (1998). Error-correction mechanism tests for cointegration in a single-equation framework. *Journal of Time Series Analysis*, *19*(3), 267–283. doi:10.1111/1467-9892.00091

Barbi, F. C. (2014). *Determinants of Credit Expansion in Brazil*. Munich Personal RePEc Archive (MPRA) MPRA Paper No. 19535. Available online at https://mpra.ub.uni-muenchen.de/19535/

Barrios, J. J., Gandelman, N., & Michelin, G. (2010). *Analysis of several productive development policies in Uruguay* (IDB Working Paper Series No. IDB-WP-130). Washington, DC: Inter-American Development Bank.

Barro, R. (1990). Government Spending in a Simple Model of Endogenous Growth, *journal of Political Economy*, *98*(5), 103-125.

Barro, R. (1990). Government Spending in a Simple Model of Endogenous Growth. *Journal of Political Economy*, *98*(5), 103-125.

Basuki, A. T. (2020). Determinants of economic growth in Indonesia: A dynamic panel model. *Journal of Asian Finance, Economics and Business*, *7*(11), 147-156. doi:10.13106/jafeb.2020.vol7.no11.147

Bayne, N. (1991). In the balance: The Uruguay round of interntional trade negotiations. *Government and Opposition*, *26*(3), 302–315. doi:10.1111/j.1477-7053.1991.tb01142.x

Beeley, W. H., & MacLachlan, C. M. (2009). *Mexicans in Revolution, 1910-1956*. University of Nebraska Press-Sample Books. doi:10.2307/j.ctt1dgn3xj

Bernardi, L., Barreix, A., Marrenza, A., & Projeta, P. (2007). *Tax Systems and Tax Reform in Latin America*. SIEP Working Paper 591. Parva: Societa Italiana di Economia Pubblica.

Biplob, M. (2018). Financial sector development and economic growth: Empirical evidence from Bangladesh. *Asian Economic and Financial Review*, *8*(6), 799–814. doi:10.18488/journal.aefr.2018.86.799.814

Boamah, J., Adongo, F. A., Essieku, R., & Lewis, J. A. Jr. (2018). Financial depth, gross fixed capital formation and economic growth: Empirical analysis of 18 Asian economies. *SSRN*, *2*(4), 120–130. doi:10.2139/ssrn.3424688

Borenstein De Gegorio, J., & Lee, J. (1998). How does foreign direct investment affect economic growth? *Journal of International Economics*, *45*(1), 115–135. doi:10.1016/S0022-1996(97)00033-0

Borio, C., & Zabai, A. (2018). Unconventional monetary policies: a re-appraisal. In *Research Handbook on Central Banking*. Edward Elgar Publishing. doi:10.4337/9781784719227.00026

Bourguignon, F. (2018). *Political and Economic Development of Tanzania: A Brief Survey – Tanzania Institutional Diagnostic*. Economic Development & Institutions.

Broich, T. (2017). *US and Soviet foreign aid during the cold war: a case study of Ethiopia*. United Nations University (UNU-MERIT) Working Papers #2017-010.

Brown, R. L., Durbin, J., & Evans, J. M. (1975). Techniques for testing the constancy of regression relationships over time. *Journal of the Royal Statistical Society. Series B. Methodological*, *37*(2), 149–192. doi:10.1111/j.2517-6161.1975.tb01532.x

Bruton, H. (1989). *Handbook of development economics*. Elsevier.

Buainain, A. M. & da Silveira, J. M. (2002). *Structural reforms and food security in Brazil*. Academic Press.

Bumann, S., Hermes, N., & Lensink, R. (2012). *Financial liberalisation and economic growth: a meta-analysis. Technical report*. EPPI-Centre, Social Science Research Unit, Institute of Education, University of London.

Carstens, A. G., & Werner, A. (1999). *Mexico's Monetary Policy Framework Under A Floating Exchange Rate Regime*. Banco de Mexico Research Paper No. 9905.

Chang, H. J. (2002). *Kicking away the ladder: Development strategy in historical perspective*. Anthem Press.

Chang, R., Kaltani, L., & Loayza, N. (2009). Openness can be Good for Growth: The Role of Policy Complementarities. *Journal of Development Economics*, *90*(1), 33–49. doi:10.1016/j.jdeveco.2008.06.011

Che, N. (2021). *Dissecting economic growth in Uruguay* (IMF Working Paper WP/21/2). IMF.

Chenery, H. B., & Strout, A. M. (1966). Foreign Assistance and Economic Development. *The American Economic Review*, *56*, 679–733.

Chingoiro, S., & Mbulawa, S. (2017). Electricity consumption and Economic growth in Botswana: A Vector Error Correction approach. Advances in Management & Applied Economics, 7(2).

Chinh, H. Q., & Chi, D. T. (2018). Analysis of Foreign Direct Investment and Economic Growth in Vietnam, *International Journal of Business. Economics and Law*, *15*(5), 2289–1552.

Chowdhury, A. (2002). Politics, society and financial sector reform in Bangladesh. *International Journal of Social Economics*, *29*(12), 963–988. doi:10.1108/03068290210447003

Chowdhury, A. H. M. Y., Hamid, M. K., & Akhi, R. A. (2019). Impact of macroeconomic variables on economic growth: Bangladesh perspective. *Information Management and Computer Science*, *2*(2), 19–22. doi:10.26480/imcs.02.2019.19.22

Cindy L. (2021). *Vietnam Trade, an Overview, Part 2: The Doi Moi Reforms Modernizing Vietnam's Trade Economy*. Academic Press.

Cubit, G. (2013). *Economic History and Practice Working Paper*. Academic Press.

Dan, D. V., & Binch, V. D. (2019). The Effect of Macroeconomic Variables on Economic Growth: A Cross-Country Study. *International Econometric Conference of Vietnam, ECONVN 2019: Beyond Traditional Probabilistic Methods in Economics*, 919–927.

Dana, S. (2017). Ethiopia moves towards privatisation. It's not about money, it's about tech. *AFKInsider*.

Daumal, M., & Özyurt, S. (2011). The Impact of International Trade Flows on Economic Growth in Brazilian States. *Revista de Economia Institucional, 2*(1), 5. Advance online publication. doi:10.5202/rei.v2i1.5

Davies, A., & Quinlivan, G. (2006). A panel data analysis of the impact of trade on human development. *Journal of Socio-Economics, 35*(5), 868–876. doi:10.1016/j.socec.2005.11.048

de Cruz, C. B. B., Floriani, D. E. & Anal, M. (2020). The OLI Paradigm as a Comprehensive Model of FDI determinants: a sub-national approach. *International Journal of Emerging Markets*. doi:10.1108/IJOEM-07-2019-0517

Dewi, S. (2018). Dynamics of financial development,economic growth, and poverty alleviation: The Indonesian experience. *South East European Journal of Economics and Business, 13*(1), 17-30. doi:10.2478/jeb-2018-0002

Dey, S. R., & Tareque, M. (2020). External debt and growth: Role of stable macroeconomic policies. *Journal of Economics, Finance and Administrative Science, 25*(50), 185–204. doi:10.1108/JEFAS-05-2019-0069

Dibal, H. S., Iyortsuun, A. S., & Haruna, H. A. (2021), Asymmetric impact of financial market development on entrepreneurship in Nigeria. In Entrepreneurial finance, innovation and development. Routledge. doi:10.4324/9781003134282-10

Dickey, D. A., & Fuller, W. A. (1979). Distribution of the estimators for autoregressive time series with a unit root. *Journal of the American Statistical Association, 74*(366a), 427 431. doi :10.1080/01621459.1979.10482531

Dobado, R., & Marrero, G. A. (2011). The role of Spanish imperial state in the mining led growth of bourbon Mexico's economy. *The Economic History Review, 64*(3), 855–884. doi:10.1111/j.1468-0289.2010.00555.x

Dosman, J. D. (2017). *Raul Prebisch and the XXIst century development challenges*. United Nations – ECLAC.

Dritsakis, N., Varelas, E., & Adamopoulos, A. (2006). The main determinants of economic growth. An empirical investigation with Granger causality analysis for Greece. *European Research Studies, 9*(3-4), 47–58.

Duasa, J. (2007). Determinants of Malaysian Trade balance: An ARDL bound testing approach. *Global Economic Review, 36*(1), 89–102. doi:10.1080/12265080701217405

Dularif, M. (2010). Financial development and economic growth: An empirical analysis of Indonesia. *Jurnal BPPK, 1*(4), 93–131.

Dunning, J. H., & Lundan, M. (2008). Instituting and the OLI paradigm of Multinational enterprise. *Asia Pacific Journal of Management, 25*(4), 573–593. doi:10.1007/s10490-007-9074-z

Dynan, K., & Sheiner, L. (2018). *GDP as a Measure of Economic Well-Being*. Hutchins Center on Fiscal & Monetary Policy at Brookings, Hutchins Center Working Paper #43.

Eckler, C. R. L. (2000). *Prevailing facets and Spanish colonialism the root of exploitation and in equality* [Latin American Honors Thesis]. University of Tennessee at Chattanooga.

Eko, L., & Abdul, M. P. (2021). Indonesia's macroeconomic and finance policy framework for structural transformation. United Nations conference on trade and development.

Emmanuel, I. (2017). Balance of Payments Constrained Economic Growth in Nigeria. *African Journal of Economic Review, 5*(2), 1–13.

Era, A., & Vuving, L. (2021). *The Evolution of Vietnamese Foreign Policy in the Doi Moi*. Harvard University Press.

Erlando, A., Riyanto, F. D., & Masakazu, S. (2020). Financial inclusion, economic growth, and poverty alleviation: Evidence from eastern Indonesia. *Heliyon, 6*(10), e05235. Advance online publication. doi:10.1016/j.heliyon.2020.e05235 PMID:33088971

Etale, L. M., & Imbazi, L. I. (2020). Influence of selected macroeconomic variables on economic growth in Nigeria (1999 – 2018). *Advances in Social Sciences Research Journal, 7*(8), 315–325. doi:10.14738/assrj.78.8811

Etebon, J. M. (2021). The Long years of Military rule in Nigeria: A Blessing or a Course. *Journal of Public Administration and Government, 11*(2), 71–84.

Faal, E. (2005). *GDP Growth, Potential, Output and Output Gaps in Mexico*. IMF Working Paper; Western Hemisphere Department WP/05/93.

Faaland, J., & Parkinson, J. R. (1976). *Bangladesh: the test case of development*. C. Hurst.

Falola, T., & Heaton, M. M. (2008). Africa, Empire and Globalization: Essays in honour of A. G. Hopkins. Academic Press.

Fforde, A. (2016). Vietnam: Economic Strategy and Economic Reality. *Journal of Current Southeast Asian Affairs, 35*(2), 3–30. doi:10.1177/186810341603500201

FGN. (1972, February). Nigeria Enterprise Promotion Decree, 1972, No. 4. *Gazette, 59*(10), 28.

Flores, R., & Telles, E. R. (2012). Social Stratification in Mexico: Disentangling Color, Ethnicity, and Class. *American Sociological Review, 77*(3), 486–494. doi:10.1177/0003122412444720 PMID:25382861

Ford, M. (2015). *Subverting democracy, producing terror: the United States and the Uruguayan cold war, 1963-1976* [MA thesis]. California State University, Fresno, CA.

Franko, P. (2018). *Puzzle of Latin American economic development* (7th ed.). Rowman and Littlefield Publishers.

Galeano, E. (1996). *Open veins of Latin America* (C. Belfrage, Trans.). Monthly Review Press.

Garrison, C.B., & Lee, F. (1995). The effect of macroeconomic variables on economic growth rates: A cross-country study. *Journal of Macroeconomics, 17*(2), 303-317. https://doi.org/doi:10.1016/0164-0704(95)80103-0

Getinet, B., & Ersumo, F. (2020). The impact of public external debt on economic growth in Ethiopia: the ARDL approach to con-integration. *Journal of Economic and Sustainable Development, 11*(11).

Ghouse, G., Khan, S. A., & Rehman, A. U. (2018). *ARDL model as a remedy for spurious regression: Problems, performance and prospectus.* MPRA Paper No. 83973, Pakistan Institute of Development Economics. https://mpra.ub.uni-muenchen.de/83973/

Gohar, M., & Butt, F. (2012). The impact of external debt servicing on the growth of low-income countries. Proceeding of International Conference on Business Management.

Gomes, L. (2020). *Brazil's economic growth strategy: the last two decades (1999-2019).* Munich Personal RePEc Archive (MPRA) Paper No. 104874. Available at https://mpra.ub.uni-muenchen.de/104874/

Gonzalez-Risotto, R., & Rodriguez, V. (1989). La importancia de las misiones jesuiticas en la formacion de la sociedad Uruguaya. *Estudo Ibero-Americanos, 15*(1), 191–214. doi:10.15448/1980-864X.1989.1.30514

Granger, C. W. J. (1969). Investigating causal relations by econometric models and cross-spectral methods. *Econometrica, 37*(3), 424–438. doi:10.2307/1912791

Green, T. (2008). *African Kingdoms: A guide to the Kingdoms of Songhay.* Oxford Cambridge & RSA A-Level.

Guedea, V. (2000). The process of Mexican independence. *The American Historical Review, 105*(1), 116–130. doi:10.2307/2652439

Gujarati, D. N. (2003). *Basic Econometrics McGrow.* Hill Publishing Ltd.

Gupta, K. (2021). The importance of financial liberalisation for economic growth: The case of Indonesia. *Bulletin of Indonesian Economic Studies, 57*(2), 175–201. doi:10.1080/00074918.2020.1747596

Gupta, V. (2019). A Case Study on Economic Development of Tanzania. *Journal of the International Academy for Case Studies, 26*(1), 1–16.

Guru, B. K., & Yadav, I. S. (2019). Financial development and economic growth: Panel evidence from BRICS. *Journal of Economics, Finance and Administrative Science, 24*(47), 113–126. doi:10.1108/JEFAS-12-2017-0125

Hackle, S. W. (1997). Land, Labor, and Production: The Colonial Economy of Spanish and México California. *California History (San Francisco), 76*(2-3), 111–146. doi:10.2307/25161664

Halder, P. (2019). Analysis of the impact of exchange rate, inflation, export and import on gross domestic product in Bangladesh. *Business, Management and Economics Research, 5*(12), 170-175.

Hall, P., & Soskice, D. (2001). *Varieties of capitalism: The institutional foundations of comparative advantage*. Oxford University Press. doi:10.1093/0199247757.001.0001

Hanoi Times. (2018). *Capital Expenditure in Vietnam*. Retrieved from https://hanoitimes.vn/vietnam-to-raise-capital-expenditure-to-u227-billion-in-2022- 318651.html

Hansjörg, H., Erwin, S., & Truong-Minh V. (2016). *The Integration of Vietnam in the Global Economy and Its Effects for Vietnamese Economic Development*. The Digital Library of the Friedrich Ebert Foundation.

Hanson, G. H. (2012). *Understanding Mexico's Economic Under-Performance*. The Regional Migration Study Group. Woodrow Wilson International Center for Scholars Migration Policy Institute.

Haruna, H. A., Dibal, H. S., & Isichei, E. E. (2023). Foreign direct investments and stock market development in Sub-Saharan Africa: Does regulatory quality moderate? *Global Business Review, 0*(0), 1–20. doi:10.1177/09721509231163712

Hepler, R. & Lutz, A. (2021). *Mexican-American War & Treaty of Guadalupe Hidalgo*. Academic Press.

Hidayatinnisa. (2021). The effect of financial literacy and financial inclusion on economic growth in Indonesia. *Jurnal Bisnis, Manajemen dan Perbankan, 7*(2), 339-359. doi:10.21070/jbmp.v7vi2.1539

Hossain, M. A., & Shirin, S. (2016). Impact of debts on economic growth of Bangladesh: An application of ARDL model. *Asia-Pacific Journal of Business, 7*(1), 1-10. https://imr.kangwon.ac.kr/apjb.7.7.201606.1

Hossin, Md. S. (. (2020). Interest rate deregulation, financial development and economic growth: Evidence from Bangladesh. *Global Business Review*, 1–14. doi:10.1177/0972150920916564

Hsing, Y. (2003). Impacts Of External Debt And Other Macroeconomic Policies On Output In Brazil: VAR Approach. *Revista de Análisis Económico, 18*(2), 97–108.

Huong, D. T. M. (2019). Real exchange rate and economic growth: An empirical assessment for Vietnam. *Asian Economic and Financial Review, 9*(6), 680–690. doi:10.18488/journal.aefr.2019.96.680.690

Hussain, M. E., & Haque, M. (2016). Foreign direct investment, trade, and economic growth: An empirical analysis of Bangladesh. *Economies*, *4*(2), 1–14. doi:10.3390/economies4020007

Igewereme, O. B. (2015). Anatomy of Corruption in the Nigerian Public Sector: Theoretical Perceptiveness and some Empirical Explanation. *SAGE Open*, *5*(2). Advance online publication. doi:10.1177/2158244015581188

Ikenna, A. A., Penzin, D. J., Nkang, N. M., & Golit, P. (2018). Impact of Oil Price Volatility on Selected Macroeconomic Indicators in Nigeria. *Editorial Committee*, *56*(1), 1.

Imoagwu, C. P., & Ezeanyeji, C. I. (2019). Financial Development and Economic Growth Nexus in Nigeria. *International Journal of Business and Management Invention*, *8*(3), 50–63. www.ijbmi.org

IndexMundi. (2021). *Uruguay economy.* https://www.indexmundi.com/uruguay/economy_overview.html

Iniguez-Montiel, A. J. & Kurosaki, T. (2018). Growth inequality and poverty dynamics in Mexico. *Latin America Economic Review, 27*(12), 1.

International Trade Administration. (2021). *Uruguay – Country Commercial Guide (Uruguay Market Overview).* Author.

Irwin, D. A. (2020). *The rise and fall of import substitution* (Working paper WP 20-10). Peterson Institute for International Economics.

Isaac, J. (2013). *Indian Geographical History.* Available online at www.encydopediaBritanica.com

Isaac, J. E. (1983). *Realism and Social Scientific Theory.* Available online www.onlinelibrary.com

Islam, J. N., Mohajan, H. K., & Datta, R. (2012). Aspects of microfinance of Grameen Bank of Bangladesh. *International Journal of Economic Research*, *3*(4), 76–96.

Islam, T., & Hossain, M. T. (2019). Exchange rates and economic growth in Bangladesh: An econometric analysis. *Trade and Development Review*, *2*(2), 79–92.

Ismail, M. S. (2015). *Indonesia finance sector assessment.* Asian Development Bank.

Istiak, K. M. (2012). Foreign aid to Bangladesh: Some iconoclastic issues. *Journal of Developing Areas*, *46*(1), 331–343. doi:10.1353/jda.2012.0005

Iyaniwura, W. (2014). Corruption and Military Rule in Nigeria: An Overview 1966-1999. *Global Journal of Human Social Sciences for Political Science.*, *14*(4), 1–7.

Jaglinska, D., & Motyovszki, G. (2010). *The Washington Consensus: A post Keynesian perspective* (Unpublished manuscript). Universiteit Van Amsterdam, Amsterdam.

James, R., & William, S. T. (1999). *The Politics and Economics of Transition to an Open Market Economy in Vietnam.* OECD Development Centre Working Paper No. 152.

Jamil, T., & Hasan Md, S. B. (2015). Foreign direct investment and economic growth: Evidence from Bangladesh. *Journal of Business Studies*, *36*(2), 171–180.

Johansen, S. (1998). Determination of cointegration rank in the presence of a linear trend. *Oxford Bulletin of Economics and Statistics*, *54*(3), 383–397. doi:10.1111/j.1468-0084.1992.tb00008.x

Johansen, S., & Juselius, K. (1990, March). Maximum Likelihood Estimation and Inference on Cointegration – With Applications to the Demand For Money. *Oxford Bulletin of Economics and Statistics*, *52*(2), 169–210. doi:10.1111/j.1468-0084.1990.mp52002003.x

Jonathan, P. (2009). Vietnam Sustaining Growth in Difficult Times. *ASEAN Economic Bulletin*, *26*(1), 11–24. doi:10.1355/AE26-1B

Jumono, S. (2021). Bank liquidity and economic development in underdeveloped regions: An empirical study in Indonesia. *Journal of Asian Finance, Economics and Business, 8*(7), 31-42. doi:10.13106/jafeb.2021.vol8.no7.0031

KalirajanK. P.SalimR. (1997). Economic reforms and capacity realization in Bangladesh: An empirical analysis. doi:10.2139/ssrn.1222343

Karahan, O. (2020). Influence of exchange rate on the economic growth in the Turkish economy. *Financial Asset and Investing*, *11*(1), 21–34. doi:10.5817/FAI2020-1-2

Kehoe, T. J., & Ruhl, K. J. (2010). *Why Have Economic Reforms in Mexico not Generated Growth?* Federal Reserve Bank of Minneapolis, Research Department Staff Report No. 453.

Kesar, A., Bandi, K., Jena, P. K., & Yadav, M. P. (2022). Dynamics of governance, gross capital formation, and growth: Evidence from Brazil, Russia, India, China, and South Africa. *Journal of Public Affairs*, *2022*(e2831), 1–14. doi:10.1002/pa.2831

Khan, M. F. H. (2021). Impact of exchange rate on economic growth of Bangladesh. *European Journal of Business and Management Research*, *6*(3), 173–175. doi:10.24018/ejbmr.2021.6.3.891

Khanom, S. (2019). Does trade openness cause economic growth in Bangladesh? *IIUC Studies*, *16*, 99–110. doi:10.3329/iiucs.v16i0.50139

Kharusi, S. A., & Ada, M. S. (2018). External debt and economic growth: The case of emerging economy. *Journal of Economic Integration*, *33*(1), 1141–1157. doi:10.11130/jei.2018.33.1.1141

Knight, A. (2004). Mexico: The Colonial Era. Cambridge University Press.

Koh, D. (2008). Leadership Changes at the 10th Congress of the Vietnamese Communist Party. *Asian Survey*, *48*(4), 650–672. doi:10.1525/as.2008.48.4.650

Kolodko, G. W. (1999). *Ten years of post-socialist transition: The lessons for policy reform*. The World Bank. doi:10.1596/1813-9450-2095

Korkmaz, S. (2015), The relationship between external debt and economic growth in Turkey, *Proceedings of the Second European Academic Research Conference on Global Business, Economics, Finance and Banking (EAR15Swiss Conference)*, 971-978.

Kose, A. M., Guy, M., Meredith, G. M., & Christophe, M. T. (2004). *How has NAFTA Affected the Mexican Economy? Review and Evidence.* IMF working paper wp 04/59.

Kose, M. A., Meredeth, G. M., & Towe, C. M. (2004). *How Has NAFTA Affected Mexican Economy? Review and evidence.* IMF Working Paper. WP/04/59

Koutsoyiannis, A. (2001). Theory of Econometrics. Palgrave Publishers St. Martin's Press.

Kuznets, S. (1955). *International Differences in Capital Formation and Financing in: Capital Formation and Economic Growth.* National Bureau of Economic Research, Inc.

Kuznets, S., Epstein, L., & Jenks, E. (1941). *National Income and Its Composition, 1919–1938* (Vol. 1). National Bureau of Economic Research.

Kwiatkowski, D., Phillips, P. C. B., Schmidt, P., & Shin, Y. (1992). Testing the null hypothesis of stationarity against the alternative of a unit root. *Journal of Econometrics, 54*(1–3), 159–178. doi:10.1016/0304-4076(92)90104-Y

Ladan-Baki, I. S. (2016). Arms procurement mirage; corruption and insurgency in Nigeria. *International Journal of Politics and Good Governance, 7*(3), 1-7.

Lanzilotta, B., Mordecki, G., & Umpiérrez, V. (2018). Political economic uncertainty in a small and open economy: The case of Uruguay (Serie Documentos de Trabajo DT 05/2018). Instituto de Economía, Uruguay.

Lequiller, F., & Blades, D. (2007). *Understanding National Accounts.* OECD Publishing., doi:10.1787/9789264027657-en

Lessa, F., & Pierre-Louis LeGoff, P. (2013). Skewed Priorities in Uruguay: Uruguay continues to Struggle With its Dictatorial Past. *Al Jazeera.* http://www.aljazeera.com/indepth/opinion/2013/11/skewed-priorities-uruguay-20131118133045296340.html

Le, T. D., Nguyen, P. H., Ho, Y. T. P., & Nguyen, T. N. (2021). The Influences of FDI, GFCF, OPEN on Vietnamese Economic Growth. *International Journal of Asian Business and Information Management, 12*(3), 1–13. doi:10.4018/IJABIM.20210701.oa26

Levine, R. (2005), Finance and growth: Theory and evidence. In P. Aghion & S. N. Durlauf (Eds.), Handbook of Economic Growth. Elsevier.

List, F. (1977). *The national system of political economy.* (Original work published 1844)

Loto, M. A., & Alao, A. A. (2016). Remittances and the Growth of the Nigerian Economy. EJBE, 6(2).

Lucas, R. Jr. (1988). On the mecanisme of economic development. *Journal of Monetary Economics, 22*(1), 2–42. doi:10.1016/0304-3932(88)90168-7

Maasho, A. (2015). *Ethiopia launches 4G mobile service in the capital.* Reuters.

Maasho, A. (2015). *Ethiopia sells off seven state firms, to offer more.* Reuters.

Macnutt, F. A. (1909). *Fernando Cortse and the conquest of Mexico 1485-1547*. The Knickerbocker Press.

Macrotrends. (2022). https:www.macrotrends.net

Madhou, A., Sewak, T., Moosa, I., Ramiah, V., & Gerth, F. (2021). Towards Full-Fledged Inflation Targeting Monetary Policy Regime in Mauritius. *Journal of Risk and Financial Management*, *14*(3), 126. doi:10.3390/jrfm14030126

Magaji, S., & Abdul-Maliq, Y. O. (2013). Dollarization of Exchange Rate Management in Nigeria: Issues, Wishes and Realities. *Proceedings of the 3rd AFRA International Conference on Critical Accounting and Finance Issues in Developing Economies.*

Maganya, M. H. (2018). Financial Development and Economic Growth in Tanzania: An Empirical Investigation. *International Journal of Academic Research in Business & Social Sciences*, *8*(8), 291–307. doi:10.6007/IJARBSS/v8-i8/4470

Mahmud, W. (2008). Bangladesh. In A. Chowdhury & W. Mahmud (Eds.), *Handbook on the South Asian Economies*. Edward Elgar Publishing. doi:10.4337/9781848441293.00009

Mahmud, W., Ahmed, S., & Mahajan, S. (2008). *Economic reforms, growth, and governance: The political economy aspects of Bangladesh's development surprise. Commission on Growth and Development Working Paper; No. 22*. World Bank. http://hdl.handle.net/10986/28037

Maiolo, S. (2014). *A Brief History of Mexico: The Classic Period to the Present.* Treaty of Guadalupe Hidalgo.

Mandalu, M., Thakhathi, D. R., & Costa, H. (2018). Investigation on Tanzania's Economic History since Independence: The Search for a Development Model *World. Journal of Social Sciences and Humanities*, *4*(1), 61–68.

Manh, C. T. H. C. N. (2019). The Relationship Between the Human Capital and Economic Growth: A Case of Vietnam. *Industrial Engineering Letters*, *9*(5), 23–30.

Manyazewal, M., & Shiferaw, A. (2019). Economic Policy and Structural Transformation in Ethiopia. Institute of Political Science and International Relations, Jagiellonian University and Jagiellonian Research Center for African Studies.

Marangos, J. (2009). The evolution of the term 'Washington Consensus'. *Journal of Economic Surveys*, *23*(2), 350–383. doi:10.1111/j.1467-6419.2008.00565.x

Martin Weinstein, M. (1988). Uruguay: Democracy at the Crossroads. Westview Press.

Matthew B. (2017). *The missing middle: A political economy of economic restructuring in Vietnam: low institute*. Academic Press.

Mbulawa, S. (2015). Effect of Macroeconomic Variables on Economic Growth in Botswana. Journal of Economic and Sustainable Development, 6(4).

Mecaa, R., Schwartz, S. B. & Grubesic, A. (2009) Race and Class in Colonial Latin American. *A critique, Comparative Studies in Society and History, 21*(3). doi:10.1017/500/0417500013074

Meraj, M. (2013). Impact of globalization and trade openness on economic growth in Bangladesh. *Ritsumeikan Journal of Asia Pacific Studies, 32*, 40–50.

Meyer, D. F., & Sanusi, K. A. (2019). A causality analysis of the relationships between gross fixed capital formation, economic growth and employment in South Africa. *Studia Universitatis Babeș-Bolyai Oeconomica, 64*(1), 33–44. doi:10.2478/subboec-2019-0003

Meza, F. (2019). *The Case of Mexico. Working Paper, Macro Finance Research Program: Wp.* A Program of Becker Friedman Institute.

Meza, F. (2019). *The monetary and fiscal history of Mexico, 1960-2017.* Macro Finance Research Programe, Making Paper. https://ssu.com/abstract=3238181

Minh, N. D. (2018). A New Decision Making Model based on the Made in Vietnam Lean Management Philosophy. *Economia e Sociologia, 1*(3), 44–66.

Ministry of Foreign Affairs. (2020). *Ethiopian history.* https://etiopien.um.dk/en/about-etiopia/ethiopia-history

Mitchell, O. S. (1996). *Social security reform in Uruguay: An economic assessment* (Wharton Pension Research Council Working Papers. 527). https://repository.upenn.edu/prc_papers/527

Mohajan, H. K. (2013). Economic development of Bangladesh. *Journal of Business Management and Administration, 1*(4), 41–48. https://mpra.ub.uni-muenchen.de/id/eprint/50663

Moller, L. C. (2015). *To continue the impressive run, Ethiopia needs to modernize the policy framework to further strengthen the foundations of its economy.* World Bank Report on Ethiopia. https://www.worldbank.org/en/news/press-release/2015/11/23/wbethiopia-a-unique-economic-strategy-delivering-high-growth

Morales-Olmos, V., & Pienika, E. (2022). Contribution of the forest sector to the Uruguayan economy: A first approach with National Accounts. *Journal of Forest Science, 68*(3), 116–119. doi:10.17221/149/2021-JFS

Mora, M., & Giambiagi, F. (2005). *Federalismo e Endividamento Subnacional: Uma Discussão sobre a Sustentabilidade da Dívida Estadual e Municipal. TD 1142.* Instituto de Pesquisa Econômica Aplicada.

MoreiraM. M. (2009). Brazil's Trade Policy: Old and New Issues. Published by the Inter-American Development Bank. Available online at https://ssrn.com/abstract=1555947

Moreno-Brid, J. C., Santamaria, J. & Valdira, J. C. R. (2005). *Mexico: economic growth export and industrial performance after NAFTA united nation publication.* CEPAL: Economic Development Unit.

Morris, I. (1976, Mar. 8). Human Rights in Uruguay and Paraguay: Hearings Before the Subcommittee on International Organizations of the Committee on International Relations, House of Representatives, 64th Cong., 2d sess., June 17, July 27 and 28th and August 4, 1976, 37; "Torture in Uruguay." *New York Times*.

Moudatsou, A. (2003). Foreign direct investment and economic growth in the European Union. *Journal of Economic Integration*, *18*(4), 689–707. doi:10.11130/jei.2003.18.4.689

Nazir, M. R., Tan, Y., & Nazir, M. I. (2021). Financial innovation and economic growth: Empirical evidence from China, India and Pakistan. *International Journal of Finance & Economics*, *26*(4), 6036–6059. doi:10.1002/ijfe.2107

Nelson, C. R., & Plosser, C. R. (1982). Trends and random walks in macroeconmic time series: some evidence and implications. *Journal of Monetary Economics, 10*(2), 139-162.

Ngowi, P. H. (2009). Economic Development and change in Tanzania since independence: The Political leadership factor. *African Journal of Political Science and International Relations*, *3*(4), 259–267.

Nkoro, E., & Aham, K. U. (2016). Autoregressive distributed lag (ARDL) cointegration technique: Application and interpretation. *Journal of Statistical and Econometric Methods*, *5*(4), 63–91.

Nugroho, D. F., Wicaksono, B. R., & Reynald, M. R. (2021). Special allocation fund and poverty rate in Indonesia. *Economics and Finance in Indonesia, 67*(2), 257-269.

Nunnenkamp, P. (2002). *Determinants of FDI in developing countries: has globalization changed the rules of the game?* (No. 1122). Kiel Working Paper.

Nwachukwu, N. E., Adebayo, R. O., Shettima, A. M., Anigwe, J. O., & Udechukwu-Peterclaver, C. T. (2016). Real effective exchange rate misalignment in Nigeria. *Central Bank of Nigeria Journal of Applied Statistics*, *7*(1), 71–91.

Nwala, M. N., & Fodio, I. M. (2019). Effect of Macroeconomic Variables on Financial Sector Development in Nigeria. *Journal of Accounting. Business and Social Sciences*, *1*(2), 1–12.

Nwanosike, D. U., Kalu, U. I., Ogbuabor, J. E., Uzoechina, B., & Ebenyi, G. O. (2016). *Economic Development Dynamics in Nigeria: Evidence from 1914- 2014*. Saudi Journal of Business and Management Studies. doi:10.21276/sjbms.2016.1.4.1

Nweke, G. O., Odo, S. I., & Anoke, C. I. (2017). Effect of capital formation on economic growth in Nigeria, *Asian Journal of Economics. Business and Accounting*, *5*(1), 1–16. doi:10.9734/AJEBA/2017/36075

Ochonu, M. (2008). Colonialist within Colonialism: The Hausa-Caliphate Imaginary and the British Colonial Administration of the Nigeria Middle Belt. *African Studies Quantory*, *10*(2&3), 95–127.

Odetola, T. O. (2008). Military Politics in Nigeria: Economic Development and Political Stability in the Developing Economics. Cambridge University Press.

OECD (2009). *National Accounts of OECD Countries 2009. Volume I, Main Aggregates.* OECD Publishing. doi:10.1787/na_vol_1-2009-en-fr

OECD. (2009). National accounting of OECD countries 2009, Vol.1, main aggregates. OECD Publishing. http://dx.doi.org/ doi:10.1787/data-00001-en

OECD. (2019). Economic Surveys: Mexico. *Online (Bergheim).* Advance online publication. doi:10.1787/9536dooe-en

Ofori-Abebrese, G., Pickson, R. B., & Diabah, B. T. (2017). Financial Development and Economic Growth: Additional Evidence from Ghana. *Modern Economy, 8*(2), 282–297. doi:10.4236/me.2017.82020

Ogunmike, O. F., & Salisu, A. A. (2012). Financial Development and Economic Growth in Nigeria. *Journal of Monetary Economics Integration, 12*(2), 91–119.

Ogunode, S. A. (2021). The Military Foray into Nigerian Politics and Nation-Building: Historical Reflections on Murtala/Obasanjo Military Regime. *West Bohemian Historical Review, X1*(2), 273–281.

Okojo-Iweala, N., Soludo, C. C., & Mukhtar, M. (2003) The Debt Trap in Nigeria: Towards a Sustainable Debt Strategy, Africa World Press, Inc.

Okonjo-Iweala, N., & Osafo-Kwaako, P. (2007). *Nigeria's Economic Reforms: Progress and Challenges.* The Brookings Institution.

Olaopa, T. (2012, Apr. 10). Nigeria: Public Service and Udoji Reform – A Review. *Daily Trust.*

Olayungbo, D. O., & Quadri, A. (2019). Remittances, financial development and economic growth in sub-Saharan African countries: Evidence from a PMG-ARDL approach. *Financial Innovation, 5*(1), 9. doi:10.1186/s40854-019-0122-8

Ongo, E. N., & Vukenkeng, A. W. (2014). Does gross capital formation matter for economic growth in the CEMAC sub-region? *EuroEconomica, 2*(33).

Onwumere, J. U. J., Ibe, I. G. & Okpara, G. C. (2012). Foreign Private Capital Inflows and Real Sector Growth: Evidence from Nigeria. *International Journal of Finance Management, 43*, 6724-6729.

Orji, A., Nwagu, G. U., Ogbuabor, J. E., & Anthony-Orji, O. I. (2021). Foreign Direct Investment and Growth Nexus: Further Evidence from Africa's Largest Economy. *Journal of Infrastructure Development, 13*(1), 65–78. doi:10.1177/09749306211024433

Oyegoke, O. E., & Aras, O. N. (2021). Impact of foreign direct investment on economic growth in Nigeria. *Journal of Management, Economics, and Industrial Organization, 5*(1), 31–38. doi:10.31039/jomeino.2021.5.1.2

Oziah, K. (2011). *God, Gold and Glory: Causes of expansion into the new world.* American Military University. AMUID4226500.

Pesaran, M. H., & Shin, Y. (1999). An autoregressive distributed-lag modelling approach to co-integration analysis. In *Econometrics and Economic Theory in the 20th Century. The Ragnar-Frish Centennial Symposium*. Cambridge University Press.

Pesaran, M. H., & Shin, Y. (1999). An autoregressive distributed lag modelling approach to cointegration analysis. Econometrics and economic theory in the 20th century. In S. Strom (Ed.), *The Ragnar Frisch centennial symposium*. Cambridge University Press. doi:10.1017/CCOL521633230.011

Pesaran, M. H., Shin, Y., & Smith, R. P. (2001). Bounds testing approaches to the analysis of level relationship. *Journal of Applied Econometrics*, *16*(3), 289–326. doi:10.1002/jae.616

Phelan, L. (2018). *Pan-Latinism, French intervention in Mexico (1861-1867) and the genesis of the idea of Latin America Historicas Digital*. https://www.historicas.unam.mx/publicacines/publicdigital/libros/114/canciencia.autenticidad/html

Phillips, P. C. B., & Perron, P. (1988). Testing for a unit root in time series regression. *Biometrika*, *75*(2), 335–346. doi:10.1093/biomet/75.2.335

Piaggio, M., Alcantara, V., & Padilla, E. (2012). *Economic structure and key sector analysis of greenhouse gas emissions in Uruguay* (Documente de Treball 12.04). Universitat Autonomia de Barcelona.

Pomesh, D. L. E. (1902). *The economic history of India*. Trench Publishing.

Preston, E., Marvin, H., & Weistein. (2011). Antigas / Uruguay. *Encyclopedia Brittanica*. https://www.brittanica.com/place/antigas-uruguay

Qamruzzaman, M., & Jianguo, W. (2017). Financial innovation and economic growth in Bangladesh. *Financial Innovation*, *3*(19), 1–24. doi:10.1186/s40854-017-0070-0

Qamruzzaman, M., & Jianguo, W. (2018). Nexus between financial innovation and economic growth in South Asia: Evidence from ARDL and nonlinear ARDL approaches. *Financial Innovation*, *4*(20), 1–19. doi:10.1186/s40854-018-0103-3

Rahman, A. (2015). Impact of foreign direct investment on economic growth: Empirical evidence from Bangladesh. *International Journal of Economics and Finance*, *7*(2), 178–185. doi:10.5539/ijef.v7n2p178

Rahman, M. M., Bashar, M. A., & Dey, S. (2012). External debt and gross domestic product in Bangladesh: A co-integration analysis. *Management Research and Practice*, *4*(4), 28–36.

Rajib, M. I., & Rahman, R. (2020). Foreign direct investment and economic growth: Evidence from Bangladesh economy. *European Scientific Journal*, *16*(10), 38–55. doi:10.19044/esj.2020.v16n10p38

Ramirez, E. G. (2021). *Mexico's parliament and other political institutions, emperies*. European Parliamentary Research Services.

Ramsey, J. B. (1969). Tests for specification errors in classical linear least-squares regression analysis. *Journal of the Royal Statistical Society. Series B. Methodological*, *31*(2), 350–371. doi:10.1111/j.2517-6161.1969.tb00796.x

Ramzan, M., & Ahmad, E. (2014). External debt growth nexus: Role of macroeconomic policies. *Economic Modelling*, *38*, 204–210. doi:10.1016/j.econmod.2013.12.014

Razzaque, M. A., Bidisha, S. H., & Khondker, B. H. (2017). Exchange rate and economic growth. *Journal of South Asian Development*, *12*(1), 42–64. doi:10.1177/0973174117702712

Ref-Kirkwood, B. (2005). *The History of Mexico New York*. Palgrave McMillian Press.

Reuters. (2012). https://www.reuters.com

Rius, A. (2015). The Uruguayan tax reform 2016: Why did it not fail? In J. E. Mahon Jr, M. Bergman, & C. Arnson (Eds.), *Progressive tax reform and equality in Latin America*. Woodrow Wilson International Center for Scholars.

Robinson, D. O., Gaertner, M., & Papageorgiou, C. (2011). Tanzania: growth acceleration and increased public spending with macroeconomic stability. Yes Africa Can, p. 21.

Roett, R. (2010). *The New Brazil*. Brookings Institution Press.

Roger Nord. (2009).Tanzania: the story of an African transition. African Dept. International Monetary Fund.

Romer, P. (1986). Increasing returns and long run growth. *Journal of Political Economy*, *94*(5), 1002–1037. doi:10.1086/261420

Romer, P. (1990). Endogenous Technological Change. *Journal of Political Economy*, *98*(5, Part 2), 71–102. doi:10.1086/261725

Ros, J. (1993). *Mexico's Trade and Industrialization Experience Since 1960: A Reconsideration of Past Policies and Assessment of Current Reforms*. Kellogg Institute for International Studies, Working Paper No. 186/January 1993.

Saganga, M. K. (2021). Financial development and economic growth in Tanzania: An ARDL and bound testing approach. *Asian Journal of Economics and Banking*, *5*(1), 46–65. doi:10.1108/AJEB-09-2020-0063

Saifuddin, M. D. (2016). Public debt and economic growth: Evidence from Bangladesh. *Global Journal of Management and Business Research*, *16*(5), 64–73.

Salisu, M. (2001). *Incentive structure, Civil Service Efficiency and the Hidden Economy in Nigeria*. United Nation University/WIDER Discussion paper No. 2001/86.

Sanchez, D. (2017). *Ethiopia moves towards privatization. It's not about money, it's about tech.* Retrieved from Moguldom Nahon: https://moguldom.com/136888/

Sarker, F., & Khan, F. (2020). Nexus between foreign direct investment and economic growth in Bangladesh: An augmented autoregressive distributed lag bounds testing approach. *Financial Innovation*, *6*(10), 1–28. doi:10.1186/s40854-019-0164-y

Sawada, Y., Mahmud, M., & Kitano, N. (2018). *Economic and social development of Bangladesh: Miracle and challenges* (1st ed.). Palgrave Macmillan Cham. doi:10.1007/978-3-319-63838-6

SaxenaH.BansalP. K. (2019), Relationship between economic factors and economic growth. Proceedings of 10th International Conference on Digital Strategies for Organizational Success. https://ssrn.com/abstract=3319961 or doi:10.2139/ssrn.3319961

Segal, T. (2021). *Import substitution industrialization-ISI.* https://tinyurl.com/2p9h4cku

Selvanathan, S., Jayasinghe, M., & Selvanathan, E. A. (2020). Exports, imports and sustainable economic growth in Bangladesh. In M. Hossain, Q. K. Ahmad, & M. M. Islam (Eds.), *Climate Adaptation for a Sustainable Economy: Lessons from Bangladesh, an Emerging Tiger of Asia* (pp. 195–218). Nova Science Publishers.

Shahzad, U., Hussain, M., Qin, F., & Muhamadi, S. (2019). Role of FDI and Foreign Remittances in Boosting Economic Growth: Evidence from Brazil. *European Online Journal of Natural and Social Sciences*, *8*(1), 118–127.

Sharma, B. S., & Jha, D. N. (2015). *The economic history or India up to AD 1200: Trends and prospects.* Available online from www.jstor.org

SharmaG. D.SinghS.SinghG. (2011). Impact of Macroeconomic Variables on Economic Performance: An Empirical Study of India and Sri Lanka. http://dx.doi.org/ doi:10.2139/ssrn.1836542

Shimul, S. N., Abdullah, S. M., & Siddiqua, S. (2009). An examination of FDI and growth nexus in Bangladesh: Engle Granger and bound testing Cointgration approach. *BRAC University Journal*, *6*(1), 69–76. https://dspace.bracu.ac.bd/xmlui/handle/10361/455

Shirazi, N. S., & Abdul Manap, T. A. (2005). Export-led growth hypothesis: Further econometric evidence from South Asia. *The Developing Economies*, *43*(4), 472–488. doi:10.1111/j.1746-1049.2005.tb00955.x

Shrestha, M. B., & Bhatta, G. R. (2018). Selecting appropriate methodological framework for time series data analysis. *The Journal of Finance and Data Science*, *4*(2), 71–89. doi:10.1016/j.jfds.2017.11.001

Shukla, S. (2017). Innovation and economic growth: A case of India. *Humanities & Social Science Review*, *5*(2), 64–70. doi:10.18510/hssr.2017.521

Shukla, S. (2020). The Impact of Macroeconomic Variables on Economic Growth: Empirical Evidence from India'. *International Journal of Current Advanced Research*, *09*(06), 22628–22632. doi:10.24327/ijcar.2020.22632.4471

SIDRA. (2018). *Regional integration in the horn of Africa: is prime minister Abiy's initiative an institution ahead of its time?* Somali Institute for Development Research and Analysis, SIDRA policy brief 08, 2018. www.sidrainstitute.org /

Simba, H. M. A., & Çankal, E. (2020). Empirical Analysis of Financial Development Institutions and Economic Growth in Tanzania: Based on ARDL Model. *Journal of Business Research-Turk, 12*(2), 1962–1973. doi:10.20491/isarder.2020.955

Singer, H. W. (1950). Distribution of Gains between Investing and Borrowing Countries. *The American Economic Review, 40*(May), 473–485.

Singh, K., & Kumer, A. (2020). Empirical analysis of India and foreign trade and economic growth. *International Journal of Research, 8*(10), 105–111.

Solow, R. (1957). A Contribution to the Theory of Economic Growth. *The Quarterly Journal of Economics, 70*(1), 65–94. doi:10.2307/1884513

Soludo, C. C. (1996). Theoretical Framework of SAPs in Africa: Some better ideas from dead economists. In A. H. Akpo (Ed.), Beyond Adjustment: Management of the Nigerian Economy (pp. 107-132). Multi-Media Publishers Ltd. Nigerian Economic Society.

Srinivasan, T. N. (1996). *Indian economic reforms: Background, Rationale, Achievements and future prospects*. Sage Publishers.

Stiglitz, J. (2002). *Globalization and its discontents*. W. W. Norton.

Stock, J. H., & Watson, M. W. (1989). New indexes of coincident and leading economic ` indicators. *NBER Macroeconomics Annual, 4*, 351–394. doi:10.1086/654119

Svirydzenka, K., & Petri, M. (2014). *Mauritius: The Drivers of Growth—Can the Past be Extended?* International Monetary Fund (IMF) Working Paper WP/14/134.

Tabassum, N., & Ahmed, S. P. (2014). Foreign direct investment and economic growth: Evidence from Bangladesh. *International Journal of Economics and Finance, 6*(9), 117–135. doi:10.5539/ijef.v6n9p117

Tada, P. R. (2001). Economic Reforms and Structural Changes in Ethiopia since 1992; An Inquiry. *International Conference on African Development*. https://scholarworks.wmich.edu/africancenter_icad_archive/18

Tariq, R., Khan, M. A., & Rahman, A. (2020). How does financial development impact economic growth in Pakistan? New Evidence from Threshold Model. *Journal of Asian Finance, Economics and Business, 7*(8), 161-173. doi:10.13106/jafeb.2020.vol7.no8.161

Tariq, R., Khan, M. A., & Rahman, A. (2020). How does financial development impact economic growth in Pakistan? New evidence from threshold model. *The Journal of Asian Finance, Economics and Business, 7*(8), 161–173.

Tashome, A. (2015). *Development Finance and debt sustainability in Ethiopia: lesson to Sub-Saharan countries*. Academic Press.

Taslim, M. A. (2008). Governance, policies and economic growth in Bangladesh. In N. Islam & M. Asaduzzaman (Eds.), *A Ship Adrift: Governance and Development in Bangladesh*. Bangladesh Institute of Development Studies.

Temiz, D., & Gokmen, A. (2014). FDI inflow as an international business operation by MNCs and economic growth: An empirical study on Turkey, *International Business Review. International Business Review*, *23*(1), 45–154. doi:10.1016/j.ibusrev.2013.03.003

Texto para Discussão. IE/UNICAMP n. 107, mar. 2002.

The Economist. (2007). https://www.economist.com

The President. (1982). The unacceptable face of indigenization. *The President, 2*.

Thilakaweera, B. H. P. K. (2011). Economic impact of foreign direct investment in Sri Lanka. *Staff Studies-Central Bank of Sri Lanka, 41*(1&2), 89–115. https://ss.sljol.info/articles/10.4038/ss.v41i1.4684

Todaro, M. P., & Smith, S. (2012). *Economic Development* (11th ed.). Pearson Education Inc.

Topik, S. (2004). The Revolution, the State and Economic Development in Mexico. *History Compass, 2*(2004), 1-36.

Tu-Anh, V. (2017). *The Political Economy of Industrial Development in Vietnam: Impact of State-Business Relationships on Industrial Performance*. Oxford Scholarship.

Tuck, J. (2005). History of Mexico-Miguel Hidalgo: The Father who Fathered a Country 1999, Mexconnect. *World History: Don Miguel Hildalgo Reading*.

Twinoburyo, E. N., & Odhiambo, N. M. (2018). Can monetary policy drive economic growth? Empirical evidence from Tanzania. *Contemporary Economics*, *12*(2), 207–222.

Uddin, K. M. K., Rahman, M. M., & Quaosar, G. M. A. A. (2014). Causality between exchange rate and economic growth in Bangladesh. *European Scientific Journal*, *10*(31), 11–26.

Ukpabi, Iyodo, & Abdul-Maliq. (2021). Financial system development in emerging economies: An array of mint economic bloc. *International Journal of Science and Technoledge*, *9*(6), 39-46. doi:10.24940/theijst/2021/v9/i6/ST2106-003

Ukpabi, I. O., Onu, C., & Abdul-Maliq, Y. O. (2021). Economic Growth in The Wake of Nigerian Financial System Development: A Model of ARDL Bounds Test. *IRE Journals.*, *5*(4), 2456–8880.

UNCTAD. (1992). Transnational corporations as engines of growth. World Investment Report. doi:10.1007/978-3-030-04200-4_67

Uruguay: Country Commercial Guide. (2022). International Trade Administration. https://www.trade.gov/country-commercial-guides/uruguay-market-overview

US Department of State, Foreign Relations of the United States, 1958-1960. (1960). In *American Republics. Volume V.* Washington DC: Government Printing Office.

Utonga, D., & Dimoso, R. L. (2019). The Nexus between Export and Economic Growth in Tanzania. *Journal of Business School, 2*, 49–59. doi:10.26677/TR1010.2019.144

Van, C. N., & Cooper, E. (1983). *Vietnam under Communism, 1975-1982*. Hoover Press.

Vijayasri, G. V. (2013). The Importance of International Trade in the World. *International Journal of Marketing. Financial Services & Management Research, 2*, 111–119.

Washington. (2020). *Reforms in Indonesia's financial sector open new economic opportunities.* Press release no: 2020/141/EAP.

Wasiaturrahma, R. M., & Ajija, S. R. (2019). Financial deepening and economic growth in Indonesia. *Media Trend, 14*(1), 24-32. doi:10.21107/mediatrend.v14i1.455225

Watson, P., Wilson, J., Thilmany, D., & Winter, S. (2007). Determining economic contributions and impacts: What is the difference and why do we care? *The Journal of Regional Analysis & Policy, 37*, 140–146.

Wilson, C. (2017). *Growing Together: Economic Ties between US and Mexico*. Development Bank of Latin America and Wilson Center Mexico Institute. Woodrow Wilson International Centre for Scholars.

World Bank Report. (2021). Africa CAN. *The World Bank in Ethiopia Special Report.*

World Bank. (1978). *Uruguay: Staff appraisal report on a vocational training and technological development project* (Report No. 1928b-UR). World Bank.

World Bank. (1994). *Adjustment in Africa: Reforms, Results and the Road Ahead.* University Press.

World Bank. (1996). *Nigeria and the World Bank: Learning from the Past, Looking into the Future*. World Bank Washington D.C.

World Bank. (2015). Ethiopia's Great Run: The Growth Acceleration and How to Pace It. *World Bank Report: A Unique Economic Strategy Delivering High Growth.*

Wubneh, M. (1993). The Economy. Ethiopia: a country study (4th ed.). Federal Research Division, Library of Congress. OCLC 25869403.

Yeasmin, F., & Chowdhury, M. N. M. (2014). Impact of foreign debt on growth in Bangladesh: An econometrics analysis. *International Journal of Developing and Emerging Economics, 2*(4), 1–24.

Yeasmin, F., Chowdhury, M. N. M., & Hossain, M. A. (2015). External public debt and economic growth in Bangladesh: A co-integration analysis. *Journal of Economics and Sustainable Development, 6*(23), 64–74.

Yeh, A., & Olagnibel, G. (2011). The Virgin of Guadeloupe: A Study of Socio-Religious Identity. *International Journal of Frontier Missiology, 28*(4), 169–177.

About the Contributors

Adekunle Alexander Balogun is an academic and researcher in the field of finance. He has a PhD in Finance and currently lectures in the Department of Banking and Finance, University of Ibadan, Nigeria. Balogun had over a decade and half career in banking, corporate finance, consulting and financial advisory services. His research interests are in corporate finance, fiscal and monetary policies and energy and infrastructural finance.

Hyeladi Stanley Dibal is a Lecturer in the Department of Banking and Finance, Federal University Wukari, Nigeria. Hyeladi is currently a PhD student in the Department of Banking and Finance, University of Nigeria, with research interest in financial development, entrepreneurial finance, non-bank financial institutions and capital markets development. He has published in high impact international and local journals.

Edward Ogbonnia Eleje is an Associate Professor in the Department of Banking and Finance, Federal University, Wukari, Nigeria. He received his Ph.D and M.Sc. Degrees in Banking and Finance from the University of Nigeria, Nsukka (UNN). He also holds a B.Sc. Degree in Banking and Finance. He is a member of the Chartered Institute of Stock Brokers and the Nigerian Institute of Management respectively. His research interests are in Strategic Financial Engineering and Development Finance. He is highly published majorly in peer-reviewed local and International academic journals and has featured substantially in many local and international seminars and conferences.

Oladapo Fapetu is a Professor of Finance in the Department of Finance, Federal University Oye-Ekiti, Ekiti State, Nigeria. He holds B.Sc, M.Sc and Ph.D in Banking and Finance. He started his teaching career on March 1, 2000 as a Graduate Assistant, Department of Banking and Finance, University of Ado-Ekiti, Ekiti State and rose to the position of Lecturer I on October 1, 2012. He was appointed a Senior Lecturer and Ag. Head, Department of Banking and Finance, College of

Management Sciences, Federal University of Agriculture, Abeokunta, Ogun State, Nigeria on June 30, 2015. Professor Fapetu was elevated to position of a Reader on October 1, 2018 and became full Professor on March 9, 2023. He is an erudite scholar who has published in reputable journals at both local and international outlets. He is a member of many academic and professional bodies, among them are Fellow, Nigeria Society for Financial Research; member African Financial Research and Development and member Chartered Institute of Personnel Management of Nigeria. His areas of research interest include international finance, development finance, informal finance, money and banking. Presently, he is the Head, Department of Finance, Faculty of Management Sciences. Federal University Oye-Ekiti, Ekiti State, Nigeria.

Habila Abel Haruna is Lecturer in the Department of Banking and Finance, Federal University Wukari-Nigeria, and a PhD candidate in the Department of Banking and Finance, Nnamdi Azikiwe University Awka-Nigeria. Research interests are development finance, capital market, and entrepreneurship.

Gbenga Olorunmade is an academic staff of the Department of Finance, Federal University Oye-Ekiti, Nigeria. He holds master's degree in Banking and Finance and currently lectures courses in finance and banking. His research interests are in corporate finance, investment and entrepreneurial issues.

Ephraim Ugwu is a Lecturer I at the Department of Economics, Federal University, Oye Ekiti (FUOYE), Ekiti State, Nigeria. He was previously a Project Manager at the Innovation and Research Centre, FUOYE. He studied Economics at the University of Nigeria, Nsukka and graduated with Bachelor of Science degree in Economics with Second Class Upper division and a Master of Science degree in Economics (Public Finance). He is currently a Ph.D student at the Department of Economics, FUOYE. As a researcher, Mr. Ephraim's interest is focused on issues relating to public Sector economics and developments especially in the developing economies.

Index

P

Q

R

S

T

U

V

www.ingramcontent.com/pod-product-compliance
Lightning Source LLC
LaVergne TN
LVHW081332300926
849161LV00008B/1951
* 9 7 9 8 3 6 9 3 1 6 1 0 8 *